973.7089 REI

AFRICAN CANADIANS
IN UNION BLUE

Studies in Canadian Military History

Series editor: Tim Cook, Canadian War Museum

The Canadian War Museum, Canada's national museum of military history, has a threefold mandate: to remember, to preserve, and to educate. Studies in Canadian Military History, published by UBC Press in association with the museum, extends this mandate by presenting the best of contemporary scholarship to provide new insights into all aspects of Canadian military history, from earliest times to recent events. The work of a new generation of scholars is especially encouraged, and the books employ a variety of approaches – cultural, social, intellectual, economic, political, and comparative – to investigate gaps in the existing historiography. The books in the series feed immediately into future exhibitions, programs, and outreach efforts by the Canadian War Museum. A list of the titles in the series appears at the end of the book.

African Canadians in Union Blue

VOLUNTEERING FOR THE CAUSE IN THE CIVIL WAR

Richard M. Reid

UBCPress · Vancouver · Toronto

© UBC Press 2014

All rights reserved. No part of this publication may be reproduced, stored in a retrieval system, or transmitted, in any form or by any means, without prior written permission of the publisher, or, in Canada, in the case of photocopying or other reprographic copying, a licence from Access Copyright, www.accesscopyright.ca.

22 21 20 19 18 17 16 15 14   5 4 3 2 1

Printed in Canada on FSC-certified ancient-forest-free paper
(100% post-consumer recycled) that is processed chlorine- and acid-free.

LIBRARY AND ARCHIVES CANADA CATALOGUING IN PUBLICATION

Reid, Richard M., author
African Canadians in Union blue : volunteering for the cause in the Civil War / Richard M. Reid.

(Studies in Canadian military history series, ISSN 1499-6251.)
Includes bibliographical references and index.
Issued in print and electronic formats.
ISBN 978-0-7748-2745-4 (bound). – ISBN 978-0-7748-2746-1 (pbk.). – ISBN 978-0-7748-2747-8 (pdf). – ISBN 978-0-7748-2748-5 (epub)

1. United States – History – Civil War, 1861-1865 – Participation, Black Canadian.
2. United States – History – Civil War, 1861-1865 – Blacks – Canada.
3. Blacks – Canada – History – 19th century. 4. Canada – History – 1841-1867.
I. Title. II. Series: Studies in Canadian military history

E540.C25R43 2014   973.7089'96071   C2014-900203-3
C2014-900204-1

Canadä

UBC Press gratefully acknowledges the financial support for our publishing program of the Government of Canada (through the Canada Book Fund), the Canada Council for the Arts, and the British Columbia Arts Council.

Publication of this book has been financially supported by the Canadian War Museum, and UBC Press is also grateful to the Wilson Prize for Publishing Canadian History for its contribution towards the publication of this book.

Printed and bound in Canada by Friesens
Set in Trajan and Sabon by Artegraphica Design Co. Ltd.
Copy editor: Deborah Kerr
Proofreader: Stephanie Vander Meulen

UBC Press
The University of British Columbia
2029 West Mall
Vancouver, BC V6T 1Z2
www.ubcpress.ca

To Susan,

who provides the motivation for so much of my work

Contents

Illustrations / ix

Acknowledgments / xi

Introduction / 3

1 British North America: Glory Land or the Least-Worst Option? / 11

2 The Black Response: What the Numbers Mean / 37

3 Blacks in the Navy: A Different Military Experience / 56

4 Promises Deferred: In the Army, 1863-64 / 83

5 Promises Fulfilled: In the Army, 1864-65 / 114

6 Black Doctors: Challenging the Barriers / 146

7 Post-War Life: Continuity and Change / 177

Conclusion / 206

Appendix: Establishing the location of black British North American veterans, 1865-75 / 213

Notes / 217

Selected Bibliography / 267

Index / 280

Illustrations

Maps

12 / British North America in 1861
167 / Contraband camp and hospital, Washington, DC, later the Freedmen's Hospital

Photographs

32 / Abraham D. Shadd
43 / Military service record form
51 / Recruitment poster for Rankin's Lancers
59 / Integrated crew on a US warship
69 / USS *Eolus*
77 / USS *Cairo*
78 / USS *Massasoit*
88 / Recruitment poster for the 54th Massachusetts
94 / Private Abraham F. Brown

95 / Private John Goosberry
103 / The 26th USCT, raised at Rikers Island
110 / Benjamin Blackburn's desertion record
118 / Abraham W. Shadd
139 / Substitute enlistment form for George Dean
154 / Alexander Augusta in uniform
158 / John Rapier in uniform
164 / Anderson Abbott in the uniform of a contract surgeon
173 / Jerome Riley
182 / George Caples
199 / Ben Jackson and Jack
208 / Anderson Abbott

Figures

1. Black enlistment and Lincoln's call for troops / 122
2. Black enlistment and the resolution of the unequal pay issue / 123

Tables

1. British North American black recruits / 48
2. British North American black sailors / 63
3. Occupation of British North American black sailors / 71
4. Occupation of British North American black soldiers / 134
5. Terms of enlistment and deserters / 136

Acknowledgments

The genesis for this study was a conversation I had with Ed Redkey some years ago, at a conference in New Orleans. We were both interested in the important contributions made by black soldiers to the emancipation struggle. He was then working on the Fifty-fourth Massachusetts Volunteer Infantry, which was made famous, or rather more famous, by the movie *Glory,* and I had started to research North Carolina's black volunteers. During our talk over soft-shelled crabs, he mentioned that more than two dozen volunteers born in the British colonies had enlisted in the Fifty-fourth, and he offered to send me their regimental records. He was the first, but far from the last, colleague who helped, encouraged, challenged, and influenced me in this project.

At the time, with a major research project already under way, I made a mental note of the information on the soldiers, thinking that it might form an interesting article. Years later, when I examined the regimental descriptive books, looking for black volunteers from British North America, I quickly realized that doing justice to the courageous black men who left their homes to join the fight against slavery would require much more than an article. I hope that this book provides at least partial recognition of their valour and contributions. Fortunately, the extensive military and pension records held in Washington allow researchers to at least partially flesh out the story of their lives and actions, although I am conscious of just how many questions remain unanswered.

The process of historical research can be lonely and isolating, with hundreds of hours spent deciphering documents and recording information, but helpful and knowledgeable staff at archives and museums can be immensely supportive. I have been very fortunate in the assistance that I have received. I am particularly indebted to the archivists and staff at the National Archives and Records Administration in Washington. Anyone who has researched there understands just how valuable they can be in identifying records that might otherwise be missed and in providing important context to the documents. Equally valuable assistance was provided by many other archives and museums. I owe a debt of gratitude to Spencer Alexander at the Buxton National Historic Site and Museum, James Barry Arnott and staff at Western University's Archives and Research Collections Centre, Pam Atwell at the West Hants Historical Society, Sharon Knecht of the Oblate Sisters of Providence Archives, and Blair Newby of the Chatham-Kent Black Mecca Museum. They all helped me find documents and illustrations that gave a face to the men who had served. The staff and archivists at the Massachusetts Historical Society and the Toronto Reference Library provided equally valuable help. I also benefitted from an exceptionally talented research assistant, Wade Cormack, who helped me identify which black soldiers could be linked to subsequent censuses in Canada and the United States or to their later pension applications.

For most writers, conceptualizing, drafting, and redrafting a manuscript can benefit immensely from the feedback of other academics. This is the collaborative aspect of the historical profession, and I have incurred many intellectual debts in the process. Sharon Roger Hepburn, Jamie Snell, and Cathy Wilson read some of the earliest chapters without snickering and even offered encouragement. Roger Sarty looked at the early version of the naval chapter, encouraged me to submit it as an article to the *Northern Mariner*, and then kindly permitted its subsequent reuse. Margaret Humphreys graciously shared her extensive knowledge of many aspects of nineteenth-century American medical history with a neophyte. Adam Arenson's careful reading and judicious comments on the manuscript greatly improved the final product. Marie Puddister once again showed her skill as a cartographer. In addition, I owe an enormous debt to David Roberts, who read the whole manuscript, offered extensive criticism, and made key suggestions as to how I might reconceptualize and improve portions of it. His editorial insights were invariably correct and to the point, damn it!

Two other people greatly facilitated the completion of this book. Emily Andrew, senior editor for UBC Press, is all that any writer could hope for in an editor. She has been supportive, encouraging, extremely well organized, and tolerant of my idiosyncrasies. Her time- and author-management skills allowed the manuscript to pass through the system in an efficient fashion. The only person more supporting and encouraging, and at least as tolerant of my idiosyncrasies, is my wife, Susan, who shares my love of history but does not understand why I do not equally share her love of gardening.

African Canadians in Union Blue

Introduction

O{N 18 MARCH 1863}, Samuel J. Robinson enlisted in the Fifty-fourth Massachusetts Volunteer Infantry. He was one of the earliest recruits in the first black regiment raised in a Northern state during the Civil War. Born in Toronto in 1841, Robinson was working as a printer in Rochester, New York, by 1863.[1] He was promoted to first sergeant within two months of his enlistment and transferred to the Fifty-fifth Massachusetts to help organize that regiment. On 24 June, he was made the regimental sergeant major, and by the end of the year he had become the quartermaster sergeant.[2] Five years after the war, Robinson was back in Rochester, working as a labourer and living with his wife, Mary, an American citizen.[3] In the year after Robinson volunteered, Joel Monroe, a thirty-four-year-old farmer, left his home in Oro Township, Simcoe County, Canada West, and joined the Twenty-ninth Connecticut Volunteer Infantry, a black regiment being raised in that state.[4] A contributing factor in his decision to enlist may have been the recent death of his wife and child. Monroe survived the war and lived for a number of years in New Haven, where he remarried. However, for unknown reasons he left New Haven and his wife and returned to his province of birth, where he died at his brother's house in April 1890.[5] Shortly after Monroe volunteered, William Jones, a young labourer from Saint John, New Brunswick, signed a contract in Portsmouth, New Hampshire, with Thomas Boyd, agreeing to serve as Boyd's substitute in the army.[6] Jones served in the

Third United States Colored Troops until he was mustered out in October 1865. He then returned to the Maritimes, and in 1871 he was living in Amherst, Nova Scotia, with his wife, Amelia.[7] Although these three men, and many others like them, were born and raised in British North America, their actions indicate that they conceived of their world as being broader than just their province. They lived in communities with complex social, economic, and intellectual ties that transcended national borders. At the same time, place mattered for many of these individuals, and "home" exerted a strong centripetal force. Their actions, and what they revealed about both the Civil War and the communities from which they came, form the core of this book.

The more that I learned about the black volunteers from British North America, the more I was convinced that their story was both interesting and historically significant. Understanding why these men voluntarily left their homes and fought in a "foreign" war at great risk to themselves gave me new insights into a range of Canadian and American issues. The men's willingness to sacrifice so very much, coupled with the knowledge that black Union soldiers faced greater risks in combat than their white counterparts, gave me a sense of how strongly the message of the Emancipation Proclamation resonated in the black communities outside the United States. Moreover, where, when, and how the men enlisted, how well they served in the military, and their decisions once the war ended gave me a fuller understanding of the complex nature of the black military experience in general. Because the numbers of volunteers who came from the various British colonies provide a rough measurement of the strength of the colonies' transnational ties, Canadian historians should find this a useful starting place for future research. Of course, the problem for any researcher is that few volunteers left personal records in the form of letters, diaries, or memoirs to explain their decision to enlist. Or if they did, much was not preserved, because the records were undervalued in the nineteenth and early twentieth centuries. As a result, scholars are obliged to infer their motives from their behaviour and to utilize other sources to flesh out their stories, as will be discussed in Chapter 2. The paucity of sources and the associated methodological problems may partially explain why little has been written about these men. This is unfortunate because their commitment to the struggle against slavery deserves to be known.

By the time the war ended, nearly 2,500 young black men from all across British North America had followed Robinson, Monroe, and Jones to become part of the Northern war effort. Most served in the infantry, cavalry, and artillery regiments of the Union army, but hundreds of others helped man vessels in the Union navy, blockading the Southern coast or searching for Confederate privateers on the high seas. These men clearly believed that they had a stake in the outcome of the bloody struggle convulsing the United States. For both black British North Americans and African Americans who lived in the British colonies, President Lincoln's Final Emancipation Proclamation of 1 January 1863 and his authorization of the use of black soldiers as an official part of the Union army symbolized the start of a dramatic if uncertain new era, one that was important to all black North Americans. Of course, these momentous changes had an uneven impact. For African Americans, especially black Southerners, emancipation ushered in a transformative phase in which old social relationships were destroyed and new hopes were raised that a more equitable set of racial associations had begun. Persons who were chattel slaves in 1861 were free Americans by the end of 1865. For black Northerners, the destruction of slavery and the Fourteenth Amendment's entrenchment of black citizenship rights opened the door for fuller citizenship than they had ever enjoyed before. Indeed, Eric Foner argues that "the decade following the Civil War witnessed astonishing advances in the political, civil, and social rights of Northern blacks."[8]

Those changes would benefit African Canadians as well. Emancipation and more equitable treatment of African Americans in the Northern states during Reconstruction inevitably expanded the world of the black residents in the newly formed Dominion of Canada and generated new social and economic opportunities for them. This process was inevitable, given the geographic and intellectual borderland in which they lived.[9] Even before the war, many black British North Americans had strong transnational ties, both physically and psychologically, to black communities in the Northern states, but prior to 1861 few were willing to move permanently to the United States.[10] Nevertheless, like Robinson, Monroe, and Jones, many blacks born in the British North American colonies believed that the war concerned them in important ways. The young men who acted on this belief and went south to fight changed both themselves and their communities. In the post-war era, the world of most black North Americans had been dramatically altered, and young black men from British North America had been part of that transformation. The destruction of slavery and the repeal of the most discriminatory laws in the Northern states ended the desire of some African Americans to leave the United States. Few Americans, black or white, migrated north after 1867, when the United Province of Canada (consisting of the administrative districts of Canada West and Canada East), New Brunswick, and Nova Scotia united to form the Dominion of Canada.[11] At the same time, the new opportunities in the United States for black residents, including the right to become an American citizen, led an increased number of African Canadians to relocate and begin a new life south of the border. In keeping with what would be a long Canadian tradition, however, these changes would have an asymmetrical impact on the various provinces.

Historians have long been aware of African Americans' movement into the British North American colonies, including fugitives fleeing slavery and free-born blacks who were disgusted with the discriminatory laws of many Northern states. Both Sharon A. Roger Hepburn and Harvey Amani Whitfield capture much of the tension, aspirations, and motivation of these borderland migrants in the decades leading up to the Civil War.[12] Even when settled in the British colonies, many African Americans experienced, in the words of Gustavo Cano, a sense of "being here and there at the same time."[13] They maintained strong ties to black communities in the United States, connections reinforced by clergy and educators, and many of them decided to return home during or after the Civil War. Fewer historians, however, have examined the transnational ties of the British North American-born black residents, especially in the years before 1861. Nevertheless, a permeable border allowed ideas and people to flow in both directions. The young black men from British North America, especially those born in the British colonies, provide a prism through which to examine both the cross-border ties and the changing nature of black involvement in the war.

As a result, one way of assessing whether black British North Americans saw the Civil War as important to their lives is to determine how many enlisted in the Union military. A small number of recruits would suggest that they were largely uninvolved and perhaps uninterested in the war, whereas a significant number would imply the existence of strong cross-border ties and would open a new area for exploration. Thus, the first goal of this study was to estimate, as accurately as possible, the number of black British North American-born soldiers and sailors who fought in the war.[14] Assessing their numbers and determining their place of residence made it possible not only to analyze their contribution to the Union war effort but also to get a sense of the engagement and transnational values of the various provincial black communities. At the very least, the information raises questions regarding whether the actions of volunteers reflected the values and ideas of their elders and neighbours. Such an analysis should also allow a more nuanced understanding of the diversity and behaviour of the black communities in British North America during the Civil War era. In addition, the actions of the soldiers provide a lens to examine the changing nature of the Union's biracial military struggle and the international response to the implicit message of the Emancipation Proclamation.

The behaviour of these young black men adds a corrective to some of the popular misconceptions regarding the war. All too often foreign-born recruits were depicted as mercenaries who joined solely for the bounty money or as dupes who were manipulated and exploited by officials in a conflict in which they themselves had little stake. Certainly, many Northern contemporaries distrusted the commitment of the foreigners who entered the army, whereas Southerners then and later portrayed the Union army as being full of foreign soldiers of fortune.[15] Subscribing to this attitude, Union officials at the time associated desertion with cities, large bounties, and foreigners. They reported as "probable" that a close examination would reveal "that desertion is a crime of foreign rather than native birth."[16] Historians no longer believe that foreign-born soldiers were disproportionately represented in the Union army and have increasingly depicted these recruits as having as many, if different, ideological reasons for entering the war as their native-born comrades.[17] Not surprisingly, much of the literature on the foreign-born soldiers in the Union army that discusses motivation, military service, or the degree of subsequent societal assimilation has concentrated on the Irish and German recruits who made up the bulk of the soldiers born outside the United States.[18] Much less has been written about the "invisible" recruits, either white or black, who came from British North America, although their reasons for volunteering were equally complex, and they faced as many decisions when the war was over. These men also represented the foreign element in the Union military. Although the black recruits from British North America were limited in number, their study nonetheless enables an understanding of the social changes that flowed out of the black military experience.

This book is organized in a way that will hopefully allow readers to better understand the varied backgrounds of the black volunteers from British North America as well as the changing nature of their participation in the war effort. Although the black communities in the five British colonies had much in common, their size and social makeup differed as did their ties to black communities in the United States. Chapter 1 examines their nature and evolution on the eve of the Civil War as a precondition to understanding the involvement of recruits during the war. Chapter 2 measures the strength of the black response outside the United States by establishing how many black British North American–born volunteers joined in the war effort. This chapter also discusses some of the methodological challenges facing researchers who wish to re-create the lives of those who left few personal records. Hundreds of black Union sailors referred to a British North American colony as their place of birth, and they are the subject of Chapter 3. An examination of their experiences shows not only that the war afloat was very different from that on land but also that their motivations and expectations differed strongly from those of black soldiers.

The men who joined the army, more than eight hundred of whom listed their place of birth as British North America, make up the largest group of volunteers studied in this book, and their experience takes up two chapters. The first of these, Chapter 4, looks at the Lincoln administration's 1863 decision to allow black regiments in the Union army and the positive response of black recruits throughout that year. The official acceptance of black soldiers and the repeated assurances during the first months of recruiting that they would be treated in the same manner as white soldiers implied a new role for them in society and promised an affirmation of their manhood. Nevertheless, in this liminal stage, a series of factors soon constrained the number of recruits who came forward. The early reports of the Union army's discriminatory policies, best exemplified by the War Department's decision to pay black soldiers half of what their white counterparts received, plus the threats from the Confederate Congress and military officials that captured black soldiers would not be treated as legitimate prisoners of war, deterred many potential new recruits. Most of the men who joined in 1863 had understood that they would face far greater risks and harsher work conditions than their white comrades, but they had not expected to be treated as second-class soldiers. When this occurred, many became angry and bitter, believing that they had been deceived by Union recruiters.

In the second half of 1864 and early 1865, the numbers of black British North American recruits increased, reflecting a renewed belief that the army would deal equitably with them. At the same time, their methods and reasons for joining may have changed, a topic that is the focus of Chapter 5. Many men, highly motivated but drawn from a working-class background, took advantage of the money being offered as bounties for volunteers or as payments for substitutes. The records reveal that a volunteer who was careful and informed about where and when he enlisted could earn hundreds of dollars upon recruitment, although not all men were careful or informed.

Chapter 6 looks at the careers of five doctors, all of whom practised or were educated in Canada West. They were among the most cosmopolitan of the men studied, and much more than the enlisted men, they tested the limits of change that American society would accept. During the war, four of them offered their medical services to the Union army and spent most of their time working in the Washington area hospitals and camps for black refugees. In very different ways, all five doctors were searching for their "place" in society, both professionally and socially. Although establishing professional stature in the United States would prove more difficult than in Canada, only one doctor chose to return to a medical practice in Ontario.

The final chapter explores the post-war lives of the veterans and their families, and tries to capture the diversity of their experiences. When the war ended, most black veterans re-entered civilian life, and many simply disappeared from the existing records. Nevertheless, the post-war world had been significantly altered for all black residents of North America. Broad demographic shifts and individual histories together give some indication as to how the black communities responded to the new opportunities and challenges of post-war North America.

Although much of this book concentrates on the war and its impact, an important theme is the movement and historical agency of the various black communities across British North America as they adjusted to the changes triggered by the war. The men who are the primary subject of this book were not mere pawns, manipulated by external forces. Rather, they were independent beings who made complex decisions in difficult situations. Many of their choices regarding when, where, and how they would serve, though constrained, were closely tied to the multifaceted dynamics of being black in nineteenth-century North America. Most of their decisions were influenced by the restrictions placed on blacks in a largely white and hostile society. And yet part of their mobility and their search for a better social and economic life for themselves and their families would resonate with other socio-ethnic groups in North America. North Americans were highly mobile, and few restrictions stopped them from crossing borders in the nineteenth century. For Canadians, it is worth remembering that John Kenneth Galbraith once wrote that to "The Scotch" of southwestern Ontario, among whom he grew up in the 1920s, Canadian identity was worth five dollars a week. When the wage difference between Detroit and home exceeded that level, he observed, people simply picked up and moved south. They preferred being Canadian, but they didn't prefer it that much. Galbraith himself left for good during the 1930s. The young black men who are the focus of this book showed at least as much agency in carving out their own lives during and after the war.

CHAPTER ONE

BRITISH NORTH AMERICA

GLORY LAND OR THE LEAST-WORST OPTION?

A<small>LTHOUGH BLACKS HAD</small> been part of Canadian history from the founding of New France and, for the English-speaking colonies, from the establishment of Halifax, most blacks in the British North American colonies came from a mixture of slaves, ex-slaves, refugees, and loyalists who had fled during the American Revolution or in the wake of the War of 1812.[1] In some colonies, this original population was enlarged by African Americans, both fugitive and free, escaping slavery in the Southern states or the increasing discrimination in many Northern states. The implementation of the Fugitive Slave Act of 1850 convinced other African Americans that until slavery was abolished in the United States, their only hope for security lay in the British colonies. Through this same period, growing numbers of blacks, even those with strong attachments to their place of birth, saw emigration as an alternative to living in a society where the Supreme Court might deny "federal citizenship to all African Americans, not just those of slave ancestry."[2] By contrast, African Americans could become British citizens after just three years of residency.[3] Yet as Barrington Walker suggests, all black residents in the British colonies lived "in a state of paradox, caught between formal legal equality and deeply entrenched societal and economic inequality."[4] Black immigrants reacted variously to this structural tension. For some, the British colonies were the start of a new life; for others, they were a way-station to a more ambitious all-black colonization scheme; and for yet others,

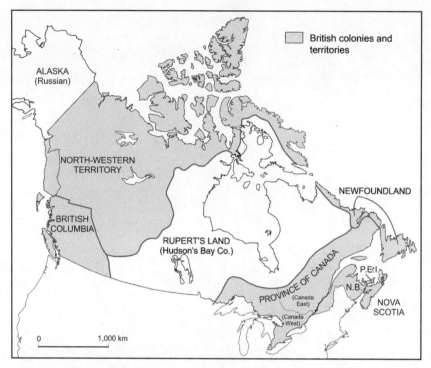

British North America in 1861

they were merely a short-term sanctuary before returning home. Of course, more African Americans rejected migration of any kind and believed that the plans to leave the United Sates were "betrayals of the African American community, and an abdication of the duty to take up the divine birthright of blacks in America."[5]

Most of the significant black migration into the Maritimes, primarily directed to Nova Scotia, had concluded by about 1825.[6] After that, population increase occurred largely due to natural reproduction, and any influx of new black settlers was matched by an out-migration of black Maritimers. Then, fifteen years after the War of 1812, when black migration into the Maritime colonies had essentially ended, a new wave of black migrants began moving into Upper Canada. Only a handful went to Lower Canada; the other colony formed out of old Quebec.[7] The makeup and timing of the various migrations helped establish the characteristics of the disparate black communities.[8]

The end of the American Revolution marked the first major incursion of blacks into British North America as the losers of the revolution sought a new life in the parts of British America that remained loyal to the Crown.[9] With the end of hostilities and the signing of the Treaty of Paris in 1783, perhaps as many as thirty-five thousand loyalists immigrated to Nova Scotia as the British evacuated New York, Charleston, and Savannah. They were part of an exodus of seventy-five thousand people who left the newly independent United States to find homes in the British Empire.[10] Nearly half of the loyalists who moved into Nova Scotia settled in the Saint John River area and on the west side of the Bay of Fundy. Complaints of government neglect soon triggered the creation of the new colonies of New Brunswick and Cape Breton (absorbed back into Nova Scotia in 1820). Another eight to ten thousand loyalists fled to the colony of Quebec, where subsequent social and political tensions led to the passage of the Constitutional Act of 1791, which divided Quebec into Upper and Lower Canada.[11]

Among the exodus from the American states were thousands of black refugees, both slave and free. Many white loyalists who rejected the vision of the revolutionaries and moved to the British colonies brought slaves with them, sometimes in significant numbers. One loyalist, who arrived at what would become Shelburne, brought 57 slaves.[12] Perhaps as many as 2,000 accompanied fleeing slaveholders who entered the British colonies – about 1,200 to the Maritimes, 300 to Lower Canada, and 500 to Upper Canada.[13] Initially, the gender balance was skewed. Male slaves in this forced migration outnumbered women three to one, a reflection of their relative financial value. Although the migrating slaveholders were greatly outnumbered by the artisans, labourers, farmers, and small merchants who made up the mass of the Maritime loyalists, they were nevertheless committed to maintaining both the institution of slavery and their position in society.[14] It was a recipe for future discord.

Approximately three thousand free black loyalists were among the refugees leaving New York City, and they moved primarily into Nova Scotia.[15] They had left with promises of freedom and support from the imperial government. What they would not receive was parity and equality. In the years that followed, as loyalist refugees adjusted to life alongside colonists whom they perceived as less committed to Britain, class and political tensions ran high, and the poorest loyalists, both white and black, faced serious hardships. Although all loyalists were entitled to compensation for their losses, what they actually received varied considerably. Too few surveyors, too little good land, and a cumbersome administration complicated the process of allocating real estate.[16] Probably less than a third of the black settlers received land from the British government, and even then it generally consisted of smaller lots of poorer quality. Hard times sparked social conflict. The difficulties, discrimination, and dangers facing the black settlers were highlighted in Shelburne in 1784 when high unemployment and economic competition goaded disbanded white soldiers to riot. Shelburne resident Benjamin Marston recorded in his diary that the white veterans had "risen against the free Negroes to drive [them] out of Town because they labour Cheapr [than] they (ye soldiers) will."[17]

Across Nova Scotia, significant black communities grew up at Birchtown, Brindly Town (near Digby), Preston (near Halifax), and Little Tracadie in what is now Guysborough County. The decades between the revolution and the War of 1812 were a period of considerable hardship, social flux, and out-migration for many original Maritime loyalists, both white and black. In Shelburne, for example, a population of approximately ten thousand in 1783 had shrunk to less than a thousand by the turn of the century.[18] Not surprisingly, the hard times weighed heaviest on the early black pioneers, who became disillusioned with their second-class status and white hostility. Some 1,200 black residents, including prominent leaders such as David George, Daddy Moses, and Thomas Peters, migrated to Sierra Leone in January 1792.[19] When they left, a majority of the remaining black settlers relocated to towns such as Halifax in search of steady employment. In 1796, they were joined by more than five hundred Jamaican maroons whom the government had expelled from their island and shipped into Nova Scotia with the expectation that they would work on the Halifax citadel. Settled as a group at Preston on land vacated by earlier black loyalists, they received plots varying from thirty to a hundred acres. By the time they had suffered through a second Canadian winter and attempts by the governor to "civilize" them, most were desperate to relocate to a warmer and more familiar climate. In 1800, virtually all left for Sierra Leone.[20]

Fewer black migrants settled in New Brunswick than in Nova Scotia, although by 1784 an estimated five hundred slaves were living in the Saint John area, many owned by key members of the colony's elite.[21] Slavery survived in the colony well into the nineteenth century, but its legality was ambiguous. No local legislation established or empowered slavery in New Brunswick, although slave owners assumed that it was state supported. An 1800 test case before the Supreme Court of New Brunswick, which involved the ownership of a slave named Nancy, ended with the bench evenly divided.[22] With no judgment entered, Nancy was returned to her owner. In 1801, two supporters of slavery introduced bills into the House of Assembly that would have established the clear legality of slavery, but the bills were withdrawn because of the resultant opposition. The lack of legal security and the increasing aversion to slavery undermined the institution within the colony and led to its demise. In 1822, the New Brunswick government claimed that no slaves were held in the province, although Jennifer Harris has challenged that assumption.[23]

Besides the slaves who were transported to New Brunswick, an unidentified number of free blacks had joined the post-revolution exodus of refugees leaving New York and Charleston by contracting themselves as indentured servants. Some came to New Brunswick. In addition, many Nova Scotia black loyalists, such as Thomas Peters and Ralph Henry, relocated to New Brunswick after becoming dissatisfied with their treatment and the delays in receiving the land allocated for black refugees.[24] Although many were given small fifty-acre parcels, the black experience there was similar to that in Nova Scotia. Blacks clustered together in small communities, generally unhappy with their land and the government's policies and support, while they watched as white settlers were given acreage that they thought had been set aside for them. When the first elections were held in New Brunswick, free blacks were explicitly excluded from the franchise.[25] Disillusioned and bitter, some joined the emigration to Sierra Leone, whereas others abandoned their allotted land and moved to Saint John and other towns in search of employment.

Despite this history, the blacks who remained in the Maritimes demonstrated their commitment to the Crown during the War of 1812.[26] In both colonies, they volunteered for militia service, and three black corps were formed to defend the colonies from possible American invasion. The end of the war also saw a significant increase in the black population of the Maritimes. In April 1814, Vice-Admiral Alexander Cochrane issued a proclamation inviting Americans to become British subjects. The proclamation did not specifically mention slaves, but its obvious intent was to attract runaway slaves and give them legal status. Cochrane's call led to a post-war influx of about two thousand new black refugees who settled in or close to Halifax and other towns, where they received limited government assistance.[27] Many remained in Nova Scotia, but perhaps a quarter of them resettled in New Brunswick.[28] Over the next decades, the black population in both colonies grew slowly. As a result of this long historical process, one of its characteristics (at least in the popular mind) was loyalty to Britain and resistance to the United States. Although blacks remained socially and economically disadvantaged in the Maritimes and were frequently denigrated by the colonial press, the image of black loyalists helped moderate the racial prejudice of white society by offering "a tangible example of the difference between Nova Scotia and the United States."[29]

Prince Edward Island has no comparable records that allow us to track the growth of its black community, which was no larger than several hundred at its maximum size in the nineteenth century.[30] The House of Assembly had legally recognized slavery on the island as early as 1781, and some loyalists who arrived in 1784 brought their slaves with them.[31] Nevertheless, until the island repealed slavery in 1825, it was ill defined there, as it was in the other colonies.[32] Records do indicate that slave sales occurred as late as 1802, but the institution was clearly moribund.[33] When the Assembly formally abolished slavery on the island in 1825, the act was symbolic as there were no slaves on Prince Edward Island.[34] Most blacks were concentrated in a part of Charlottetown whose name, the Bog, said much about their status in the colony. The first Canadian census to include Prince Edward Island was conducted in 1881, and it enumerated only 181 black islanders.[35]

By about 1830, the pattern of black demography had been well established in the Maritimes, at least as revealed by the various censuses.[36] On the eve of the Civil War, the black population in the Maritime colonies was less than 10,000, a small fraction of the 663,000 people living there.[37] Nova Scotia's black population was four to five times that of New Brunswick, but the two groups shared a common background formed by the American Revolution and the War of 1812. In Nova Scotia, census statistics reveal a black population growing slowly by natural increase during the decades before the Civil War: In 1851, 4,908 blacks lived in the colony, with females (2,587) outnumbering males (2,321). That population reached 5,927 in 1861. New Brunswick's census records from 1824 to 1861 show a generally stable black population holding well below 2,000.[38] In 1851, the official figures listed only 1,058 black inhabitants, of whom 505 were male and 553 were female.[39] By 1861, the population had grown to 1,581, made up of 730 males and 851 females.

Although the black populations of Nova Scotia and New Brunswick differed markedly in size, their gender balance did not. All the existing census records for both colonies that indicate the sex distribution of the black population list slightly more females.[40] This suggests a largely indigenous and stable population. The preponderance of females, coupled with the fact that successful American runaway slaves were disproportionately male, strongly indicates that there had been no large influx of fugitive slaves into the Maritimes.[41] Unfortunately, the censuses for both provinces list place of origin only for the general population, not for subgroups. Nevertheless, Nova Scotia had only 1,950 US-born residents in its total population, whereas the New Brunswick census had a catch-all category of "Other Foreign Countries" that totalled just 3,594. Thus, it is reasonable to assume that very few African Americans lived in these provinces.

Nonetheless, it is very likely that some black fugitives arrived in Nova Scotia and New Brunswick, because escapees from the Upper South frequently went by sea.[42] Moreover, there were a number of very visible black fugitives who reached the Maritimes, most of whom had arrived on boats from the United States.[43] Certainly, the provincial press mentioned them.[44] In one case, George Lewis, an escaped slave from Virginia, settled briefly in Albany before abolitionist friends helped him relocate to Boston, where his daughter Lizzie was living. Lewis worked for three years as a carpenter in a Boston shipyard while attempts were made to get his wife and five other daughters out of slavery. With the increased anxiety created by the passage of the 1850 Fugitive Slave Act, Lewis opted to move his family to Nova Scotia.[45]

His decision was uncommon, but a few other African Americans did follow his example. Escaping from Baltimore in 1839, Jesse Coleman went to Halifax, where he became a preacher and founder of the Zion Methodist Church. A few years later, John William Robertson also used the maritime route, stopping at Baltimore, Philadelphia, Hartford, and Boston before he reached Halifax, where he worked as a servant for a British officer in the garrison.[46] In 1842, Robert J. Patterson fled from his Virginian owner onboard a packet-boat, first to New York and then Boston, where he lived for ten years before concerns about the Fugitive Slave Act prompted him to relocate to Saint John in 1852. He remained there for the rest of his life, becoming a prosperous and respected member of the urban community.[47] A fourth fugitive, Thomas H. Stone, used the Maritimes as a brief sanctuary. Born in North Carolina and owned by a merchant, Stone managed to save enough money to purchase his wife's manumission and ultimately send her to Brooklyn. He later stowed away on a ship bound for New York, where he was reunited with his family. After the passage of the Fugitive Slave Act, Stone, though not his family, moved to Saint John. Three years later, however, he rejoined his family in Massachusetts, where he remained.[48] Other African Americans may also have used the Maritime colonies as a refuge, but few chose them as a permanent home in the 1850s.

Conditions were very different in the Canadas. By the time of the Civil War, their black population was considerably larger than in the Maritimes, although initial growth had been slow. In the years immediately following the American Revolution, the perception and reality of the black experience there, as in the Maritimes, was fluid and ambiguous. Some loyalists had moved into the British-controlled areas along the Detroit and Niagara frontiers, bringing hundreds of slaves with them. The 1791 division of Quebec into Upper and Lower Canada left the vast majority of blacks living in the former, but slavery, involving both blacks and Amerindians, also existed in Lower Canada.[49] In that colony, which was overwhelmingly French speaking and Catholic, the black subpopulation showed little signs of significant growth, although government officials initially encouraged the use of slaves. In 1784, a census of slaves in what would become Lower Canada enumerated 304, although, again, this was probably a significant undercount.[50] During the mid-nineteenth century, official records show a continuous decline in the colony's black residents, from 266 in 1844 to 163 in 1861 and only 148 in 1871. Even if their numbers were several times what the officials recorded, few African Americans moved into this province during the 1840s and 1850s. Those who found a new home around Montreal settled into a complex society, where separation, not only by race and ethnicity but also by religion and language, was the norm.

Although Upper Canada initially had a small black population, that quickly changed. Some writers have estimated that by 1792, the slaves brought into the province numbered in the hundreds.[51] Indeed, in the first decade of the new colonies, slave owning was widespread among the elite. John Butler, Sir John Johnson, and many of their soldiers had brought slaves to Upper Canada.[52] Mohawk leader Joseph Brant owned thirty or more slaves, and other Native leaders also held slaves.[53] At least nine members of the Legislative Council and five of the Executive Council were slave owners.[54] From the early 1790s to 1812, black bondsmen secretly crossed the border in both directions, seeking freedom. A small but growing number of African American slaves entered Upper Canada, hoping to escape slavery and their owners, only to be offset by Upper Canadian slaves who were fleeing in the other direction, hoping to find freedom in the United States.[55] When the Upper Canadian government established a gradual abolition act in 1793, it freed not the slaves themselves but those of their children who were born after 9 July 1793 – and only when they turned twenty-five.[56] As a result, slaves existed in the colony until Britain abolished slavery throughout the empire in 1834.[57]

African Americans who crossed through the Niagara region often settled in the area of St. Catharines or Hamilton, although many subsequently moved on to Toronto. Those who crossed at Detroit congregated, at least initially, near Windsor, Chatham, or London. In many ways, these early fugitives shared experiences that resembled those of blacks in the Maritimes, enduring difficult times even as they demonstrated a commitment to the British government. As in the Maritimes, during the War of 1812 many recently arrived black settlers in Upper Canada enlisted to defend their new home. A company of black soldiers made up primarily of fugitive slaves, which was incorporated into the First Lincoln Militia Regiment, served at the start of the war as a pioneer unit.[58] They also served as infantrymen during the battle at Queenston Heights, in the unsuccessful defence of Fort George in May 1813, and the June 1813 victory over the Americans at the Battle of Stony Creek.[59] Moreover, black soldiers were part of the Third and Tenth Regiments of York Militia and the Glengarry Light Infantry, and another fifty fought with Joseph Brant's Native warriors.[60] Blacks demonstrated a very public loyalty and commitment to their new home through their military service during the War of 1812, the Rebellion of 1837, and even the Crimean War.[61]

From 1800 to about 1830, the black communities in all the British North American colonies shared important similarities. Their small but growing populations endured the economic privations common to cash-poor and landless refugees while dealing with local discrimination and hard times. Although the institution of slavery had been abolished, the stigma connected to it all too often remained. In both the Maritimes and the Canadas, blacks could claim to be part of a loyalist tradition, although that contention was made more frequently for the Maritimes.[62] During the War of 1812, black men in all the colonies had been quick to defend the Crown. When rebellions broke out in 1837 around Toronto and then in the London District, both sides agreed that the black residents in the province strongly supported the government. William Lyon Mackenzie grumbled that "nearly all of Upper Canada's Blacks are opposed to every species of reform" because "they are so extravagantly loyal to the Executive."[63]

Although both Upper Canada and the Maritimes housed black populations that identified with Britain, white perceptions of black settlers in Upper Canada, or Canada West as it became in 1841, increasingly differed from those in the Maritimes. The public image (and a good deal of subsequent historical literature) became dominated by stories of American fugitive slaves and the efforts of their owners to reclaim them. Accounts that focused on the Underground Railroad as an important conduit for runaways also depicted Canada West as their typical destination.[64] Not surprisingly, on the eve of the Civil War, Canada West's black community was portrayed as the most Americanized in the colonies, with the largest numbers of refugees from American slavery. This raises important questions regarding their identity. Some writers have assumed that most of the black residents were merely sojourners rather than citizens with a deep commitment to the British colony, although the term "transmigrants" perhaps better describes them.[65]

The popular perception in Canada West that the black community consisted primarily of American fugitive slaves was the product of several factors. As early as 1819, various settlements were established in the colony specifically to assist black migrants, especially African Americans. In Oro Township, northeast of Barrie, a government-sponsored attempt to settle black veterans of the War of 1812 was largely stillborn, and subsequent waves of black migrants who arrived after 1826 failed to establish a more prosperous or larger community. At its peak, Oro's black settlement reached only 150.[66] Later ventures, with greater black input, were more successful, and although the Wilberforce settlement north of London and the Dawn settlement near Dresden fell short of their organizers' goals, the efforts to establish a black community at Buxton in Kent County fared well. Moreover, all three of these enterprises received considerable public attention due to the growing importance of anti-slavery rhetoric in both the United States and the British colonies.[67]

The impetus behind most of these schemes was the discrimination against African American communities in the United States during the decades immediately before the Civil War. Sometimes the catalyst was a specific event, as was true of the Wilberforce settlement. After the growing influx of fugitive slaves into Cincinnati triggered white-on-black violence in 1829, the city required black residents to provide certificates of freedom and to post five-hundred-dollar bonds.[68] In response, the Cincinnati Colonization Society sought to send black colonists to Upper Canada. It reached an agreement with Sir John Colborne, the lieutenant governor of Upper Canada, and the Canada Company to purchase land in Biddulph Township north of London to form the Wilberforce settlement. Although several thousand blacks purportedly left Cincinnati, only 460 came to Canada, and of these, only 6 families joined 15 families from Boston to establish Wilberforce.[69] Eventually, about 200 blacks did join the community, but many left within a few years.[70] In 1852, the Anti-Slavery Society of Canada reported that only 20 black families still lived at Wilberforce and portrayed them as struggling, an assessment confirmed by other sources.[71]

Several other black settlements, established during the 1840s, were given additional impetus by the fear generated in African American communities due to the passage of the Fugitive Slave Act.[72] Josiah Henson, an ex-slave who had lived in Canada West since 1830, and Hiram Wilson, a white American abolitionist, established the British-American Institute in Dawn Township near Dresden. Although the Dawn settlement reached a population of perhaps five hundred at its peak, the institute was always short of funds, and it shut down in 1868. Moreover, both Henson and Wilson lacked critical leadership skills, and both would face accusations of mismanagement.[73] Other attempts were made to settle African Americans in the Windsor area. In 1852, abolitionists in Ontario and Michigan founded the Refugee Home Society, with Mary and Henry Bibb as its managers. Donations were collected on both sides of the border with the goal of purchasing fifty thousand acres of government land "for the homeless refugees of American Slavery to settle upon."[74] Although the original plan proved unrealistic, the Refugee Home Society ultimately bought approximately two thousand acres in Sandwich and Maidstone Counties close to Windsor.[75] Each family was to receive twenty-five acres; five were free and the remaining twenty were to be paid for in nine annual installments. Financial mismanagement and controversies dogged the society, and many black settlers viewed it with considerable skepticism. Perhaps as a result, fewer than 150 remained on the land by 1855.[76]

The settlement established at Buxton, about twelve miles south of Chatham in Kent County, was the most successful of these projects.[77] The driving force behind it was William King; born in Northern Ireland in 1812, King came to the United States in 1833, first to Ohio and then to Louisiana. For the better part of a decade, he taught school in the South before deciding to enter the Presbyterian ministry. In 1845, while in Scotland training to become a clergyman, he inherited slaves from his father-in-law in Louisiana. Following the death of his wife and children, he accepted a position in Toronto, manumitted his slaves, and took steps to establish them as free settlers in British North America. Although he had rationalized slave holding while in Louisiana, the death of his immediate family was a turning point for him.[78] He managed to obtain support from the Presbyterian Synod and to recruit local businessmen to assist his plan. In 1849, the "Elgin Settlement" purchased 4,300 acres around Buxton on which to settle freed and fugitive African Americans. Its backers believed that other similar ventures had failed because they depended on "voluntary contributions" and were poorly managed. They asserted that a sense of community and a personal and financial commitment to Buxton by all of its members would be crucial to its success.

In little more than a decade, Buxton had almost a thousand inhabitants and included several businesses. In addition to a saw and gristmill, a brickyard, and small manufacturing works, it boasted a post office, a bank, a store, four churches of differing denominations, and three schools. One of these, the Buxton Mission School, quickly attained exceptional quality, producing some remarkable graduates. Staffed by teachers in training from Knox College in Toronto, it swiftly achieved financial and academic stability, and its pedagogical reputation led white parents to enrol their children there. Although the exact reasons for Buxton's achievements are debated, it was the most successful black settlement in the province.[79] Nevertheless, despite the high visibility of these communities, their members constituted only a small part of Canada West's black population.

The well-publicized attempts of Southern slaveholders to reclaim fugitive slaves and of runaway African Americans to reach freedom north of the border also created a high profile for African Americans in Canada West. Because they were widely covered by the press and became part of the narratives told by abolitionists at open meetings, there was considerable public awareness of the British colonies as legal havens for escaped slaves. Indeed, the forcible transportation and sale of Chloe Cooley to an American in March 1793 by her Niagara-area owner had played a key role in convincing Lieutenant Governor John Graves Simcoe to push the Upper Canadian Legislature to enact legislation that year for the gradual abolition of slavery in the colony.[80]

An 1833 act passed by the Parliament of Upper Canada to allow the extradition of persons accused of certain crimes in foreign countries quickly produced several test cases involving African Americans who had fled slavery in the United States.[81] In June 1833, Thornton Blackburn, a fugitive slave from Kentucky who had been arrested in Detroit but freed by armed supporters, managed to reach Upper Canada. An American extradition attempt was refused on the grounds that he had not participated in the rioting that facilitated his escape and therefore could not be charged with any of the crimes specified in the act of 1833.[82] Blackburn remained in Toronto for the rest of his life. Four years later, two other fugitive slaves faced extradition from Upper Canada. In the first case, the Upper Canadian government ordered that Solomon Moseby (also spelled "Molesby" and "Mosely"), who had escaped on his owner's horse and reached Upper Canada, be returned to the United States. The governor of Kentucky had requested his extradition on the grounds that he was a horse thief, and Upper Canadian officials could find no technicalities to deny the request. Before he could be expelled, however, black supporters forcibly rescued Moseby and soon got him to England. Years later he would return to live in Niagara.[83] In a similar case involving Jesse Happy, a Kentucky fugitive, the Executive Council decided that the evidence submitted was insufficient to determine his guilt, and Happy was released.[84] The court also ruled that any extradition under the 1833 law applied only if the alleged offences were crimes under Upper Canadian law and raised the possibility that actions taken by an escaping slave might be viewed as self-defence, not a felony.[85]

A new extradition case, in July 1841, inflamed public opinion in both the Canadas and Britain, when a Canadian court ordered Nelson Hackett, a fugitive from Arkansas, returned to his owner. Because he had fled with his owner's horse, coat, and gold watch, Hackett was treated as a thief. After his extradition, abolitionist societies in Bristol and Liverpool attempted to purchase his freedom, but their efforts failed because they were unable to discover his whereabouts. With the intent of appeasing public concern, British officials promised that they would henceforth "follow the most liberal interpretation of British law in maintaining protection for ex-slaves."[86] The last extradition case in Canada West concerning a fugitive slave dealt with John Anderson, a Missouri runaway who had stabbed and killed Seneca T.P. Diggs when he had tried to arrest him. Years later, while Anderson was living in Caledonia, Canada West, he was arrested and held pending a hearing. Under the Webster-Ashburton Treaty of 1843, Britain and the United States agreed to return individuals who had been charged with murder. Anderson's supporters argued that under British law an attempt to enslave someone could be resisted with lethal force. After a series of trials attended by hundreds of black and white sympathizers, the Court of Common Pleas in Toronto ruled in favour of Anderson, citing technicalities involving the wording of the writ.[87] On his release, British abolitionists invited Anderson to give a series of lectures throughout England. Following that, at the end of 1862, he sailed for Liberia and disappeared from historical records.[88]

It was not only extradition cases that caught the Canadian public's attention in the years prior to the Civil War. Community groups hostile to slavery frequently hosted lectures by both white and black abolitionists in provincial towns and cities.[89] Canadian papers also carried frequent stories concerning the plight of fugitives, the evils of slavery, and attempts to re-enslave black residents. In one such article, a Kingston paper warned that "three negro boys were enticed away from Prescott into the U.S. to be sold into slavery."[90] A more famous case appeared in the *Montreal Gazette* in 1855. The city's chief of police published a letter sent by John H. Pope of Maryland proposing that fugitives be lured or coerced to the border where Pope "would be there to pay cash."[91] This was one of several letters sent to officials in various Canadian cities, and though both the police chief and the *Gazette* denounced Pope, the Marylander later claimed that he had "secured eight of her Majesty's loyal black subjects."[92]

Public sympathy for African Americans in British North America was sufficiently great that some feared its exploitation by the unscrupulous. In 1841, Reverend R.V. Rogers warned readers of the *Kingston Chronicle and Gazette* "against the imposition of a coloured man who claims to be a runaway slave raising money to buy his child."[93] Whether Rogers was correct is not known, but imposters did exist. A decade later, after Butler's Real Ethiopian Serenaders put on a concert in Montreal "for the benefit of the fugitive slaves," five members of the city's real fugitive slave community published a warning "that the benefit given for them" was an apparent fraud and that they had received no money from Butler. They warned that Butler "may try to play the same game in some other City of Canada if it is not made known to the public."[94]

Canadian papers also printed stories about attempts in Northern states to enforce the 1850 Fugitive Slave Act that threatened to trigger widespread violence. These accounts resonated across British North America. The editor of the *Halifax British Colonist* believed that the arrest of an escaped slave in Detroit had aroused so much anger that he "would not be at all surprised to hear of a war of extermination breaking out between the races."[95] In February 1851, a largely black crowd freed Shadrach Minkins from a Boston court before he could be returned to his Virginia owner, spirited him out of the city, and put him on a train to Canada East. Unlike other fugitives who soon left the colony, he stayed in Montreal, where he married an Irish woman and raised a family. Having created a new life and identity for himself, Minkins remained in Montreal until his death in December 1875.[96] In the fall of 1851, a Missouri fugitive slave, William "Jerry" Henry (or McHenry), was arrested in Syracuse, New York, by one of the federal commissioners created by the Fugitive Slave Act. Fortunately for Henry, numerous abolitionists were in the city at the time, attending a Liberty Party meeting.[97] They quickly organized and freed him, in what became known as the Jerry Rescue. Within a few days, Henry and several of his liberators had reached Kingston, Ontario, where he lived until his death in 1853.[98]

At almost the same time as the Jerry Rescue, a more violent and widely publicized confrontation unfolded near Christiana, Pennsylvania. Attempts by a Maryland slaveholder, Edward Gorsuch, to arrest four of his fugitive slaves ended in a gun battle that saw Gorsuch killed and his son badly wounded. The black participants, including William Parker, another escaped slave who had assisted Gorsuch's runaways, fled north before crossing the lake to Kingston. Many stayed in Toronto, although Parker and his neighbour Abraham Johnson relocated to Buxton, where they became prominent members.[99] Parker's role in the riot, his escape, and subsequent settlement in Buxton, which he later recounted in an *Atlantic Magazine* article, fed Southern anger while reinforcing the image of Canada West as a sanctuary for fugitive slaves.[100]

The "Battle of Christiana" and the public response to it convinced President Franklin Pierce that the Fugitive Slave Act had to be enforced if American unity were to be preserved.[101] Pierce's determination to apply the law led to the most publicized fugitive slave case, the seizure of Anthony Burns and his return to slavery in May 1854. Burns had escaped from Virginia to Boston but unwisely wrote to his brother, also a slave. His letter was intercepted and his location revealed.[102] Pierce subsequently used the full authority of his office to arrest and return Burns in an attempt to prove to Southerners that the law would be enforced "even in Boston." A bloody rescue attempt failed, offers to buy Burns's freedom were rejected, and only the presence of a large military escort enabled authorities to get him onboard a steamer and returned to his owner.[103] Ultimately, supporters in Boston purchased Burns's freedom, and he became a minister. He preached briefly in Indianapolis but was forced out by Indiana's black laws, which barred out-of-state African Americans from becoming residents. In 1860, Burns took over the congregation at the Zion Baptist Church in St. Catharines, Canada West, where he preached until his death in July 1862.[104]

The 1850s featured heightened anxiety, not just for recently escaped fugitives but also for many African Americans in Northern states. "Fugitive slaves who had lived for many years safely and securely in western New York and elsewhere," wrote Frederick Douglass, "were suddenly alarmed and compelled to flee to Canada for safety."[105] Across the North, black churches recorded a sudden drop in membership as many parishioners felt the need to relocate their families.[106] Nevertheless, Burns's trial and transportation had transformed and energized resistance across the North. He was the last fugitive slave to be officially returned from anywhere in New England, and nine Northern states quickly passed new personal liberty laws to protect African Americans.[107] The number of runaways who were returned to their owners, never a large amount, fell off after passage of the liberty laws, although some were still seized and returned without legal process.[108]

Although fewer fugitives sought refuge in the British colonies by the late 1850s, that did not necessarily halt the northward flow of all African Americans. Many more free blacks made strategic moves across the international border. The new Fugitive Slave Act was just one factor in their decision. Equally important was the legal and social discrimination to which they were subject in many Northern states. Across much of the North and particularly in Indiana, Ohio, and Illinois, regulations were increasingly implemented to restrict the rights of blacks in the areas of immigration, residency, suffrage, education, military service, and equal standing in the courts. The regulations were designed to discourage African Americans from moving into those states and to encourage black residents to leave. Only in New England did blacks and whites have equal voting rights. In most Northern states, blacks could not serve in the militia, and educational segregation was increasingly the norm.[109] By contrast, though prejudice certainly existed in the British colonies, the laws and the courts seldom sanctioned it.

The decades before 1861 may have been identified in the public mind with the plight and flight of fugitive slaves, but historians have disagreed over what that influx actually meant for the black communities in Canada West. Indeed, the exact size and makeup of Canada West's black population in 1861 has been the subject of considerable debate. The disagreement pivots on methodological differences and the favouring of certain types of sources. The image that has captured the popular and historical imagination, based largely on anecdotal evidence drawn from newspapers and published accounts, is that of thousands of African Americans, both fugitive slaves and free Northerners frightened by the powers given to "slave catchers" under the Fugitive Slave Act, seeking sanctuary and freedom in British North America.[110] Adding to the mystique is the idea of an Underground Railroad managed by committed abolitionists, both black and white, who risked much by putting principle over personal safety. The image is particularly appealing for many Canadians, concerned as they are with the differences between their country and the United States, because it depicts British North America as the long-sought-after "Glory Land," an asylum for blacks fleeing American intolerance.[111]

Central to the debate is the question of the size and makeup of Canada West's black population. In the 1920s, Fred Landon, a pioneer in African Canadian history, laid out what became the standard narrative on this topic. He believed that 15,000 to 20,000 African Americans fled north between 1850 and 1860, swelling the black population in "the British provinces from about 40,000 to nearly 60,000."[112] He argued that most settled into Essex and Kent

Counties in Canada West and that many returned to the United States when the Civil War ended. Landon drew most of his data from sources such as the *Boston Liberator*, the *Windsor Voice of the Fugitive*, and the reports of the American Anti-Slavery Society, which commonly referred to the numbers of fugitives heading for British North America.[113] His arguments have been supported by recent writers who claim that "at least 30,000 to 40,000" fugitives reached Canada via the Underground Railroad.[114] As a result, the typical depiction of Canada West's black population in 1861 is that of approximately forty to sixty thousand people, most of them African American fugitives who clustered in a few areas of the province and returned in large numbers to the United States once the Civil War was over.[115] Thus, Jason H. Silverman states that after the war, "the fugitive slaves departed from Canada West almost en masse."[116] The problem is compounded by the censuses of 1861 and 1871, which disagree. The 1861 census reported only 11,223 blacks in Canada West, but many scholars dismiss it as too flawed for reliability; by contrast, the 1871 census, which listed 13,435 blacks and supports the return migration argument, is accepted largely uncritically.[117]

Robin Winks, the most widely cited authority on the black community in Canada, sought to correct the higher estimates in *The Blacks in Canada*. Asserting that the numbers and nature of Canada West's black community can never be accurately known, he dismisses the exaggerated estimate of some contemporaries that as many as sixty thousand fugitive slaves lived in the province on the eve of the war.[118] Nevertheless, he concludes that the 1861 black population "may have reached forty thousand, three-quarters of whom had been or were fugitive slaves or their children."[119]

Michael Wayne challenges almost all these assumptions. He systematically examined the nominal census schedules filled out by the enumerators who collected data for the 1861 Canadian census. Nominal census schedules, which contain detailed information on names, ages, origins, religion, occupation, and other factors, form the basis of the published census. In column 13 of the 1861 schedules, enumerators were to make a note for every black resident and were instructed to be especially diligent in recording them. On the basis of his research, Wayne claims that the four major tenets of the standard interpretation – a black population of forty thousand made up primarily of fugitive slaves and their children, clustering in a few areas and returning en masse to the United States after the war – are all incorrect. For Wayne, the key was the size of the 1861 population. He discovered that census enumerators of that year had listed 17,053 black residents on their forms, a much larger number than what the clerks ultimately recorded in the published report.[120] Gary Collison later observed the same pattern in Montreal's enumeration process. He found that although the published census listed only 46 black residents in that city, the census forms filled out by the enumerators identified 228 Montrealers as black.[121]

Also, both Wayne and Collison assume that a significant part of the black population, perhaps up to 20 percent, was missed by the enumerators in the field. This rate for black underenumeration was the upper limit found in many North American censuses. Adding the undercount, and allowing for some individuals who passed as white, Wayne estimated Canada West's black population at a maximum of twenty-three thousand.[122] Within it, 41 percent gave Canada West as their place of birth, whereas 57 percent were from the United States. Since many African Americans had entered the province as free persons, and given the equal gender balance mentioned above, Wayne estimated that only about a third of the American-born group – about 20 percent of all blacks in the province – were fugitives. In addition, if he is correct about the size of the black population in 1861, comparing that figure with the one given in the 1871 census demonstrates that fewer blacks left the province after the Civil War than has generally been assumed.

How are we to resolve the very dissimilar population estimates made by these historians? Part of their disagreement is rooted in differing perceptions as to which evidence is most trustworthy, and part is based on which population numbers are actually being estimated and when. Although the problem of underreporting plagues all censuses, and some are more accurate than others, historians and demographers have demonstrated that the degree of error in specific censuses can be estimated with considerable precision. The figures will always be approximate, but the approximation will be a systematic one, with greater reliability. By contrast to Wayne's finding, the anecdotal evidence regarding the numbers of "fugitives," "Negroes," "runaways," and/or "slaves," as provided by contemporary writers and newspapers, suggests widely divergent population figures, sometimes refers to different categories of black residents, and offers little effective method of assessing its own reliability.[123] Thus, someone such as Samuel Gridley Howe, a member of the American Freedmen's Inquiry Committee who made two trips to Canada West in 1863 to report on its black communities, could, after talking with abolitionist groups there, accept that the black population was larger than his own research suggested. After a careful assessment, Howe "concluded that a figure of from 15,000 to 20,000 was reasonable; but he uncritically accepted a highly generous estimate that some 30,000 or 40,000 black immigrants had come to Canada West since 1800."[124]

Some later writers accept the high number for the 1861 black population because they believe that the African Americans who entered the Canadas during the decades prior to 1861 remained in the province until the time of the census. Most assume that little or no black out-migration from British North America occurred during the 1850s and the early 1860s. In fact, black mobility was far more dynamic and complex than such a simple paradigm suggests. Blacks moved into British North America for many reasons, and they responded to its conditions in very different ways. Whereas some remained for the rest of their lives, others saw the province as a short-term sanctuary and left within a few years or even months. It may have been "Glory Land" for some, but for others it was simply the "least worst" option.

Understanding black mobility and agency may explain why historians have differed regarding the size of Canada West's black population. As systematically as possible, Wayne has captured its numbers at the time of the census. Writers who disagree with his conclusions have focused on newspaper reports, letters, and published accounts regarding the movement of African Americans into British North America during the 1850s and have assumed that all of them remained there at least until the Civil War began. In addition, the sources used by these writers, which reflect contemporary agendas, may have exaggerated their totals.[125] Of critical importance is the fact that the numbers of fugitive slaves who could possibly have reached British North America are quite limited. Tales of flight and rescue, capture and triumph, made for sensational reading in newspapers and published accounts, but only a thousand or fewer slaves successfully escaped their American owners each year, and most came from the Upper South.[126] Since most found permanent refuge in the Northern states, there was a relatively small pool available to immigrate to British North America. Of course, free African Americans also considered relocation, but that was an equally complicated decision.[127]

Historians who assume that African Americans who came to British North America tended not to leave it before 1863 ignore the complex ebb and flow of blacks in North America. Clearly, after the passage and initial implementation of the Fugitive Slave Act, many African Americans considered departing the United States, and most, but certainly not all, favoured the British provinces. However, the uncertainty of life as a fugitive had faced many blacks since the revolution, although the situation was now much more critical. In times of crisis, many blacks contemplated migration, or at least short-term relocation, but leaving the United States was always a contentious issue in their communities.[128] Nevertheless, during the 1850s, increasing numbers of them, led by men such as Martin Delany and James Theodore Holly, proposed various schemes involving emigration to places such as Canada West, the West Indies, or Africa, although their motives were frequently very different.[129] American newspapers often reported that black residents were planning to move north, but few verified whether they actually had. In October 1850, the *Boston Daily Evening Traveler* noted that "quite a number of families, where either the father or mother are fugitives, have been broken up, and the furniture sold off, with a view of leaving for safer quarters in Nova Scotia or Canada."[130] How many actually did leave, however, was never reported. A black conference held in Toronto in September 1851 urged fugitive slaves and free blacks to move to Canada West, but the impact of this is hard to measure.[131]

Although large numbers of African Americans immigrated to the British colony during the 1850s with the intent of becoming permanent residents, and many were recently escaped slaves, others were merely sojourners who often came north for very specific and time-limited reasons before returning to the United States. John H. Rapier, a prosperous businessman in Florence, Alabama, sent his sons north to be educated and also to get them out of the South. The first two boys, Henry and Richard, attended school in Buffalo and then in Canada West before they set out for California in 1855. The other two sons, John Jr. and James, were sent to the Buxton Mission School, where they lived under the care of their uncle, Henry Thomas.[132] John Jr. left Canada West after he graduated, but James, his "hell-rake" brother who had found religion, remained in the province for some years. After graduating from Buxton in 1860, James continued his studies in Toronto, where he earned a teaching diploma. He then returned to teach at Buxton. He voiced the ambivalence of African Americans living in the British colony. In 1860, James was selected to deliver an address to the Prince of Wales, who had stopped in Buxton during his North American tour. After describing the crucial refuge that the province offered to African Americans, James highlighted the importance of Buxton: "Here we enjoy true freedom, a blessing denied us in the land of our birth." Yet his first thoughts on hearing that South Carolina had fired on Fort Sumter in the spring of 1861 were "The year of jubilee has come, return, you exiles, home."[133] In 1864, James left for the South and never again lived in British North America.

Other African Americans, who felt unable to continue living in the United States, crossed the border during the 1850s, seeking a more tolerant society. Not all stayed. Martin Delany, frustrated by the widespread racism in

American society and his inability to get into an American medical school, moved to Chatham, Canada West, in February 1856. There he offered his medical services to fellow African Americans and became politically active, while at the same time supporting the idea of a back-to-Africa movement.[134] In the spring of 1858, he provided limited support to John Brown by helping to organize a convention at Chatham, although he was aware that many blacks in Canada West were deeply skeptical of Brown's actions. Delany's stay in the British province was brief, and in May 1859 he sailed from New York to Liberia as head of the Niger Valley Exploring Party. Nevertheless, he maintained many ties to Chatham, and in 1861 he recruited eighty-six people from Chatham and Buxton to go to Africa, although many subsequently decided not to go.[135]

Why other black emigrants chose to leave the United States is not always clear, as is the case for William Howard Day. He was born in New York City and with the assistance of a white guardian he obtained a liberal education that his parents could not otherwise have provided. As a newspaperman, publicist, and member of the black elite of Cleveland, Day experienced considerable achievements as well as setbacks. Yet in the fall of 1855, he decided to move to Canada West and buy a small farm near Dresden, for reasons that are not clear. One biographer speculates that "poor health, the failure of his second newspaper venture, continued discrimination, and America's dogged resistance to pleas of blacks for their rights, all contributed to his decision to seek his fortune elsewhere."[136] He did not last long as a farmer and soon moved to London, to St. Catharines, and finally to Chatham, where he taught for a short time in Buxton. He was involved in printing the final version of John Brown's constitution, but when Brown attacked Harper's Ferry in 1859, Day was in England on a fundraising trip. When he returned to North America, he went to New York rather than Canada West.[137]

For some, the move north was a necessity, if only for a short time. Samuel R. Ward claimed in his widely read *Autobiography of a Fugitive Negro* that by 1851 he "had already become hopeless of doing more in my native country; I had already determined to go to Canada."[138] He had some knowledge of the province, for he had visited Windsor, Kingston, Niagara Falls, and Queenston during the 1840s. However, the catalyst for his October 1851 move to Canada West was his participation in the Jerry Rescue and the fear that he would be arrested. He worked as an agent of the Anti-Slavery Society of Canada, giving lectures across the country. In less than two years, however, the society encouraged him to go to England to help raise funds and awareness of its work.

Abraham D. Shadd, a free-born African American abolitionist from Delaware, brought his family to Buxton in the early 1850s. The transnational character of the family, which had extended ties and influence in both the United States and Canada, was reflected in the prominent careers of members such as Mary Ann Shadd, I.D. Shadd, Abraham W. Shadd, and Emaline Shadd. *Courtesy of the Stanley Smith Collection, Western Archives, Western University.*

He never returned to British North America and spent the last eleven years of his life in Jamaica, where he died in 1866. Ward was not the only prominent African American to cross the border in search of temporary refuge from possible criminal prosecution in the United States. One of the most famous was Frederick Douglass. In the aftermath of John Brown's raid on Harper's Ferry, Douglass and several other abolitionists crossed the border, fearing that they might be arrested for their support of Brown. After moving "from town to town, trying to decide what to do," Douglass ended up in Clifton, New Brunswick, where he sailed for England in November 1859. Nor were blacks the only fugitives. Three of the "Secret Six" followed Douglass across the border, in quest of short-term asylum.[139]

The two black papers in Canada West, Windsor's *Voice of the Fugitive*, which was established by Henry Bibb, and the rival *Provincial Freeman* set up by Mary Ann Shadd, Samuel R. Ward, and others, reflected the differing attitudes of blacks who had emigrated from the United States. The *Voice* appealed to those who saw themselves as exiles waiting for a time to return.[140]

Thomas H. Jones, a Nova Scotia resident, expressed this sentiment in an 1851 letter to the *Boston Liberator*. "So long as nature prompts me," he wrote, "I shall look back to my native clime with anxiety, sorrow, and devotion. My personal friends, my flesh and blood, are there ... I am now in exile."[141] By contrast, the *Provincial Freeman* argued that blacks in Canada West should see themselves as British citizens, not as transient American émigrés. Of course, some who initially agreed with the paper may have changed their minds.

Whether African Americans left the United States in search of a freer life or a better job, their experiences in British North America varied considerably.[142] In 1855, a New Bedford black explained why two of his friends had returned from Canada West: "Times are very hard in Canada ... Every thing are so high and wages so low They cannot make a living."[143] Most free and fugitive blacks who came to the British provinces did so for a spectrum of reasons. Many who felt exiled or were discouraged by the poor job prospect in British North America returned to the United States prior to the Civil War. Moreover, by the late 1850s, many Northern states had created real barriers to the capture and return of fugitive Southern slaves, and even slaveholders who were passing through Northern states with their slaves ran the risk of losing them.[144] As a result, by the late 1850s blacks living in Northern states felt less pressure to emigrate to Canada or elsewhere. At the same time, some black residents in Canada West saw their quality of life declining due to increasing prejudice in pockets of white society.[145] In addition, a late 1850s recession in the Canadas may have driven many Canadians, both white and black, to migrate to the United States for economic reasons.[146] Certainly, some black British North Americans saw US conditions as so appealing that they moved south well before 1861.

Historians have long been familiar with the migration of tens of thousands of people from British North America to the United States. By 1860, about a quarter of a million US residents had been born in British North America. Little has been said, however, about the black members of this group. During the 1850s, hundreds of British North American–born blacks moved to Northern states. Certain Northern cities, such as Boston, were particularly attractive to them. By 1850, 16 percent of Boston's black residents were foreign born, and of these a majority came from the British provinces. Ten years later, while some African Americans were still looking north, foreign-born blacks made up more than a quarter of Boston's black population, "with most of these from Canada."[147] Nor was Boston unique. The 1860 US census, which listed the place of birth of those enumerated, included hundreds of black residents who gave Canada as their birthplace. Like most censuses, it would significantly have underrecorded the actual numbers of black residents, both native and foreign. Nevertheless, it listed 1,249 "black" or "mulatto" individuals who gave a British North American colony as their place of birth.[148] Not surprisingly, many clustered in states that bordered British North America, such as Michigan (173), New York (193), and Ohio (54). Massachusetts had the largest number (216), almost 60 percent of whom lived in Boston, and another 25 percent lived in nearby towns such as Lynn, Cambridge, and Brookline.[149] In the states adjacent to the Canadas, British-born blacks could be found in towns scattered from Jackson, Michigan, and Toledo, Ohio, to Geneva, New York, although the heaviest concentration was in urban centres such as Detroit (42), Niagara (47), New York (35), and Buffalo (18). Black British North Americans lived in most of the other Northern states as well, with the greatest number (42) in California. At least 3 had chosen to reside in a slave state. Henry Berryman, age twenty-nine, James Johnson, age fifty-six, and Mary James, age twenty, were all living in Baltimore in 1860.

Given the number of black families that had moved south to the United States by 1861, it is not surprising that some of the British North America–born soldiers and sailors were already resident there when they volunteered. A few examples highlight the diverse experiences of this group. Born in St. Catharines, William Hardy soon moved to the United States with his parents. After the war, he testified that he "was born in Canada, Jan. 2, 1846 and lived during the years 1850 and 1860 with his parents, John and Pamela Hardy, on Main Street" in Geneva, New York. Complicating matters, the 1850 census manuscript gives his age as two. Whether Hardy left St. Catharines before he was two or when he was slightly older, he had little recollection of it. Certainly, it is unlikely that he defined himself as British North American, and there is no evidence that he returned to Canada after the war.[150]

Hardy's case was not unique. When Henry Brown enlisted in the Eighteenth United States Colored Troops at St. Louis, Missouri, on 23 August 1864, he revealed a similar background. He testified that he was born in Chatham in 1840 and that he had moved to the United States in 1852, where he lived in Buffalo, New York City, and New Orleans before moving to St. Louis. Perhaps because he was serving as a substitute for N. Samuel Greene, Brown swore before a justice of the peace that he had "never declared my intention of becoming a citizen of the United States, and have not exercised the right of suffrage by voting in any election in any State."[151]

Moreover, in the years before the Civil War, transplanted black British North Americans could be found in increasing numbers in small American towns near the Canada West border. Ypsilanti, Michigan, a town near Detroit, provides one such case. The 1860 census shows that it had a black population of 227, of whom 43 were children born in "Canada." This group amounted to about 19 percent of the town's black population.[152] Sixteen black families in Ypsilanti had at least one child who was born in Canada. The fathers of virtually all these children came from a Southern state, whereas a few of the mothers were born in Canada West. The picture is one of fugitive slaves moving north, sometimes in stages, and residing in Canada West for a number of years. While there, they had one or more children, and they returned to the United States before 1860. The Safford family conforms to this pattern. Richard Safford, age thirty, was born in Virginia, and his wife, Martha, age twenty-two, was from South Carolina. Their children were Mary Jane, age seven and born in Indiana; Maloina, age five and born in "Canada"; Lyman, age three, and William, age two, both born in Michigan. The Hall family offers a variation on the pattern. John W. Hall was a thirty-nine-year-old cooper from Kentucky, but his twenty-four-year-old wife, Earline, was born in "Canada." Their first two children were born there as well, but the last two, the oldest of whom was two in 1860, were born in Michigan. Some Ypsilanti families, such as that of David and Amanda Travers, had spent more time in Canada West. All six of their children were born there. Because the oldest was fifteen and the youngest was two, and the family left the province some time after 1858, David Travers must have arrived in Canada West by 1845.[153] There were also six young Canada West–born women who worked in Ypsilanti as servants. Only three young men from Canada West worked there, but the low figure may merely indicate that they were often out of town, engaging in seasonal occupations.

One young Canada West–born black resident of Ypsilanti, Elijah McCoy, would become a highly celebrated inventor. His parents, George and Mildred McCoy, were fugitive slaves from Kentucky who managed to reach Canada West and settled in Colchester. Elijah was born there in May 1844, but only three years later the family moved to Ypsilanti. In 1859, Elijah was sent to Edinburgh, where he trained as a mechanical engineer. He subsequently returned to Michigan and worked for the Michigan Central Railroad as a fireman and oiler. An inventor by nature, McCoy developed an automatic lubricator for locomotive steam engines, although he received little recognition from the railroad. By the end of his life, he had obtained patents on fifty-seven inventions, mostly related to lubrication, and had set up the Elijah McCoy Manufacturing Company. Because of the quality of his products, some have argued that the term "the real McCoy" should be associated with his inventions.[154]

A few of the British North American–born men who would ultimately enlist in the Union army or navy had moved to the United States as adults. One such example, James M. Harrison, was born and raised in Halifax, and lived briefly in New York City before the war. Harrison did not give the date of his move to New York and was not enumerated in the 1860 census, but he was resident there when he joined the navy in July 1864. After his discharge in late 1865, he remained in New York for just over four years and subsequently moved back to Nova Scotia, first to Halifax and then to Shelburne. There he married and lived until his death in March 1908. Despite Harrison's sojourn in the United States, his roots were in the Maritimes.[155] In other cases, the pre-war moves were of limited distance and short duration. Some men, such as Isaac Hardy from South Colchester, Canada West, crossed the border to take advantage of temporary employment opportunities. Hardy and his friends would leave home for several months during the winter to cut wood in the shanties around Ann Arbor, Michigan. This was a way for Canadian farmers to augment their incomes.[156] In many cases, information regarding an individual's movements is very limited. Thomas W. Brown was born in Montreal on 2 July 1843. He left Canada at some point and was living in New York City when he joined the Twenty-ninth United States Colored Troops in 1864; like Harrison, he does not appear in the 1860 census. Unlike Harrison, however, he remained permanently in the United States after his discharge, living in either New York City or Brooklyn until his death in 1914. By then, Brown would probably have viewed himself as an African American.[157] Ultimately, the individual histories given above all suggest that, among blacks in the British colonies, those of Canada West had the strongest transnational ties. This would become clear when they had a chance to volunteer.

CHAPTER TWO

THE BLACK RESPONSE

WHAT THE NUMBERS MEAN

HISTORIANS OF THE Civil War have increasingly stressed the importance of its transnational dimensions and the ways in which it resonated in other countries.[1] Certainly, Abraham Lincoln claimed that the war involved more than just American interests. What was at stake, he believed, was the question of whether a constitutional republic could maintain its territorial integrity, an issue for all men who wanted "a fair chance in the race of life."[2] Of course, Confederate spokesmen, also appealing to an international audience, argued that the South was fighting for self-determination and the right of free citizens to decide their political future, and that these too were issues of world-wide significance. When the Lincoln administration used the Emancipation Proclamation to depict its war efforts as a struggle on behalf of liberty and equality, it gained vocal support in some quarters in Europe and the British Empire, just as it generated cynicism elsewhere.

After the release of Lincoln's Preliminary Emancipation Proclamation in September 1862, the *New York Evening Post* predicted its impact: "It puts us right before Europe ... It animates our soldiers with the same spirit which led our forefathers to victory under Washington; they are fighting today, as the Revolutionary patriots fought, in the interests of the human race."[3] By contrast, much of the English press, led by the *London Times*, was hostile to the proclamation, or at least to what it perceived as the political calculations that lay behind it. The *Times* warned of a possible bloodbath and depicted the proclamation as a scheme for subjecting "an Anglo-Saxon people to horrors equalled only by those which fell upon the English in India five years ago." Many papers were skeptical of Lincoln's motives. In a cartoon labelled "Abe Lincoln's Last Card; or Rouge-et-Noire," *Punch* depicted him as a desperate gambler playing his last card.[4] Even anti-slavery papers, such as the *London Spectator,* saw little to endorse in the proclamation. "It is only a hopeful promise," the paper editorialized. "The principle asserted is not that a human being cannot justly own another, but that he cannot own him unless he is loyal to the United States."[5]

Many British North American papers were also unimpressed with the proclamation and the man who drafted it. The *Halifax Morning Journal* described Lincoln as "a mere pettifogging third-rate country lawyer," and the *New Brunswick Reporter* claimed that the proclamation was grounded in military necessity, not morality.[6] The *Hamilton Evening Times* agreed that it arose not "out of any hostility to the system of slavery, from any consciousness of its injustice or from love of the negro, but simply that it is for the punishment of disloyal masters."[7] The *Saint John Morning Freeman* was quick to point out the paradox of the proclamation, and the *Kingston Daily News* likened it to the "Pope's bull against the comet."[8] In early February 1863, the *News* assessed the impact of the proclamation, stating that the "first month of its operation has been very barren of results favorable to the Federalists."[9] Many papers warned that the proclamation might unleash a race war. The *Toronto Globe* differed from the norm, giving a more favourable account of Lincoln's actions. His pronouncements, the editor believed, were "wise and right; the whole force of freedom must be arrayed against the slave power." Emancipation was crucial because "nothing short of the actual undoing of Slavery, and the inauguration of universal freedom can either compensate the sacrifices or destroy the causes of this war."[10]

Although foreign governments and press seldom saw the proclamation as a humanitarian call to arms, many individuals, especially in the black community, perceived it differently. For them, the president's call was revolutionary in both scope and content. Anderson Abbott decided to volunteer after he "learned by our city paper that it was the intention of the government of the United States to raise 150,000 colored troops."[11] Black communities across the hemisphere as well as the abolitionist movement of the Atlantic world increasingly saw the conflict as more than a struggle to eradicate slavery. For them, it was a fight for universal rights and equal justice. They understood that the Emancipation Proclamation was a powerful symbol indicating that the destruction of slavery and the right to civic membership for black

Americans had become a central part of war goals. They believed that a historical moment of enormous significance had been reached, and they framed their collective responses accordingly. Although young black men throughout the hemisphere became more emotionally and intellectually engaged with the growing reality of a war against slavery, how this translated into actual behaviour is less clear. The international dimension of their occupation enabled black sailors in the Atlantic world to join the struggle. John Robert Bond, a sailor of African and Irish background, left his Liverpool home in 1863 to join the Union navy and, as his family remembered, "to help free the slaves." Seriously wounded during his service, Bond remained in the United States after the war.[12] Certainly, the men who filled the ranks of the black regiments perceived that they were fighting for more than the freedom of enslaved Southerners, although that was part of their motivation. Charles W. Singer, a sergeant in the 107th United States Colored Troops, was one of many who argued that the war's significance extended beyond the United States. "Remember, soldiers," he wrote, "we are fighting a great battle for the benefit not only of the country, but for ourselves and the whole of mankind." The struggle was of crucial importance, he suggested, because "the eyes of the world are upon us."[13]

His comments raise the question as to how intently "the whole of mankind" was listening or the world was watching. Did the rhetoric depicting the war as a human rights crusade of global significance translate into actual physical support, especially from foreigners of African descent? Examining the British North American–born black recruits who entered the Union army and navy provides part of the answer. Their decision to enlist enables us to measure the transnational ideological involvement of black communities outside the United States. Black foreigners who left their homes to fight, at considerable personal risk, were probably responding to the powerful message of the Emancipation Proclamation. Thus, if British North America yielded a significant number of black recruits, as a proportion of its black population, the incorporation of emancipation into Union war goals probably resonated strongly with them, becoming a major motivator for action.[14] Calculating their number, however, is a complicated task.

Although historians have made many assumptions about black recruits from the British provinces, few have conducted a serious analysis of these men, a fact that is also true for white British North American recruits who served in the war. Thus, the apparently simple question of how many recruits, black or white, should be credited to the British colonies remains the subject of considerable debate. There is even less consensus regarding their motivation. In part, this disagreement is grounded in the fact that the answer is inextricably tied to the ambiguous concept of national identity. This has been aggravated by the need of some historians to fit their demographic estimates into an overarching interpretation of events before, during, and after the war. As a result, the estimates cited for the total number of British North Americans who served in the war, on both sides of the conflict, have varied from a low of fifteen thousand to a more generally accepted figure of fifty thousand.[15] Historians have been even less precise concerning the number of black recruits from British North America.[16] Robin Winks states simply that "many Canadian Negroes served in the Northern army – largely for Massachusetts, New York, and Michigan regiments."[17] Greg Marquis refers to the "scores of blacks from Canada West" who joined the Fifty-fourth Massachusetts or "the U. S. Colored Troops" but gives no specific number and focuses his discussion on a handful of black recruits from the Maritimes.[18] General surveys of Canadian histories often merely note that "many African Americans left Canada at the outbreak of the Civil War to help the northern side."[19] In addition, most writers who explore the numbers (and motives) of black British North American recruits tend to ignore sailors, focusing almost exclusively on soldiers.

In part, the disagreement concerning numbers is driven by a debate over personal identity and the question of who is to be designated a British North American (or even the more ambiguous "Canadian").[20] Many historians have relied on the apparently uncomplicated component of nativity to establish national identity, a task aided by the fact that most military records list the birthplace of black Civil War recruits. Other historians, however, believe that long-term residence better defines identity, and thus they argue that many British North Americans who settled in the states well before 1861 should really be considered Americans.[21] Many Civil War draft officials concurred.[22] Whether one chooses nativity or residence as a determinant of identity has a direct impact on estimates of the number of white and black recruits. During the 1850s, tens of thousands of white British North Americans and hundreds of their black counterparts started new lives in various American states, while at the same time thousands of African Americans, both free and fugitive, migrated north, overwhelmingly into Canada West, in search of greater social and civil freedom. Thus, using nativity to count British North American recruits undoubtedly inflates their number. By contrast, many American-born black recruits who returned briefly to the United States to serve in the military, men like James Newby, a free African American who had come to Buxton just before the war, may no longer have seen themselves as Americans, identifying instead with their new home.

Of course, historians have differed not just on the numbers of British North American volunteers but also on their motivation. Robin Winks believes that only "several thousand" white British North Americans enlisted in the Union military due to ideological reasons.[23] The rest, he argues, joined for the bounty money, sold themselves as substitutes, or were the victims of unprincipled recruiting agents. Even historians who accept that ideology was a strong impetus have concentrated on the controversial, shocking, or exceptional cases involving British North American recruits. Crimping, bounty-jumping, and desertion are favourite topics in discussions of white recruits. By contrast, examinations of blacks who volunteered have asserted or assumed that most did so in hopes of ending slavery.[24] Financial incentives, commonly linked to white enlistees, are seldom mentioned in connection with black volunteers.

Clearly, establishing just how many black British North Americans enlisted in the Union military is a challenging task. Part of the reason for the lack of scholarly attention is that, with a few notable exceptions, such as letters published in newspapers, black enlistees wrote little about their actions and incentives that has survived. Literacy was higher among black British North American volunteers than among most African American soldiers, but even the former left few personal records.[25] Moreover, what records they did leave were not highly valued by most repositories in the late nineteenth and early twentieth centuries. Because of this, only a few letters and diaries from black Civil War participants have survived into the twenty-first century. Marginalized groups with limited literacy leave fewer records of all sorts, be they probate documents or land transaction deeds; nor do they tend to figure in local histories.[26] Building a complete account of their life experience is therefore difficult. The shortage of personal records forces a greater reliance on information gathered by government bodies. The compiled military service records for each Union soldier and the pension applications that many filed after the war allow a partial re-creation of their lives. In addition, longitudinal data from American and Canadian manuscript censuses provide critical evidence for this task. As the disagreement regarding the accuracy of the 1861 Canada West census clearly reveals, not everyone sees census data as a useful source of information. However, the large body of literature on the analysis and use of census manuscripts allows for a sophisticated and careful interpretation of those data. In the end, there are only two ways of establishing the size of any particular population – one can guess, or one can count. Of course, there are wise guessers and poor counters, but a systematic rendering of numbers, even by poor counters, possesses an important characteristic that is unavailable in anecdotal evidence – it is possible to estimate the degree of error embedded in census records with some considerable accuracy. Determining the accuracy of any given individual's assessment of size is much harder.

A systematic analysis of the young black men who left the British colonies to volunteer in the American Civil War allows for a better understanding of both British North American black communities and the rapidly changing roles of black participants in the conflict. The primary focus of analysis is the men who named a British colony as their place of birth when they enlisted in either the Union army or navy. Clearly, birthplace is just one factor in an individual's self-identification, but it is powerful nonetheless, often more important than place of residence. A focus on British North American–born black recruits, though not without problems, combines practical benefits with necessity. Like the census, military records routinely include place of birth among their data. Thus, with considerable work, it is possible to identify and compile virtually every recruit who gave a British North American colony as his place of birth. However, the records do not differentiate between African Americans who were living in the United States and those who were resident in British North America when the war began. Black Americans who returned to the United States to enlist can be identified only by anecdotal evidence, and it is therefore impossible to be precise regarding their numbers. It is assumed, however, that they had as many ties to American black communities and were as concerned about events in the United States as were British North American–born blacks.

Although the military records provide a valuable approximation of the numbers of recruits, they must be used with caution, as is the case for most historical sources. The details recorded by the army enlisting officers, like the data compiled by census enumerators, were provided by the persons being questioned. Both enlisting officers and enumerators were to record the information as it was given to them. As will be discussed below, not all the information was truthful. Nonetheless, the place of birth given by the soldiers and sailors allows researchers to understand a recruit's starting point, both personally and geographically. Identifying a group of black participants who were born outside the United States opens the possibility of comparative study. When this information is used in tandem with other historical sources that track their subsequent careers, we can better understand the nature of

When young Ben Talbot enlisted in the 5th United States Colored Troops in August 1864, he did so under the alias William Therman because he had joined without his parents' consent. Decades later, when he applied for and received a pension, he persuaded the Pension Office to use his correct name. *Courtesy of the National Archives and Records Administration.*

black mobility in North America and how these individuals identified themselves in the context of the changes sweeping the continent. It also provides a measurement of the international response to the appeal for black equality.

Although military records note physical characteristics – age, height, colour of eyes, hair, and complexion – that would allow deserters to be recognized, they do not refer to race. However, establishing the number of black soldiers who enlisted is relatively easy because army units were not integrated at this time. Black artillery, cavalry, and infantry regiments were led by white officers.[27] The regiments were designated as United States Colored Troops (USCT), except for a few that retained their state designations.[28] The only white enlisted men who served in such units were a handful of senior non-commissioned officers, usually first sergeants or regimental non-commissioned staff members, who were added to bridge the gap until suitable black non-commissioned officers could be trained to replace them. The physical characteristics recorded in the regimental descriptive books allow researchers to catch these exceptional cases. Thus, it is possible to be quite accurate about the number of black soldiers in the Union army, although discovering exactly where they came from is sometimes impossible.

Identifying black sailors is more arduous because Union naval vessels were integrated, thereby mixing both white and black crewmembers. The descriptive information, therefore, becomes crucial in establishing race, although it is problematic. Individuals who are recorded as "Negro," "Colored," or "Mulatto" can safely be categorized as black. Those whose complexion is recorded as "Yellow" or "Swarthy" are more difficult to classify, especially because the navy enlisted sailors from many parts of the world. Furthermore, naval muster rolls for 1861 often fail to include a physical description of recruits. As a result, an accurate estimate of all black sailors, let alone black British North American sailors, is extremely difficult to achieve. Fortunately for this study, the Civil War African American Sailors Project, a special research partnership between Howard University, the Department of the Navy, and the National Parks Service, which is headed by Joseph Reidy, has identified all the black sailors who served in the Union navy during the Civil War.[29] Researchers working for the project sifted through thousands of pages of enlistment records and quarterly muster rolls of navy vessels, looking for descriptive terms that indicated the African ancestry of recruits. The project's stated policy was to err on the side of inclusion. Although its findings are the most precise to date, extracting racial identity from records that ignore race will always be problematic, and some individuals were probably missed.[30] To date, the project has identified nearly 18,000 black sailors, including 348 who were born in British North America. Even this intensive screening did not catch them all, and at least another four have been identified from other sources.[31] These men were among the 1,500 foreign volunteers who joined the Union navy, with the largest numbers coming from the islands of the Caribbean.

Whereas many foreigners may have enlisted at least in part to fight slavery, historians have detected more self-serving reasons for joining the military. Forty-five percent of naval recruits were foreign born, whereas in the army, the figure was just 27 percent.[32] Of course, the navy had a long tradition of national diversity among its crews, but historians have emphasized other factors to explain the large number of foreign sailors. Michael Bennett suggests that "getting clean" and making money were the most common motives for both white and black sailors. "Getting clean" meant participating in the war with minimum risk of personal hardship or death. The benefits of joining the navy extended beyond regular pay and rations to the chance of acquiring "big money," a share of prize money, and "ready money" (a salary advance).[33] Regardless of why they enlisted, most sailors would not have perceived entering the Union navy as a transformative act. Life at sea remained much the same, even if their purpose for serving had not. For black civilians who opted to become soldiers, life changed a great deal.

Unfortunately, no systematic attempts have been made to identify foreign-born black soldiers who joined the Union army. As a result, the first step in determining the number of black British North Americans who did so was an examination of the regimental descriptive books for the black units that were likely to have recruits from the British colonies, starting with those raised in the Northern states.[34] The books give every recruit's height, colour of hair and eyes, and complexion as well as place of birth and occupation before enlistment. This information, along with other scattered data on enlistment, service, desertion, and promotions, was recorded for any soldier who gave a British colony as his place of birth. Although there was space on the form for him to supply his town or county of birth, most simply gave "Canada." It is assumed that in the vast majority of cases, this indicated Canada West, although some recruits may have meant Canada East. For example, when Thomas Kennedy enlisted in the Third United States Colored Heavy Artillery Regiment, he gave his birthplace as "Montreal, Canada."[35] In a much more unusual case, John Littlefield, a sailor from Nova Scotia who enlisted in New York in July 1864, said he was born in "Cape Breton, Canada."[36] It is assumed, however, that few Maritimers would have given "Canada" rather than "New Brunswick" or "Nova Scotia."

Once the records of the Northern regiments had been scrutinized, the next step was to examine a representative sample of regiments raised in Southern states. Where there were indications of recruits from a British colony, all descriptive books were inspected for that state. For example, Virginia's black regiments were found to have a significant number of "Canadian" recruits, so all Virginia regiments were checked.[37] Because not all black regiments, especially a few units organized late in the war, were examined, a few black British North Americans may have been missed. The compiled numbers, therefore, represent a low estimate. Once all the information was accumulated, it was checked, wherever possible, against the soldier's compiled military service record to verify and augment the data in the descriptive books.³⁸

It is important to be clear that though we can precisely count the number of soldiers who gave British North America as their birthplace, that figure should nonetheless be seen only as a close approximation because some birthplaces may be incorrect. Explanations for this error range from deliberate falsehoods to confusion over the question to carelessness in recording the data. Recruiting officers who filled out the forms may have asked for place of origin rather than place of birth, and some recruits may have confused place of origin with place of residence. This was clearly the case for James Bailey, who volunteered for the Fifth Massachusetts Cavalry and gave "Canada" as his birthplace before correcting himself and citing "Kentucky." He was in fact an African American, although perhaps one who identified himself with his new home.³⁹ The regimental descriptive book record for Silas Garrison, who enlisted in Company A, Fifty-fourth Massachusetts, gives his birthplace as Canada, but his company descriptive book lists it as St. Louis, Missouri, though with an additional notation – "Single, Chatham, Canada West." Garrison was reported as missing in action after the assault on Fort Wagner in the summer of 1863, and there are no further records to explain the discrepancies regarding his nativity.⁴⁰

In instances where a black recruit tried to enlist but did not serve, that individual was not included among the number credited to the British colonies. Such was the case for James Firman, a thirty-six-year-old labourer from Saint John, who was documented, on the only card in his compiled military service records, as being mustered into the Twenty-third USCT on 30 June 1864 as a substitute for Isaac P.F. Edwards of Massachusetts. On the back of the card, however, is the notation "name not taken up on rolls of reg't." His file contained no evidence of military service, and he did not apply for a pension after the war. Although Firman is not included in this study, his name does appear on the African American Civil War Memorial in Washington, DC.⁴¹

Some black recruits deliberately gave inaccurate information to the recording officers. Many knew that, as British subjects, they were violating British law by enlisting in a foreign army during time of war. Although this law was not often enforced in the British colonies and remained more a threat than a punishment, some black veterans were charged or prosecuted under it.⁴² Thus, it seems plausible that some volunteers prudently chose to hide their identities or lie about their place of birth. In some instances, more personal reasons lay behind the use of an alias. Such was the case for Benjamin

F. Talbot of Seaforth, Canada West; enlisting as a substitute in Toledo, Ohio, in August 1864, he gave his name as William Therman, or Thurman, when he joined the Fifth USCT.[43] He had volunteered without the permission of his parents, so he used an alias, although he returned to Canada West as soon as he was mustered out. John E. Hart gave his correct birthplace but used the alias Franklin Howard because "he had run away from [home] and had enlisted under the name as he did not want his family to know that he had enlisted."[44] Enoch Dennis, who grew up in Colchester Township, Essex County, testified that some men of his acquaintance "did use fictitious names" when they joined the army.[45] Because a recruit under the age of twenty-one was legally a minor requiring parental consent to enlist, some recruits found it easier to lie about their age and place of birth. The British Consul in Buffalo recorded one such case of a sixteen-year-old volunteer from Canada West who had passed himself off "as eighteen and swore to that effect, also that he was from Cleveland, a place he had never seen in his life."[46] By contrast, some African Americans may falsely have claimed British North American nativity, assuming that doing so would help them qualify as substitutes. Among the more than two hundred black British North Americans who served as substitutes, there could be a number of erroneous nativity claims.

Finally, for many recruits and the officers who recorded their data, birthplace was not necessarily a critical issue. Some recruits may not have known, or remembered, where they were born. Certainly, the records for Luke Fizer, a soldier who served in the 102nd USCT, suggest this. Among the papers in his military records and his pension file, his place of birth is variously given as Baltimore, Windsor, and Kentucky. One of his deponents, John Price, swore that he had grown up with Fizer in Detroit, whereas another, Leonard Johnson, who was born and raised in Chatham, also remembered that Fizer lived there for a few years before the war.[47] Other pensioners left equally conflicting information regarding their place of birth, even when there was no apparent personal benefit in doing so. The cumulative effects of these cases may not significantly alter the total numbers of black British North Americans, but the nativity of some individuals under discussion may be incorrect.

Table 1 lists the total number of British North American–born volunteers, as identified in the military records. It also estimates the number of African American residents in Canada West who returned to the United States to fight in the war. The numbers of recruits show that the issues raised by emancipation and black enlistment resonated strongly in some black communities

Table 1
British North American black recruits

Colonies	Black population 1861	BNA-born recruits		US-born recruits	Recruits as % of black population
		Soldiers	Sailors		
Canada West	17,053	725	220	1,247*	13.7
Canada East	163	16	7	–	14.1
Nova Scotia	5,927	46	73	–	2.0
New Brunswick	1,581	46	49	–	6.0
Prince Edward Island	No census	2	3	–	–

* Estimate

outside the United States. At least 835 black soldiers and 352 black sailors – almost 1,200 men – who served during the Civil War claimed a British colony as their place of birth. Although most came from Canada West, every British colony was represented in both the Union army and navy. Nova Scotia, home for most blacks in the Maritimes, contributed at least 46 soldiers and 73 sailors, whereas New Brunswick, with a much smaller population, yielded 46 soldiers and 49 sailors. Even the two colonies whose black population was very small, Canada East and Prince Edward Island, contributed men to the Union military. Sixteen soldiers and 7 sailors claimed Canada East as their place of birth, and 2 soldiers and 3 sailors came from the tiny black community on Prince Edward Island. Not surprisingly, Canada West, which had British North America's largest black population and the strongest and most complex ties with adjacent states, yielded the greatest number of British North American–born recruits. At least 725 soldiers and 220 sailors gave this colony as their birthplace. Most were from the southwestern region of Canada West, but volunteers came from almost all parts of the province, including urban centres as diverse as Toronto, Hamilton, Kingston, Georgetown, Fort Erie, and Owen Sound.

However, the figure for Canada West would have been higher than this. The 945 volunteers who came from Canada West were all drawn from the 41 percent of the black population, slightly over 7,000 people, who gave that province as their place of birth in the 1861 census. Even larger numbers of American-born blacks lived in Canada West, and anecdotal evidence indicates that many of them returned to the United States to enlist. The 1861 census shows that African Americans made up a little over 57 percent of the province's black population, or approximately 9,800 people.[48] Assuming that they were as likely to enlist as Canada West–born blacks, we can conclude that at least another 1,247 men, sojourning African Americans, left British North America to serve in Union regiments and warships. Because the military records did not document their place of residence, we cannot precisely determine their numbers, although they left considerable anecdotal evidence of their service. African Americans did live in the other British colonies but in much smaller numbers, although some would probably have returned to join the Union military. In total, almost 2,500 black British North Americans and resident African Americans served as soldiers and sailors in the Union war effort.

The numbers of black recruits who came from British North America are all the more remarkable in light of the British government's efforts to prevent them from doing so. Under British law, it was a crime to join, or to encourage others to join, a foreign military in time of war. When Britain declared its neutrality at the start of the Civil War, its government evoked the seldom used Foreign Enlistment Act of 1819, which prohibited its citizens from serving in the army or navy of other nations at war, from arming or equipping ships of war for any belligerent, and from breaking any lawful blockade.[49] During the war, the enlistment of Britons in both the Union and Confederate armies, though significant, was politically less inflammatory than the actions of Confederate agents in Britain who tried to circumvent the neutrality law by purchasing ships to use as commerce raiders.[50]

Ironically, even as Union officials demanded strict neutrality from Britain, Union recruiters were busily trying to get British citizens resident in the various Northern states to join the army.[51] Indeed, at the start of the war, British officials foresaw the problems that would ensue. Richard Bickerton Pernell, or Lord Lyons, Britain's de facto ambassador to the United States, warned Foreign Secretary Earl Russell in 1861 that various states would probably enact laws to compel both foreigners and citizens to serve in the military. "Should it be done," wrote Lyons, "the claims for exemption on the part of real and pretended British Subjects will be very numerous."[52] Over the next year, Lyons focused more on the issue of underage Britons who had apparently enlisted without their parents' consent than on the general enlistment of British North Americans.[53] The records suggest that he was not particularly troubled about the number of British citizens who wanted to enlist, perhaps because in the first months of the war, Secretary of War Simon Cameron turned down various offers from civilians in Montreal, Quebec City, and Halifax to volunteer or to raise troops for the Northern army.[54]

Nevertheless, as the war progressed, the Union army's voracious need for more men increasingly drew British North Americans into the conflict.

Although British officials might look the other way, their counterparts in Canada West indicated by the fall of 1861 that they were willing to enforce the Foreign Enlistment Act, at least in the most egregious cases. A prominent Windsor mining entrepreneur and politician, Arthur Rankin, was arrested in October 1861 on charges of violating the act. In July of that year, Rankin, himself a militia colonel in Canada West, had approached American officials with a plan to raise a regiment of lancers, many of whom would be Canadians, to serve in the Union army. The American government accepted his proposal, he was commissioned a Union colonel, and Canadian recruits were surreptitiously transported to Detroit.[55] Rankin's subsequent arrest reflected the public outrage in some quarters that a member of the Canadian Parliament and a provincial militia officer would behave in such a manner. Although Rankin asserted that the Foreign Enlistment Act applied only to governments, not individuals, his freedom depended less on his arguments and more on the difficulty of enforcing the act in British North America. A man of "Quixotic eccentricities," he was not convicted of the charges, but he ultimately lost both his American and Canadian commissions, and his proto-regiment of lancers was disbanded.[56] In December 1861, as the debate over Rankin's action continued, the Adjutant General's Office in Washington warned the mustering officer in Detroit "not to muster into service any recruits who may have been imported from Canada for the purpose of filling up the regiments now organizing in your vicinity, and not to muster in the men of any regiments unless satisfied that all of the recruits have been enlisted within the limits of the United States."[57]

In other cases, provincial authorities may have used the Foreign Enlistment Act as a threat to discourage recruitment efforts in the British colonies. This may have been true for Josiah Henson, the fugitive slave who had helped found the black settlement at Dawn. His *Autobiography* describes his early encouragement of black enlistment and the repercussions that ensued. When it became possible in 1863 for black British North Americans to enlist in the Union army, the elderly Henson, who was physically incapable of military service himself, told his black neighbours "that the young and able-bodied ought to go into the field like men, that they should stand up to the rack, and help the government."[58] When the first group of black volunteers headed off to enlist at Detroit, Henson offered to provide assistance to the families of any needy volunteers "till they could send bounty-money to them." When the second group of would-be recruits left for the United

This poster was used in Arthur Rankin's unsuccessful attempt to raise a regiment of lancers in Canada West to serve in the Union army. Rankin was arrested in October 1861 in Toronto for violating the British Foreign Enlistment Act of 1819, although he was not convicted. *Courtesy of Library and Archives Canada.*

States, Henson accompanied them, in order, he claimed, to safeguard their bounty money. A man named John Alexander was to have joined this group, but he changed his mind at the last moment and stayed home.

Henson soon discovered that Alexander had complained to the magistrates "that [Hensen] had tried to induce him and others to enlist."[59] While in the United States, Henson received a letter from his wife that urged him "to remain in Boston, and not return, for a writ was ready to take me as soon as I appeared in Dresden, and if the charge was proven, the penalty, by the

Foreign Enlistment Act, would have been seven years' imprisonment."[60] Despite this warning, Henson returned to Dresden, in part because he believed that he had worked "for the cause of Christ," but almost as soon as he arrived, he was charged with violating the Foreign Enlistment Act. According to Henson's account of the case, his conviction was predicated on the credibility of Alexander, who had argued that Henson's aid to his family was a bribe to encourage his enlistment. When a witness testified that Alexander was "a rogue" and had "no character," the magistrates released Henson.[61]

Although he had escaped conviction for violating the Foreign Enlistment Act, Henson had been well warned and he changed his attitude toward enlistment in the Union army, at least in public. When his friend and neighbour Alexander Pool asked Henson to help his son and brother-in-law enlist at Detroit, Henson replied, "I do not intend to subject myself to another trial on that score. I do not care if they enlist or not." Although he was finally persuaded to accompany the two young men to Detroit, he made it clear to them that he was not urging them to enlist: "It is not my wish that you should enlist, but for your father's sake I will go to Detroit with you to protect you from the sharpers."[62] After this final incident, Henson's autobiography contains no further mention of encouraging black men to leave the province and join the war, but he may have continued to do so quietly. Certainly, the Anglican minister in Dresden, Reverend Thomas Hughes, believed that in April 1865 Henson had been responsible for getting William Wheeler, a black resident from Kent County, out on bail and over "to the American side and sold as a substitute."[63]

Henson's case reflected some of the difficulties involved in convicting British subjects of violating the law. Reports circulated of vessels anchored at Quebec City that were planning to run the Union blockade, but in "the absence of any positive evidence, the Government cannot take proceedings under the Foreign Enlistment Act." Eventually, a ship was searched and nothing illegal was found, but the *Hamilton Evening Times* suggested that it was "doubtful if the Government could have legally detained the steamer, even if powder had been discovered on board, so lax is the law."[64] In 1864, the *Times* noted that Canada West residents who faced provincial government prosecution under the act had "in most instances been able to evade punishment."[65] Despite the difficulties in getting convictions, British officials believed that "the preliminary imprisonment before trial acted as a salutary warning to parties who had been arrested and served to deter others from following the same course."[66]

During the fall of 1864, the government made further efforts to enforce the act. In November, two men in Canada East were convicted of enticing civilians to enlist in the Union army. One of them paid a $450 fine and the other was sentenced to six months in jail.[67] Early in 1865, the provincial parliament passed new legislation to facilitate the prosecution of recruiting agents and crimps (those who enticed or forced men into military service).[68] Perhaps because of this change, one of Buxton's black residents, Lucien Boyd, was arrested in early 1865 and charged with violating the Foreign Enlistment Act. In his case, the government and the court were determined to apply the law. Boyd was convicted and sentenced to two years in Kingston Penitentiary.[69] Although he was not alone in being convicted under the law, his punishment was more severe.[70]

Despite the periodic threats of government prosecution, hundreds of young black British North Americans joined the Union war effort, a fact that reflects the importance attributed to the war against slavery by many in the black communities. Nevertheless, it is also true that the levels of response differed from colony to colony, which shows that the local did matter. When the numbers of recruits from each colony are compared with the black population of that colony, as given by the census, the results are striking. In Canada West, as much as 13.7 percent of the total black population joined either the Union army or navy.[71] In Canada East, the rate was even higher at 14.1 percent, although the small numbers involved need to be interpreted cautiously. In the Maritimes, by contrast, the enlistment rate was only 2.0 percent in Nova Scotia, the Maritime province with the largest black population, and 6.0 percent in New Brunswick.[72]

What this dramatic difference in rates of volunteering indicates, at the very least, is that local conditions significantly influenced black decision making. The response in each colony reflected the history and dynamics of its own black population, its social and economic relationship with communities in the United States, and its broader attitudes regarding the conflict.[73] The black communities of the Canadas were much more socially, culturally, and economically integrated into their counterparts in the United States. African Canadians shared close ties of friendship and kinship with the black communities in contiguous American states, which were reinforced by their constant ebb and flow across the border. Among other things, this made Canada West a major theatre for American and British abolitionists and lecturers, who frequently visited it. Certainly, some contemporaries believed that Chatham, Canada West, was "the headquarters of the Negro race in Canada," a claim for Chatham that historian Gerald Horne argues could apply to the entire continent.[74] Although there is much puffery in this contention, Chatham was one of the places that John Brown visited in search of support, and it was there, in May 1858, that he convened a constitutional convention prior to his raid on Harper's Ferry. No town in Nova Scotia or New Brunswick carried the same cachet or was as closely linked to African American activities. Although the border between the Maritimes and the United States was just as permeable, and there was a good deal of interaction among all groups of people, the exchanges between black communities there were less significant than for Canada West, although that would alter after the war. As a result, whereas enlistment officials who worked on behalf of the Northern states frequently undertook recruiting trips to Canada West, they rarely visited the Maritimes.

That the rate of black volunteering varied from colony to colony raises important questions about the makeup of the separate British North American black communities and their response to the struggle for emancipation. However, left unanswered is the question of the significance of an enlistment rate of 14 percent in Canada East, 6 percent in New Brunswick, and 2 percent in Nova Scotia. One way to measure the importance of these rates is to compare the responses of the black British colonists with the corresponding black response in some Northern states. This can be done by contrasting the number of black recruits who enlisted as a percentage of the total black population.[75] Several Northern states with a large black community provide a useful standard of comparison.[76] Of these, Pennsylvania had the largest, and by the end of the conflict the War Department credited it with enlisting 8,612 black soldiers and 1,175 sailors, a rate of 17.2 percent of its overall black population.[77] New York, whose black inhabitants totalled 49,005, was credited with 4,125 soldiers and 1,288 sailors, a rate of 11.0 percent. Ohio's black population of 36,372 sent 7,161 men into the army and 157 into the navy, a rate of 20.1 percent, whereas New Jersey, which had 25,318 black residents, was credited with enlisting just 1,185 soldiers and 433 sailors, a rate of only 6.4 percent. Almost 226,000 black people lived in the Northern states, and the War Department's records show that 37,723 black soldiers were raised across the North, for an army service rate of 16.7 percent of the black population. At the very least, these comparisons reveal that, on a per capita basis, Canada West yielded as many black soldiers as some of the Northern states and that even New Brunswick's rate almost equalled that of New Jersey. Overall, the enlistment levels suggest that black recruits from the British colonies had a very strong predisposition to support the Northern cause once emancipation became a Union war aim. What makes the figures even more impressive is that all of these men were volunteers who freely chose to enlist. By contrast, during the last year of the war, many African Americans who lived in the Northern states, and who might not necessarily have joined the military, did so because they were subject to the draft and preferred to volunteer rather than be conscripted.

The differing volunteer rates in the British colonies also raise questions as to why some men chose to enlist, whereas others did not. Just as the various black communities had multiple and overlapping identities formed by class, culture, geography, and historical background, so individual motivation must have been equally complex. The broad generalizations that are commonly offered by historians, such as "fighting against slavery," satisfying "a desire for excitement," or being "lured by financial considerations," do little to explain the very disparate responses from Nova Scotia and New Brunswick, which will intrigue some Canadian historians.[78] Indeed, if the generalizations apply – if young black men were naturally willing to risk their lives in the fight against slavery or were attracted by large bounties and financial inducements – enlistment rates should be much the same in all the British colonies. Or at least, if the motivation to enlist were primarily financial, rates of volunteering should be greatest in poverty-stricken areas. The aggressive Union recruiting efforts in Canada West only partially explain the high enlistment rate for that province. What is clear, however, is that an examination of the timing and terms of these men's enlistment indicates that many saw their military service as much more of a negotiated arrangement than is often supposed. Young black men were willing to join the fight for emancipation and greater equality, but they exercised personal agency regarding how and for what length of time they would serve. Events in the last two years of the war would bear this out. During its first year, however, black British North Americans who wished to fight the Confederacy were obliged to join the navy.

CHAPTER THREE

BLACKS IN THE NAVY

A DIFFERENT MILITARY EXPERIENCE

WHEN THE CIVIL WAR began and young black men attempted to join the Union army, the Lincoln administration refused to accept them. A series of factors caused Lincoln to conclude that enrolling black soldiers might cost him the war. Prejudice was deeply entrenched across much of the North. In addition, Lincoln understood the critical strategic importance of the "Loyal Slave States," Maryland, Missouri, and especially Kentucky, and was willing to compromise his values to keep them in the Union. Finally, most Northerners believed that the conflict would be a short and successful struggle to preserve the Union. In the spring of 1861, few Americans were willing to wage war to end slavery. As a result, the Union army was not open to most black men until early 1863, including black men from British North America. For sailors, however, the situation was very different. Indeed, when and why they joined as well as the nature of their service provides a useful foil for the wartime experiences of black soldiers.

On 16 May 1861, just one month after the fall of Fort Sumter and the start of the American Civil War, John Anderson, a twenty-one-year-old "mulatto" from Nova Scotia, enlisted in the Union navy at a rendezvous station in New York City. Anderson gave his occupation as "none" but was rated as an "ordinary sailor," which indicates that he had extensive maritime experience. He signed on for three years, although there is little record of the ship or ships on which he served.[1] Indeed, not much more is known of Anderson, but that is not remarkable. Very little is known or has been written about the hundreds of blacks from British North America who served in the Union navy during the Civil War. The best general or regional studies, such as Robin Winks's *Civil War Years* or Greg Marquis' *In Armageddon's Shadow,* give little more than brief anecdotes of black involvement in the war and virtually ignore black sailors.[2] None attempt a systematic measurement of how many men joined the navy, perhaps because the naval war is the forgotten sister in most Civil War accounts but also because employing black sailors, unlike black soldiers, was not a revolutionary act that held out the promise of a new racial norm. Nevertheless, a discussion of who these men were, how and where they joined, and the agency that they displayed in selecting their service speaks not only to the nature of British North America's black communities but also to the changing character of the war.

Of course, sailors from the British colonies, including black sailors, had served in the Union navy long before the Civil War broke out, despite official attempts to ban the use of foreigners. The navy seldom had a sufficient number of suitable recruits, especially in prosperous years, for mariners could find other employers. During peace, the merchant marine paid higher wages, and in time of war privateers ran fewer risks, courted danger for briefer periods, and offered greater chances of reward. Nevertheless, sailors frequently joined the peacetime navy, completed an enlistment term, and subsequently hired out their services to a new employer. This practice was common for both career and short-term sailors.[3] William Hall, the son of black refugees who came to Nova Scotia during the War of 1812, is one such example. His father was a sailor who worked at the shipbuilding yards at Half-Way River (Hantsport), and William followed his trade. After crewing on ships out of Half-Way River, he served in the American navy for some years during the late 1840s. He then joined the Royal Navy in 1852 as an able seaman. After twenty-four years of exceptional service, he retired at the rank of quartermaster and returned to Nova Scotia, a recognized hero.[4] How many other Maritimers served in the American navy before the war is extremely difficult to determine, but Hall was certainly not unique. In September 1860, when the navy sloop USS *Levant* disappeared without a trace while en route from the Hawaiian Islands to Panama, Maritimers were among its two-hundred-odd crew.[5]

Almost as soon as the Civil War began, willing black volunteers, including men from British North America, began entering the Union navy. This was possible because the traditions and practices of the navy had long been very different from those of the army. Following the passage of the federal

Militia Act of 1792, a prohibition that remained in force to the time of the Civil War, the army officially refused to enrol black soldiers.[6] By contrast, the navy had employed black sailors since the American Revolution and also racially integrated them on all its vessels. In the ensuing years and despite official trepidation, the navy continued to rely on black sailors in times of crisis, including some slaves whose owners enlisted them and pocketed their wages.[7] Very early on, the navy had tried to prohibit the enlistment of both black and foreign sailors, but the policy proved impractical. In August 1798, Secretary of the Navy Benjamin Stoddard had issued orders to block the recruitment of black crewmen.[8] Nevertheless, the chronic shortage of experienced sailors made strict enforcement almost impossible. In 1807, during the aftermath of the *Chesapeake* incident, when the HMS *Leopard* seized British deserters from the USS *Chesapeake*, Congress banned the enlistment of foreign nationals but, for the first time officially, allowed that of free African Americans.[9] Although in 1813 Congress repeated the ban on the enlistment of aliens, large numbers of immigrants continued to enter the navy, some of whom were black.[10] In 1828, Secretary of the Navy John Branch complained that foreign seamen were "a distinct class of people from those useful citizens who have sought protection under our institutions ... Very few of them have their interests located here, or are bound to us by all the ties which connect a man with his country."[11] Fortunately for those who wished to evade the regulations, fraudulent certificates of citizenship could be purchased, often for as little as fifty cents. In addition, American recruiters commonly assigned "purser's names" to foreign sailors, anglicizing their surnames and making it difficult to estimate their numbers.[12] In any time of necessity, need trumped theory. In 1861, Secretary of the Navy Gideon Welles told members of the House of Representatives that, because of the need for sailors, the law banning foreign enlistment had "not been rigidly observed," but he added that efforts were made to enlist only experienced sailors.[13]

Despite an equal reluctance to enlist African Americans, naval records show that black sailors saw action during the Quasi-War with France, the campaigns against the Barbary States, the War of 1812, and the Mexican War.[14] In 1816, about 15 percent of the crew of the frigate USS *Java* were black.[15] Nevertheless, in 1839, as a result of the serious recession created by the panic of 1837, Isaac Toucey, the acting secretary of the navy, capped black recruitment at 5 percent of monthly totals and banned the practice in which slaveholders enlisted their slaves and received the wages. The quota had a significant impact on black volunteering, and by 1861 the percentage of

Crewmembers cluster on the foredeck of the USS *Miami*. Although most Civil War naval vessels had integrated crews, black sailors, especially ex-slaves, were often marginalized, as is suggested in this photograph. *Courtesy of the National Archives and Records Administration.*

blacks on federal warships had fallen to 2.5.[16] For men who had worked at sea before 1861, however, signing on at a naval rendezvous to serve on a Union navy vessel would have seemed similar in many ways to joining a commercial ship.

Although the total number of Civil War enlistments in the Union navy can be precisely identified, at 118,044, the number of black sailors is much more difficult to establish because the navy did not record racial identity. As a result, researchers who wish to isolate black sailors are obliged to use the physical descriptions normally included on the enlistment forms. Some entries clearly indicate African descent; others do not. Even after the naval documents that were created during the career of a recruit are cross-tabulated, the racial identity of some sailors may not be absolutely established.

As a result, we will probably never know exactly how many Union sailors who enlisted during the Civil War were of African descent, much less how many came from British North America.[17] The first rough estimate was made early in 1902 by the secretary of the navy in response to a congressional request. Senior officers who were veterans of the war remembered that a quarter of sailors were black, so the secretary divided the total enlistment by four and calculated that 29,511 sailors were black.[18] Many decades later, David L. Valuska conducted a detailed examination of the naval records for the various rendezvous stations and revised the number of black sailors downward to 9,596, or about 8 percent of the total force. He also identified 111 men from British North America.[19] Although his figures were research-based and more systematic than earlier estimates, they encompassed only those sailors who had signed up at a rendezvous station, which meant that they omitted the many men who had enlisted onboard naval vessels or whose records were missing. More recently, the Civil War African American Sailors Project has produced the most precise figures to date, identifying nearly 18,000 black service men, including 348 sailors who were born in British North America.[20] They were part of the 1,500 foreign volunteers, most from the Caribbean islands, who joined the Union navy. The project examined enlistment records and quarterly muster rolls of navy vessels, searching for descriptive terms that indicated African ancestry.[21] Despite its painstaking approach, however, some black sailors were missed. Indeed, Valuska names three British North American black men who were not identified as such by the project.[22] The omission of one well-known black Nova Scotia veteran by both studies suggests that even more British North American men have been missed. Ben Jackson, a black sailor from Lockhartville, Nova Scotia, enlisted as a substitute under the name Lewis Saunders and was wounded while serving as a gun captain on the USS *Richmond*. After his discharge, he returned to his home province and lived in Lockhartville for the rest of his life.[23] Both sources failed to identify Daniel Crowell, a sailor on the USS *Brooklyn* who was a former playmate of Jackson as they grew up in Nova Scotia.[24] How many other black British North American sailors have been missed remains unclear.[25]

At the outbreak of the war, the navy, like the army and other branches of the government, was largely unprepared for the type of conflict that would ensue. The small pre-war navy, primarily a "blue water" fleet tasked with protecting American commercial interests around the world, had very limited resources in terms of both men and ships. In the spring of 1861, many of the ninety vessels that the navy had on its books were in storage or unserviceable. Only forty-two were commissioned and in service, and all but twelve were posted in Asia, South America, and Africa.[26] Moreover, Isaac Toucey, the secretary of the navy during the secession crisis, refused to recall some ships to American waters lest it be seen as an act of aggression against the South.[27] As a result, President Lincoln learned from his secretary of the navy, Gideon Welles, in late March 1861 that he had only a dozen vessels at his immediate disposal to cover the Gulf of Mexico and the Atlantic.[28]

Despite what is sometimes suggested, the navy was beginning the process of modernization on the eve of the war. The United States Naval Academy had been established in 1850, in part to professionalize its officer class.[29] Inspired by European examples, the navy understood the need to change from sail to steam and had begun that transition. After experimenting with paddlewheel warships, it concluded that propeller-driven vessels were more efficient and that their engines were less vulnerable to enemy fire, although paddlewheel vessels would remain an important part of the Civil War navy. During the 1850s, six large screw frigates and a number of steam sloops were built that compared favourably with similar examples in any European fleet.[30] These ships, however, were essentially unarmoured sailing vessels with an auxiliary propulsion system that was to be used when necessary. Marine engines were often unreliable, coal was expensive, and wind was free. As a result, these naval vessels required a large complement of experienced seamen to serve and sail them. These were the warships that were expected to protect the widespread Northern merchant marine from possible Southern privateers and Confederate raiders.

The navy had another problem that quickly became evident when the war started. Except for its auxiliary craft, none of the ships in service were suitable for use on America's river system or for close-in work on coastal estuaries. Indeed, Southern senators had ensured that the draft of the new vessels the navy was building was too deep for effective use in most Southern harbours and rivers.[31] Successful prosecution of the Civil War, however, would require blockading fleets that were capable of operating close to shore, often under fire from enemy batteries, to seal the more than 3,500 miles of Southern coastline and all its ports and river mouths. In addition, the navy quickly realized that it had to develop a military capacity to control the inland waterways in support of the army. All this demanded a dramatic expansion of its size and capacities. Different types of vessel and new recruits to crew them were desperately needed. Whereas the existing frigates and sloops, such as the USS *Minnesota* and the USS *Hartford*, would always require a crew of experienced mariners, the application of steam and armour in the navy's newly created "brown water" fleet on the inland rivers allowed for a deskilling of servicemen.[32] The creation of a freshwater fleet especially brought the navy into contact with escaping slaves, or "contrabands."[33] Given the chronic shortage of crewmen and the eagerness of Southern blacks to serve, Gideon Welles soon authorized navy recruiters to tap this pool, as long as they were enlisted at the rating of "boy," a restriction that he removed in December 1862.[34] Both parts of the new navy provided opportunities for men from the British colonies. Driven by the urgent need for more sea power, the navy radically expanded its fleet, purchasing or chartering merchant vessels while speeding up the construction of new warships. By early July 1861, it had 82 commissioned ships, a figure that reached 264 by the end of the year. A year later, the number was 427, and by war's end the navy had almost 700 ships of every kind. Its annual expenditures kept pace with the enlargement of the fleet, swelling from $12 million to $123 million.[35]

If these new ships were to be used effectively, thousands of recruits had to be found, and the navy had to compete with an army clamouring for men. When the war began, the navy had only 7,600 seamen in uniform, and though few sailors opted to leave and serve the South, many officers did. One-fifth resigned their commissions to join the Confederacy. As a result, naval numbers were woefully inadequate.[36] Lincoln immediately authorized an expansion of an additional 18,000 seamen, but given the army's competition for manpower, where they were to come from was not clear. The urgent necessity to expand the naval roster and the army's voracious demand for white troops forced the navy increasingly to utilize black sailors, whether they were Southern contrabands, Northerners, or foreign volunteers. Although precise numbers are difficult to assess, the percentage of black sailors in the navy rose rapidly. As the war progressed, they made up an increasingly large component of naval personnel. By the end of May 1861, after a burst of new enlistment, 8 percent of the naval roster were black, a figure that peaked at approximately 23 percent in the fall of 1864 and slowly diminished to around 17 percent at war's end.[37] Almost 5 percent of the black seamen in the Union navy were born in British North America.[38] Although black seamen became more numerous as the war progressed, they were never a homogeneous group; nor were they evenly distributed throughout the service. The actual percentage of black sailors who crewed any particular ship varied enormously, both by theatre of service and type of vessel. In the European

Squadron, which hunted Confederate commerce raiders in the North Atlantic, about one in ten sailors was black. In the squadrons blockading the Southern coast, that number was one in four, whereas in the freshwater fleet, blacks accounted for more than a third of mariners. The nature and duties of naval vessels also influenced where blacks served. Their numbers were limited on the frigates and sloops of war, but they were disproportionately represented on the barks and schooners that supplied and supported the active warships.[39] For black British North Americans, this factor raises a range of questions about background and motives, when and where they joined, where they served, and how they were perceived by their white crewmates.

As the navy sought ways to expand its manpower, the pattern and growth of general black enlistment was mirrored by that of black volunteers from the British colonies. Slightly more black sailors entered the navy in 1862 than in 1861. Following the Emancipation Proclamation, physical and psychological barriers to black service crumbled, and enlistment among African Americans increased in 1863 and surged in 1864. By January 1865, as the navy had achieved most of its objectives and the end of the war seemed imminent, it began cutting back its complement of sailors.[40] Table 2 shows a pattern of enlistment that was quite similar for Canadian and Maritime sailors.

In 1862, 30 black sailors from British North America joined the navy, and 31 more enlisted the following year. That number rose to 259 in 1864, primarily made up of recruits from Canada West. This increase coincided with a

TABLE 2
Enlistment of British North American black sailors

	1861	1862	1863	1864	1865	Total
Canada West	2	12	9	191	6	220
Canada East	–	–	1	6	–	7
Nova Scotia	10	14	14	31	3	72
New Brunswick	6	4	7	29	3	49
PEI	–	–	–	2	1	3
Total	18	30	31	259	13	351

NOTE: All recruits who gave "Canada" as their place of birth are credited to Canada West except for those who listed a Quebec city, such as Thomas Bryant, who named "Quebec, Canada" as his birthplace. As a result, some sailors who were born in Canada East may have been credited to Canada West. One Nova Scotia–born sailor, William Maxwell, has been omitted from the table because his records supply neither date nor place of enlistment.

change in regulations that allowed bounties, previously offered only to soldiers, to be paid to enlisting sailors, who were also credited to a district's draft quota.[41] The Enrollment Act of 1863 had established a national draft to fill the army's ranks, but it excluded the navy. Federal bounties, supplemented by many communities, had been paid to soldiers almost from the start of the war, but sailors had not been eligible for this money. The Amendatory Act of February 1864 ended this inequity. Under its terms, new sailors could receive federal bounties, and because they were now credited to the draft quota, communities had greater reasons to support naval enlistment.[42] Although the monetary incentives remained in place, the enlistment of black British North Americans dropped to only thirteen in 1865. Nevertheless, the sailors who joined during the final months of the war frequently served the peacetime navy well after its conclusion. After war's end, men such as Abraham Bankster and Israel N. Dolman, both experienced seamen from Nova Scotia who crewed on the USS *Hartford*, served for years in the Pacific Squadron. Two of the three sailors from Prince Edward Island, John H. Thompson and Charles H. Trust, enlisted together at Portsmouth, New Hampshire, near the end of 1864 and joined the crew of the iron-hulled side-wheel gunboat, USS *Mohongo*. In May 1865, they helped sail the ship through the Straits of Magellan during a severe gale to take up serving with the Pacific Squadron.[43]

When sailors decided to enlist, their first task was to determine how long they would serve, for unlike most soldiers, they could choose the length of their term. This could range from one to three years or could last for the duration of the war; many ex-slaves in the Mississippi Valley chose the latter option. Steven Ramold argues that recruits based their choice of term on their perceptions of how long the war would last. In 1861, during the first year of what many people thought would be a brief engagement, most recruits joined for three years; in 1862, with enthusiasm ebbing for the war, many selected a one- or two-year term. The result was that by 1864, the year in which most black British North Americans volunteered, the navy was trying to fill new warships and to replace veteran seamen whose time of enlistment had expired.[44]

Black British colonial sailors differed only slightly from their American counterparts in choosing their terms. In 1861, two-thirds of the eighteen colonists who enlisted did so for three years, and of this cohort, more than half came in at the rank of landsman. In the next year, the thirty volunteers split between three-year and one-year terms. Only one chose two years, and for the first time, two men enlisted for the duration. Numbers of recruits held steady in 1863, but the selection of term altered. All but two men signed on for just one year. The following year, 1864, saw a turnabout in both numbers and choice of term: 259 black British North Americans entered the navy, three-quarters of whom were from Canada West. Two hundred and two men elected to serve for three years, 38 signed on for one year, and 19 chose two years. Only 1 man enlisted "for the war." This pattern is consistent with that of sailors from outside the United States. "More than half of foreign sailors enlisted in the last two years of the war," and most joined at the port cities of the mid-Atlantic and New England.[45]

Everyone who enlisted in the navy was assessed and assigned a rating, rather than a rank, when they enrolled. Ratings were based on experience and skills. The most expert recruits, men with at least five years of maritime service, were rated "able seaman" and paid sixteen to eighteen dollars a month. They handled the sails and rigging, steered the vessel, and provided critical leadership throughout it. Men like John Anderson, a Nova Scotian who was rated as ordinary seaman, generally had two years or more of maritime experience and were paid fourteen dollars per month. They manned the guns, operated the ship's boats, and supervised the landsmen. Landsmen, the most common rating in the Civil War navy regardless of race, had negligible naval experience and were expected to learn their skills on the job, as the navy had no dedicated training facilities. They earned twelve dollars a month. When the war began, recruits who were under eighteen were rated as first-, second-, or third-class "boy," with wages of ten, nine, or eight dollars a month, depending on their age and skills. They undertook light labour, served the officers, carried ammunition during combat, and completed any other tasks assigned them by the commander.[46] When the navy began to enlist ex-slaves, or contrabands as they were called, they were initially required to sign on as boys. As the navy continued its transition to steam power, two other ratings became more common. Firemen (first and second class) managed the boilers, monitored steam pressure, and, under direction, helped repair machinery. They made thirty or twenty-five dollars a month, depending on their classification, in line with their years of experience.[47] Coal heavers, who were paid eighteen dollars per month, required little previous skill but great endurance. Using shovels and wheelbarrows, they ensured that the load of coal was evenly distributed in the bunkers, and they fed the boilers. It was heavy and demanding work in extreme temperatures.[48]

When John Anderson, the first black British North American to join the wartime navy, was rated as an ordinary seaman, this not only guaranteed him greater status, higher pay, and more skilled tasks, it also suggests that when he gave "none" as his occupation, he meant to indicate that he was unemployed, not that he was unskilled. Anderson was probably between "berths," and this was perhaps true of many other sailors who entered "none" as occupation, judging by the way in which they were subsequently rated.[49] Just two days after Anderson enlisted, John A. Johnson, a twenty-one-year-old from Saint John, signed on in Boston for a year. Johnson, who also gave his occupation as "none," was rated as landsman, like most new recruits. Precisely why these two individuals joined the navy is unknown, but they seem to fit the enlistment pattern identified by Michael Bennett, who argues that sailors, unlike soldiers, seldom volunteered for ideological reasons such as patriotism or a desire to combat slavery. Instead, he claims, their decision was grounded in a mix of practical factors including guaranteed employment, regular wages, and a chance at prize money.[50] Both Anderson and Johnson may have been unemployed when they volunteered, and Johnson's choice of a one-year term was uncommon in 1861. At that time, most sailors signed up for three years. Before the year ended, another sixteen black British North Americans also joined the navy. Eleven of them opted to serve for three years, three signed on just for one year, and two chose a two-year term.

Whatever their motives, the eighteen black British North Americans who entered the Union navy in 1861 differed significantly from the average American naval recruit in terms of skills. Slightly more than half of them were rated as ordinary seamen or higher, at a time when 78 percent of new American recruits and 80 percent of black American recruits were assessed as having "absolutely no skill or experience in things nautical."[51] Due to their hard-earned skills, many of the black Maritimers who joined in 1861 were assigned to the existing frigates and sloops of war. Some were placed on the USS *Hartford* and USS *Brooklyn*, but others found berths in the newly expanding navy. David Campbell, a sea cook from Halifax, served his enlistment on the USS *Vanderbilt*, a two-mast, side-wheel transatlantic passenger ship given to the government by Commodore Vanderbilt in 1861. Because the *Vanderbilt*'s role was to hunt for Confederate commerce raiders, Campbell saw Rio de Janeiro, Port Louis, Mauritius, Cape Town, Halifax, and the West Indies.[52] By contrast, Berry Chever, an experienced seaman from Halifax, served much of his enlistment on the USS *General Bragg*, a river gunboat patrolling the Mississippi.[53] He might have considered himself less fortunate than Campbell, for his ports of call included Helena, Arkansas, Greenville, Mississippi, and Natchez-Under-The-Hill.

Most black sailors from the British colonies who joined the Union navy did so by presenting themselves at naval recruiting stations called "rendezvous," which were set up in the major seaports of the northeast.[54] Usually situated in areas where sailors lived, drank, and whored, and regular citizens avoided, rendezvous often employed recruiting agents, or "runners," as well as local boarding house operators to locate potential enlistees and to encourage them to join up. The runners received three dollars for every acceptable sailor whom they brought in and were not heavily weighted with scruples. Their activities frequently scandalized middle-class citizens, including businessmen in Manhattan's lower east side, who protested at their tactics: "There is hardly a day that passes, that the most corrupt and outrageous means are used by these runners to decoy the citizens into the U. S. Navy, and when expostulated with, they are very insulting."[55] No doubt, some black British North Americans who ended up in the federal navy were plied with alcohol and promises of prize money and lied to about their terms of enlistment, or in extreme cases, even shanghaied, or kidnapped. Nineteenth-century port towns were notorious for their "crimping" establishments. At best, the recruiters were sailor-brokers or agents who matched demand with supply. At worst, they were "bold, brutal, and unrestrained" in their manipulation of sailors.[56] Canadian and Maritime sailors may have been preyed on by recruiters in the United States, just as they were in Quebec City, Halifax, and Saint John, but the stories of young men being forcibly removed from their homes in the British colonies, though sensational, are based on a few cases, judging by the enlistment records of black sailors.

Nevertheless, some men believed that they had been coerced. In September 1864, nine of them wrote to the British consul in Boston, claiming that they had been made drunk in Quebec City boarding houses and persuaded to ship aboard a vessel there. They testified that they had "been sold at Lebanon, New York, for bounty money." They were bitter that they had received only two hundred dollars, whereas those who victimized them had got one thousand.[57] In Digby, Nova Scotia, a local youth was reportedly drugged, taken aboard a schooner for Boston, and saved only by the prompt action of Digby citizens.[58] In another case, John Bland Allinson, a fifteen-year-old orphan, alleged that while on the way to his home in Niagara Falls a stranger approached and then drugged him. He later had "some sort of recollection of passing places, trees, etc., and a man asking if I felt better." His clearest memories came only after he found himself a newly enlisted sailor aboard the USS *Michigan*, a side-wheel gunboat operating on Lake Erie. Fortunately, his guardians, a grandmother and an aunt, along with the help of the British consul in Buffalo, were able to secure his release.[59] In fact, only one black sailor from Canada West, John Ryde, a thirty-five-year-old cook, enlisted at the Buffalo rendezvous during the entire war, and though many others joined in Boston, a line of drugged bodies being carried off vessels in the Boston harbour would have attracted attention.[60]

Moreover, few British North American sailors signed on in a border town. Three-quarters of all black Maritime sailors enlisted at either New York or Boston, and though most of the remainder joined at Philadelphia, Baltimore, and New Bedford, there were a few exceptions. John Lewis from Nova Scotia enlisted at Acapulco and served out his term on a Pacific Squadron store ship, the USS *Farallones*. Jacob Tucker, an experienced sailor from Halifax, joined at Antwerp and chose a one-year term. By contrast, almost three-quarters of recruits from the Canadas (160 out of 227) enlisted in New York, whereas less than 10 percent (19 out of 227) did so in Boston. More men joined in Brooklyn (24) than in Boston, and others enlisted at rendezvous in Cairo, Cincinnati, Chicago, and other western cities. The surge of naval enlistment in late 1863 and 1864 was possible, in part, because of the deskilling associated with the change from sail to steam. The need for experienced men who could reef sails in heavy weather declined while the demand for untrained manual labour grew. By 1863, the navy was hiring civilian recruiters to locate the specific labour that it needed. These agents, some runners and some crimps, got "three dollars for each seaman or ordinary seaman but ten dollars for each landsman or coal heaver" whom they brought to the rendezvous.[61]

When naval recruiters, runners, and crimps were trying to persuade young men to choose the navy rather than the army, they used the alluring prospect of prize money to sway the eager and the gullible. All Confederate warships and any merchant vessel that attempted to evade the blockade of Southern ports were subject to seizure by Union ships as legitimate prizes of war. The Prize Law, established by the US Navy in 1798, set out the rules for both the capture of ships that violated a legal blockade and the subsequent auction and sale of the vessels and their cargos.[62] After deducting court costs, which could vary significantly in differing jurisdictions, the Navy Department passed on half of the prize money to be distributed among the crew of the vessels that had seized the ship.[63] All federal vessels within signal distance of the ship that made the capture received a share. In practice, this meant that all Union warships within six miles took a portion of the prize money. The commander of the blockading squadron received 5 percent, and the captain of the capturing warship got 10 percent. The remaining 35 percent was divided among the crew or crews, according to their rating.[64]

The USS *Eolus* was a side-wheel steamer outfitted as a gunboat. Besides participating in the North Carolina blockade, it carried men, messages, mail, and supplies between the larger vessels in the squadron. She is depicted here capturing the *Lady Sterling*. *Courtesy of the US Navy, NH 2041.*

For a lucky crew off a busy blockade-running port, the potential reward could be significant. Benjamin Jackson was one of these fortunate sailors, for his obituary claimed that he had earned nine hundred dollars in prize money during his service.[65] William Brown of Nova Scotia was even luckier. He enlisted in Brooklyn on 8 August 1864 and joined the crew of the USS *Eolus*, a small side-wheel steamer built as a merchant vessel in 1864 with a complement of just over fifty men. Because of its good speed and low silhouette, the *Eolus* was used for close-in work on the blockade of Wilmington, North Carolina. Two months after Brown joined the *Eolus*, it intercepted the side-wheel steamer *Hope*, which was running the blockade with a cargo of machinery. After a sixty-five-mile chase, the *Eolus* captured the steamer. The amount of prize money for distribution was ruled at $263,296.83, and each seaman on the ship received over $1,000.00. Just nine days later, the *Eolus*, along with USS *Calypso*, captured another ship, *Lady Sterling*, and this time the shared prize money amounted to $494,891.29. Brown, a Nova Scotian, may have seen the irony of aiding the capture of a blockade-runner based out of Halifax.[66]

Brown, however, was more fortunate than most. The experience of the four British North American black sailors who crewed on the screw frigate USS *San Jacinto*, a particularly successful prizewinner with a complement of 278, was more typical. John W. Price of Nova Scotia joined the *San Jacinto* in December 1863, thus missing the capture and prize money from the steamer *Alabama*, which was worth $120,951.[67] By that time, legitimate prizes of enemy vessels were fewer, and chases more frequently resulted in their destruction rather than seizure.[68] However, Price was eligible for prize money from the capture of *Edwards* ($2,139), *Magnolia* ($430), *Roebuck* ($8,096), and *Lealtad* ($38,880). When William B. Johnson from Nova Scotia, John Backus of Canada West, and Elijah Nellis of Saint John joined the *San Jacinto* in October and November 1864, it was finishing repairs in Portsmouth, New Hampshire. When it returned to the Gulf blockade, legitimate prizes were scarce, and one of the few credited to it was valued at only $7.08. Although the four sailors did not share equally in the prize money, they did share the hardships and danger when the *San Jacinto* struck a reef and foundered near Grand Abaco Island, Bahamas, on 1 January 1865.[69]

Black sailors from the Maritimes and the Canadas may have enlisted in the Union navy with the hope of getting rich from prize money, but most would have been disappointed. Sailors who were not on warships in American waters, involved in a blockade, or working on the many auxiliary vessels that served the fleet had little chance of seeing prize money. Some ships were too old or too slow to capture an enemy vessel; some were stationed in places where they would never encounter a potential prize. Moreover, many British North American sailors had enlisted late in the war, when fewer prizes were taken.[70] Captains and sailors may have dreamed of plunder, but the navy made it very clear that destroying a blockade-runner was preferable to risking its escape. As a result, the number of destroyed Confederate steamers (85) began to approach the number captured (136).[71] Of the more than 160 vessels on which black sailors from British North America served, less than a third ever took a prize. Even ships on some of the blockading stations had little hope of ever seeing a blockade-runner, much less catching one. William Keeler of the USS *Florida* expressed pity for the ships stationed along the Gulf coast:

> As I saw the solitary blockaders watching this dreary stretch of naked sand, cut off from the world for such long periods of time, not even blockade runners to chase or rebel batteries to watch to relieve the monotony of their life & too far apart for an occasional visit to each

other, I thank God that my lot has been with the N.A.B. [North Atlantic Blockading] Squadron.[72]

Of course, even sailors who had little chance of receiving prize money clung to their faint hopes of it because they had few other financial resources.

Northern mariners overwhelmingly came from the poor working-class conditions that helped fuel popular attitudes about sailors, "the lowest class of humanity."[73] Black British North American sailors differed from them in many ways, but they shared a similar hardscrabble manual-labour background, although there were some significant variations, as Table 3 indicates.

The recruits' occupational self-identification can be fitted into six broad categories. Fifty-three claimed to be mariners, and of these, thirty-seven were given a rating as seamen. Among the Maritimers, only four, all under twenty-one, were not rated as such. James Sullivan, a thirty-year-old mariner from Nova Scotia who enlisted in October 1864, was the highest rated of all the black British colonists who joined the navy, signing on as boatswain's mate.[74] The navy was a little more skeptical of some men from Canada West who claimed to be seamen, boatmen, or watermen. Only twelve of the twenty-three who volunteered were rated as ordinary or able seamen.[75] Some recruits were too young to have much experience on the water or had listed "mariner" as one of their two occupations. In addition, the navy may have been trying to save money by "under rating" enlistees, and recruiting officers in

TABLE 3
Occupation of British North American black sailors

	Mariner	Labourer	Farmer	Tradesman	Service	None/Blank	Total
Canada West	23 (12)	37	21 (2)	32 (3)	75 (4)	31 (2)	219
Canada East	–	4	–	–	3	–	7
Nova Scotia	20 (17)	5	–	10 (2)	20 (4)	18 (13)	73
New Brunswick	9 (8)	3	–	7 (2)	20 (3)	10 (5)	49
PEI	1 (1)	–	–	–	1	1	3
Total	53 (37)	49	21 (2)	49 (7)	119 (11)	60 (20)	351

NOTE: The numbers in parentheses indicate how many men in each group were rated "ordinary seaman" or higher when they enlisted, indicating previous maritime experience. Because he gave his occupation as "slave," George Mallory is not included in this table. When he enlisted in Napoleon, Arizona, on 21 February 1863 for one year as a second-class boy, he gave his place of birth as Toronto and his age as thirty-five.

the eastern ports may not have seen freshwater sailors as real mariners. Nevertheless, the number of young black men from Canada West who claimed a maritime occupation speaks to how important river and lake shipping was to the province.

Most of the forty-nine recruits who claimed to be labourers were rated as landsmen at the rendezvous. Those who said they were farmers came only from Canada West, and though most were rated as landsmen, two were designated as seamen, indicating that they had previous experience at sea. A significant number of volunteers from all colonies gave their occupations as tradesmen – shoemakers, tanners, carpenters, blacksmiths, barbers, and painters – and slightly more than 15 percent received a seaman's rating. Most recruits had worked in various service occupations, typically as cooks, waiters, and stewards, but only eleven were rated as such. Cooks and stewards earned considerably more than seamen (twenty-five or thirty dollars per month), and they were technically petty officers, although some functioned more as personal servants.[76] Many cooks and stewards managed shipboard accounts, purchasing small order supplies and assisting the paymaster with monthly stipends.[77]

Another sixty volunteers either listed their occupation as "none" or left the column blank, probably to indicate that they were unemployed. However, many enlistees had clearly worked in multiple occupations. Thomas Bryant of Quebec, who said he was a "barber/pistol maker," or Hosea J. Easton of Canada, who was a "waiter/shade painter," were among the many who cited two occupations. Moreover, twenty individuals who claimed non-maritime employment were rated as ordinary seamen or higher, indicating that they too had seafaring experience. Not surprisingly, Maritimers who had multiple occupations were more likely than their counterparts from the Canadas to have spent time on the water. Not only did more New Brunswick and Nova Scotia recruits claim to be seamen, 30 percent compared to 12 percent for Canada West, but even those who said they had no occupation were also more likely to have been sailors. Two-thirds of the Maritimers with no job were subsequently rated as seamen, whereas only two of the thirty-one Canadians who claimed no occupation were rated above landsman.

The military and social culture of the navy differed strongly from that of the army. Many recruits, both black and white, joined the army as a group, as was the case for the young men from Buxton who entered a Michigan infantry regiment. New recruits often came from the same community, which meant that many British North American men served with comrades from their own province and commonly with friends or kin, a fact that reinforced their ties to home. Moreover, they frequently shared an ideological commitment to save the Union, to fight against the institution of slavery, and to prove that black men could make effective soldiers. For them, enlisting was a transformative act. Most were civilians who had to adjust to the strict discipline of army life. In addition, the experience of living in the United States plus the bonds they formed with fellow soldiers could encourage many foreign volunteers to see the United States as a potential future home. Thus, as soldiers served through the war with some old friends and relatives, they slowly developed new ties to the communities in which they served. By contrast, recent studies of Civil War sailors have found little romanticism or altruism among naval recruits. As Michael J. Bennett puts it, "The typical Union sailor was a hard, pragmatic, and cynical man who bore little patience for patriotism, reform, and religion. He drank too much, fought too much, and prayed too little."[78] For other historians, this depiction of sailors as hard men who were cut off from the bulk of society seems a little too harsh and too close to the stereotypical depiction of sailors as drunken and violent misfits in conflict with genteel society. Thus, Eric W. Sager presents their essential character as a workingman's resistance to a difficult world. To their struggles against arbitrary authority and unfriendly elements, mid-nineteenth-century sailors "brought the capacity for adaptation and survival of men who were literate, migratory, self-reliant, and tenacious in defense of assumed rights. They were not brutalized or enfeebled by their workplace," but found their strength through common cause.[79]

Ironically perhaps, for men who would form tight bonds with their shipmates, recruits entered the navy, as they generally joined merchant ships, overwhelmingly as individuals.[80] A few sailors, such as John H. Thompson and Charles H. Trust from Prince Edward Island, and Philip Bushlaw and Edward Johnson from New Brunswick, enlisted together, served in the same vessel, and left the navy together, but they were the exceptions.[81] More frequently, black sailors joined independently and were then dispersed throughout the fleet as the navy needed them. They seldom managed to serve on ships with black sailors whom they had known before the war or who had come from their home colony, let alone their hometown. Because seamen were spread throughout the fleet and confined to one vessel for varying lengths of time, their sense of belonging and identification was more to a ship's complement than to a region, state, or country. When the ship was decommissioned or the sailor's term of enlistment expired, that particular sense of community ended as well. Not surprisingly, the black sailors from British North America saw service in virtually every part of the Civil War navy, in more than 160 vessels. Unlike soldiers, who normally spent the war in just one regiment, sailors typically moved from ship to ship. Some, such as Thomas B. Jackson from "Canada," who enlisted on 12 August 1864 for three years, might serve their entire time on one vessel, but that was not the norm. More common was the experience of Isaac Layton of Montreal, who served on five ships, or George Powers from Saint John, who served on six.

Because they did not enter the navy as a collective group, few black British North American sailors could expect to serve alongside other black men from their home province, although they would have encountered many more white sailors from British North America. Indeed, only four Union ships ever had more than five black British North Americans on their roster during the war. Almost forty served on the frigate USS *Minnesota*, generally for brief periods, but that was a unique case. A few Nova Scotia recruits, most of whom were rated seamen, joined the *Minnesota* in the first part of the war and served for extended periods, but most of its foreign black recruits, all of whom were landsmen or boys, came from Canada West and volunteered in July and August 1864 as navy enlistment soared. Stationed at Hampton Roads, the *Minnesota* acted as a receiving ship for them, and they were quickly moved to other vessels, some staying for only a few days or weeks.[82] Indeed, only four of them, Samuel Fuller, James Monroe, Reuben Randall, and Henry Staats (or Stoats), were still aboard the *Minnesota* when it participated in the attack on Fort Fisher, North Carolina, on 13-15 January 1865.[83] They were among the fewer than 24 black sailors who made up the ship's crew of 562.[84] However, they may have formed a common bond with the 42 white British North Americans onboard, who were from Canada West, Nova Scotia, and New Brunswick.[85]

One ship, the USS *William Badger*, an old whaling vessel that the navy had purchased at the start of the war, may have been the only craft whose complement consisted largely of black sailors from a British colony. From the summer of 1864 to the fall of 1865, thirteen black sailors from Canada West, one from Nova Scotia, and one from New Brunswick were stationed on the *Badger*, during a time when it was used as a "supply hulk" at Beaufort, North Carolina.[86] The *Badger* and two other old vessels, the USS *Arletta* and the USS *Release*, were dismasted and lashed together as a floating storehouse.[87] Life aboard the *Badger* would not have been pleasant. Described as "totally unfit for the preservation of government property," it "was rotten and leaked and was infested with rats that destroyed the stores."[88] A vessel of the *Badger*'s size, 334 tons, normally had a crew of about twenty-four, so its British North Americans outnumbered their shipmates.[89] In addition, two other black Canadians, Aaron Jordan and Charles Vail, plus Levine T. Baynard from New Brunswick, served on the *Arletta*.

The only other naval vessel with more than five black sailors from the British colonies was the USS *Potomac*, an aging frigate built in 1822. Carrying a complement of 480, it performed a wide range of tasks. For part of the war, it escorted convoys of "California steamers" on the route "from New York to Aspinwall [in Panama] and back."[90] Later, it was a stores ship for the Gulf Blockading Squadron and then a receiving ship. Most of the twelve black British North Americans who served on the *Potomac* did so only after the start of 1865, when it was stationed in the Pensacola Naval Yards as a receiving vessel. Only two had joined the ship in 1864, Aaron M. Brown and Thomas B. Jackson, both from Canada West, and they arrived months after the *Potomac* had received credit for its last prize, the schooner *Champion*.[91]

Although black Canadian and Maritime sailors who joined the Union navy could be found in virtually every theatre of the war, most served either in the blockading squadrons in the Atlantic, concentrated at Wilmington and Charleston, or along the Gulf coast. Far fewer served with the Mississippi Squadron, the "brown water" navy that patrolled the inland waterways in support of the Union army. Men who expected that being part of a blockading squadron would guarantee excitement and prize money soon learned otherwise. Even for those who were located off an active blockade-running port such as Wilmington, boredom dominated. "It is to be one dull monotonous round, day after day, week after week, yes & month after Month ... No papers, no letters, *no nothing*," lamented William Keeler on the *Florida*. "Up & down the coast just within sight are others of the fleet going through the same dull routine of duty as ourselves."[92] Ships on the blockade of Charleston found life just as tedious. "Nothing broke the monotony," recorded Commander John Marchand of the USS *James Adger*, "and I became heartsick and tired."[93]

Given their divergent service, black colonial sailors were involved in many key events of the maritime war. John Anderson was aboard the frigate USS *Congress*, part of the Union fleet at Hampton Roads in March 1862, when the Confederate ironclad CSS *Virginia* attacked the Union vessels.[94] After sinking the USS *Cumberland*, the *Virginia* attacked the *Congress* and set fire to it after it ran aground. Although Anderson was not among the 120 sailors who were killed, he was seriously injured. A shipmate, Joseph Coombs, described what happened to him: "John Anderson was a shipman of mine on bord the uss frigate Congress Laying at Newport News, Va., a few miles above Hamden roads while in an Engagement with the merry mack *[Merrimack]* on the 8 of march 1862 he received a shell wound of left leg." As Coombs explained, this was only part of Anderson's injuries: "In the same battlefrom the smoke and concushion of the Guns met with ingury to the eyes and face as his face was swollen and his eyes read and watery. Also impressed that he was quite deff from the dreadful roar of the Canading."[95]

In the final great naval campaign of the war, the assault on Fort Fisher, which guarded the last blockade-running port of the Confederacy, black British North Americans served on two ironclads, eight frigates and sloops of war, three double-ended side-paddle gunboats, four screw gunboats, and more than a dozen auxiliary craft. Although some of these ships were repeatedly hit by Confederate fire, the damage was generally limited. The USS *Mackinaw*'s port boiler was ruptured by a Confederate shell, and ten men were scalded, but neither George Douglas from Hamilton nor John A. Jarvis of Nova Scotia, both members of its crew, were hurt.[96] Crews of other warships had more to fear from their own guns than from Confederate fire. Defective iron-cast guns burst on the USS *Juniata, Mackinaw,* and *Quaker City,* injuring dozens of sailors. On the *Juniata* alone, eighteen officers and crew were killed or wounded when a hundred-pound Parrott rifle burst.[97]

Some sailors had more adventuresome, or at least more dangerous, service than those who crewed supply vessels or blockading ships. John W. Mitchell was a twenty-nine-year-old sailor from Saint John who enlisted in Boston in March 1862. In October, he was mustered into the crew of the USS *Cairo,* one of the first river ironclads, becoming one of the few black Maritimers to serve in the Mississippi Squadron. Although he was the only black British North American in the crew of 159, 7 of the white sailors had been born in "Canada."[98] On 12 December 1862, while clearing mines in preparation for an attack on Haines Bluff, Mississippi, the *Cairo* struck a torpedo, or mine, which was exploded by Confederates hiding onshore.[99] It became the first armoured warship claimed to have been destroyed by an electrically detonated mine.[100] Mitchell survived the explosion and was transferred to the USS *Rattler,* a tinclad river gunboat. He was serving on the *Rattler* when its commander, Acting Master Daniel W. Glenny, tried unsuccessfully to deliver the ship and its crew into Confederate hands in exchange for cash, a hundred bales of cotton, and the command of a blockade-runner.[101] Then, only a few months after avoiding Confederate capture, the *Rattler* was driven ashore in a heavy gale near Grand Gulf, Mississippi, where it holed on a snag and sank. Mitchell survived this, his second shipwreck, one of the few sailors who did so during the war.

A river ironclad, the USS *Cairo*, on which John Mitchell served, was part of the Union army's Western Gunboat Flotilla, which was used on the Mississippi and Ohio Rivers. These gunboats were so hot and unreliable that sailors commonly referred to them as "federal bake ovens." *Courtesy of the US Navy, NH 61568.*

Another brown water sailor from Canada West was not as fortunate. William Johnson, a twenty-six-year-old experienced mariner who enlisted at Boston in July 1864, joined his new ship, USS *Massasoit*, a Sassacus-class gunboat performing picket duty on the James River in Virginia. Five months later, it participated in the 24 January 1865 duel with Confederate batteries at Howlett's House and took several hits.[102] Johnson was wounded by shell fragments. After a long convalescence at the Norfolk Naval Hospital, he was discharged from the navy for reasons of disability.[103]

Although most black British North American sailors spent all of the war in American waters, a few served on ships tasked with tracking down Confederate raiders in the North or South Atlantic or intercepting vessels carrying slaves from Africa. William H. Thomas of Saint John was one of the first sailors to enlist, volunteering in December 1861. He joined the newly refurbished USS *Onward*, a sailing cruiser that was ordered to help in the Charleston blockade. As a sailing ship, the *Onward* was of minor usefulness in the blockade, although it did manage to destroy two small schooners,

A side-wheel steamer, the USS *Massasoit* was initially used to patrol the New England coast and was then part of the North Atlantic Blockading Squadron. When William Johnson joined its crew, the *Massasoit* was serving on picket duty on the James River. *Courtesy of the US Navy, NH 100991.*

Chase and *Sarah*, by driving them ashore.[104] The *Onward* was then ordered to join in the hunt for Confederate commerce raiders in the South Atlantic.[105] In March 1863, along with the USS *Mohican*, the *Onward* blockaded two Confederate supply vessels, CSS *Agrippa* and CSS *Castor*, in Bahia, Brazil, forcing them to sell the supplies that they carried for the Confederate raiders CSS *Alabama* and CSS *Georgia*. Due to the actions of the *Onward* and *Mohican*, the effectiveness of the two Confederate raiders was greatly reduced.[106]

Jacob Tucker of Halifax, by contrast, served his one-year enlistment onboard the USS *Niagara*, a screw frigate attached to the European Squadron. Tucker, who was already in Europe, joined the frigate when it stopped at

Antwerp while searching for the Confederate cruisers built in British and French shipyards. Too late to join the USS *Kearsarge* in the destruction of the CSS *Alabama*, the *Niagara* was frustrated in its attempts to intercept the ironclad ram CSS *Stonewall* as it left Ferrol, Spain.[107] February 1865, as the frigate waited for the Confederate warship to leave port, was a stressful month for the crew, and a number deserted. One black crewman recorded the general mood in his diary: "All of the talk is of the Ra[m]. We expects that she is an ugley customer to handle, but we will not be dismayed."[108] Fortunately for Tucker and his shipmates, the *Stonewall* managed to slip out of port unnoticed, and the *Niagara* never tackled the Confederate ironclad in battle. Despite arguments that sailors were little motivated by ideology and despite the fact that Tucker's enlistment may have been opportunistic, he was one of several black seamen who contributed money to the *New York Anglo-African*, to be used to aid the freedmen.[109]

Even as the resources of the Union navy were stretched to their limit during the war, the combination of the Lyons-Seward Treaty of 1862 and a separate agreement signed with Denmark forced it to become more active in the suppression of the international slave trade. Twenty-four naval vessels "were designated as available for suppression of the African slave trade."[110] A dozen black British North Americans served on seven of these ships.[111] Although it is not clear how many saw action against slave-trade vessels, at least one black Nova Scotian, Henry Forman from Halifax, served in the West Indies. He joined the USS *Powhatan* in October 1864 at Cape Haytien (Haitian) in Haiti while the warship, part of a ten-vessel squadron, was on patrol in the Caribbean.[112] Before his one-year term was up, however, the *Powhatan* was back in American waters as part of the assault on Fort Fisher.[113]

Historians have debated how black sailors were viewed by their white crewmates and the extent to which they faced less animosity than black soldiers. Because the navy, unlike the army, allowed black enlistment from the start of the war, had racially integrated ships, and paid black sailors the same wage as white sailors, some historians have suggested that they were treated substantially better than white soldiers. Steven J. Ramold makes the most persuasive argument for a less racist navy. In his monograph on African American sailors during the Civil War, he suggests that, in the context of mid-nineteenth-century America, they were treated remarkably well. In addition to integrating crews, "the navy ensured equal pay and benefits, promotion opportunities, standard of living, and health care to its African American sailors, in sharp contrast to the experience of many black soldiers."[114] Although individual sailors demonstrated prejudice in numerous ways, none of the navy's official policies were racist. By contrast, historians such as Michael J. Bennett have argued that racism was an integral and ever present part of the Union navy. Steeped in racial stereotypes, white sailors rejected contrabands as crewmates, and the tensions of an integrated ship triggered violent confrontations, or "frictions," in which they targeted black sailors. By contrast, white soldiers may have used violent language in their objection to black enlistment, but Bennett asserts that their reactions "to the introduction of slaves into the army were relatively nonviolent." Of course, army units were segregated and had limited interaction. The very integration of racially mixed crews in confined quarters exacerbated the tensions on ships. Here, Bennett agrees with David Valuska that close contact created "an atmosphere conducive to hostility between the races."[115]

However, the debate about whether the army or the navy was preferable for black recruits often ignores the complex dynamics of racism, class, and skill. Although most white Americans, indeed most white North Americans, held various degrees of bias against people of African descent, their attitudes were never monolithic, consistent, or static. Prejudice varied considerably by region and by economic and cultural groups. Moreover, much greater prejudice was directed at blacks who were, or had been, slaves, on the reasoning that they had been "scarred" by the institution of slavery and had not benefitted from life in a free Northern society. Samuel Gilbert Webber, the surgeon of the USS *Nahant*, which had two black cooks from Canada West, expressed in a letter to his wife the outlook of many whites regarding ex-slaves: "Though I do not believe the negro equal to the white or that the african race will approach the caucasian in intelligence until after many years of training; yet I do believe them entitled to freedom." Webber conceded, "It may be that after many generations the degradation of slavery, its debasing & lowering influence will be overcome & they will rise higher than most expect; but if this ever happens it must be after long training first."[116] Given such widespread attitudes toward slavery and ex-slaves, the worst of the racial harassment and the most violent incidents, the very ones cited by Bennett, overwhelmingly targeted contrabands. Edward W. Hammond, a white boatswain of the USS *St. Mary*, recalled years later the "intense race hatred" directed at the ex-slaves by some white crewmen. Sailors normally used the evening dog watches to relax on the main deck, but a group of white rowdies made sure that the black sailors would be excluded by throwing gun chocks at any who showed his face above deck. Hammond remembered that even he and other white sailors who normally gathered around the steerage hatchway or open deck areas were in danger of being hit. He wrote that by "setting down on deck with our backs to the after side of a gun, we were comparatively safe."[117]

By contrast, free blacks from the North were perceived as more independent and intelligent, and better able to integrate into white communities. How white Americans tended to view black British North American sailors is unknown, for the records are silent on this issue. The sailors had the advantage of being identified as the beneficiaries of a free democratic society but were also lumped into the category of "foreign sailors." Four of them served on the USS *Florida*, whose crew was described by one of its officers as "a motley collection for a crew – from all parts of the world – England, Ireland, France, Spain, Portugal, Russia, Austria, Poland, Norway, Sweden, have representatives onboard. Besides these we have a Lascar, a Mexican, Sardinian, Italian, one from Maderia [sic], one from Manila, another from Peru &c."[118] Moreover, black British North Americans benefitted from both the racial hierarchy of maritime culture and the equally important class structure that was based on skill, experience, and background. All were free-born members of a culture that was both different from and equal to that of the Northern states, and many had extensive maritime training. Thus, they were seen as very different from the ex-slaves whose presence on Union ships generated the ugliest signs of racism in the navy. Indeed, their separateness was one of their chief characteristics.

Although significant numbers of black British North Americans served in the Union navy during the war, they remained, in important ways, distinct from the larger American society or even the African American community. In this light, the views of both historian Michael Bennett and Secretary of the Navy John Branch, who described foreign sailors as a distinct class with few ties to the United States, seem correct. Very few black sailors were bound to the United States in the ways that Branch mentioned. Instead, they were part of a fluid class of maritime workers whose attachments were more to their form of employment than to their specific employer. Enlistment was a hardnosed decision grounded in their own best interests, and they exercised considerable agency in selecting when to join up and how long to serve. During their post-war lives, most were only marginally involved in American society. Like everyone who fought for the Union army or navy, they became eligible for Civil War pensions decades after the conflict had ended. Approximately 90 percent of white American veterans and three-quarters of African American veterans had at least one successful application.[119] Only perhaps 10 percent of black British North Americans who had served in the navy bothered to request a pension.[120] This reflected their lack of involvement in American society generally. They had served the Union navy well but only as part of their employment career. By contrast, many men who entered the army, marched across America, and lived for months if not years with African American comrades saw their lives fundamentally altered by that shared experience.

CHAPTER FOUR

PROMISES DEFERRED

IN THE ARMY, 1863-64

ONCE THE WAR BROKE OUT, the Lincoln administration received a series of requests and petitions from black Americans and sympathetic abolitionists, all asking that blacks be allowed to enlist in the Union army. Some appeals were self-serving, such as that from a would-be colonel in Ohio who guaranteed that he could raise a regiment "of 1000 *colored men*, three fourths of whom are bright mulattoes" if only he received approval and, perhaps more importantly, a commission.[1] More frequently, however, the appeals came from black Northerners who simply wanted to be part of what they saw as a campaign against slavery. Such was the case for W.T. Boyd and J.T. Alston from Cleveland, Ohio, who wrote to Secretary of War Salmon P. Chase in November 1861. Describing themselves as two "Colard men, (legal voters)" who had "voted for the presant administration," they asked Chase to "allow us the poor priverlige of fighting – and (if need be dieing) to suport those in office who are our own choise." They promised to provide a thousand other names, enough to form a regiment, if they were permitted to enlist.[2] Petitioners often stressed the alleged advantages that black soldiers had serving in a Southern climate that was "So unhealthy to the [white] Soldiers of the *North*."[3]

Throughout 1861, however, all offers of black assistance were rejected. When black men tried to enlist in Cincinnati, an angry constable warned them that they were not wanted. "We want you damned niggers to keep out of this," he told them. "This is a white man's war."⁴ In the first year of the war, racial relationships were not to be challenged. Nevertheless, Northern blacks, wherever they lived, continued to organize and prepare in the expectation that they would eventually be allowed to fight.⁵ By early 1862, requests to allow blacks to enlist came even from London, Canada West. In May, Garland H. White, a minister of the African Methodist Episcopal Church and pastor of the mission in London, informed Secretary of War Chase that he had been "called upon By my peopl to tender to your *Hon* thir willingness to serve as soldiers in the southern parts during the summer season or longer if required." An African American living in Canada West, White was one of those who would have identified himself as a sojourner rather than a permanent resident. As he told Chase, "It is true I am now stopping in canada for awhile but it is not my home."⁶ Born a slave some time around 1829 in Hanover County, Virginia, he had been sold in his youth to Robert Toombs, a leading pro-slavery Democrat and secessionist from Georgia. Once Toombs became a congressional senator, he brought his slave with him to Washington, and White escaped from the capital in late 1859.⁷ By October 1861, he had been appointed "to the Pastoral Charge" of the London African Methodist Episcopal (A.M.E.) mission. The United States, however, drew him back. As he told Chase, despite the fact that he was a "man who are free from all the calumities of your land," his willingness to serve the Union was "not for speculation or self interest but for our love for the north & the government at large."⁸ By early January 1863, White had left Canada West and was preaching in a church at Toledo, Ohio. Perhaps he always saw his time in the province as temporary, but his departure coincided with a church schism in Canada West that reflected differing attitudes among black residents.⁹

Despite the lobbying efforts by men such as White and by the African American communities and their abolitionist allies, black men from Northern states and British North America would not enlist in the Union army until the start of 1863. Although President Lincoln personally opposed slavery, he believed that his actions were limited by the Constitution and that, as long as slavery was not prohibited, he was therefore compelled to defend the right of loyal Southerners to hold slaves. Equally important, he feared that linking the war to emancipation in 1861 would alienate many whites, slaveholders and non-slaveholders alike. This was especially important in the loyal border states.¹⁰ Convinced that the loss of these states would cost him the war, he moved cautiously on the issue of black participation. The potential for black involvement increased during the summer of 1862, when Congress passed two important acts. The Second Confiscation Act, passed on 17 July 1862, allowed the president to free slaves of persons who were "engaged in rebellion" and to employ blacks "in such manner as he may judge best." The Militia Act, of the same day, empowered him to employ blacks "for any military or naval service for which they are found competent."[11] Most people assumed, as did Iowa governor Samuel J. Kirkwood, that Lincoln would now allow blacks to serve in the army but only as labourers. Just after the passage of the two acts, Kirkwood transmitted a request from a colonel in one of his state regiments. The colonel wanted to replace white soldiers who were doing fatigue duties with black workmen: "We do not need a single negro in the army to fight but we could use to good advantage about one hundred & fifty with a regiment as teamsters & for making roads, chopping wood, policing camp."[12] Despite the greater flexibility that Lincoln now possessed, his administration did not reverse itself on the question of enlisting black soldiers until the Final Emancipation Proclamation of 1 January 1863.[13]

Public attitudes regarding black involvement in the war were gradually changing by the end of 1862 as antipathy toward the South intensified. The bloody losses incurred during the battles at Bull Run, Shiloh, Fredericksburg, and Antietam had seemingly brought victory a little closer but had cost the North heavily in its young men. War weariness, a new awareness of the hardships of army life, and a booming economy drastically reduced the number of men who were willing to volunteer for army service.[14] Ominously, more than a hundred short-term Union regiments were due to be discharged in the summer of 1863.[15] The government's response was to begin drafting a selective conscription law that was subsequently passed as the Enrollment Act of 3 March 1863. All able-bodied male citizens between the ages of twenty and forty-five, including immigrants who had filed for citizenship, were to be enrolled, establishing each district's quota of potential draftees. After the president called for more troops in July, federal officials set the number of new recruits that would be required from each congressional district. In several ways, the draft encouraged men from British North America and other foreigners to enlist. If a quota was not met, a lottery draft was held to fill it out. Any man who was selected in the lottery became liable for military service. If district officials could persuade a British North American to enlist, he was added to the district's quota, which meant that one less local citizen had to be found. A draftee might be ruled exempt for physical disabilities or family reasons.[16] Failing that, however, he could legally avoid service only by hiring a substitute who was not eligible for the draft or by paying a commutation fee of three hundred dollars.[17] Since African American males were bound by the terms of the Enrollment Act, at least in theory, most could not legally serve as substitutes. Both black and white British North Americans, however, could do so under American law.

To encourage volunteering, state and municipal governments, over time, greatly increased the size of the local bounties and financial support that they offered to men who volunteered, while they withheld it from those who were conscripted. The hope was that encouraging voluntary enlistment, especially of men from outside the district, would allow local citizens to avoid the draft. As white citizens increasingly faced the prospect of conscription, the idea of filling a district's quota with black volunteers became more palatable. In addition, as the sums being offered to volunteers increased, Union army service became more attractive to many British colonists, especially those who were coping with hard times.

Like a growing number of Northerners, Lincoln believed that African Americans should be used in the war effort, but he was not convinced that they would be effective in combat. Their role, he believed, would be to support white troops. Thus, he added a clause to the Final Emancipation Proclamation, which went into effect on 1 January 1863: it stated that such people of African descent, "of suitable condition, will be received into the armed services of the United States to garrison forts, positions, stations, and other places, and to man vessels of all sorts in said service."[18] Abolitionist groups in the North immediately pressed the administration to allow the creation of black regiments in the Northern states. The *Toronto Globe* understood the importance of the moment for black residents: "The freemen of the North have it in their power, if they are worthy of their cause, to destroy root and branch the monstrous growth which has cursed their country."[19] Accordingly, during January 1863, Secretary of War Edwin Stanton authorized the governors of Connecticut, Massachusetts, and Rhode Island to raise regiments of black soldiers that would be commanded by white officers.[20]

The first stage in the organization of black troops was a mixture of exhilaration and hesitancy, commitment and caution. Some saw the Union's use of black soldiers as a vindication, whereas others viewed it as a dangerous experiment. All, however, recognized it as a radical break with the past. Nevertheless, in the early summer of 1863, whether black recruits would perform as effective combat troops or unreliable soldiers best used for garrison duties was unknown. Even the government's treatment of the first black recruits was inconsistent. Although early promises were made of equal pay and comparable equipment, it was obvious that equality would not apply to other matters, especially eligibility for bounties and other financial benefits.

In May 1863, as Northern governors launched their first appeal for black volunteers, skepticism in the black communities was so strong that only the most idealistic or dedicated came forward.

John Andrew of Massachusetts was the first governor to begin enlisting black soldiers, and in mid-February he turned to the abolitionist communities of the North for help. So few black men of suitable age lived in Massachusetts that raising even one black regiment would be difficult. The 1860 census recorded that only 1,973 black men between the ages of eighteen and forty-five lived in the state. If they volunteered at the same rate as white men, the state stood to gain a maximum of only 394 new soldiers, well short of the 1,000 needed to form a regiment.[21] If Andrew were to reach his goal, recruits from outside the state had to be attracted.[22] The attitude of other governors, however, made it difficult for him to recruit outside his state. Captain Luis Emilio of the Fifty-fourth Massachusetts explained the issue: "The delicacy of the situation, as well as its absurdity, lay in the fact that these other governors, though themselves refusing to enlist the negro, still claimed him, as soon as he manifested his intent to enlist elsewhere, as potentially part of their quota."[23] Sending Massachusetts officials into Northern states to recruit black soldiers would inevitably generate complaints from their governors. This problem made the pool of potential black recruits in Canada West, a number inflated by many abolitionist accounts, doubly appealing to Massachusetts recruiters. Massachusetts's efforts to recruit them make an interesting case study when compared to the experience of other states. Not only was it the first to actively and aggressively recruit black regiments, but it also attempted to tap the manpower north of the border.

One of Andrew's first acts, after receiving authorization to raise black regiments, was to create a committee of prominent abolitionists whose mission was to organize and gather financial support for a recruiting drive that reached beyond the state border. To head the committee and act as its agent, Andrew chose George L. Stearns, who himself had once sought sanctuary in British North America.[24] In addition to Stearns, the committee, soon known as the Black Committee, included prominent abolitionists from throughout New England and New York.[25] The efforts of these private citizens to find black recruits and assist them in travelling to Massachusetts for enlistment could not be directly opposed by other state governors. The committee quickly raised $5,000 to publicize the call for volunteers and to support Stearns's recruiting efforts. In late February 1863, a week after the committee was established, Stearns left Boston and headed west to begin organizing the network that would be needed to gather volunteers. After stopping in

This broadsheet, urging patriotic black men to enlist, promised wages that equalled those of white soldiers. It was a promise that would be delayed for more than a year. Moreover, the state aid mentioned in the poster was available only to men whose families were living in Massachusetts. *Courtesy of the Massachusetts Historical Society.*

Rochester to get critical assistance from Frederick Douglass, Stearns set up a series of recruiting centres that were connected to his headquarters at Buffalo. With Douglass's help, he soon had the support of prominent African Americans across the Northern states, who used their influence in the black communities.[26] Men such as Henry Highland Garnet, John Jones, John Mercer Langston, and Martin R. Delany would provide most of the recruiting impetus, and they were responsible for much of the actual recruitment.[27]

Besides appealing to the patriotism of black men, recruiters outlined the financial benefits available to those who enlisted. The Massachusetts government promised to remunerate recruiters two dollars for every volunteer and to give each enlistee a fifty-dollar bounty when the regiment was mustered in.[28] Governor Andrew also promised black soldiers that they would receive thirteen dollars a month, the same rate as white privates in the Union army. The committee would cover all transportation costs to the camp in Readville, Massachusetts, and would even shoulder the return costs for any recruit who was rejected by the regimental surgeons. In addition, under An Act in Aid of the Families of Volunteers, the state assembly guaranteed support payments of up to twelve dollars a month to the families of all Massachusetts soldiers while they were serving. Local communities might provide even more.[29] Unfortunately for the men from British North America, the aid to families was available only for "inhabitants" of Massachusetts. No benefits were paid to their dependants. This was an especially cruel irony, given the aggressiveness with which state officials recruited African Americans from other jurisdictions. Certainly, Colonel Robert Gould Shaw of the Fifty-fourth Massachusetts understood that it would cause some men to think twice about joining. He confided to his father that the "want of State aid for the men's families will be a great drawback to their enlistment in other States. Only Massachusetts men can get it."[30]

Shaw's comment highlights an important factor. Potentially, there was a large number of young black men, in both the United States and British North America, who were willing, for a range of motives, to serve in the Union army. Hoping to appeal to them, Frederick Douglass published an article titled "Why Should a Colored Man Enlist?" in the April 1863 issue of his *Douglass' Monthly*. His most persuasive arguments focused on the transformative power of joining the struggle. "Enlist for your own sake," he urged, for doing so would be a means of recovering self-respect and enforcing equality in a society steeped in prejudice and malice. Military service was the most effective repudiation of the claim that African Americans were fit "only to be a servile class." By becoming a soldier in the Union army "against rebels and traitors," Douglass claimed, "you are defending your own liberty, honor, manhood and self-respect."[31]

Young black men may have been willing to enlist, but this did not equate with handing a blank cheque to white recruiters. For them, joining the army meant considering a spectrum of factors, ranging from personal and family obligations to the situation they would encounter in the military. They expected to be treated equitably by the authorities. A few individuals in the

Massachusetts regiments may have volunteered for fear of being drafted, but certainly no black British North American was liable to the draft.[32] Like thousands of young black men across America, they would consider joining the Union army but only if they were accorded fairness and respect. In large part, they were the architects of their own destiny. One example illustrates this point. When Robert E. Lee's Army of Northern Virginia thrust into Maryland and Pennsylvania in the summer of 1863, it triggered alarm and panic in the North. Near the end of June, when Southern troops were approaching the outskirts of Harrisburg, the capital of Pennsylvania, Governor Andrew Gregg Curtin issued a proclamation urging Pennsylvanians to come forward in defence of their government. On 17 July, ninety black volunteers from Philadelphia arrived at Harrisburg, ready to protect the capital, only to discover that the governor and the commanding officer preferred to use them as labourers rather than soldiers. In addition, Curtin apparently instructed them to maintain a low profile. They were "to keep very quiet, lest a democratic convention, then in session, should have its attention drawn to the fact of black soldiers being in town." Angered by this insulting and discriminatory approach, the men promptly returned to Philadelphia.[33] Black British North Americans who contemplated service in the Union military had at least as much control over their actions as African Americans, and they took their own best interests into account when they assessed enlistment opportunities. Throughout much of 1863, many questioned whether joining the military lay in their best interests.

By contrast, white recruiters often seemingly felt that black British North Americans would automatically flock to the Union colours. In February 1863, George Stearns had told Governor Andrew, "If you will obtain funds from the Legislature for their transportation, I will recruit you a regiment among the black men of Ohio and the Canadian West."[34] Shortly after setting up his headquarters in Buffalo, Stearns crossed the Niagara River, hoping to find large numbers of recruits in Canada West. His biographer argues that after he arrived in Toronto, "he worked quietly because secessionist sympathy was strong there," but his caution may also have reflected his awareness that he was violating the Foreign Enlistment Act.[35] Hostility toward foreign recruiters was also growing. The anger was fed by stories in the provincial press of unscrupulous agents who preyed upon gullible young men. The most inflammatory articles dealt with men who were drugged and taken across the border to be forcibly enlisted.[36]

Thus, when Stearns headed to Toronto in the summer of 1863 to find black volunteers, there was already considerable public concern over the actions of foreign bounty brokers and local crimps operating in the Canadas. Throughout the war, a bounty broker was defined as an agent who, capitalizing on the naive, arranged for young men to enlist in the army and then received a large fee for his service. A "crimp," as defined in the Canadian press, was a Canadian broker who brought willing, or sometimes unwilling, volunteers to American recruiting stations in the Northern states.[37] Brokers and crimps have generally been depicted as predators and swindlers, driven purely by profit and happy to provide volunteers whom they knew to be bounty-jumpers – men who enlisted for the bounty and then promptly deserted. The activities that most outraged British officials, however, were attempts to get British troops to desert and cross the border.[38] All this may have forced Stearns to keep his head down in Canada West, but nevertheless, on his return to Buffalo he claimed to have "already one hundred and twenty promises to leave" the province. Encouraged by the response that he believed he had found in Canada West, he returned to Boston to acquire additional funds for recruiting in New York and the Canadas.[39]

Despite Stearns's optimism, there were a number of important reasons why potential black recruits in the summer and fall of 1863 would carefully consider their decision to enlist. All Civil War soldiers risked death or disability from battle wounds or disease. However, black Union soldiers faced a danger that was seldom a reality for their white counterparts. Even if they came from British North America, black men in uniform would not be treated as legitimate prisoners of war if they were captured and might simply be killed or sold into slavery. During the war, few Confederates accepted the legitimacy of black troops. As early as 1862, the very suggestion that they might be used in the Union army elicited violent threats from white Southerners. "For many Southerners," Dudley Cornish explains, "it was psychologically impossible to see a black man bearing arms as anything but an incipient slave uprising complete with arson, murder, pillage, and rapine."[40]

Speaking for the Confederate government, Secretary of War James Seddon announced that black Union troops "cannot be recognized in any way as soldiers subject to the rules of war and to trial by military court." The *Richmond Examiner* voiced Southern anger when it warned, "Should they be sent to the field, and put in battle, none will be taken prisoner. Our troops understand what to do in such cases."[41] In May 1863, the Confederate Congress resolved that all white officers who led black units were guilty of inciting insurrection and that they should "be put to death, or otherwise punished" if captured.[42] Canadian newspapers reported the threats, and the *Hamilton Evening Times* noted that "the failure of the United States

Government to guarantee protection to its colored soldiers, has retarded the enlistment of that class of troops."[43] In the wake of the Fifty-fourth Massachusetts's failed assault on Fort Wagner and amid rumours of the mistreatment of captured black soldiers by the Confederates, many supporters of the black troops were angered. Frederick Douglass announced that he would not encourage black men to volunteer so long as the administration failed to protect its black soldiers. "How many 54ths," he wrote, "must be cut to pieces, its mutilated prisoners killed and its living sold into Slavery, to be tortured to death by inches before Mr. Lincoln shall say: 'Hold, Enough!'?"[44]

Despite Confederate bravado, both Southern officials and soldiers were soon constrained by Lincoln's public threats of retaliation and the willingness of federal officers to mete out a similar fate to Confederate captives. In July, the president issued General Order No. 252, which declared that the Union government would protect all its soldiers, black or white, who were captured. He gave notice that "for every soldier of the United States killed in violation of the laws of war a rebel soldier shall be executed, and for every one enslaved by the enemy or sold into slavery, a rebel soldier shall be placed into hard labor."[45] Atrocities against black troops persisted until the war ended, but they were never authorized, at least officially, by the Confederate command.[46] Only as the war progressed, however, did the Confederate treatment of captured black troops become a known quantity. In the first summer of enlistment, it was not yet clear, and the Confederate threats remained an all-too-real possibility.

Indeed, the *Toronto Globe* ran sensationalized accounts of the failed 18 July 1863 assault on Fort Wagner that might have made some black men think twice about enlisting. The paper reported that the black soldiers of the Fifty-fourth Massachusetts charged the fort bravely, "but the rebels made a dash towards them with all their bitter feelings against negro troops aroused ... They took some prisoners, slaughtering many." Two days later, the *Globe* added, "Unofficial reports say the negroes have been sold into slavery, and that the officers are treated with immeasurable abuses."[47] Given this, it was not surprising that a prominent African American in Oxford, Massachusetts, informed Governor Andrew near the end of 1863 that rather than enlisting in the Fifth Massachusetts Cavalry Regiment then being formed, some potential recruits "think they would rather wait and see if the Gov't is not going to take some measures to protect the colored man if he got taken prisoner. You see it is a little discouraging for a colored man to enlist."[48] Many black British North Americans may have shared this view. Ultimately, more than fifty would serve in the Fifth Massachusetts, but only a handful joined in 1863.

Black men in British North America would also have known that their enlistment would impose financial hardship on their families. Almost all of them came from working-class backgrounds, and most either farmed or worked as labourers. Few could support their families if they left home for an extended period, a fact that was especially germane for married men. Unlike those of African American soldiers, their families would receive no state aid during the war. Like other soldiers who joined the Massachusetts regiments, they could expect a fifty-dollar bounty paid by the state. In addition, those who signed up for three years would receive a hundred dollars from the federal government but only at the end of their term of service.[49] This was small financial compensation for those who left dependants in British North America without a source of income for several years. Moreover, when Lincoln first authorized the use of black soldiers in 1863, they were not eligible for full federal enlistment bounties.[50] Only later in the war would increased financial inducements be offered to recruits in various forms of bounties or payments for substitutes, and even these varied considerably from region to region.[51] In the summer of 1863, black recruits could expect little in the way of financial benefits when they enlisted.

Black British North Americans who were being urged to join the Massachusetts regiments had to ponder all these factors. Certainly, their 1863 enlistment in the two Massachusetts infantry regiments and the black cavalry regiment indicates that the early optimism of recruiters such as Stearns was exaggerated. Although a significant number did serve in the Fifty-fourth and Fifty-fifth Massachusetts and the Fifth Massachusetts Cavalry, they were only a small fraction of what Stearns and others had hoped to get. Of course, the military records make it almost impossible to identify the African Americans who were resident in British North America in 1863 and who chose to return south. Many of them may have joined the Massachusetts regiments.

While Stearns was canvassing the North for more men, the first recruits arrived at the Readville regimental camp, just south of Boston. On 23 February 1863, Colonel Robert Gould Shaw of the Fifty-fourth Massachusetts wrote to his fiancée, Annie Haggerty, describing the opening of the camp. The first twenty-seven men had arrived; moreover, he told Annie that "to-day three men are going on a campaign into Canada."[52] The three men, who were recruiting agents, may have been successful, for the first black volunteer from British North America, John W. Moore, reached Readville on 13 March. A twenty-two-year-old gunsmith from Dundas, Canada West, Moore had left his wife at home to serve in the war.[53] A year later, he would be the "regimental armorer," although he was soon discharged because of an injury to

Private Abraham F. Brown was born in Toronto, where he worked as a sailor before enlisting in the 54th Massachusetts in April 1863. He died of an accidental gunshot wound four months later. *Courtesy of the Massachusetts Historical Society.*

his left arm.⁵⁴ In the month after Moore joined the Fifty-fourth Massachusetts, nine more men followed him to Readville. In mid-March, Shaw wrote his mother that "Mr. Stearns, who is at home for a few days from Canada, says we can get more men than we want from there." The same day, he told Annie that men were beginning to arrive from "Western New York and Canada," and that "our recruiting agent [George Stearns] up there says he can get enough to make two or three regiments, if the Governor is authorized to raise them."⁵⁵

Although Massachusetts eventually raised three black regiments, and British North Americans were among their earliest recruits, they were not

A sailor from St. Catharines, Private John Goosberry joined the 54th Massachusetts at age twenty-five. He wears his uniform as a company musician and holds his fife.
Courtesy of the Massachusetts Historical Society.

the first choice of most black British colonials. In fact, the Black Committee's recruiting agents had only moderate success in attracting men from British North America. Twenty-eight British North American–born men joined Massachusetts's first black regiment, and of the twenty-seven who came from Canada West, twenty-five had enlisted by mid-May 1863. Two more followed suit before the year's end, and the remaining man, John Robinson, a twenty-two-year-old sailor from Halifax, did not join the regiment until 14 February 1865.[56] Because regimental records do not list a recruit's place of residence, it is unknown whether these men were living in the United States before they enlisted. More is known about the members of the state's second black regiment, the Fifty-fifth Massachusetts. Volunteering had been so great that the Fifty-fifth was quickly established after the Fifty-fourth was full. The regimental descriptive book indicates that eighteen black men from British North America joined this unit. Moreover, because a history of the Fifty-fifth Massachusetts was published after the war, we know a little more about their place of residence. At least six were living in the United States when they joined the Fifty-fifth.[57] It is reasonable to assume that a significant number of the British North Americans who enlisted in the Fifty-fourth Massachusetts were also living in various Northern states.

Although the forty-six colonial soldiers who joined the Fifty-fourth and Fifty-fifth Massachusetts may have been fewer than recruiters expected, their numbers were reasonable, given the factors they had to consider. By the late summer of 1863, Rhode Island, Connecticut, and Pennsylvania were all in the process of organizing their own black regiments and vying for enlistees.[58] Moreover, by that time, not even romantic young men could see the war as a brief and largely bloodless conflict. The bloody harvest of battle was revealed in the casualty reports published by the newspapers and by the invalids who filled up Northern army hospitals. Men across North America more fully understood the harsh conditions, danger, and cost of war, and white volunteering rates had fallen off as a result.

Potential black recruits had even more issues to contemplate. How the Northern government would treat them was not yet clear. The Final Emancipation Proclamation, which stated that they would be used "to garrison forts, positions, stations, and other places," implied that they would perform a secondary role, and many senior officers obviously saw them largely as a labour force. General William T. Sherman was representative of many senior officers in his disdain for their military value. He would willingly employ them to dig entrenchments, "but he was convinced that they were useless as soldiers," a view shared by most of his men.[59] Indeed, when black regiments participated in the July 1863 siege of Charleston, South Carolina, they were initially given far more fatigue duties than white troops.[60] In October, the *Philadelphia Christian Recorder* carried a report outlining the hardships faced by men in the Third United States Colored Troops (USCT), a regiment containing men from Canada West, New Brunswick, and Nova Scotia. The men described how "with spade and shovel [we] dug up to the very parapet of the rebel fort under a heavy fire of grape and canister shell from the rebel batteries."[61] Although by the end of the year the men could report that their duties as diggers and sappers were less onerous, some potential black recruits who expected equal treatment and opportunities were angered by the use to which many black soldiers had been put. Troops who served farther south may never have seen an improvement in their use. Months later, an anonymous soldier in the Twentieth USCT, a New York regiment with sixty-five black British North Americans, wrote to the president. He complained, "We are treated in a Different manner to what other Rigiments is Both Northern men or southern Raised Rigiment Instead of the musket It is the spad and the Whelbarrow and the Axe cutting in one of the most horable swamps Louisiana stinking and misery."[62]

Published accounts in the Northern press ensured that by the late summer of 1863 and early 1864, British North Americans were aware of the situation facing black soldiers. In addition, any hope that they might be promoted to the rank of officer, a possibility raised when the regiments were first formed, was dimmed by the fall of 1863.[63] Making matters worse, reports in the *New York Weekly Anglo-African* during the spring of 1863 disclosed that the few African Americans who held commissions, the well-educated and cultured officers in the Louisiana Native Guards, were being systematically purged by senior white officers.[64] In May, even as men were joining the Fifty-fourth and Fifty-fifth Massachusetts, Surgeon Alexander T. Augusta, a black doctor who had left Toronto to join the Union army, sent a story to the *Christian Recorder*, which recounted his experience, while in uniform, of being attacked by thugs at the Baltimore railroad station.[65] Many young black men may not have wished to sacrifice so much for a society that offered them so little.

In the summer of 1863, what particularly angered black soldiers and their white supporters was the issue of unequal pay. It both labelled them as second-class soldiers and undermined their ability to support themselves and their families. In the first months of 1863, Governor Andrew, Secretary of War Stanton, and many recruiting officers had all promised that black recruits would receive the same wages as white soldiers – thirteen dollars a month for privates, plus a clothing allotment of three dollars. On 4 June 1863, after consulting with Solicitor William Whiting, the War Department announced that the Militia Act of 1862 was the authorizing legislation for the enlistment of black men in military units. According to Whiting, the act specified a lower rate of pay for all African Americans and also precluded bounties.[66] Thus, black soldiers would receive only ten dollars a month, with three dollars deducted for clothing. Moreover, unlike their white counterparts, black non-commissioned officers would receive the same wage as privates.[67] Captain Luis Emilio wrote that the black soldiers of the Fifth Massachusetts Cavalry had not complained when they "were not paid the portion of United States bounty paid to other volunteer regiments in advance," but the lower pay nonetheless implied lower status.[68] In July 1863, the black soldiers in Massachusetts regiments grew increasingly angry when they learned that they would not receive the wages that Governor Andrew had promised them when they enlisted.[69] Provoked by what they saw as an issue of principle, they repeatedly refused to accept the unequal pay, even when the state offered to make up the difference.[70]

The resentment felt by many enlisted men was so great that some white officers feared potential mutiny. Although the black troops could decline their pay, as soldiers during wartime they could not refuse to obey orders. In November 1863, a crisis ensued when Sergeant William Walker of the Third South Carolina Colored Infantry persuaded his men to stack their arms and refuse service because of the pay issue. He argued that because the army had failed to uphold its promises, the men were released from duty. The army disagreed. Charged and convicted of mutiny, Walker was executed on 1 March 1864.[71] Joseph Glatthaar believes that Governor Andrew provided the most fitting epitaph for Walker: "The Government which found no law to pay him except as a nondescript and a contraband, nevertheless found law enough to shoot him as a soldier."[72]

A soldier in the Fifty-fifth Massachusetts summed up the bitterness felt by most black soldiers regarding their treatment during the summer of 1863: "No Chance for promotion, no money for our families, we are little better than an armed band of laborers with rusty muskets and bright spades."[73] Samuel Robinson, the Toronto-born first sergeant, voiced the same frustration after a few months of service, although money was not his major concern. He was concerned about the other ways in which they had been treated as second-class soldiers. In particular, he was frustrated that talented black non-commissioned officers were denied any hope for promotion. The soldiers' anger was constrained solely by assurances from their supporters in Congress that if only they remained patient, the injustice would be resolved.

By December 1863, when the Fifth Massachusetts Cavalry Regiment was beginning to form, black British North Americans had a more accurate idea of what they might experience once they put on a Union uniform, yet many enlisted. Some white recruiters were not as realistic, or perhaps not as honest. In November, after announcing that he wanted to create a cavalry unit in his state, Governor Andrew met with a "Dr. Ross of Canada," who claimed that he "could raise five hundred men from the British colony." Andrew replied that "he could take about two hundred and fifty to fill up the vacancies in the Fifty-fourth and Fifty-fifth, but could accept no more men because no new organizations were authorized." Whether Ross ever produced any soldiers is unknown, but Andrew used his promise as leverage to get Stanton's authorization for the black cavalry regiment.[74] By that time, foreign recruits were coming from elsewhere than Canada West. Whereas the black British North Americans in the Fifty-fourth and Fifty-fifth Massachusetts were overwhelmingly from that province (only one of the thirty-five soldiers came from elsewhere), the situation was different in the cavalry regiment. Among its fifty-six black troopers from the British colonies, twenty-five came from the Maritimes, including Nathaniel Williams, a nineteen-year-old "student" from Prince Edward Island who enlisted in May 1864.[75]

As Massachusetts recruiters fanned out across the North in search of black volunteers, officials in Rhode Island and Connecticut also began to compete for them. In July 1863, Governor James Y. Smith of Rhode Island was authorized to organize a company of black soldiers.[76] When the company quickly filled, it was expanded to a battalion and then a full regiment of heavy artillery, the Fourteenth Rhode Island Heavy Artillery.[77] Long after the war, an officer of the Fourteenth explained the reasons for its creation: "In the summer of 1863, white men were no longer eager to enlist for a war the end of which none could foresee; but nevertheless the war must be prosecuted with vigor; another draft was impending and the State's quota must be filled."[78] The black enlisted men who filled the ranks during the summer were more enthusiastic than many of their white officers. Lieutenant Joshua Addeman remembered his indecision in accepting a commission in the regiment: "In common with many others I did not at the outset look with particular favor upon the scheme. But with some hesitation I accepted an appointment from the State as a second lieutenant and reported for duty at Camp Smith."[79] Once its ranks were filled, the first battalion of the regiment manned fortifications that it constructed on Dutch Island to guard Narragansett Bay while the second battalion was being organized. Then the first battalion was shipped to Texas, the second battalion occupied Dutch Island, and the final battalion was formed. Months later, during the early summer of 1864, the regiment reunited in Louisiana, where the men spent the remainder of their service in manning forts on the Mississippi River, from New Orleans to Plaquemine, just below Baton Rouge. The Fourteenth Rhode Island never saw battle, but the Plaquemine region, where much of it was stationed, was "infested with guerilla bands" and the threat of raids and reprisals remained a constant.

One black Canadian who joined the Fourteenth and served in its second battalion was Charles L. Clayton, a nineteen-year-old farmer from "Black Rock," Canada West.[80] He enlisted in Providence, Rhode Island, and accompanied the regiment in January when it left for New Orleans on an army transport that "had long since seen its better days." The voyage south was particularly difficult, with "men packed like sheep in the hold," seasickness, scanty rations, and the little water that could be distilled from the boilers.[81] Once the regiment disembarked, it went into camp fifteen miles south of New Orleans at an unhealthy spot called English Turn. Clayton was among the many men who fell ill there. On 6 March 1864, he died in the battalion hospital of phthisis pulmonalis, or pulmonary consumption. The records indicate that he "died possessed of no effects" and was buried on the riverbank.[82] He had been a soldier for just six months. The other sixteen Canadians who joined the regiment were more fortunate than Clayton, for none died although several were ill enough to be discharged for disabilities before their term of service was complete.[83] They may have considered themselves fortunate because the Fourteenth had one of the highest mortality rates among all black regiments.

A sergeant captured the plight of his men: "The mortality down here is very great; no less than two or three dying every day ... Out of one hundred and forty, one hundred and twelve remain, and if we stay in these swamps we will all die."[84] More than just the environment and excessive fatigue duty were to blame for the illness and deaths. The sergeant believed that badly needed supplies provided by the Sanitary Commission were being diverted elsewhere. In addition, he stated, though many of the doctors and nurses were competent and kind, the hospital stewards were another matter: they "held the lives of the men in their hands" but were incompetent alcoholics.[85]

Many Canadians who enlisted in the Fourteenth Rhode Island served as non-commissioned officers. Henry A. Berryman, a barber from Hamilton, was appointed sergeant in November 1863, on the same day that he enlisted, perhaps because he was literate.[86] Another Hamilton man, John Jackson, was made corporal when he signed up, became a sergeant two months later, and served as acting sergeant major during the fall of 1864.[87] Four other men from Canada West served as corporals for at least part of their time in the army. Several of these soldiers had difficulty in keeping their stripes. The boredom of garrison and guard duty, the tension of working in the midst of Confederate sympathizers, and the proximity to urban areas may have been major factors in some of their demotions. Nelson Dunkerson provides one example. A twenty-six-year-old labourer from Canada, he enlisted in

September 1863 and was made corporal only two weeks later. A year afterward, however, while the regiment was based at Plaquemine, he was court-martialled for being absent without leave and for "lying out of quarters." More specifically, he was accused of "lying out of quarters ... at the house of one Ellen Barker (colored) between the hours of 8½ and 12 o'clock on the night of 16th November 1864."[88] A patrol from the regiment had searched the nearby town before locating him in Barker's bedroom. When the door was finally opened, Dunkerson was found hiding between the bed and the wall, dressed only in his pants. The court found him guilty of the charges and decided to make an example of him.[89] Reduced to the ranks, Dunkerson forfeited a month's pay and was forced "to work at hard labor on the fort at Plaquemine, La., Thirty days (30) one third of the time with a ball weighing Thirty-two (32) Pounds attached to his left leg by a chain three feet long."[90]

Another Canadian non-commissioned officer who lost his stripes was John Jackson, the regiment's acting sergeant major in late 1864. He, however, exercised some personal control in his demotion when he publicly voiced his distaste for his senior position. The first charge against him was conduct prejudicial to the service in that he apparently claimed, "I want to be sent to my Company and if they do not send me, I will do something to make them. I have got tired of hanging around the God damned miserable Head Quarters." Jackson got his wish and was returned to his company as a private.[91] He was still a private when he mustered out in October 1865.

The Fourteenth Rhode Island had at least one African American who had made a new home for himself in Chatham, Canada West, before the war began. Sergeant Alexander Atwood was singled out for praise in the official history of the regiment, in part because he died in the battalion hospital on 28 August 1864, to the sorrow of men of all ranks. Noting that Atwood "was known as a modest and conscientious man, and greatly respected by both officers and men," the regimental historian added that his "patriotism was unquestioned, having journeyed from Canada to enlist in the Union Army in the States." His sacrifice was seen as all the greater because he had left behind a family and a prosperous grocery store. Indeed, just before he died, his wife "had come from her far northern home" to visit him in Louisiana.[92] Although Atwood was born in Prairie Bluff, Alabama, he had established himself in Chatham after he married Priscilla Hartsill in Ripley, Ohio, in June 1854.[93]

The third New England state to raise black troops, Connecticut, began recruiting in August 1863. Initially, its success in attracting British North Americans was limited, and by the time the Twenty-ninth Connecticut

Regiment was mustered in March 1864, only six had joined its ranks. The first to enlist was Alfred McIntosh, an eighteen-year-old porter from Kingston who joined the regiment on 19 December 1863. Made corporal in March 1865, he survived both the war and the regiment's difficult Reconstruction service in Texas, and was mustered out in October 1865.[94] Five other men, including William Anderson from New Brunswick, also enlisted during the first months of 1864. Anderson had been living in Mansfield, Vermont, before he joined the Twenty-ninth Connecticut.[95] James A. Myers, a thirty-eight-year-old butcher born in "Canada" but married and living in Hartford, joined the regiment in January 1864. He would not see his wife again. He died in the Tenth Corps base hospital in September 1864 of chronic diarrhea and was buried at City Point, Virginia.[96] Other British North Americans, including twenty who signed up as general recruits in August and December 1864, all survived the regiment's campaigning in the siege efforts around Petersburg and Richmond, Virginia.

Although the New England states were the first to recruit black soldiers, other Northern states eventually proved at least as successful in drawing black volunteers from north of the border. In part, this was because the men were free to choose where they served, and they volunteered for multiple personal reasons. New York State sent no official recruiters to the British colonies but still managed to attract many black enlistees from the Canadas. Denis Donohoe, the British consul in Buffalo, captured some of the optimism being spread by Buffalo newspapers in late 1863 as well as the reason that many residents wanted to attract black volunteers from Canada West. "No one doubts that at least a regiment of colored soldiers might be raised within six weeks here in Buffalo, by employing proper agencies among the colored people of Canada," Donohoe quoted from the newspaper, "and such a help towards filling up the quota of Buffalo and the averting of another draft for her people is not to be regarded with indifference nor neglect."[97] While the paper's prediction was not realistic, by the end of the war, more than 170 black men born in the British colonies had enrolled in New York's black regiments. The Twentieth USCT, organized in early 1864 at Rikers Island, had 65, and the Twenty-sixth USCT, also raised on the island, had 37. The Thirty-first USCT, a New York regiment that incorporated the partially formed Thirtieth Connecticut Colored Regiment, had at least 70.

Other Northern states also enrolled significant numbers from British North America. The nine black infantry regiments organized in Pennsylvania, beginning with the Third USCT, enlisted more than two hundred. The Sixth USCT, from Philadelphia, had twenty-two, and the Twenty-fifth USCT,

The men of the 26th United States Colored Troops on parade in camp. Thirty-seven British North Americans served in this unit, which was raised at Rikers Island in early 1864. Like all black regiments, it was led by white officers. *Courtesy of the National Archives and Records Administration.*

raised a few months later at Camp Penn, had seventy-one.[98] The march of the Sixth USCT through Philadelphia reflected just how quickly white attitudes changed regarding the use of black troops. When the first black regiment, the Third USCT, marched through the city in September 1863 on its way to the front, city officials compelled the men to march without arms and in civilian clothes for fear that the mere sight of black soldiers would trigger white violence. Less than a month later, the Sixth USCT, in full uniform and carrying arms, paraded throughout Philadelphia past a largely supportive crowd as it headed off to war.[99]

Some black regiments were unable to acquire recruits from British provinces, even though they seemed to have a connection to the colonies. Garland White, the minister who preached in London, Canada West, became a very active recruiter of black soldiers in 1863. He later claimed that he "recruited colored men for every colored regiment raised in the north" and that he had "canvassed the entire north and west urging my people to enlist."[100] He was particularly active in recruiting for the Indiana regiment being raised in late 1863, in part because he expected a commission as its chaplain. He informed Secretary of State William H. Seward in May 1864 that he himself had recruited nearly "half the men in the 28th U.S. Colored Infantry Regiment raised in Indiana."[101] Indeed, he may have been correct, but he was also actively self-promoting. Receiving his commission took considerably more time than he had anticipated. Although the first recruits for the Twenty-eighth USCT were mustered in on 24 December 1863, the regiment was only partially complete when it left the state four months later, and until it was full White could not get his commission.[102] He was forced to enlist as a private in Company D so that when the tenth company was finally filled, he would be available to become chaplain. The last four companies were slow to fill, in part because of a lack of willing recruits in Indiana.[103] Only after the War Department provided about four hundred men who filled the last companies, and with strong recommendations from his colonel and eighteen regimental officers, did White finally become chaplain. Interestingly, though White had preached in Canada West, touted his abilities as a recruiter, and had travelled, as he said, across "the entire north and west" in his efforts to recruit, not a single soldier in the Twenty-eighth USCT gave a British North American colony as his place of birth.[104]

During the summer of 1863, the Union started to recruit black soldiers in the South, and a few black British North Americans enlisted in regiments south of the Mason-Dixon Line, although the records do not reveal why they chose these units. The First USCT was organized on Mason's Island in the District of Columbia during the summer of 1863, and two of its five black Canadians were among the first to enlist. Jerry Marks, an eighteen-year-old unmarried harness maker from Chatham, did so in July. He survived the war, apparently without injuries, and was mustered out on Roanoke Island, North Carolina, at the end of September 1865.[105] James Peak joined the regiment a month before Marks, and his records raise more questions than they answer. A twenty-three-year-old cook from St. Catharines, Peak enlisted in Company E on 17 June. Almost immediately, he was detailed to help recruit in Baltimore and was promoted to first sergeant in mid-July. Nevertheless, four months later he was court-martialled, found guilty of riotous and disorderly conduct, "reduced to the ranks ... and sentenced to hard labor during his remaining term of enlistment and to forfeit all pay and allowances due or to become due from the U.S." Six months later, the "unexpired portion of sentence [was] remitted by order of Genl B. F. Butler from May 4 '64." Indeed, he was again appointed sergeant only three weeks afterward. He still held that rank when he was wounded near Fair Oaks, Virginia, and he spent the next eight months in hospital. He finally rejoined his regiment before it was mustered out in North Carolina in September 1865.[106]

Not all the Canadians who joined the new regiments were black. Thomas Kennedy was one of these rare exceptions, and his role in the Third United States Colored Heavy Artillery (USCHA) was duplicated in a number of black regiments raised in the South. A twenty-year-old blacksmith born and raised in Montreal, Kennedy had joined the 117th Illinois Volunteers in August 1862 and been promoted to corporal. A year later, he was discharged from the white regiment so that he could become a first sergeant in the Third USCHA, which was being organized in Memphis, Tennessee, during the summer and fall of 1863. Like many black regiments, it desperately needed experienced non-commissioned officers to help train its new troops. Moreover, since so many Southern recruits were illiterate, sergeants who could handle the mountain of paperwork, maintain company records, and reply to correspondence were in short supply. Men such as Kennedy accepted positions in black regiments with the expectation that they would ultimately receive a commission as regular officers. Kennedy's hopes were not disappointed. In April 1865, he was promoted to second lieutenant in the Third USCHA. Like many Canadian recruits who served in the South, Kennedy became ill, suffering from "intermittent fever of long continuance." Unlike the black enlisted men, however, Kennedy, now an officer, could apply for and receive an extended leave "to visit [his] home in Montreal," where he recovered.[107]

Of the USCT regiments, the First Michigan Colored Infantry, later redesignated the 102nd USCT, was most able to attract British North Americans. Its success was grounded in its proximity to Canada West, the timing of its organization, and the financial offers that it made to enlistees. In addition, unlike most black regiments, it continued to recruit in its home state. Many black British North Americans were drawn to the First Michigan by the ties of kinship, friendship, and culture that were grounded in the social and economic network spanning the border. Although the First was similar in many ways to other black regiments, its genesis offers a valuable contrast to that of its Massachusetts equivalents.

Unlike most Northern black regiments, which owed their existence to the state governor's office, the First Michigan was initially promoted by a private citizen, Henry Barnes, editor of the *Detroit Advertiser and Tribune*. His idea found support among sympathetic groups such as the black quasi-military organization called the Detroit Liberty Guards, but Michigan's white residents, among whom ran a deep streak of racism, were bitterly divided over the issue.[108] Not surprisingly, they tended to split along political lines; Republicans generally favoured the use of black soldiers, whereas Democrats opposed it. In 1862, the Michigan legislature had passed an act to prohibit the enrolment of African Americans in the state militia, a measure that underscores the antipathy toward the very idea of black soldiers.[109] Many Michigan whites saw the Civil War as a "white man's war," a view shared throughout the United States. Lieutenant John C. Buchanan of the Eighth Michigan expressed the prejudice of many when he wrote that he had found "none of these Colored Gemmen as yet who would be capable of fighting & will venture the assertion, such is their servility, that fifty of their masters would put to flight a Reg. of them."[110]

In the early months of 1863, even as Henry Barnes was using the *Detroit Advertiser and Tribune* to promote the idea of a black regiment for Michigan, numerous black men were leaving the state and travelling to Massachusetts, where they could enlist.[111] Once there, they were credited to the draft quota of Massachusetts.[112] When Michigan's Republican governor, Austin Blair, turned down Barnes's request to raise a black regiment, Barnes appealed directly to Secretary of War Stanton. In August 1863, Stanton instructed Blair to raise the regiment and suggested that he consider Barnes as its organizer. On 12 August 1863, Barnes finally received authorization to raise the regiment of black soldiers.[113] The newspaperman's ability to get his regiment properly organized and into action in a timely fashion was handicapped by Blair's lukewarm support for the venture. The governor voiced his inherent racial prejudices during a speech that he gave in Adrian, Michigan. "I am utterly unable to see why," he declared, "it is not proper to use a rebel's sacred nigger ... I am entirely unable to see, too, why Sambo shouldn't be permitted to carry a musket."[114] It speaks to the nature of mid-nineteenth-century politics that someone such as Blair, who was active in founding the Republican Party and who has been described as a Radical Republican, would think nothing of using the racist language of his day.[115]

Volunteering in the new regiment was slow, which suggests that many members of the black community were skeptical about what was being offered, offended by white racism, and fully aware of their other economic opportunities. In the summer of 1863, the state of Michigan, various cities, and even urban wards were all offering a range of enlistment bounties to boost volunteerism, but these were available only to white soldiers. Local officials soon changed this policy, but federal bounties would not be given to black recruits until mid-1864. By contrast, the wartime economy had opened up new opportunities for black civilians who chose not to volunteer.[116]

Recruits trickled in during the late summer and early fall of 1863, and the first volunteers from Canada West arrived in September, led by Alexander Brown from Kent County and Elijah Johnson from London.[117] By the end of October, the regiment had enrolled about three hundred men, some of whom came from the Buxton settlement, crossing the border and enlisting in two separate groups.[118] By the end of the war, the Michigan regiment had enrolled 137 men who gave Canada West as their place of birth. Most were living in the province when they decided to enlist, although some were residing in Michigan. In addition, numerous African American residents of Canada West, friends and neighbours of the Canadian recruits, also left the province to join the First Michigan. Among the first group of thirty who left Buxton and entered the regiment, only seven were born in Canada West. The rest were African Americans who had lived in Buxton for varying lengths of time. All told, perhaps as many as seventy black recruits came from the Buxton area.[119]

Barnes had failed in his attempts to convince either Michigan or Detroit to provide enlistment bounties for his volunteers, but attitudes changed once Lincoln called for more troops in October 1863. Threatened with a draft lottery to select more white recruits, several Michigan communities who felt that they had already sacrificed enough offered bounties to black volunteers who would then be credited to their congressional district. Wayne County, where Detroit was situated, soon followed suit, although its bounty initially took the form of a bond that was redeemable at the end of service.[120] In the following months, as more municipalities made financial inducements available to prospective volunteers, black men could choose among them in order to maximize their financial interest. Their decisions were made more complex by the presence of unscrupulous agents who preyed on the naive and by warnings in the *Detroit Advertiser* that some states did not honour their promises of bounties.[121]

The case of one black soldier highlighted the financial issues that volunteers had to assess. In June 1865, George G. Freeman wrote to the chief justice of the United States to complain about his treatment in the army and to request a compassionate discharge. He had left a wife and two children behind, and he felt that he had been misled when he enlisted. He claimed that

> my famley Receives no Relief from my states as was Promesed me For I was stolen from my town of Enrollment and creaded to the city of Detroit ... I could tell you Of a great deal of rascality that has Ben a going on in the Regiment that I belong if it was nesicary but I only want obliging my self.

Because he had enlisted in Detroit, his wife and children were apparently not eligible for the family financial support provided by their district. Freeman's commanding officer, Captain E.J. McKendrie, told a different story. Only part of the soldier's claim was correct, McKendrie stated, for he had been "accredited to a certain ward in the City of Detroit at his own request because he was aware that he could get a larger Bounty in the City of Detroit than he could in a rural District where his family resided." It was unfortunate for Freeman's family that his choice had deprived them "of certain local appropriations which were generally made by the several towns in the State of Michigan to the families of those who enlisted during the late war."[122] In his opinion, Freeman had made a financial decision that turned out not to benefit his family. He did not comment on Freeman's other charges.

Other black recruits may have questioned their decision to volunteer much sooner than Freeman did. In the fall of 1863, the *Detroit Free Press* declared that Barnes was abusing and bullying his new recruits. It added that soldiers who received bonds as their enlistment bounties were forced to sign them over to him for a fraction of their face value. Defending himself in print against the claims of the rival paper, Barnes said that "he secured the bonds to protect the recruits from unscrupulous speculators, and that the regiment was fully aware of his attempt to protect the full worth of the bonds for their benefit."[123] In November, a meeting of Detroit's black community at the Second Baptist Church endorsed Barnes and spoke out against the *Free Press*.

Nonetheless, by the time the regiment's 895 men were mustered into the Union army on 17 February 1864, serious problems had emerged within it and would simply intensify as it waited another six weeks before leaving for Annapolis, Maryland.[124] Not only were the men required to adjust to a dreary routine of drill and fatigue duty but they also endured atrocious living conditions in the barracks at Camp Ward.[125] One report claimed that "the barracks were unfit for human habitation and there was not a barn or pig-sty in the whole city of Detroit that is not better fitted for human habitation than Camp Ward."[126] Blankets and clothing were always in short supply, the roofs leaked, the barracks had no flooring, and sickness spread through the regiment during the particularly cold winter of 1863-64. In addition, the black soldiers who had come forward in 1863 to help preserve the Union and end slavery encountered white hostility and indifference in a city that had a reputation for intolerance. Without a clear victory over the Confederacy, Frederick Douglass warned, the North might "be but another Detroit, where every white fiend will with impunity revel in unrestrained beastliness towards people of color; they may burn their houses, insult their wives and daughters, and kill indiscriminately."[127]

White residents, by contrast, saw black soldiers as the root of the problem. When the soldiers clashed with white civilians in the bars and streets of Detroit, especially when they tried to enter "white only" establishments, the newspapers depicted the conflict as arising inevitably from undisciplined and uncontrollable black troops.[128] The *Detroit Free Press* warned that the "practice of allowing members of Colonel Barnes's Darkey regiment to parade the streets ... is fast approaching a stage where it should be declared a nuisance ... They enter saloons and eating houses, where it has always been the custom to refuse selling to niggers, and if not accommodated, commence preparations for a fight."[129] Whereas white civilians complained about the disorderly and abusive behaviour of the First Michigan, the men themselves were exasperated by the lack of respect accorded them. As soldiers defending their country in a time of crisis, they expected different treatment. The indignities were highlighted in March 1864, when the men of the Tenth Michigan Infantry, a white unit, refused to participate in a military parade because they would have to march behind the black regiment's band.[130]

Perhaps unsurprisingly, the regiment experienced a wave of desertions between December 1863 and March 1864. By the end of March, when it left for Maryland by train, 122 men had deserted, including 20 from Canada West.[131] One of these was Benjamin Blackburn, a twenty-six-year-old farmer who had been among the first to enlist in September 1863. Why he deserted in November of that year is unknown, but he was no "bounty-jumper," for he knew that a bounty would not be available to him and that he would be paid less than a white soldier. Perhaps he had expected neither the intense prejudice that greeted black Canadian soldiers in Michigan nor the miserable conditions of Camp Ward.[132]

Although the First Michigan left the state in March 1864, primarily for service in South Carolina and Florida, its ties to potential volunteers from Canada West were not severed. Unlike most states, Michigan continued to recruit new soldiers from within its borders and to forward them to its regiments in the field to replace men lost through casualties, disease, and desertion.[133] Once they left their state of origin and were on active duty in the

When Benjamin Blackburn joined the 1st Michigan Colored Infantry in September 1863, he gave "Canada" as his place of birth. Although other black Canadians deserted from Camp Ward because of the dreadful conditions, Blackburn appears to have had more complex reasons. *Courtesy of the National Archives and Records Administration.*

field, most black regiments received their replacements from a general pool of men who had volunteered at the various recruiting depots in the North. However, in July 1864, officers of the First Michigan opened a conversation with their lieutenant governor and governor about how, with the aid of officers seconded from the regiment, they might recruit men from Michigan. Lieutenant Edward Cahill explained the need: "Our aggregate, which has been as high as a thousand men *within six months,* is this morning 720." He also claimed that an additional two hundred men were sick and that only a third would ever return to the regiment.[134] The lobbying succeeded. In practice, this meant that when a third group of men, including Lorenzo Rann and Peter Scipio, left Buxton in August 1864, they knew they would join their friends and kin in the First Michigan, even though it was then stationed in the South.[135] As a result, the First had more British North Americans and African Americans who had lived in Canada West than any other black regiment. Their shared experiences and sense of connection may have ameliorated the difficult adjustment to army life and the deep anxiety of impending combat.

In other important ways, the wartime experiences of the First differed from those of the Massachusetts regiments and were much closer to those of the other black regiments. Shortly after the First reached South Carolina in April 1864, its name was changed to the 102nd USCT. With a few exceptions, the names of all black regiments were changed from a state designation, such as the First Michigan Colored Infantry, to a numbered USCT designation early in 1864.[136] This development arose from the formation of the Bureau of Colored Troops in May 1863. Once the government had authorized the establishment of black regiments, the War Department quickly found itself inundated with requests for information, guidance, appointments, details on the state of regiments being raised, and a host of other paper-generating subjects. The demand on staff time, the growing mass of paperwork, and the need to systematize the process prompted the War Department to create the Bureau of Colored Troops, with Major Charles W. Foster in charge, to handle all matters related to the organization of black units.[137] As black enlistment increased, Foster decided to rechristen all the black regiments in the Union army. They were given a number and designated "United States Colored Troops."[138] The only regiments to retain their state designations were the Fifty-fourth and Fifty-fifth Massachusetts Regiment, the Fifth Massachusetts Cavalry, and the Twenty-ninth Connecticut Regiment. Only Massachusetts and Connecticut maintained the important symbol that linked their black soldiers to state citizenship.

The role of the First Michigan was similar to that played by other black regiments and markedly different from that of the Massachusetts infantry units. Black soldiers fought in hundreds of bloody skirmishes during the war but rarely participated in major battles. In the summer of 1863, military leaders were reluctant to use them as front-line combatants, seeing them more as garrison troops or common labourers. In contrast to Governor Blair and many other state governors, John Andrew campaigned relentlessly to get the

Fifty-fourth and Fifty-fifth Massachusetts sent to an active theatre, where they would function as combat troops and thus prove that black soldiers were as effective as white soldiers. As a result, the Fifty-fourth and Fifty-fifth took part in the siege of Charleston, the symbolic starting point of the Civil War. The staunch behaviour of the Fifty-fourth during the 18 July 1863 assault on Fort Wagner justified the governor's belief in its martial ability, and abolitionists cited its courage as proof that black soldiers were valuable. By contrast, the First Michigan spent its first seven months in South Carolina, where it drilled, picketed, and built fortifications, though it did take a two-week break in August to join a raid into Florida.[139] For much of its time, many of its companies were off on detached service. The First was involved in just one major engagement, the Battle of Honey Hill; only three hundred of its men participated, though reports claimed that the regiment "fights well."[140] Senior officers gradually came to believe that black regiments were effective in combat. Late 1864 would see a greater use of them in the fierce fighting around Richmond and Petersburg.

However, before that day came, black soldiers could expect a disproportionate amount of heavy fatigue duty. Uncertain regarding their abilities and espousing racist attitudes, senior officers more frequently used them as labourers than as combat troops. The day after the Fifty-fifth Massachusetts arrived at Folly Island, South Carolina, in early August 1863, a black corporal recorded, "the regiment was introduced to Messrs. Shovel and Spade, a firm largely interested in building rifle pits, breastworks and batteries."[141] General Israel Vogdes drew so many fatigue parties from among the black regiments, including men to erect tents for white soldiers, that General Quincy Adams Gillmore overruled him and prohibited "the employment of colored troops to perform menial or unmilitary service for white troops." Long after the war, a junior officer explained Vogdes's behaviour to a former member of a black regiment: "I do not know of any reason for the ill treatment that Vogdes served out to your regiment except the general disgust of all the old West Pointers against the use of Colored Troops. That became plain to me in many ways when later on I was Brigaded with Regular Officers of the 25th Corps in Texas."[142]

The excessive fatigue duties demanded of many black regiments wore out clothing, undermined moral, compromised health, and cut into the men's training and drill.[143] An unsigned letter sent to the president by a trooper in the Twentieth USCT, a regiment with almost seventy British North Americans, outlined the soldiers' plight: "Men are Call to go on fatiuges wen sum of them are scarc Able to get Along the Day Before on the sick List." His letter ended, "Remember we are men standing in Readiness to face thous vile traitors an Rebeles who are trying to Bring your Peaceable homes to Destruction. And how can we stand them in A weak and starving Condition?"[144] Military necessity and progressive leadership reduced but never ended the disparity in the use of black troops. For example, though Adjutant General Lorenzo Thomas issued Order No. 21 to forbid the disproportionate employment of black troops in fatigue duty so that they would have more time for combat training, it was not always implemented at the local level. Nor were junior officers alone in ignoring such direction. In August 1864, while commanding the Army of the Potomac, General Major George Meade pulled a division of black soldiers "to use these troops in the construction of Warren's redoubts, as they work so much better than white troops, and save the latter for fighting."[145]

Black British North Americans were well aware of many of the problems that beset black soldiers, a fact that affected their decision making. The complaints of Sergeant Samuel Robinson that competent black sergeants could not hope for commissions were symptomatic of a growing conviction that the army would never treat black soldiers fairly, as was the desertion rate in the First Michigan during the winter of 1863-64. Black men from the British colonies came forward more slowly than their American counterparts. Only eight volunteered in April 1864, and just ten during the next month. A year after the secretary of war had authorized the creation of black regiments, and at a time when the Fifty-fourth Massachusetts had been bloodied at Fort Wagner and the First Michigan was ready to muster in, fewer than 15 percent of the British North Americans who would ultimately serve in black regiments had enlisted. Not until Congress and the War Department displayed greater willingness to treat black soldiers more equitably did men in the British colonies show a renewed willingness to volunteer.

CHAPTER FIVE

PROMISES FULFILLED

IN THE ARMY, 1864-65

IN THE EARLY SUMMER of 1864, black recruitment from British North America reached its nadir. The initial burst of enthusiasm, when enlistment became possible and black regiments were authorized, had passed. For some, a sense of disillusionment had set in. Certainly, by early 1864 there were abundant reasons why a potential black recruit from British North America might hesitate to enlist, even though the financial incentives increased as the rate of white volunteerism declined. These included the army's discriminatory treatment of black soldiers and threats from Confederate officials regarding the fate of black prisoners. For months, supporters had urged black soldiers to be patient, promising that conditions would improve. Men who were already in uniform and governed by military law had few options, but black civilians in British North America had more choices.

Stories sent home by early volunteers had revealed that black regiments were little more than gangs of labourers and had highlighted the soldiers' growing anger at the government's broken promises. As a result, some potential black volunteers in the British colonies held back. In the Northern black regiments as a whole, and in the Massachusetts units in particular, no issue had generated more resentment or seemed to better symbolize the black soldiers' subordinate status than differentiated wages. Throughout 1863, the contrast in treatment of white and black soldiers had been stark. The early promises of equal dealing had seemed to symbolize a more equitable treatment of all African Americans, and thus the sense of betrayal spread beyond the ranks of the military. When Lincoln authorized the governor of Iowa to organize a black regiment in July 1863, he specified not only that the pay rate would be lower but that "to these troops no bounty will be paid."[1] By contrast, white soldiers who received thirteen dollars a month plus clothing were promised "one month's pay in advance and in addition a bounty and premium amounting to $302."[2] Those who contended that black volunteers deserved bounties were largely ignored. In this climate, General Benjamin Butler had to use all his influence to get permission to offer a ten-dollar bonus to black recruits in the Department of Virginia and North Carolina.[3]

By early 1864, the sense of injustice felt by the enlisted men had become so palpable that white officers worried about the possibility of widespread mutiny. In February 1864, officers in the Fifty-fifth Massachusetts were informed of "a rumor that the 54th had refused to obey orders and had stacked their arms; that ours would be very likely to follow their example."[4] The rumour was false, but matters seemed to be reaching a critical stage by April. When one of the soldiers, Sampson Goliah, was told to be quiet after taps, he replied that he would not stop "for any damn officers" and claimed that "you Massachusetts men have bene humbugging us long enough." In the ensuing conflict, Goliah "snapped a pistol at an officer."[5] Although Goliah's insubordination could have been deemed a capital offence, the court chose to sentence him to hard labour for the remainder of his service, forfeiture of pay, and a dishonourable discharge. The forfeiture of pay was a bitter irony, for Goliah's anger was fuelled by the fact that he had not been paid for two years, that he was destitute, and that he believed "he was got in the service under false pretenses."[6] Nevertheless, he was more fortunate than some black soldiers who protested.

Some of the anger and disappointment with the government was moderated, or at least held in abeyance, by assurances that Congress would rectify the situation, even though the pace of change seemed frustratingly slow. Lincoln met with Frederick Douglass in August 1863 and told him that black troops would eventually receive the same wages as white soldiers. However, he added that at a time when the white population was deeply divided on the issue of black enlistment, unequal wages helped "smooth the way."[7] Even the *New York Weekly Anglo-African,* an influential black newspaper with a circulation in Canada West, urged the soldiers to show patience: "Shall our enemies and the enemies of our country, say that even you are fighting for money? God forbid. Let not the smell of this taint be found on your garments ... Your country will the sooner acknowledge your magnanimity and render that justice which is pre-eminently your due."[8]

Some influential officials offered their support. In December 1863, Secretary of War Edwin Stanton urged Congress to correct the "inequality and injustice" in wages.[9] In April 1864, US attorney general Edward Bates gave Lincoln his opinion that the black soldiers should receive the same rate of pay as similar white soldiers.[10] In that month some officers in the black regiments felt that a crisis point had arrived and that their units would not continue "in the service if Congress adjourns without making due provisions for the payment of the men; the families of some are in actual want."[11]

Finally, in June 1864, over Democratic and conservative Republican opposition, Congress passed an act to equalize pay for all Union soldiers, although ex-slaves would receive retroactive pay only to 1 January 1864, not to the date of their enlistment.[12] Only if the soldier had been free on 19 April 1861, which encompassed all British North American recruits, was the pay retroactive to his date of enlistment. However, another month would elapse before legislation was passed to guarantee black recruits the same federal bounties as white troops.[13] When the president issued his call of 18 July 1864 for 500,000 volunteers, the new bounties were announced: "For recruits, including representative recruits (white or colored) – for one year, $100; for two years, $200; for three years, $300."[14]

However, the wrath of some enlisted men did not immediately subside, and news of the new policies took time to reach British North America. Indeed, in July 1864, after Congress had adopted its equal pay bill, First Sergeant Samuel J. Robinson, a Toronto native, and the rest of Company D, Fifty-fifth Massachusetts, petitioned Lincoln for redress. They believed that they had enlisted under the laws that governed all volunteer regiments. Refusing to accept the lower remuneration, they had served without pay for more than a year. Even when the Commonwealth of Massachusetts offered to make up the difference in wages, they declined it. For them, the issue was one of principle because "to us money is no object we came to fight for Liberty justice & equality. Those are gifts we prize more Highly than gold. For these We left our Homes, our Families, Friends & Relatives most Dear to take as it ware our Lives in our Hands To Do Battle for God & Liberty." They wanted both their back pay from their date of enlistment and an immediate discharge, "having Been enlisted under False Pretence." They warned that "if imediate steps are not taken to Relieve us we will Resort to more stringent mesures." They then signed their petition "your Obedint Servants."[15] The administration took no action; the pay issue had been resolved and Lincoln had no intention of releasing troops.

In part, the anger and suspicion lingered in July for the simple reason that black regiments had not been informed of the new pay regulation. Finally, after many unfounded rumours, the War Department notified them in August, at which point the soldiers could sign for their retroactive pay.[16] However, before they could receive it, they were required to swear an oath that they had been "free on or before April 19, 1861." Although this proviso disqualified only a few men from receiving full pay, many saw it as unjust, and it merely reinforced their sense of betrayal. As the lieutenant colonel of the Fifty-fifth Massachusetts explained, "So many times had the men been deceived, intentionally by their enemies, unintentionally by their friends, that they feared some deception, some few going so far even as to consider the whole thing as a trap to ascertain who had been held as slaves, in order to return them to their masters at the end of the war."[17]

Other forms of discrimination incensed soldiers. By the end of 1863, the army had made clear that even talented and qualified black sergeants would not be raised to the rank of officer.[18] Sergeant Robinson, who had been promoted to regimental sergeant major in June 1863, explained the situation early the next year in a letter to the *Boston Liberator*. Although he praised the behaviour of the state of Massachusetts, he was affronted by the War Department's assumption that black enlisted men were "incapable of acting for ourselves." This assumption was made obvious in army policy, which was to select sergeants from white regiments and promote them to the rank of lieutenant or captain in the black regiments rather than to consider black sergeants for commissions. Robinson, the highest ranked sergeant in his unit, found the policy deeply offensive:

> We, as a race, have been trodden down long enough. Are we, who have come into the field of bloody conflict, and left our quiet homes the same as white men, for the sake of our country, and to beat down the rebellion – are we to be put down lower than these, many of whom have not enlisted with as good motives as we have? If we have men in our regiment who are capable of being officers, why not let them be promoted the same as other soldiers?[19]

The War Department moved even more slowly on this issue than it did on the pay dispute, and the Canadian sergeant may have been penalized for his dissent. Soon afterward, he was "reduced to ranks for drunkenness at Folly Island ... Mar. 1/64."[20]

The son of Abraham D. Shadd, Abraham W. Shadd was an exemplary soldier, ending the war as the sergeant major of the 55th Massachusetts. Governor Andrew commissioned him as a second lieutenant, but, as was the case for a number of black sergeants, the regiment was mustered out before he could officially receive his commission. After the war, he became a prominent lawyer in Mississippi. *Courtesy of the Buxton National Historic Site and Museum.*

Governor Andrew subsequently used his authority to offer commissions to several black sergeants in the Massachusetts regiments, but Robinson was passed over. Despite the governor's action, the sergeants could not take up their commissions until they had been formally mustered out as enlisted men, and the War Department simply ordered the local commander not to discharge them. Another year would pass before the War Department changed its policy and the first men received their commissions.[21] During this time, more heated letters appeared in the *Boston Liberator* and the *New York Weekly Anglo-African*. In August 1864, one anonymous soldier in the Fifty-fifth Massachusetts cited the recent casualties suffered by the regiment during a battle on James Island and added bitterly, "Yet our noble government will still deny us just treatment." Although the regiment's colonel had recommended three enlisted men and the governor had commissioned them, still "the U.S. government has refused so far to muster them because *God did not make them white*. No other objection is, or can be offered. *Three cheers for 'our country.'*"[22]

Those who were already in the army had few options other than to accept the lower wages, greater fatigue duty, inferior medical care, inadequate weapons, worn-out equipment, and frequent antagonism from white soldiers wearing blue. They could write to allies, plead for justice, and hope for improvements, or even desert, but they lived under military regulations, where obedience was enforced and violations were punished. Black civilians in British North America, however, could shun military service and take advantage of the wartime economy's new financial prospects. At the end of 1863 and into the first months of 1864, black volunteerism slowed as potential recruits chose to wait until they received more credible assurance of equitable treatment and respect.

Other men may have been deterred, in early 1864, by widespread reports of a series of Confederate atrocities. The alleged mass killing of black soldiers at Fort Pillow in April 1864 was the most notorious of these, but other incidents occurred at Plymouth, North Carolina; Poison Spring, Arkansas; Olustee, Florida; and elsewhere.[23] Accounts were soon circulating in the British colonies, especially of the events at Fort Pillow. On 16 April 1864, just four days after the battle, the *Toronto Daily Globe* revealed that black soldiers had been killed while trying to surrender. The paper's extended coverage of the atrocity culminated in a front-page article titled "The Massacre at Fort Pillow."[24] It announced that the "Federal Government threatens to retaliate for the massacre of the negro garrison at Fort Pillow." Although the *Globe* editor hoped that the Union government would not respond in kind, he did agree that such threats evinced "a determination – from which the Federal Government has never swerved – to enforce on behalf of the negro soldiers the observance of the rights of war."[25] The *Perth Courier* also carried "graphic accounts" of the atrocity and reported that black soldiers who had dropped their guns and pleaded for mercy "were all shot down in cold blood."[26] In the Maritimes, the *Saint John Morning Freeman* stated that, "alluding to the Fort

Pillow massacre," the president "declared [the] Government's determination to protect colored troops and visit retribution on a barbarous enemy. Great applause greeted this."[27]

Whereas Fort Pillow was the most widely reported atrocity, provincial papers also ran detailed stories on the 20 April fall of Plymouth and the killings that ensued when the Union soldiers surrendered. Under the heading "Fort Pillow Massacre Re-enacted," the *Toronto Daily Globe* explained that only a few black recruits were at Plymouth when it fell and that "the few unfortunate blacks thus butchered were merely laborers for the government."[28] The *Saint John Morning Freeman* also picked up accounts of the atrocity. It reported that white Union soldiers from North Carolina "were mostly shot after surrendering; also all colored men in uniform."[29]

Of course, black Canadians did not receive all their news from local papers. Many subscribed to American publications. An April 1864 letter in the *New York Weekly Anglo-African*, directed to the "lady from Canada West" who wanted more information about the situation of the Fifty-fifth Massachusetts, described the feelings of the regiment when faced with Confederate threats:

> As far as this regiment is concerned we will ask no quarter, and rest satisfied that we will give none. Where is the wounded that fell into the enemy's hands at the battle of Olustee? Echo answers, "Where?" We will never forget the cry of "Kill the G——d d——n s——s of b——s," when the 54th Massachusetts Volunteers went into the fight.[30]

Although major atrocities were few in number and Lincoln's threat of retaliation had its desired effect, black regiments remained vulnerable to violence outside the laws of war. The soldiers in the Eleventh USCHA, a unit raised in Rhode Island that had more than a dozen men from Canada West, learned what might happen to anyone who was captured. On 6 August, while the regiment was posted along the Mississippi above New Orleans, Texas cavalry attacked the outskirts of its camp and scattered its pickets. Although the Confederates were quickly driven off, they managed to seize three black soldiers. Captain Joshua M. Addeman later recalled, "We understood, the next day, that our men were shot in cold blood ... Subsequently we learned that the raiders were Texans who boastfully declared that they asked no quarter and gave none."[31]

Despite the various concerns that deterred some black men from volunteering, black Americans and Canadians were enlisting in greater numbers by the second half of 1864. The army's voracious demand for men and the heavy losses due to combat death, disease, and disabilities, coupled with the declining rates of white volunteering in the summer of 1863, forced the federal and local governments to change their policies regarding black recruits. The Enrollment Act of 3 March 1863 had effectively transferred recruitment and national conscription to federal control while saddling local leaders with the burden of stimulating enlistment.[32] In some states, officials initially disagreed that the Enrollment Act encompassed African Americans, and very few black residents were enrolled and drafted during its first year.[33] Clarification came only after an amendment of the Enrollment Act ordered by Lincoln confirmed that "all able-bodied male colored persons" between the ages of twenty and forty-five should also be enrolled.[34] As the legislation indicated, whenever the president issued a new call for a specific number of men, enlistment quotas were assigned to each congressional district on a pro rata basis and broken down into subdistricts. Districts usually had fifty days to meet their quota. If a subdistrict failed to provide its quota by that time, a draft lottery, drawn from the enrolled names, would be held to make up the difference. Depending on the patriotism of residents or the activities of recruiting committees, some districts might have to hold a draft lottery, whereas others did not.

The ability of districts to find new volunteers was sorely tested throughout 1864. Exercising his powers under the Enrollment Act, the president had called for 300,000 men on 17 October 1863. All districts met their quotas by the 5 January 1864 deadline, and enlistments were sufficiently high that Lincoln was able to postpone the scheduled draft. However, on 14 March 1864, he called for another 200,000 soldiers to serve for three years. Before the year ended, he made two more major calls for additional troops, one for 500,000 men on 18 July and another for 300,000 more on 19 December.[35] In these later calls, perhaps to encourage the hesitant, volunteers were allowed to choose between one-, two-, or three-year terms.[36] Many of the black British North Americans would opt for just one year.

The growing difficulty of satisfying the demands for more soldiers was reflected in the numbers of districts that were forced to employ the draft lottery. Just over 50 percent of the 180 congressional districts did so during the first two drafts. By contrast, more than 77 percent (139) held lotteries to meet the July 1864 call for troops. The 19 December 1864 call for 300,000 men was suspended on 13 April 1865 and was never fully completed, but the ability to find recruits had further diminished by that time.[37] Increasingly, men whose names were pulled in the lottery simply failed to report to their draft board.

Figure 1
Black enlistment and Lincoln's call for troops

The enlistment of black British North Americans during 1863 and early 1864 was more closely linked to the recruiting efforts of specific regiments than to Lincoln's early calls for more men. Only after the highly symbolic pay issue was resolved did enlistment closely correlate with the presidential troop calls.

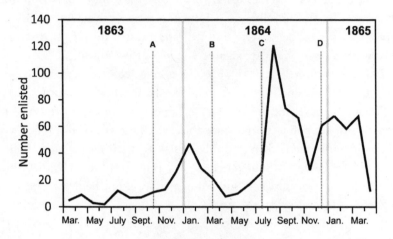

President's draft calls:
A 17 Oct. 1863 (300,000)
B 14 March 1864 (200,000)
C 18 July 1864 (500,000)
D 19 Dec. 1864 (300,000)

More than 161,000 never appeared and were ultimately classified by the War Department as deserters. Districts in New York and Pennsylvania, which had some of the highest rates of non-reporting draftees, were particularly interested in encouraging recruits from the British provinces. Compounding the problem was an expanding war economy and a severe shortage of labour in the North.[38] This confluence of factors meant that, in the summer of 1864, a young man of military age who was not liable to the draft was an extremely marketable commodity. The new financial inducements to enlist, coupled with a growing belief that the government was finally treating black soldiers more equitably, encouraged greater black enlistment.

Figures 1 and 2 show the enlistment of black British North Americans from March 1863, when the first volunteers joined the Fifty-fourth Massachusetts, to April 1865, when the army stopped enlisting men. The timing of

FIGURE 2
Black enlistment and the resolution of the unequal pay issue

The graph clearly illustrates that the vast majority of black enlistment from British North America occurred only after the black soldiers received more equitable treatment, symbolized by the resolution of the pay dispute.

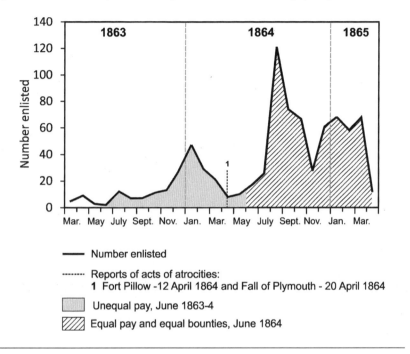

— Number enlisted
------ Reports of acts of atrocities:
1 Fort Pillow -12 April 1864 and Fall of Plymouth - 20 April 1864
▨ Unequal pay, June 1863-4
▨ Equal pay and equal bounties, June 1864

their entry into the war provides a lens through which we can examine their reasons for participation. Canadian historians have suggested that ideology was their prime motivator, but tracking their timing of enlistment indicates that several factors prompted their decision to fight for the Union army.

During the spring and summer of 1863, while recruiters were encouraging young black men to enlist in specific regiments, responses north of the border were slowly improving. The announced organization of the Fifth Massachusetts Cavalry and the First Michigan Colored Volunteers, coupled with Lincoln's call for more men in October 1863, spurred enlistment for several months. However, because many Northern officials believed that the Enrollment Act did not apply to African Americans, it had a limited impact on black recruitment during 1863. In the spring and early summer of 1864, the enlistment of black British North Americans declined despite the president's

March appeal for 200,000 more men. A number of factors suppressed their volunteerism at this time. They knew that black soldiers were paid inequitably and that bounties were not available to them. They knew of the anger in Northern black regiments concerning their treatment by the army. And thanks to the diligence of the press, they knew of the Confederate atrocities that targeted black soldiers in April 1864. This period of uncertainty and resentment marked the nadir of black British North American enlistment. By the time that Lincoln issued his July 1864 call for additional men, Congress had authorized equal pay for black soldiers, with retroactive pay to the level of white soldiers of the same rank. Clearly, black soldiers would now enjoy something approaching financial equality with their white equivalents. With this, as Figure 2 reveals, a major obstacle to their enlistment was removed. At the same time, growing war weariness in the Northern states ensured that the financial benefits offered to willing volunteers would reach new heights. The result was that a wave of black British North Americans enlisted during the second half of 1864, a turnout that remained high for the rest of the war.

During 1863, black British North Americans may have enlisted to fight against a slave regime, to prove their manhood, or to satisfy a youthful and romantic sense of adventure, but few did it for monetary reward. Yet, enlistment placed a heavy financial burden on their families. By the late summer of 1864, few could view the war as a thrilling adventure, and the economic and personal costs to families who had lost fathers and sons were all too clear. Black colonists may have had the same ideological motivation, but now they could maximize their monetary benefits by making complex decisions about a host of options. The size of bounties and substitute payments differed from region to region, and they had to choose when and where to enlist as well as which branch of the army to join.

In making these decisions, they considered the localized nature of the market for volunteers. Although districts had almost two months to meet their quotas, much of their activity took place during the last few hectic weeks as they tried to enlist the necessary men. By the summer of 1864, many young Northerners had been killed or maimed, and finding white volunteers was increasingly difficult. Both urban and rural communities hoped that by offering local bounties to augment the federal ones, they could attract willing volunteers, especially from outside their district. After the draft calls in 1864, some men did immediately come forward, but they were seldom enough. Potential recruits had learned to wait until local recruiting committees, fearing a possible draft, had organized patriotic meetings, canvassed enumerated men for funds, and levied real estate taxes, all with the goal of raising the maximum possible bounty.³⁹ How much money a community could raise, or needed to raise, and therefore the amount of bounties that could be used to entice volunteers, varied considerably across districts and over time. In the Tenth District in Massachusetts, the average bounty paid during the call of 14 March 1864 was $492.91, whereas it was only $8.00 in the Fifth District.⁴⁰ In some districts, appeals to patriotism and financial self-interest generated sufficient volunteers to meet the local quota, which meant that the draft lottery would not be held.

Because the local bounties varied widely, from community to community and from draft to draft, it is difficult to know how much most recruits received. At the high end, a knowledgeable volunteer in late 1864 who chose wisely might earn $1,000 or more by combining local, state, and national bounties.⁴¹ Of course, researchers must be cautious not to collapse the multifaceted decision making into a single motive resembling financial determinism. One microhistory of Civil War recruiting and recruits in Midland County, Michigan, found that the men from British North America had a higher enlistment rate than native-born men (38 percent compared to 21 percent), but their dominant impetus did not appear to be financial. It is possible, the study explains, "that some of the late-arriving Canadians signed up for service while still living in Canada. However, as other communities' bonuses were larger than those offered in Midland, it seems probable that many of these late enlistees from Canada had moved to Midland before they enlisted."⁴² Moreover, since as aliens they could enlist wherever they pleased, their choice of Midland County rather than a community with higher bonuses suggests that their decisions were grounded in more than financial factors alone.⁴³

Late in the war, some enlistment forms recorded the amount of local bounties, enabling us to form an idea of what black British North Americans could receive if they enlisted strategically. Three men, all of whom joined the Twenty-fourth USCT for a one-year term, illustrate how much bounties could vary, depending on where and when one volunteered. James Robinson, a twenty-seven-year-old seaman from Saint John, enlisted at Philadelphia on 10 March 1865. He was credited to the Sixth Ward in Pennsylvania's First Congressional District, and he received $400 as his local bounty. By contrast, William E. Stratton, a nineteen-year-old waiter from Canada, enlisted at Lancaster on 4 April 1865, was credited to the forty-third subdistrict, the town of Paradise, in the Ninth Congressional District, and he received $500. Paul Western, a twenty-four-year-old seaman from Canada, waited three days longer than Stratton before he too joined at Lancaster. He was credited to the forty-ninth subdistrict in the Ninth Congressional District and was paid $550 as his local bounty.[44] In addition, all three men were also eligible for the $100 federal bounty that accompanied a one-year term.

For three men who enlisted in New York, the difference was even greater. All were from Canada West and all signed up for three years. Francis Warren, a forty-year-old labourer, did so on 27 March 1865 at Lockport and was credited to the town of Castile, the twenty-eighth subdistrict in New York's Twenty-ninth Congressional District. His local bounty was $550. Alexander Carter, a thirty-five-year-old farmer who had enlisted at Lockport five days earlier, was either luckier than Warren or more astute. He was credited to the town of Bethany, the seventeenth subdistrict in the Twenty-ninth Congressional District. Because Carter opted for Bethany, his local bounty was $875.[45] In addition, Warren and Carter's choice of a three-year term meant that both stood to receive another $300 in bounty installments from the army. The two men joined the Sixth USCT. Another Canadian, Major Rose, a twenty-seven-year-old waiter, chose a different time and place to volunteer, with less financial reward. Rose joined the First US Colored Cavalry at Poughkeepsie, New York, and was credited to the town of LaGrange, part of New York's Twelfth Congressional District. Perhaps because he signed up on 6 January 1865, when the threat of a draft was still well off, or because LaGrange could not or would not pay a large bounty, Rose received only $300 along with the first $100 installment of his federal bounty.[46] Except for Stratton, all these men signed their names with a fluid penmanship.[47] Because they were apparently literate and because the amount of the local bounties was recorded on the enlistment forms that they signed, they knew how much money they would receive. Although some of it may have gone to recruiting brokers, these men would have been fully aware of the size of the deduction.

Of course, even recruits who were paid their full bounty when they enlisted might not manage to keep it all. Some of the first men from Canada West who joined the black Michigan regiment "lost their bounty-money through 'sharpers' lying in wait for them."[48] As a result, when the son and brother-in-law of Alexander Pool, a friend of Josiah Henson, decided to enlist in Detroit, the elder Pool urged Henson to go with them to safeguard their money. Henson finally agreed to accompany them, although he thought incorrectly that they intended to desert after enlisting. The two men signed up and were paid at least six hundred dollars each. Leaving them with a hundred dollars, Henson took the rest, returned home, and delivered the money to Alexander Pool, who gave him four hundred dollars "for my expenses and trouble." Unfortunately for the soldiers, Henson claimed, the remaining seven hundred dollars were "squandered in dissipation" by Alexander Pool. The two veterans eventually returned home to find their bounty money gone.[49]

The terms and conditions of the Enrollment Act provided a second route to financial reward for British North American recruits. After a district had failed to meet its quota, held a public lottery, and selected the necessary number of men, their names were publicized and they were contacted. They were given ten days to take care of personal business before they had to appear at their enlistment station. Some may not have known that they had been drafted, but anyone who failed to report was ultimately declared a deserter.[50] Many more reported and were deemed exempt from service due to physical disabilities, age, "alienage," or other factors.[51] Indeed, James Geary found that out of 776,829 men whose names were drawn, only 206,678 were "held to service." That is, they presented themselves to enlistment officers and were not ruled exempt from military service. However, only a quarter of them, 46,347 to be exact, actually entered the army, for they had two options if they wished to escape service.[52]

Both of these were firmly rooted in American military custom and precedent. In the 1863 lottery draft, men whose names were pulled from the drum had ten days to pay a commutation fee of three hundred dollars or to hire a substitute.[53] In the draft of early 1864, the commutation fee applied solely to that specific draft. Before the final calls for men in July and December 1864, the fee was abolished, in part because it had generated so much condemnation. As the *New York Herald* claimed in July 1863, the draft was unfair "inasmuch as the rich could avoid it by paying $300, while the poor man, who was without the 'greenbacks' was compelled to go to war."[54]

In the first drafts, a potential conscript could be excused from service for three years by providing a substitute who would take his place. Describing substitution as "an old and well known practice," Lincoln believed "that there would have been great objection if that provision had been omitted." He also believed that charging three hundred dollars for commutation would prevent the price of substitutes from becoming prohibitive for all but the rich. Lincoln thought that the "money provision enlarges the class of exempts from actual service simply by admitting poorer men into it."[55] He may have been correct. In November 1862, the *Quebec Mercury* reported that, in the Pennsylvania counties holding a draft, "the trade in substitutes is very brisk. Prices range from $75 to $200. The supply is plentiful at $150 to $200." It added that "substitutes are now plentiful in Baltimore at three hundred dollars each."[56] Lincoln was not alone in believing that repealing the commutation fee would allow substitutes to demand exorbitant amounts, pricing their service beyond all but the few. In the summer of 1864, an Irish resident of Cincinnati predicted that the end of the commutation fee would drive the cost of substitutes to $2,000.[57] He was wrong, but its termination and the stricter rules regarding who qualified as a substitute did force prices upward. Until February 1864, anyone who was eligible for the draft but whose name had not yet been drawn could be a substitute. After that date, such men became ineligible and acceptable substitutes came primarily from a smaller pool – those who were under twenty years of age, discharged veterans, or aliens. In August 1864, the *St. Catharines Constitutional* carried a report from Detroit that noted that the "purchasing of substitutes goes forward more slowly now. Those who have bought them are wealthy and good business men." With few men available or willing to be substitutes, prices were rising. The highest amount, the paper claimed, was "paid for two substitutes on Tuesday, at $1,500 each. The lowest yesterday was $850."[58]

Even as the pool of candidates shrank, the demand for substitutes, or "representative recruits," increased with each new call for troops. A significant number of men, including President Lincoln himself, paid someone to be their representative recruit.[59] Indeed, some men who were eligible for the draft purchased a substitute even before the draft was held.[60] Most historians no longer hold the simplistic view that the drafted men were cowards who shirked their patriotic duty by hiring untrustworthy mercenaries or sickly seniors. Yet all too frequently the purchasing of a substitute has been seen as avoidance of civil responsibility, the polar opposite of enlisting, and the substitute himself has most commonly been portrayed as a second-class soldier.[61] The purchase of a substitute and the perception of this act are best understood in a local context, where those who hired substitutes might be approved by neighbours who valued their contribution to the community. This might explain why in Albany, city officials "bought substitutes for all who could not afford them" or why the New York City Council appropriated $3 million "to exempt poor men from the draft by furnishing substitutes."[62] This financial and emotional aid reflected the communities' desire that certain men not be forced to enlist. The motivation of substitutes would have been as complex or diverse as that of those who paid them, especially given their large numbers. From 1863 to the end of the war, 118,010 substitutes enlisted.[63] Because self-interest inspired local recruiting committees to draw men from outside their community, and because enrolled but undrafted men were no longer eligible substitutes for most of 1864, British North Americans, white or black, became a highly desirable commodity. By the end of the war, 282 black British North Americans had signed on as substitutes.

Initially, however, only a few were able to do so. During the summer of 1863, the War Department ruled that because there was a difference "in the matter of pay, bounty, and other allowances between soldiers of African descent and other soldiers," African Americans could serve as substitutes only for other African Americans, few of whom needed or were looking for substitutes.[64] In Congress, members who were sympathetic to black recruitment, such as Senator Charles Sumner, argued that it seemed "obvious that colored substitutes should be encouraged" and also that "a substitute is a substitute whether black or white." Nevertheless, perhaps because Sumner suggested that "all persons drafted must have the same pay," at a time when Congress was wrestling with that contentious issue, the question of African Americans as substitutes was largely ignored.[65] Only after the resolution of the pay issue could newspapers along the border announce that white men could hire black substitutes as long as they were not eligible for the draft.[66]

Even before that time, some black recruits from the British provinces did succeed in becoming substitutes, but the records do not reveal whether this was due to their status as foreigners or because draft officials ignored or misunderstood the regulations. Aliens, including black British North Americans in some specific cases, were subject to different regulations or to a different interpretation of the regulations. Under existing orders, "aliens not subject to draft who voluntarily offer themselves for substitutes will be accepted as substitutes if physically qualified."[67] During 1863, despite the War Department's ruling on black substitutes, at least seven black British North Americans were hired as substitutes, and there were more in the first months of 1864.

The case of one such substitute, Samuel Sylvia, is illustrative. A twenty-two-year-old sailor, Sylvia agreed in August 1863 to act as a substitute. His place of birth was recorded as Garsberry, Nova Scotia, but it was probably Guysborough, a community that had a sizable black population in 1860. Sylvia enlisted on 19 August 1863 in Concord, New Hampshire, as a substitute for Horace S. Moody.[68] Moody was a twenty-three-year-old white resident of Chichester, a town just outside Concord, who had given his occupation as "farm laborer" in the 1860 census.[69] Hiring Sylvia, or at least hiring a foreigner, was not unusual in New Hampshire. Many of its towns contributed three hundred dollars toward the purchase of a substitute, preferably an alien, for any citizen who had been drafted. Indeed, on a proportional basis, the Granite State had more substitutes than any other.[70]

Sylvia's enrolment apparently created a quandary for the local recruiting officials. Although his complexion was recorded as "black," he was initially put in with recruits being forwarded to the Third New Hampshire Regiment, an all-white unit. New Hampshire had no black regiment, which compounded the subsequent dilemma of what to do with Sylvia. Ultimately, the War Department solved the problem by sending him outside the state, where he was "turned over to detachment for 54 Mass. (Colored) Reg't, by order of Gen. Devens in accordance with instructions from the War Department, Sept. 22, 1863."[71] He finally joined the Massachusetts regiment in South Carolina at the end of November. He served with his unit until he was severely wounded in his right ankle at the fight at Boykins Mill, South Carolina, on 18 April 1865, nine days after General Robert E. Lee surrendered the Army of Northern Virginia to General Grant at Appomattox. Sylvia convalesced in a New York hospital throughout the summer and fall, and was mustered out when the men of the Fifty-fourth Massachusetts were mustered out in August, but he was not discharged from the hospital until 29 November 1865.[72] At that point Samuel Sylvia disappeared from the existing records.

The problem that men such as Sylvia had created for local officials was solved in the summer of 1864. War Department regulations were modified "to permit alien substitutes to select their regiment, their selection being limited, however, to such regiments as the acting assistant provost-marshal-general of the State may designate as suitable for recruitment in this matter."[73] This gave future substitutes greater leeway in selecting both where they enlisted and which unit they joined.

Two other men who claimed birth in British North America, enlisted in 1863 and assigned to Company H, Eighth USCT, underscore the danger of stereotyping substitutes as dubious soldiers. William H. Miner (or Minor) and William S. Boyd joined the regiment as substitutes, but their service records could not have been more different. A "boatman" from Saint John, Miner was twenty-nine on 20 August 1863, when he enlisted at Schenectady, New York, as a substitute. Within two months, he had been promoted to corporal and was made sergeant in April. During the summer and fall of 1864, he saw action in Virginia at Deep Bottom, Chaffin's Farm, and Darbytown Road, although he escaped serious injury. Then, at the conclusion of the Civil War, the Eighth USCT was sent to the Mexican border as part of the all-black Twenty-fifth Corps.[74] Illness, especially scurvy, swept through the black units there, and Miner spent part of the summer in the general hospital.[75] He would remain a sergeant until he was mustered out with the regiment in November 1865.[76] Years later he would apply for and receive a pension. By contrast, Boyd served much less time in the regiment, although he enlisted in New York City just two months after Miner. He gave his age as twenty-six, his birthplace as "Canada, B.A.," and his occupation as carpenter. Unlike Miner, he deserted after only two weeks with the regiment. Appearing on a subsequent descriptive list of the regiment's deserters was the curt notation, "Probably be found in Canada."[77]

Much of the historiography on the use of large bounties and substitutes has emphasized the financial waste and inefficiency involved, the fraud practised by bounty agents and recruiting officials, the poor quality of the enlisted men, and the widespread avoidance of service associated with the process. In such accounts, men like Boyd receive more coverage than those who behaved like Miner. Eugene Murdock, who has written extensively on the bounty system, claims that, "designed to spur enlistment and thus make the draft unnecessary, bounties were soon a national disgrace."[78] The system, it is argued, spawned a bidding war for marginally acceptable recruits who, like the avaricious substitutes, deserted at the first opportunity. Not only were substantial sums allocated to the state and local bounty system, but the full amount was also paid at the time of enlistment to attract the largest number of recruits. Historians who have seen the emergence of "bounty-jumping" as the inevitable result believe that using the same money to increase soldiers' wages would have been more efficient and more equitable. Historians no longer believe that the Enrollment Act of 1863 fell with disproportionate severity on immigrants and the working class, but during the war many Americans felt that it did.[79] Others have emphasized the extent to which dishonest brokers defrauded gullible recruits of most of the money due to them. Canadian historians have highlighted many of the same issues. Robin Winks, who estimates that only a few thousand men from British North America volunteered because of their principles, argues that many more served only because they were illegally crimped or because they were lured by the high bounties.[80]

Many contemporaries were equally harsh in their criticism. General Grant believed that many conscripts and late volunteers were nearly worthless as soldiers, but he was even more incensed by bounty-jumpers who enlisted for the money and deserted at the first chance. "Of this class of recruits," he complained, "we do not get one for every eight bounties paid to do good service."[81] Stanton believed that the increased prices for substitutes, up to nine hundred dollars and more by August 1864, meant that corruption and bribery had become rife among the surgeons who conducted the physicals.[82]

The provost marshal in Frederick, Maryland, believed that men of good character simply did not become substitutes, who were "a very unreliable and worthless class."[83] Many in Canada West held an equally pessimistic view of the men who enlisted for money. The *Toronto Daily Globe* cited a report claiming that fewer convicts had been sent to the penitentiary in 1864 than in 1863, a change that it attributed directly to the Civil War. The explanation was "that great numbers of the low and wandering population have left the Province for the United States, being attracted there by the reports of high wages for the laborers and excessive bounties given for substitutes to serve in the army of the Northern States."[84] Certainly, American newspapers understood that salting their pages with sensational items designed to titillate or outrage would help sales while convincing readers that the late recruits were unreliable. Otherwise staid publications such as *Moore's Rural New Yorker* relayed the confession of a bounty-jumper who had been arrested in Baltimore and "who boasted that he had made over $15,000 since he commenced jumping" or of a "negro boy [who] was put up at auction by his mother in Hudson, N.Y., recently, for a substitute, and was bought by a lawyer for $1,000."[85]

The case of two young brothers from St. Catharines, Henry and Richard Williams, captures some of the complexities involved in establishing the motives of many of the black substitutes. In early January 1864, the brothers left St. Catharines and joined the Union army. They served together in Company H, Twenty-sixth USCT, for the remainder of the war. They chose, however, to enlist at slightly different times and in different enrollment districts, perhaps because of the difference in bounties being offered. Henry gave his age as nineteen when he enlisted on 2 January 1864 in the Thirtieth District, and Richard, claiming to be eighteen, enlisted three days later at Pomfret, a small town just west of Buffalo in the Thirty-first District. The differences in their enlistments suggest that they were not merely the gullible pawns of a recruiting agent but rather acted to maximize their own benefits.[86] The two young men may have subsequently had a change of heart or enlisted without their parents' consent. In early 1864, a lawyer from St. Catharines, representing "friends of these youths," claimed that the brothers had been "seduced by improper means" and fraudulently and improperly enrolled in the US army. He asked for their release.

An investigation by the British consul in Buffalo revealed that the youngest brother was under the age of fifteen and that both recruits had lied about their age. Given their appearance and height (both were just over five feet), the enlisting officer should have realized that they were underage. The British official personally travelled to St. Catharines to investigate the case. He returned to Buffalo, however, convinced that the two boys had left voluntarily "for the purpose of enlisting in the United States Military Service, and that to enable them to do so they swore before the mustering officers falsely, as regards their age."[87]

The Williams brothers remained in the army. Whatever led them to enlist, they served well. Despite their age and size, both men became corporals during the war, but Henry lost his stripes and was demoted. Both also spent considerable time in regimental hospitals during their service. Both, however, were listed in the ranks when the regiment was mustered out at Hilton Head, South Carolina, on 28 August 1865.[88]

As this case suggests, black substitutes from British North America should not be facilely stereotyped. Unlike African American men of military age, they were not obligated to serve in the army. If they fought for the Union (or as they might put it, against the Confederacy), they did so by choice. They could join at a recruiting station and collect the associated bounties, or they could become substitutes and receive a mutually agreed payment, perhaps with local bounties. The timing of the influx of black British North Americans into the army, as demonstrated in Figure 1, indicates that though money may have been important, it was not the critical factor. After Lincoln called for more men in March 1864, sizeable sums for bounties and substitutes were available to entice men, but relatively few black volunteers came forward in April, May, and June. Only after the pay issue was resolved in the late summer and faith was renewed that the army would accord its black troops more equitable status did black British North Americans volunteer in record numbers. Proof of impartial treatment was more important than large bounties.

Of course, the fact that principle outweighed money for most recruits did not mean that all were motivated solely by ideology or that money was not a significant factor. Some men enlisted because of financial necessity or other imperatives. Some did so to avoid jail. During the spring of 1865, William Wheeler faced charges of sexual assault in Chatham. When his friends managed to get him released on bail, he promptly escaped across the border, where he reportedly signed on as a substitute.[89] Although Wheeler fled to evade prosecution, once in the United States he could opt to enlist as a volunteer or sign on as a substitute. Whatever their reasons for joining the army, recruits had to consider the financial implications for themselves or their families. Whether they signed up as volunteers or substitutes, their working-class background influenced their decisions.

Table 4
Occupation of British North American black soldiers

	Mariner	Labourer	Farmer	Tradesman	Service	Other	Total
Canada West	61	269	173	56	112	16	687
Canada East	6	6	2	2	–	–	16
Nova Scotia	26	5	2	4	9	–	46
New Brunswick	12	15	7	3	9	–	46
PEI	1	–	–	–	–	1	2
Total	106	295	184	65	130	17	797

NOTE: The "Other" category consists of small proprietors, students, and professed professionals.

Table 4 captures the occupational self-identification of the black British colonists who served in the Union army, including both volunteers and substitutes. In addition to the men listed in the table, another thirty-eight, all of whom gave "Canada" or Canada West as their birthplace, had no recorded occupation and are thus excluded from the table. Most may have been unemployed when they joined up, though some may not have given their occupation or may not have been asked for it by the recording officer. The information regarding occupation is valuable because it reveals the background of recruits, but it is not always precise. A man who had been a farm labourer might declare himself as either labourer or a farmer, and a self-declared mariner might have been a sailor for a relatively brief part of his career. Moreover, holding multiple occupations was common in the nineteenth century, and most of the men could expect to work in a variety of activities during their lives.

Not surprisingly, the occupational status of these men was lower than for white Union soldiers. About half of all the men in the Union army described themselves as farmers, and another quarter claimed employment as mechanics. Only about 10 percent said they were labourers.[90] By contrast, only about 23 percent of the black soldiers from British North America worked as farmers, and 37 percent were labourers. Sailors made up a little over 13 percent, and tradesmen, including masons, millers, coopers, blacksmiths, carpenters, and printers, amounted to only about 8 percent. Men who worked in the service sector, primarily as waiters, hostlers, cooks, and barbers, constituted another 16 percent.[91] A few men, who may have owned small establishments or sought to enter a profession, are grouped in the "other" category. Eight gave "tobacconist" as their occupation, and Moses Jackson described himself as a "doctor." Nathaniel Williams, a nineteen-year-old from Prince Edward Island, said he was a student, and Thomas Ward gave his profession as druggist.[92] A few other men named occupations such as surveyor, engineer, clerk, and musician.

The records clearly show that black recruits from British North America were drawn overwhelmingly from the working class. Most performed wage work for other people and for limited periods, particularly in non-agricultural jobs. Those who were contemplating enlistment in the Union army or navy and who had dependants – a spouse, aging parents, siblings, or others – faced a difficult decision. Once enlisted, they would be absent for at least a year and more frequently for three. Most men who did wage work had little financial capital to support a family while they were away. For them, a bounty or a substitute fee might facilitate enlistment because it provided economic security for dependants.

The experience of Hannah Weeks, a Chatham resident and mother of a black recruit, exemplified the plight that dependants of the men going off to serve might face. Hannah and her husband, John Weeks, were African Americans who had moved to Chatham some time before the birth of their son, John Jr., in 1844. In 1861, in the census, Hannah listed her age as forty-eight years old and said she was working as a cook. Her husband gave his occupation as "labourer," although at age sixty-two his ability to earn a wage had become very limited.[93] Hannah increasingly relied on the money brought in by John Jr., who also worked as a cook. John Jr.'s enlistment in the Fifty-fourth Massachusetts Regiment in April 1863 deprived the family of important financial support. His death in the assault on Fort Wagner months later was a bitter emotional and financial blow to his aging parents.[94] Although Hannah and John Weeks continued to live in Chatham, their names do not appear in the 1871 census. They apparently moved out of the frame house they had shared with John Davis, perhaps for financial reasons. Where they lived remains a mystery. However, a pension application by Hannah details her growing destitution in the absence of her only son.[95]

Although a young, black resident of Chatham who was considering enlistment in 1864 might not have predicted the callousness of the Pension Office, he would have been aware of Hannah Weeks's dire economic plight. For him, securing a large bounty as a volunteer or a substantial fee as a substitute would ensure that his dependants were better cared for than Hannah Weeks.

It was clear that those who decided to enlist had to address a series of questions. Was it better to volunteer or to serve as a substitute? Should they

Table 5
Terms of enlistment and deserters

	BNA-born recruits	Volunteers	Substitutes	Deserters	1-year term	2-year term
1863	97	90	7	12	0	0
1864	515	348	167	63	49	3
1865	213	105	108	47	56	1
Total	825	543	282	122	105	4

NOTE: Thirty-five of the men who deserted in 1865 did so after April (that is, after Lee surrendered the Army of Northern Virginia). Three additional men deserted in 1866 and one in 1867.

opt for the standard three years or for a shorter term? Once in the army, some of the men faced a new question. If they were being treated like second-class soldiers or if their conditions of service were dreadful, should they serve out their full term, or were they justified in deserting? As Table 5 indicates, their answers varied considerably.

Most of the 825 men who enlisted did so as volunteers, but almost 300 signed on as substitutes. A substitute was to be thoroughly vetted at enlistment. He and the principal who was hiring him were normally required to appear together, and the substitute underwent a physical and personal screening by a physician. The recruiting officer was also supposed to ensure that both the substitute and the principal understood their financial arrangement.[96] The substitute had to sign an oath indicating that he was eligible to serve as a substitute, although the exact wording varied from district to district. When George Crosby, a twenty-year-old sailor from Prince Edward Island, enlisted at Tarrytown, New York, on 25 January 1865 as a substitute for Lewis Jones, he simply had to swear that he was "between the age of eighteen and forty-five years, and not subject to the draft by means of being an alien."[97] By contrast, when John Brown enlisted at Oswego at almost the same time, his deposition was more detailed. He had to swear that he was a native of Canada, had "never declared his intention to become a citizen of the United States," and had "never exercised the right of suffrage by voting in any election in any States of the United States." In addition, he testified that he was not a deserter from the army or navy and that he was an alien who owed allegiance to Great Britain.[98]

Isaac Maynard, a soldier who served in the Forty-third USCT, provides one example of the enrolment process for many substitutes. In September 1864, the ninth subdistrict in the Twenty-ninth District of New York failed to meet the quota specified in the president's July call for more men, and officials were forced to hold a draft. One of those whose name was selected in the 22 September lottery was Henry R. Webber, a thirty-two-year-old resident of Royalton in Niagara County. Two days later, Maynard enlisted as Webber's substitute at nearby Lockport. Whatever fee they had agreed upon was not recorded. Three days afterward, Maynard was forwarded from Lockport to the draft rendezvous at Elmira, New York, a notorious prisoner of war camp. The choice of destination was in keeping with popular perceptions of the substitutes and drafted men who signed up at that time. Several weeks later, Maynard finally joined the Forty-third USCT, a Pennsylvania regiment serving in the campaigns around Petersburg and Richmond. After service on the Rio Grande frontier in late 1865, Maynard and his regiment were mustered out in October 1865, transferred east, and finally discharged in Philadelphia in November.[99]

Maynard himself may have been a competent soldier, but the government feared that many late recruits were not. Despite extra precautions, reports abounded of bounty-jumping and of substitutes who deserted as soon as they pocketed their money. As a result, some districts delayed payment, at least until soldiers reached the general rendezvous. This was the case in the Sixteenth and Seventeenth Congressional Districts of New York, which withheld bounty money until enlistees arrived at the rendezvous.[100] The federal government tried to manage the situation in December 1864, when Provost Marshal General James Barnet Fry issued a general order that all funds in excess of twenty dollars were to be taken from the volunteers and substitutes, and returned to them only when they reached their units.[101] The new policy may have reduced desertion or bounty-jumping and may have provided a safe place for recruits to bank their funds. Yet it imposed a hardship on the families of men who had few assets and who needed the money immediately for their support.

The government did not determine the amount that substitutes received, although setting the commutation fee at three hundred dollars was intended to keep the substitute fee at a similar level. When the commutation fee was discontinued and the demand for substitutes persisted, a price escalation quickly ensued that varied considerably by time and place. In most cases, government officials did not record either the amount paid by the principal or that received by the substitute, especially if a broker were involved. However, after Fry's general order, at least some black substitutes deposited their funds with the paymaster, using him as a de facto bank. These amounts varied widely and would not have included the full substitute fee if a broker were involved. The paymaster of the Twenty-fifth USCT, a regiment raised in Pennsylvania, was particularly diligent in recording these sums. Some were relatively small. The paymaster credited $54.59 to James Brown, a labourer from "Canada," but recorded that George Kennedy, a New Brunswick farmer, had deposited $650.00.[102] The amount that Kennedy received was at the high end of the spectrum; most men left between $300 and $400 with the paymaster. James Blackman, a labourer from "Canada" who had been hired as a substitute prior to the draft, deposited $212.50.[103] John Hope, who enlisted as a substitute a few days earlier than Blackman but in a different New York congressional district, was credited with $538.43.[104] Andrew Johnson signed up at Syracuse, hired by Alexander Coffin as a substitute prior to the draft, and he gave the paymaster $444.40 for safekeeping.[105] The differing amounts deposited by these and other substitutes suggest that knowledge and personal agency were key to maximizing a recruit's financial benefits.[106] Perhaps because of their variability, some people in Canada West developed inflated ideas about what a substitute might clear. Near the end of the war, Chatham residents believed that "sometimes as much as $750 and even $1000 are obtained for substitutes."[107]

Writers have frequently portrayed the substitutes and "big bounty" men who entered the army in 1863 and 1864 as poor soldiers "without patriotism or honor." They generally agree with the private in a New York regiment who claimed that "those *money* soldiers are not worth as much as they *cost* for when you heer firing ahead you may see them hid in the woods."[108] Although this stereotype may apply for a majority of American substitutes, it does not fit most who came from British North America. Many of them made good soldiers. Indeed, some made very good soldiers and were recognized as such by their commanding officers. As a result, many were promoted to the rank of corporal or sergeant, or given administrative functions. William H. Miner (or Minor), the twenty-nine-year-old "boatman" from Saint John who joined the Eighth USCT, was just one example of the British North American substitutes who became successful non-commissioned officers. Sergeant Miner effectively led his men in combat before being mustered out with his regiment at Brownsville, Texas, in November 1865.[109]

Henry Allen was a twenty-three-year-old "tobacconist" when he agreed to be a substitute and joined the Twelfth USCT in September 1864. Six months later, he was made first sergeant, the senior non-commissioned officer in a company, and retained that rank until he was mustered out "at the expiration of his term of service" in September 1865.[110] John A. Benson, who was born in

In August 1864, George Dean agreed to enter the army as a substitute for Gove Porter, a Detroit man who had been drafted. For an undisclosed amount of money, Dean enlisted in the 102nd USCT and served faithfully until his unit was mustered out in September 1865. *Courtesy of the National Archives and Records Administration.*

Hamilton in 1848, was working as a teamster in New York when he joined the Union army, in part because of the attractive substitute payments being offered at Wilmington, Delaware. Enlisting on 13 December 1864 for one year as a substitute for James M. Pride, he joined Company I, Twenty-ninth USCT. He appears to have been a good soldier, for he was quickly promoted to corporal and was "present with company during Appomattox campaign." When he was mustered out at Brownsville, Texas, in November 1865, he had been a sergeant for four months.[111] Years later, he would apply for and receive a pension.[112] Stephen Ray, a twenty-two year-old native of Nova Scotia who gave his occupation as steward, enlisted in the Twenty-fifth USCT late in the war as a substitute for a New Yorker. Because of his skills, he was soon seconded to work as a clerk in the adjutant's office, until he was discharged with the regiment on 6 December 1865.[113]

Most black troops completed their military service faithfully and were mustered out with their regiments, but some did not. A few even behaved like stereotypical bounty-jumpers. John Lewis, William Jackson, and the aptly named William Unpleasant all enlisted as substitutes in late 1864 and early 1865, were assigned to the Twenty-fifth USCT, and absconded while en route to the regiment.[114] Whereas their desertion was premeditated, such was not the case for others, but desertion was not uncommon. As Table 5 indicates, well over one hundred black soldiers from British North America deserted, a rate of 14.6 percent.[115]

Throughout the war, the problem of desertion plagued both the Northern and Southern armies. From 1861 to 1865, the Union army recorded 268,530 desertions, although the provost marshal general believed that a quarter of them represented men who were unintentionally or unavoidably absent. Of the 201,397 soldiers who were rightfully reported as deserters, 76,526 subsequently returned, or were returned, to their units.[116] The desertion rate among white troops in state and regular army regiments varied considerably, but the overall rate for all soldiers was about 10 percent.[117] Many desertions were prompted by the daily hardships of war, short or inedible rations, and unhealthy camp conditions where disease flourished. Men also left because of poor leadership, desperate letters from family members, the frustration of inactivity, and the fear of death, all aggravated by homesickness and a growing concern for kin. It must be remembered that the vast majority of men on both sides of the conflict were not professional soldiers. Instead, they saw themselves as volunteer citizen-soldiers who entered into a contractual relationship with their government during a time of crisis. For soldiers more than sailors, the transition from civilian to military life was one of many trying adjustments.[118] Not surprisingly, some men believed that when the army failed to honour its promises, the citizen-soldier could exercise his personal agency. All the factors that influenced white desertion also applied to black desertion. However, certain factors specific to the experience of black soldiers also played a role in their departures.

Defining desertion was a seemingly straightforward task. A deserter was one who left his unit or post of duty without permission and with the intent of not returning. Yet what desertion meant in practice and what motivated soldiers to leave their units varied considerably during the war. When Lincoln decided to use black troops in the conflict, many saw this as heralding a new era for all black residents of the United States, with an implied promise of equality. As a result, the motives of some black soldiers who felt betrayed and who subsequently deserted may have been quite different from those of white soldiers. Having volunteered to defend their nation, black soldiers expected to be treated in a fashion similar to white troops. When they received unequal pay, disproportionate fatigue duty, and defective equipment, many became bitter upon realizing that the government had violated its contract with them. Some white civilians, including Governor John Andrew of Massachusetts, agreed with them. As he put it, black soldiers "were raised, enlisted, mustered, sworn in, and used under the laws for raising and accepting volunteers. They stand in every respect ... upon the same law which supports the rights of white soldiers." Because they were recruited under the regulations and laws that applied to all state volunteers, Andrew argued, "the laws for the payment of the volunteer army of the United States apply to these men, or they apply to nobody."[119] Some officers in the black regiments of Massachusetts believed that if Congress did not resolve the pay issue, the units would have to be mustered out of service.[120]

As a result, some soldiers who believed that they had been deceived when they enlisted opted unsurprisingly for flight. In May 1865, one black deserter who had been imprisoned for six months in Fort Jefferson, Tortugas, wrote to the secretary of war, asking to be released. He claimed that "when I enlisted I had no other entention then perform my duty faithfully as a soldier and would fermily have done so if we had not ben treatted in such ill fashion and was subject to all kinds of missrepresentations." Like many soldiers, he had a family that depended on him for financial support, a consideration that was part of his original decision to enlist. He explained that General Benjamin Butler had promised the men thirteen dollars per month pay and a bounty of fifty-eight dollars. The promise had not been kept, and he asked, "if a genl promas or assureance is paid no respect to how much less could there be expected of a poor soldier." The prisoner concluded by saying, "I do not wish to justify my[self] in an act of desertion ... but we tried every way and could not get no redress."[121]

Although the unequal pay issue was resolved in June 1864, soldiers who believed that at enlistment they had been promised equal treatment in all things, not just wages, still had grievances. They believed that the pay issue was grounded in the principle of equal rights for blacks as soldiers and thus had entailed more than "the mere attainment of dollars and cents."[122] Pay had been standardized, but the overarching principle was still being ignored. For competent black sergeants, watching their white counterparts receive commissions that they themselves had been denied was particularly demeaning. A sergeant in the Fifty-fourth Massachusetts wrote that it was the source of "much hidden discontent." The final insult for these men, he continued, was the November 1864 promotion to second lieutenant of Private Charles L. Roberts, a white soldier in the Thirty-fifth Massachusetts.[123] His promotion came at a time when several black sergeants, commissioned by Governor Andrew, had not been released by the War Department, a necessary step before they could take up their commissions. For Sergeant Gabriel P. Iverson of the Fifty-fifth Massachusetts, this was the last straw. The regimental surgeon had described Iverson, and several other black sergeants, as "superior in all respects to many white officers that I have seen and I trust they may be promoted." Private Roberts was promoted just after Iverson received a thirty-day furlough. The sergeant who "sometime previous to enlistment was a resident of Canada" never rejoined his regiment and after the war was reported to be living back in Canada.[124]

At times, black recruits who were initially eager to serve became disillusioned by their unfair treatment. One regiment, the Michigan-raised 102nd USCT, is the best example of such a case. Although it began enlisting soldiers in August 1863, it did not leave the state until 28 March 1864. By then it had lost more than 120 men from desertions, including 20 from Canada West. Many had never experienced the virulent white bigotry that they encountered in Detroit; nor were they prepared for the atrocious living conditions in their barracks, which killed or sickened dozens of men. As they suffered through a Detroit winter with little sign that they would ever see military action, men began to leave. Some had lasted only a few months, others even less. Yet, once the regiment was on active duty, desertion largely ceased. Only eight other Canadians deserted throughout the remainder of the unit's service. Two of them, William Harrison and Elijah M. Johnson, both of whom had enlisted in 1863, absconded during the summer of 1865 after the fighting was over.[125]

Indeed, the behaviour of men such as Harrison and Johnson raises questions about what it meant to desert after Lee's April 1865 surrender at Appomattox. Because the black regiments were among the last to be raised, many were held in service while white regiments were being mustered out. Black soldiers who had enlisted to fight Confederate armies and who had done so faithfully before Lee surrendered did not feel that they should be expected to serve indefinitely as an army of Southern occupation. Of the 122 black British North Americans who deserted, 39 did so only after Lee's surrender. If the 39 are excluded, the desertion rate for black British North Americans is 10.5 percent, comparable with that of most Civil War soldiers.

Peter Jackson, a twenty-three-year-old native of Saint John who had joined the Fifth Massachusetts Cavalry in September 1864 as a substitute, deserted eight months later. However, he abandoned his unit only after Lee's surrender had ended the war in the east and at a time when officials were deciding to ship the all-black Twenty-fifth Corps to the Texas-Mexico border for extended Reconstruction service. Nevertheless, Jackson rejoined his regiment in May, spending much of his post-war service confined in a Texas military hospital because of poor health.[126] Thomas Leslie, a twenty-seven-year-old private in the Thirty-eighth USCT, was perhaps the last black British North American to desert. Organized in early 1864, his regiment spent most of its service in Virginia. In May 1865, at the end of the war, it was moved to Texas. Leslie finally abandoned it in late August 1866, despite the fact that the regimental paymaster was holding $243 for him.[127] He may have been pushed to desert by the conditions in the regiment, which had "suffered a total collapse of discipline as the result of crimes committed by dozens of its officers," including the lieutenant colonel, who withheld bounty money owed to some of his men.[128] The regiment was not mustered out until January 1867.

Eventually, Congress also came to believe that post-war desertions should be treated differently. After the war, everyone who applied for a pension had to supply proof of an honourable discharge, a stipulation that obviously excluded deserters. In 1888, however, politicians were persuaded that men who had deserted after the surrender of the Confederate armies should be eligible for pensions. In 1889, Congress approved an act "to release certain appointed or enlisted men of the Army, Navy and Marine Corps from the charge of desertion."[129] Those who were eligible for this category had to have served six months or more and to have deserted after 1 May 1865. As a result, James Jones, an eighteen-year-old labourer from Chatham who had enlisted in the Fifth Massachusetts Cavalry and deserted in May 1865 became entitled to apply for a pension. The Adjutant General's Office ruled that the "charge of desertion of May 1865, against this soldier has been removed and he is discharged to date May 28, 1865, under the provisions of the act of Congress approved March 2, 1889." Unfortunately for Jones, his discharge certificate was "prepared by the War Department July 11, 1923," only after he died. Neither Jones nor his wife received a pension.[130]

Of course, we will never know why many men chose to desert. William H. Noble, a twenty-year-old shoemaker from Malden, Canada West, enlisted in August 1864 in the Forty-fifth USCT for three years, only to desert from Camp William Penn before the end of his first month. He had contracted to serve as a substitute for a white Pennsylvanian, Joseph Powell. Noble's sudden flight could indicate that he had enlisted only for the easy money and had always intended to desert. Perhaps he did, but his officers thought enough of him during his short time with the regiment that they made him a sergeant.[131] For other deserters, such as James L. Williams, we can speculate on their motives. A thirty-five-year-old recruit from Chatham, Williams had enlisted in Chicago on 27 January 1864, and his commanding officer obviously felt that he had important skills, for Williams was appointed first sergeant in Company F, Twenty-ninth USCT, on 1 February 1864. He was reduced to the ranks on 22 July 1864, although his records do not reveal why. His demotion occurred just a week before the Twenty-ninth USCT participated in the Battle of the Crater, a bloody conflict that has been called the Civil War's worst massacre.[132] Williams survived the battle, although the regiment lost 128 of its 450 men.[133] A little more than a week later, on 6 August 1864, Williams abandoned his unit.[134] Perhaps his decision was driven by the loss of his stripes, or of so many comrades killed, or his feeling that Union authorities had done little to protect black soldiers from Southern atrocities.

An enlisted man who served in the Fifth Massachusetts Cavalry described the details of his desertion but did not mention his motives. William E. Howard was a twenty-two-year-old shoemaker from Hamilton who enlisted in June 1864 for three years. As he explained,

> I received $325.00 bounty. I served with my Regt until on or about the 20th of April 1865 when I left my Camp without permission at or near Richmond, VA., and was absent until arrested by the Officer of the Day in Richmond on or about 20th of April 1865, who took me to the Provost Marshal at Castle Thunder and by him I was committed to prison. I was then sent to City Point where I was placed in the Bull Ring and then forwarded to this place.[135]

The men who deserted during the last months of the war may have done so due to homesickness or because they still feared for their well-being. Those who enlisted in the final months of the conflict could expect greater financial rewards and fewer risks than the early volunteers, but even their risks were not negligible, as proved true for John Simons. An eighteen-year-old farmer from Canada West, John enlisted in Syracuse in February 1865. Perhaps he chose Syracuse because of the bounties being offered by the Cortland County officials, for he deposited $299.25 before he left New York. Three weeks later, he joined Company I, First USCT, which was stationed in the South. On 4 June, he was admitted to the general hospital at Goldsboro, North Carolina, where he died of consumption a month later.

He was two months shy of his nineteenth birthday.[136] Perhaps the unluckiest black volunteer from Canada West was Holman Singleton, a twenty-two-year-old labourer who enlisted as a substitute in October 1864. A year later, he was discharged with his regiment, the Third USCT, in Jacksonville, Florida, only to suffer an accidental "gun shot wound through the liver." The hospital records indicate that "this patient died on the eve of the Regt sailing after being mustered." He was buried in Jacksonville on 5 November 1865.[137] Singleton was the last of the more than fifty black soldiers from British North America who died during the war.

CHAPTER SIX

BLACK DOCTORS

CHALLENGING THE BARRIERS

THE CONTRIBUTIONS OF BLACK soldiers to the war effort changed the perceptions of many white North Americans concerning black capacities. The racial assumptions of both white citizens and soldiers had significantly altered by 1864, and more people accepted black combat soldiers as a legitimate and important part of the army. These new attitudes, however, had clear limits and a class dimension. The vast majority of black soldiers, both African Americans and British North Americans, came from a working-class background, and the societal expectations were that once in the army, they would serve as rank-and-file soldiers under the command of white officers. A very small core of black medical professionals challenged those assumptions and revealed the limits of progressive change within the army. These professionally and socially ambitious physicians had attained their medical education prior to the war despite North America's endemic racial prejudice. By the time that black regiments were authorized, the army was desperately short of trained medical personnel. Yet when black doctors sought commissions as regimental surgeons, the army was reluctant to accept their service. Their careers disclose much about the corrosive attitudes toward race in the last half of the nineteenth century.

A significant number of doctors from British North America served in the Civil War. Men born in British North America or who had received their medical training there worked in many Union regiments and hospitals, and a few were even employed in the Confederate medical system.[1] Significantly, among the dozen or so black physicians who practised either in the Union army as regimental surgeons or in various Northern hospitals and refugee camps as contract surgeons, at least four had close ties to Canada West, and they all ended up in Washington.[2] Two of them, Alexander Thomas Augusta and John H. Rapier, were born and raised in the United States and came to Canada West for the education offered there. The other two, Anderson Ruffin Abbott and Jerome Riley, had been raised in the British colony, although they had complex links to the United States.[3] In addition, a fifth man, Martin Delany, who practised medicine for a short time in Canada West during the late 1850s, is an example of a black man whose medical ambitions would be thwarted by the prejudices of nineteenth-century America. The careers of these five men provide a useful study of ambitious individuals who attempted to improve their social status and financial futures by creating niches in a fluid medical profession and in the face of deeply ingrained racism. When they sought to become surgeons in the Union army, they challenged white attitudes concerning black men in positions of authority. Although they were personally ambitious, they also believed that their education and advancement left them with an obligation to help newly freed African Americans.

Their experiences before and during the Civil War reflect the ways that prejudice influenced perceptions of proper medical preparation, and their wartime careers underscore the widespread opposition among both soldiers and civilians to commissioning black officers in the army. The Emancipation Proclamation had opened the army to black soldiers and held out the promise of a new era. The black doctors and their supporters assumed that in this time of crisis and transformation, the government would proceed to commission qualified black physicians as officers, giving them the authority and professional respect that the rank conferred. The army was desperately short of qualified physicians, and these black doctors had all the necessary credentials. Being offered commissions would symbolize a true sea change in American racial attitudes. It was not to be. As events would show, most Americans accepted the idea that black men could command other black men, but few whites agreed that they should have authority over white men. Although a few black doctors were commissioned early in 1863 because of the overwhelming need for medical practitioners, that policy was soon reversed due to white opposition. The issue of race was difficult enough to overcome, but the combination of race and class would prove virtually insurmountable.

The five doctors who had ties to Canada West were men of exceptional ambition and achievements, but their attitudes about the society in which they lived reflected the diversity of black communities. Through much of their careers, Martin Delany and John Rapier were deeply pessimistic about the likelihood that any black person could lead a satisfactory life in North America. Alexander Augusta, who always identified himself as an American, saw Canada West primarily as a vehicle to further his professional career, whereas Anderson Abbott and Jerome Riley, who were both raised in the province, had differing views as to whether it constituted home. All recognized that social and professional advancement entailed geographical mobility. Collectively, their lives illustrate the boundaries of the possible and the spectrum of the black experience, including frustrations and self-identification, in mid-nineteenth-century North America.

By about 1850, the opportunities for black North Americans to practise medicine were marginally greater than at the start of the century. Of course, there was no consensus in 1850 regarding who could or should claim to be a doctor; nor was there agreement about the proper treatment of any specific ailment. In both the United States and British North America, medical education and licensing were chaotic, competitive, and changing. Formal medical education, largely unregulated, could vary widely in length, content, and structure, and some persons who claimed to be doctors were entirely self-taught. Various groups of medical providers across North America offered a diverse body of therapeutic knowledge and practices. Practitioners offering medical service were often identified with a particular "school" or "sect" of medicine – urban and rural doctors, allopaths, homeopaths, Thomsonians, and eclectics – and most drew on dissimilar training. Not yet an elite professional group, doctors were usually educated through a combination of schooling and apprenticeship.[4] In the United States, the era saw a rapid growth of small proprietary medical schools that demanded little in the way of entrance requirements and emphasized practical skills based on the apprentice system. All too frequently these schools "were merely diploma mills whose main raison d'etre was to make money for their faculty."[5] Often run by doctors who themselves were the product of the apprentice system, at best they offered "training" rather than a medical education. By contrast, the medical schools connected with universities in the Eastern states offered perhaps better but more expensive medical education, although most did not accept African American students.[6]

At the start of the nineteenth century, most state legislatures had chartered state medical societies whose power to license practitioners incorporated at least a nominal penalty for practising without a licence. However, during the 1830s and 1840s, "almost all legislatures reversed themselves and removed all restrictions on medical practice."[7] This reluctance to empower any one set of doctors as gatekeepers of the profession was also evident in Canada West. An 1851 attempt to abolish the Medical Board of Upper Canada and to eliminate any licensing requirements failed, though by just one vote, perhaps because the initiative would have moved Canadians closer to the American model.[8] Nevertheless, though many practitioners could offer a range of services, only a limited number ever achieved financial success or broad social recognition. Both patients and institutions wanted doctors who had "proper attainments," a demand that increasingly meant medical training at a recognized university. The crucial difficulty facing black aspirants was that most universities, especially those in the United States, would not admit them. Although more than twenty-eight thousand people graduated from the various US medical schools between 1840 and 1860, only about fifteen can be identified as African American.[9]

Medical education and regulations were equally divisive issues in the British colonies. They had the same spectrum of practitioners who claimed the right to treat patients, but local factors created additional concerns. Upper Canada had fewer practitioners per capita than either the United States or Britain, although the urban centres were generally well serviced.[10] The issues of loyalty, elitism, and institutional rights complicated the situation, as British physicians jealously guarded their special privileges. Thus, though the Medical Board of Upper Canada, established in 1819, had the power to examine all physicians before licensing them to practise, this did not apply to everyone. Those who held a diploma or licence from a designated British university, belonged to the Royal College of Physicians and Surgeons in London, or had served as a surgeon in the British forces were exempt from medical board review and automatically qualified to practise in the colony.[11] Given the competing claims of differing groups of practitioners, many opposed the creation of a self-regulating medical society with monopolistic control. Dr. Christopher Widmer, head of the medical board, believed that Canada West's population was best protected, as elsewhere, by "the corrective influence of public opinion."[12] An act of 1839 established the College of Physicians and Surgeons of Upper Canada, which had examining and licensing authority, but a year later the British government disallowed the act on the grounds that it infringed on the rights of the London licensing authorities. Even had the act remained in place, it provided no legal penalty for practising medicine without a licence.[13] Thirty years would elapse before the province established the self-regulating College of Physicians and Surgeons of Ontario.[14]

Given the social attitudes in Canada West, it is not surprising that the board's function was to screen applicants for more than just their medical knowledge. It also had to be satisfied with a candidate's loyalty and good morals. Following the Rebellion of 1837 in Upper Canada, medical education became entangled in the questions not just of loyalty but also of whether to publicly fund one major medical school, aid separate college schools, or encourage privately run schools. John Rolph, who had founded the private Toronto School of Medicine, or "Rolph School," advertised that "medical students who do not intend to enter the University will be as heretofore received by the subscriber, conducted through the usual course of medical studies ... and prepared for their diploma from the Medical Board."[15] For a time, his school flourished. Reformers such as Rolph objected to the Anglican establishment funding medicine in "one great university" and championed "the salutary influence of the competition which other similar institutions would induce."[16] Although historian Michael Bliss paints an unflattering picture of medical education in Toronto before the Civil War, it was probably as good as that of most places and better than many. In the decades before 1861, Toronto had had two or three rival schools, "all of them proprietary, some at times affiliated with the University of Toronto, Trinity College, or the Methodists' Victoria University." None had anything approaching modern libraries or laboratories. Bliss notes that "students paid their fees directly to the professors, listened to their lectures over a few short terms, did some dissecting, and saw a few live patients on the wards of the Toronto General Hospital."[17]

In the Canadas, the best or at least the most rigorous medical school was at McGill University, which closely followed the British system and put a strong emphasis on high academic and professional standards.[18] The teaching sessions offered by faculty members were longer than at most schools, and students, who took courses in a proscribed order, required four years to graduate. Getting into the program, however, was very difficult. Admission requirements, though certainly onerous, were not the only hurdle for some would-be students. The culture of the program is reflected in the fact that no black or female student would graduate from McGill's medical school until the twentieth century. The only other pre–Civil War college-based medical school in the colonies was the Medical College of Queen's University, whose first class started in 1855. In Canada East, two other institutions, the School of Medicine and Surgery of Montreal (l'École de médecine et de chirurgie de Montréal) and the St. Lawrence School of Medicine, challenged the dominance of McGill.[19]

Given the limited space in the medical schools and the growing public attitude that university-trained physicians were the true professional doctors, there were seldom enough of them to meet all the health needs of the colonies. Especially in the rural areas, people with little formal training but some skills could offer a range of medical services according to the local demand. An 1837 letter written by B. Aldren, a Guelph resident who would have been seen as a "country doctor," underscored the way in which the market shaped who could offer medical services. In the early 1830s, Aldren, a recent immigrant from England, was living near York, Upper Canada, and was supporting his family as a carpenter. During the spring, "a kind of rash Fever became prevalent particularly among the Children. I undertook a case or two and succeeded. This soon brought me into the practice of Medicine in which Providence highly favoured me and I was very successful." Over the next few years, Aldren continued to offer his services to the community on a part-time basis. During this time, he relocated twice but continued to support his family primarily as a farmer. Following his final move to Guelph, he explained, "I left off dabbling in Medicine when I came to Guelph, as here are 3 regular Surgeons, and consequently no room for poor I, except in my own Family."[20]

The presence of self-trained practitioners with little or no formal medical education may explain why Moses Jackson, a twenty-two-year-old recruit from "Canada" who served in Company A, Twenty-ninth Connecticut Regiment, gave "Doctor" as his occupation when he enlisted.[21] Perhaps Jackson was a country doctor or possibly a shaman, for his military records provide more information regarding his medical services and his ethnic background. His certificate of disability, which describes his complexion as "copper," also gives his occupation when enrolled as "Indian Doctor."[22] Although he might have practised medicine, he would have done so only in his local community.

This contested medical landscape at mid-century had to be negotiated by any black doctor who hoped to establish himself as a competent and authoritative professional who would be accepted by broader society. Martin Delany's life offers a cautionary example of the ways in which a bright and talented black man could see his hopes for a medical career and public recognition shattered by the hostility of white society. Better known to historians as an early black nationalist, Delany was born in Virginia in 1812 to a free black woman who moved her family to Chambersburg, Pennsylvania, when he was ten. Then, in 1831, Delany moved to Pittsburg, where he worked as a barber and labourer, though his real desire was to become a physician. He apprenticed with an abolitionist-minded doctor, Andrew McDowell, and by 1836 was offering his services to the public as a cupper, leecher, and bleeder.[23] His ambition, however, was to obtain a university medical degree and be recognized as a fully trained physician. After being turned down by a series of medical schools but encouraged by Dean Childs of the Berkshire Medical College in Pittsfield, Delany arranged a meeting with Oliver Wendell Holmes, dean of the medical faculty at Harvard in November 1850. The Harvard Medical School had just admitted two black students, Daniel Laing Jr. and Isaac H. Snowden, who were sponsored by the American Colonization Society, for the winter course of lectures. At the end of his meeting with Holmes, Delany was also admitted and he moved to Boston.[24]

Some students, however, objected to the presence of the three black students. On 10 December 1850, the white medical students met en masse to discuss the issue as well as the possible admission of a female student.[25] Their morning meeting generally supported the right of the faculty to admit "whom they pleased to their lectures," but a smaller afternoon meeting was more exclusionary. Thirty-four of the sixty students who attended it voted in support of a resolution to expel Laing, Snowden, and Delany. The meeting found "the admission of blacks to the medical lectures highly detrimental to the interests, and welfare, of the institution" and claimed that it would "lower its reputation in this and other parts of the country." The students argued, "we cannot consent to be identified as fellow students with blacks; whose company we would not keep in the streets, and whose Society as associates we would not tolerate in our houses."[26] Somewhat incongruously, they added that they had "no objection to the education and elevation of blacks."[27] When university officials hesitated to act, many students threatened to transfer to other medical schools, and Laing, Snowden, and Delany were eventually asked to leave. Dean Holmes explained the decision to expel them: "The intermixing of the white and black races in their lecture rooms is distasteful to a large portion of the class and injurious to the interests of the school."[28] In March 1851, after just one term of study, an embittered Delany left Harvard. For him, his experience was further proof that African Americans had little hope for a better life in the United States and that the logical solution lay in emigration.[29]

When Delany and his family moved to Chatham in early 1856, the *Provincial Freeman* welcomed his arrival and promoted his medical services: "As a physician his skill is not excelled by any in this town – charges moderately, and should always be well-patronized."[30] However, given his growing commitment to his emigrationist goals, Delany worked only sporadically as a cupper and leecher in Chatham's African American community. Not surprisingly, the financial returns and social status available to him in this role were very limited. Although many of his contemporaries and later writers referred to him as Dr. Delany, he made no further attempt to enter a medical school. Despite his wife's suggestion, he did not practise medicine after the war, because he believed that "he would never be more than a country doctor."[31]

Delany's experiences highlighted the enormous difficulties that confronted aspiring black physicians. Nineteenth-century medicine promised them little in the way of wealth, but it did offer them greater social status and an opportunity to move in circles otherwise closed to them. Yet, at a time when virtually anyone could set up shop as a healer, consumers quickly constructed a hierarchy of medical practitioners. Given the depth of nineteenth-century prejudice, a black doctor who wished to be recognized and employed beyond his local community desperately needed the legitimacy of a medical degree from an established university. Only with impeccable credentials could he hope for broad social acceptance.

The first black doctor who actually graduated from a medical school in British North America was Alexander T. Augusta. He is an example of the African Americans who crossed the Canadian border due to strategic career decisions that did not alter their self-identification as Americans. Ironically, his early life was remarkably similar to that of Delany. He was born a free black in Norfolk, Virginia, in 1825 and later moved to Baltimore, where he worked as a barber. His wages enabled him to pay for private medical tutoring, a choice that reflected his commitment to education as a means of social uplift. Intending to further his training, he moved to Philadelphia, only to have his application to the University of Pennsylvania medical school rejected because of his colour.[32] He had demonstrated sufficient abilities, however, that one of the university doctors allowed him "to study medicine in his office."[33] Following this period of apprenticeship, Augusta again applied to a medical school, this time in Chicago, but was rejected once more because he was an African American. He then moved to California for three years and subsequently returned to Philadelphia.[34]

Having concluded that he could not receive proper medical training in the United States, he chose to emigrate. In 1850, Augusta and his wife, Mary Burgoin, moved to Toronto, where he entered Trinity Medical College in 1853.[35] Perhaps he chose Trinity in part because of its advertised claim that its course of instruction was recognized "by the leading schools of medicine in the United States."[36] When Augusta received his bachelor of medicine in

Alexander Augusta was one of the few black surgeons to receive a regular commission in the army during the war. He is shown here in the uniform of a US surgeon with the rank of major. *Courtesy of the Oblate Sisters of Providence Archives.*

1856, he was the first black candidate to graduate from a British North American medical school.[37] John McCaul, the second president of the University of Toronto, remembered Augusta as a man "who did very well in medicine."[38] Following his graduation, Augusta remained in Toronto for six years, practising medicine and heading the Toronto City Hospital, a twenty-five-bed charitable hospital that was heavily in debt.[39] During this time, he also opened a pharmacy.[40] In addition, he helped establish the Association for the Education and Elevation of the Coloured People to improve the educational opportunities available for black students in the province. With

Isaac Cary and Wilson Abbott, who were also members of the association, Augusta championed an integrated educational system and was a strong supporter of the Buxton school established by Reverend William King to educate both black and white students.[41] Augusta had created a well-established professional niche in Canada West, but events would show that he never lost his American identity.

Because of Augusta's strong support for the Buxton Mission School, it was natural that he became both a friend and mentor for one of its first graduates, Anderson Ruffin Abbott. Abbott's parents, Wilson and Ellen Abbott, both free blacks from Alabama, had left that state after whites had pillaged their successful grocery store in 1831 during the aftermath of the Nat Turner Insurrection. Initially, the Abbotts moved to New York but encountered discrimination there and relocated to Toronto in 1835.[42] In Canada West, Wilson Abbott accumulated considerable real estate.[43] Although most of his business dealings were in Toronto, he was a strong supporter of the newly incorporated Buxton settlement and of the educational goals of Reverend King. The settlement's only black director, he moved his family to Buxton in 1850 so that his children could attend King's school, where black students received a classical education in an integrated setting.[44] Anderson Abbott joined a remarkably gifted group of scholars that included Jerome Riley and John H. Rapier, both future doctors with whom he would work in Washington. After graduating from Buxton, he spent three years at the Toronto Academy, an affiliate of Knox College, where he "was successful in carrying away either prizes or honors in all my classes."[45] Abbott then studied in the Preparatory Department of Ohio's Oberlin College in 1856 before returning to Toronto. The next year, he studied chemistry at University College in Toronto and enrolled in the King's College Medical School the following year.[46] The records indicate that he did not complete his degree at this time but rather undertook four years of practical training from Dr. Augusta.[47] John McCaul remembered Abbott as a medical student "who got along very well."[48] In 1861, he became the first Canadian-born black doctor who was licensed to practise by the Medical Board of Upper Canada.[49]

Abbott's friend and fellow schoolmate at Buxton, Jerome Riley, also earned the right to practise medicine in Canada West in 1861. The third of the doctors from Canada West who would serve in Washington, Riley belonged to one of the first families to settle at Buxton. His father, Isaac Riley, had left Missouri because he feared re-enslavement, and brought his family north to Chicago, Detroit, and St. Catharines. In December 1849, after reading a handbill advertising the proposed all-black settlement at Buxton, Isaac Riley took his family there.[50] An active member of the community and an elder in the Presbyterian Church, he was determined that his children would obtain the best possible education. The expectation that a high-quality integrated school would be established at Buxton was a main reason for his move there.[51] His faith was rewarded.[52] Jerome Riley was part of the remarkable graduating class of 1856 that included Anderson Ruffin Abbott, John H. Rapier, and Alfred Lafferty.[53] Although King had hoped that Riley, one of his best students, might enter the ministry, the young man's initial interests lay in medicine.[54] In 1861, Riley received his licence to practise medicine in Canada West.[55] Like Abbott, Riley appears not to have completed a medical degree when he began treating patients in Chatham.

The fourth doctor in this remarkable group, John H. Rapier Jr., had the briefest ties to Canada West, although he formed a strong friendship with both Abbott and Riley. His father, John Rapier Sr., was a manumitted slave who had relocated to Florence, Alabama, where he had prospered as a barber. By 1830, he owned the house that was both his residence and his shop, held substantial savings, and was involved in several successful real estate and railroad investments.[56] In 1831, he had married Susan, a free black woman from Baltimore, whose status guaranteed that their children would be free.[57] Rapier was determined that his sons would receive the best possible education. In 1843, he sent John Jr. and a younger brother James to the only black school in Nashville, where both boys did well. However, when King's school opened at Buxton, both boys were sent to live with their uncle, Henry Thomas, a resident of the settlement, to benefit from its quality education and freedom from discrimination. Although their time at Buxton was relatively short, the school and the settlement's strict moral code had a major impact on the brothers, most notably James. A self-admitted gambler and drinker, he underwent a conversion at Buxton and in late 1858 wrote John that "I have not thrown a card in 3 years touched a woman in 2 years nor drunk any liquor in going on 2 years."[58]

Of the four black doctors who would end up in wartime Washington, John Rapier was the most international in his aspirations and the most pessimistic about life for a black man in North America. In late 1854 and early 1855, he explored, but ultimately rejected, the possibility of going to Liberia under the auspices of the American Colonization Society.[59] The following year, however, he decided to join another uncle, James P. Thomas, who was moving to Central America.[60] In 1856, Thomas and Rapier sailed from New Orleans, only to return within a few months. Although Rapier was disillusioned by the poverty and hardships facing blacks in Central America and was frustrated by the disorganization of the venture, he found life in the United States, where he worked as a freelance journalist in Minnesota, equally disenchanting. By 1858, he was again considering emigration and publicly urged fellow African Americans to abandon this "land of inexorable prejudice, degradation, and alienation" in favour of other countries that were "more congenial, more liberal, and more willing to provide the blessings of liberty and equality."[61] There is no indication that Rapier's time at Buxton led him to believe that the northern British colonies met this standard. Instead, he looked much farther south and moved to Haiti in late 1860, where he worked for a few months as an English teacher and part-time journalist before moving on to Kingston, Jamaica. Always optimistic, at least in his letters home requesting funds, he threw himself into a series of unsuccessful schemes. After contemplating the possibility of becoming a cotton planter, he apprenticed himself to Dr. William Becket, an expatriate Canadian, to train in dentistry and anatomy.[62] A few months later, during which he lived hand-to-mouth with virtually no income, he decided to study medicine under the supervision of Dr. James Scott, perhaps because it was socially more respected and financially more rewarding than dentistry.[63]

Rapier's discussions with Scott, and his subsequent plan of action, shed light on contemporary ideas about the best way of establishing one's professional credentials as a doctor. Rapier's first plan was a fairly standard one for the time. It involved both an initial stage of study and apprenticeship with Scott, followed by formal education at one or more universities to earn one or two degrees. Scott proposed that Rapier take his first degree in the Canadas and follow it up with a second one in Britain. The stumbling block was that Jamaica recognized credentials earned only at English, Scottish, or Irish medical schools. The Jamaican medical profession was particularly concerned about an influx of questionably trained practitioners churned out by some of the American medical schools. Most Canadian medical degrees offered few benefits to anyone who intended to practise in Jamaica and in some cases were considered a liability. Only two medical schools in British North America, those connected to McGill and Queen's Universities, were fully recognized and would exempt a candidate from preliminary examinations for obtaining a diploma to become a member of the Royal College of Physicians and Surgeons of England.[64] Unfortunately, neither school admitted black students.[65]

Ultimately, Rapier returned to the United States the following year, where he became the first African American student in the University of Michigan's medical school. He had given his residence as Kingston, Jamaica, so

Dr. John Rapier during his service as an acting assistant surgeon, or contract surgeon. *Courtesy of the Anne Straith Jamieson Fonds, Western Archives, Western University.*

that, as a foreign student, he would be admitted regardless of race. Although some faculty members were impressed by his ability, the presence of an African American student on campus triggered an uproar among the white students. "Whoever heard of such impudence," he wrote his uncle angrily. "They say I am nothing but a 'nigger.'"[66] Like Delany at Harvard, he was soon forced by student protests to leave the university. After a few months of enduring their antipathy, he withdrew from Michigan and entered the medical program offered by the Iowa College of Physicians and Surgeons in Keokuk. Even before receiving his medical degree from the college in June 1864, he planned to join the "Medical Service." In April, he wrote to the surgeon general, asking for information on "the proper method of making application" and stressing that he was black.[67] Two months later, when he applied for a position "as a[cting] a[ssistant] surgeon, U.S.A.," he felt the need to add that he was "a Quadroon of Southern birth."[68] By the end of June, he had reported to Dr. William Powell at the contraband hospital in Washington, where he would be reunited with his friends from Buxton.[69] By that time, the War Department's policy toward black doctors had hardened.

When the Final Emancipation Proclamation went into effect in January 1863 and the Lincoln administration began to enlist black troops, the door seemed to be open for the War Department to commission black doctors as army surgeons. For a black doctor with professional ambitions, this would entail formal government-endorsed recognition of his professional competence and new social status.[70] It also allowed those who had achieved much to help others in greater need. Most North Americans assumed that white officers would command the all-black regiments then being formed, and the War Department had rejected early attempts to commission black company officers.[71] However, because regimental surgeons and chaplains were outside the normal regimental command structures, black doctors could fill these positions.[72] Competent surgeons were in high demand. Every regiment carried one surgeon and two assistant surgeons as part of its staff, and raising hundreds of white regiments had exhausted the pool of available and competent surgeons. Although there were only a few black doctors in North America in 1863, their appointment to the black regiments seemed a logical way of addressing the manpower shortage.[73] Indeed, at least for a few months, the War Department allowed the appointment of a few black surgeons and chaplains, who hoped that a new era had begun. They were quickly proven wrong.

Like most black residents of British North America, Alexander Augusta closely followed events in the United States after war was precipitated by the secession of Southern states. As the conflict dragged on, hopes increased that blacks would be allowed to participate in it. Immediately after the Final Emancipation Proclamation of 1 January 1863 was issued, Augusta wrote to Lincoln. Like many other Americans, he believed that the proclamation signalled the government's intent "to garrison the U. S. forts &c with colored troops."[74] If this occurred, he wanted to secure a position as surgeon in a new black regiment or as a physician in a camp being established for the freedmen. He explained that he had been "compelled to leave my native country, and come to this on account of prejudice against color" in order to fulfill his goal of becoming a doctor. He offered to provide references as to his character and competence from some of the best doctors in Toronto, who were familiar with his years of private and public practice.[75] On the same day, he wrote a similar letter to Secretary of War Edwin M. Stanton, explaining that he "would like to be in a position where I can be of use to my race, at this important epoch.[76] In mid-January, the War Department told him to contact the Surgeon General's Office to arrange a time for his medical examination, which he did.[77] However, no one notified C. Clymer, president of the Medical Board, that the candidate to be examined was an African American. After Clymer met Augusta, the agitated and angry examiner immediately wrote to Surgeon General Hammond: "I believe there has been a mistake in this case and I respectfully ask that the within invitation be recalled." Clymer's argument was that Augusta "is a person of African Descent" and that "no member of the Vol. Med. Staff are of his descent or Colour." The white doctor also asserted that Augusta "is an alien & a British subject – & his entrance into the US Military Service is an evident violation of her Britannic Majesty's Proclamation of Neutrality."[78] When asked, Augusta indicated that he had never hidden his colour and that he was not a British national and therefore not subject to the neutrality law. The assistant secretary of war directed the surgeon general to have the medical board "examine Dr. Alex T. Augusta (colored) a candidate for the office of Surgeon in the Negro Regiments now being raised."[79] On 1 April 1863, the board examined Augusta, found him exceptionally qualified, and recommended that he be appointed surgeon. He was soon "assigned to duty with the Contraband Camp near Alexandria, Va.," where he worked from late May until the start of October.[80]

Augusta quickly discovered that the sight of an African American in an officer's uniform generated remarkable enmity, some of it from Southern civilians. In May 1863, he published a letter in the *Washington National Republican* that detailed an assault made on him by Baltimore ruffians when, wearing his major's uniform, he tried to board a train for Philadelphia. Two men tore off his shoulder tabs, the symbols of his rank, while eight or ten more threatened to beat him up. Although a policeman refused to intercede, Augusta ultimately managed to get help from the federal provost marshal, whose soldiers arrested several of the perpetrators. However, when Augusta and a small guard returned to the train station, he was again attacked and punched in the face. The blow was hard enough to stun him for a moment and cause "the blood to flow from my nose very freely."[81] A number of involved civilians were arrested, tried, and convicted of assault. Augusta did finally reach Philadelphia, but only after several fellow officers, with revolvers drawn and ready for use, accompanied him on the train. Many Baltimore residents, especially in the early days of the war, were unfriendly to the Union cause, but the attack on Augusta was overt and very public. Nevertheless, despite his injuries and humiliation, he believed that the episode had established "that even in *rowdy Baltimore* colored men have rights that white men are bound to respect."[82]

He was perhaps too optimistic about the way in which white civilians would treat African Americans, even those in the Union army. Early the next year, the driver of a Washington city railroad prevented Augusta, who was in full uniform, from boarding a designated "all white train." Once again, Augusta refused to accept being treated as a second-class citizen. He communicated his anger to sympathetic Republican senators Henry Wilson and Charles Sumner, as well as to the military judge advocate.[83] The senators not only read Augusta's letter into the Senate records but they also helped push legislation through Congress that made discrimination illegal on Washington public transit.[84] Unfortunately for Augusta's military career, and for other blacks who hoped to become officers, the violence of Southern sympathizers and the prejudice evidenced in the civilian workforce were not the greatest hurdles.

Augusta and other early black officers faced equal prejudice and resistance from Union officers, an attitude that spurred the War Department to change its policy regarding black doctors. After a period of service in the Alexandria contraband camp, Augusta was appointed senior surgeon of the Seventh United States Colored Troops (USCT) on 2 October 1863. He was one of the last black doctors to be commissioned, however, as the War Department buckled under pressure from racist white officers and reversed its policy of commissioning black doctors. Almost as soon as Augusta was appointed to the Seventh USCT, the assistant surgeon, Joel Morse, began to complain.[85] He soon took action.

In February 1864, President Lincoln received a petition from six white surgeons and assistant surgeons in the Seventh, Ninth, and Nineteenth USCT, all of whom had been commissioned and assigned after Augusta's appointment and who were therefore junior in rank to him. The three regiments in which these doctors served were part of General William Birney's command at Camp Stanton, and Augusta was the senior surgeon in the camp. As the six doctors explained, "Judge of our surprise and disappointment, when upon joining our respective regiments we found that the *Senior Surgeon* of the command was a Negro." All six professed to support "the elevation and improvement of the Colored race," and all claimed a willingness to sacrifice much "in so grand a cause." Nevertheless, they felt that their self-respect was severely compromised in the current situation. "Such degradation," they wrote, "we believe to be involved, in our voluntarily continuing in the Service, as Subordinates to a colored officer." They therefore strongly requested "that this *unexpected, unusual,* and most unpleasant relationship, in which we have been placed, may in *some way* be terminated."[86] The War Department did not formally respond to the white doctors, perhaps because Augusta had been transferred away from his regiment after just two weeks. For the remainder of the war, he served on detached duty in Maryland.[87]

Even Augusta's detached service was not enough for Morse, who wanted to have him permanently reassigned so that he himself could be promoted to surgeon of the regiment. In May 1864, he sent a long, angry letter to Senator John Sherman, protesting the "amalgamation or miscegenation in the appointment of officers."[88] Morse was unsuccessful in his appeal to the surgeon general "that a white man may be appointed Surgeon of the 7th U.S.C.T. in place of Dr. Augusta, colored." Thus, at least in theory, Augusta remained the regiment's senior surgeon.[89]

Augusta experienced a further indignity, one shared by all black British North American soldiers who served in 1863, when the army paymaster decided that his pay rate would be that of a black private (after clothing deduction).[90] In early April 1864, Augusta explained to Republican senator Henry Wilson, a long-time abolitionist and chairman of the Senate's Committee on Military Affairs, that the paymaster at Baltimore "refused to pay him more than seven dollars per month." A furious Wilson immediately wrote to Secretary of War Stanton, and within a few days an order was sent to the paymaster general that Augusta was to be salaried "according to his rank."[91]

The handful of other black officers encountered similar prejudice and hostility. Collectively, these controversies forced the War Department to review its decision to use African Americans as regular officers or even as surgeons. In early 1863, before the army established systematic regulations concerning black enlistment, a few African Americans had received commissions, including several doctors such as Augusta.[92] Commissioning black doctors, and thereby giving them authority over white officers and men, generated a groundswell of complaint, and the War Department very quickly stopped commissioning blacks, with the exception of a few chaplains.[93] Thus, when the organizers of the Twentieth USCT, forming in New York, asked the War Department for permission to commission black chaplains and surgeons in late 1863, they were refused. The department explained that although chaplains might "be appointed without regard for color," surgeons were another matter. "The practice of the department," wrote Assistant Adjutant General C.W. Foster, "has been to appoint white men only." When the organizers persisted in their request for a black assistant surgeon, they were informed that "colored medical officers will not be appointed."[94]

As a result, when the remaining doctors with Canadian connections applied to the War Department to become regimental surgeons, they discovered that they would be accepted only as contract surgeons, a civilian appointment lacking the rank, privileges, and pay of a commission. Some had not completed their medical degrees, which made a successful appeal unlikely, although partially trained white doctors were being appointed as regimental surgeons. In April 1863, Augusta published a letter in the *New York Anglo-African*, urging black doctors to enlist, but now he became noticeably quiet on the topic, at least in public.[95] When Anderson Abbott, Jerome Riley, and John Rapier were denied commissions as army surgeons, they had to decide whether the importance of the cause outweighed the indignity of accepting symbolic second-class status. For Abbott and Riley, the dilemma was especially difficult, since they had established practices in Canada West that they were putting aside to volunteer in the war. Ultimately, they chose to serve as contract surgeons and followed Augusta to Washington, where they worked in the Freedmen's Hospital and the nearby contraband camps.

In February 1863, before it was clear that the War Department was reversing its policy on black commissions, Abbott, now twenty-five, followed the example of Augusta and applied to Secretary of War Edwin M. Stanton for a commission as an assistant surgeon in one of the newly forming black regiments. He explained that he had "been engaged in the study and practice of medicine [for] five years" and that he was a licentiate of the College of Physicians and Surgeons of Upper Canada. He also indicated that he planned "to go up for my degree of 'Bachelor of Medicine' in the spring."[96] Perhaps because he knew of Augusta's experience when he applied for a commission in January (or because his actions violated British law), Abbott did not mention that he was a British subject. Nevertheless, his request for a commission did not succeed. Two months later, undeterred by the refusal, he requested to be appointed as a medical cadet. Congress had created this position in 1861 to use medical students who had studied medicine for two years and who had completed one course of lectures at a medical school. This measure reflected the serious shortage of trained medical personnel.[97] Abbott's application may suggest that he saw the incompleteness of his medical degree as the

Dr. Anderson Abbott in the uniform of a contract surgeon, with a green sash designating his position as a medical doctor.
Courtesy of Toronto Reference Library.

reason for his first rejection. He was again turned down. Nonetheless, service in the war was important enough to Abbott that he persevered and finally managed to secure a position in Washington as a contract surgeon.[98]

Contract surgeons, civilian doctors who were employed by the army, played an important role in the war, although many early studies criticized the care that they provided.[99] By 1865, the Union army had employed well over five thousand contract surgeons, or acting assistant surgeons to use the more formal designation, who made a key contribution to the enormous network of major military hospitals.[100] Some writers, however, have stressed that the vast majority of them were employed primarily in the rear area hospitals because few had any real surgical training. Hired by the army, they held no official military rank or authority, although many chose to wear a special contract surgeon uniform. Until 1864, they received only $80 to $100 a month, less than assistant surgeons who, as commissioned officers with the rank of lieutenant or captain, received $100 to $130, plus allowances if they were assigned to hospital service.[101] Abbott's proposed contract, which he received in June 1863, specified that he would receive $80 per month, "which shall be his full compensation and in lieu of all allowances and emoluments whatever."[102] Eighty dollars was at the low end for contract surgeons, especially for a licensed physician with practical experience, but the small sum may have reflected American attitudes about medical training in Canada West. Because Abbott was a civilian employee of the War Department, his appointment, and that of other contract surgeons who were British subjects, did not violate the Foreign Enlistment Act.

Accompanied by Mrs. Augusta, Abbott left Toronto on 10 July 1863 en route to Washington. They had to pass through New York City, where tensions were running high. The Enrollment Act, passed in March 1863, had fuelled anger among the Northern working class, especially the controversial clause that allowed wealthy men to avoid the draft by paying the three-hundred-dollar commutation fee.[103] Many opponents depicted the war as "a rich man's war and a poor man's fight." Whereas the authorities had expected that the July implementation of a draft would generate some protests, they had not foreseen the violence of the response. When Abbott and Mrs. Augusta arrived in the city on 11 July, the first draft lotteries had been conducted without incident, but the wrath of many New Yorkers was palpable. Late that night, while waiting in the station for a connecting train to Washington, they came close to experiencing the violence that had engulfed Dr. Augusta two months earlier. Abbott later recalled the incident:

> While Mrs. Augusta and I were standing in the Depot a man came pretending to be drunk, fell up against Mrs. Augusta. I pushed him off. He then approached me with a threatening attitude but did not dare to strike me. After indulging in considerable violent language and profanity he went out and brought in a big Irishman who began to abuse us in the coarsest language threatening to stamp our lives out and do many other dreadful things.

When two soldiers entered the station, Abbott and Augusta seized their opportunity to escape down dark deserted streets until they found busy avenues crowded with people. They delayed their return until the station was full of people and the train was ready to leave.[104] Only later did Abbott realize the full extent of their peril. Two days after they left New York, the second lottery was held and bloody rioting broke out, leaving at least 120 people dead and hundreds more wounded. Many were African Americans and many others fled the city in terror.[105] Abbott was convinced that he and Augusta had been marked out as the first victims of the riot and that they had just barely escaped with their lives.

Once in Washington, Abbott presented himself to the Surgeon General's Office and arranged his paperwork. However, he did not finalize his employment with the War Department until 2 September 1863, after which he joined Augusta in his work with the black refugees in the camps around Washington. The contraband camp to which Abbott was assigned was bounded by R and S and Twelfth and Thirteenth Streets in the northwestern part of the city.[106] Established in late 1862, Camp Barker was initially a one-storey building. When Augusta first arrived there, its conditions were abysmal and he reported to his medical director that "the water inside the camp appears to produce diarrhea, and the wells in the neighborhood where we receive our supply from, are drying up." He also recommended a new water system, "as there is a great danger should a fire take place" that the facility would be destroyed.[107] Subsequently expanded and improved, the camp was renamed the Freedmen's Hospital by the Quartermaster's Department of the army. In September 1863, Augusta was placed in charge of it, the first African American to head a hospital in the United States.[108] Abbott continued to work at the hospital after Augusta was reassigned.[109] "The Hospital," Abbott wrote, "contained a capacity for 300 beds. It was used for the treatment of Freedmen and Colored soldiers. It was fully equipped with a competent staff of nurses, laundry women, cooks, stewards, and clerks, etc. and was situated about 3 miles from Washington."[110] By the spring of 1864, the hospital had begun admitting wounded and sick soldiers as well as freedmen, and for a brief time that year Abbott acted as its chief executive officer.[111] At the end of the war, the "transfer of Freedmen's Affairs" to the newly created Bureau of Refugees, Freedmen, and Abandoned Lands, better known as the Freedmen's Bureau, forced the Medical Department to annul Abbott's contract so that he could sign a new one.[112] During the reorganization, control of the hospital passed from the War Department to the Freedmen's Bureau, and after several moves, the hospital was permanently established in a large brick building of four and a half storeys, with additional outbuildings for the sick.[113]

While Abbott was working in Washington, both Rapier and Riley joined him. After Rapier received his medical degree from Iowa College, he too had

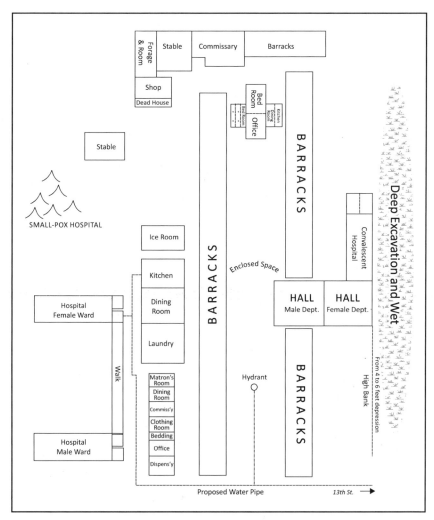

Contraband camp and hospital, Washington, DC, later the Freedmen's Hospital. The contraband camp and hospital provided care to former slaves and black soldiers, employing the largest number of black doctors among the US military hospitals. The facility consisted of tents and wooden barracks that served as hospital wards and temporary housing for the contraband and recovering soldiers.

applied for a commission in the Union army, outlining his training in both dentistry and medicine, and stressing his talents and accomplishments.[114] He described himself as a quadroon from Alabama, perhaps because he knew that previously commissioned black officers were almost entirely mulattoes. Nevertheless, the War Department was no longer issuing commissions to African Americans, regardless of their training or appearance, so Rapier accepted a position as acting assistant surgeon. In June 1864, he reported to the Freedmen's Hospital in Washington and was soon caring for the wounded and dying. Much of his work involved "attending to the out door patients" in Washington.[115] "I never worked so hard," he wrote in August 1864, "had so little rest, and felt so tired as I do now."[116]

Less is known about why Jerome Riley went to Washington. He had received his licence to practise medicine in Canada West in 1861, and had done so for a time in Chatham. In 1864, he left Chatham and joined the Freedmen's Hospital as a contract surgeon, where he ministered to black refugees.[117] He left no record to explain his decision. Indeed, none of the doctors explained why they chose to join the war effort, except for Augusta, who wished to be "of use to my race" and Abbott, who remarked that the conflict was "a war for humanity."[118] Rapier too may have been motivated by ideology, but he was more pessimistic about his decision to become an acting assistant surgeon: "I do not like the U.S. Service. However half loaf is better than no loaf."[119] He understood that, in setting aside their practices and going to Washington, the doctors were risking much.

Although the black doctors continued to face hostility from some Washington residents, they also enjoyed a reception that was impossible by earlier racial standards. Unsurprisingly, as educated and professional men, they were welcomed into the upper ranks of Washington's African American community. More surprising, however, is that Augusta and Abbott, who were "determined to visit the President at the next Levee that he held," managed to achieve their goal.[120] The president, though perhaps not all his family, seemed pleased to see them. As Abbott later recalled, he and Augusta had presented their cards to Mr. B.B. French, a commissioner of the Treasury Department, and were then conducted

> with all the urbanity imaginable to the President who was standing inside the door ... Mr. Lincoln on seeing Augusta advanced eagerly a few paces forward, grasped his hand, and as he held the Doctor's hand, Robert Lincoln, who had been standing beside his mother about six paces off, came up to the President and asked a question

very hastily, the purport of which I took to be – "Are you going to allow this innovation?" The President replied "Why Not?" Nothing more was said.

Abbott, if not Augusta, felt uncomfortable as the focus of attention:

> I suppose it was because it was the first time in the history of the U.S. when a coloured man had appeared at one of these levees. What made us more conspicuous of course was our uniforms. Coloured men in the uniforms of U. S. military officers of high rank had never been seen before. I felt as though I should have liked to crawl into a hole.[121]

Lincoln's attitude stood in sharp contrast to that of many white doctors. In the fall of 1864, Dr. William Powell accused Rapier and Abbott of misusing alcohol. On 28 November, Rapier wrote to Surgeon C.W. Hornor from the Freedmen's Hospital to protest "the charges maliciously preferred by Dr. Powell" against Abbott and himself that they had been "indulging in the use of intoxicating drinks in the Matron's room."[122] He mentioned that Abbott had forwarded testimony from the matron, which rebutted the allegation.[123] Rapier also denied the claim that he and Abbott, both members of the committee to arrange events "on the night of the celebration of Free Maryland," had sent one of Powell's friends "to purchase and introduce whiskey into the 15th St. Church." He also denied assertions of Abbott's drunkenness. He testified that he had known Abbott for "14 years and had never known him to be drunk or a habitual tippler."[124] Nothing further came of the episode, but it may explain why Abbott collected letters from his subsequent superiors, testifying to his ability and character.

Despite the enmity that they found in the army, the four doctors, like many others in Washington, were convinced that the government should and, with enough pressure, would commission black officers to lead the black soldiers. Pressure was increasing on several fronts. Governor John Andrew of Massachusetts had commissioned a handful of black lieutenants in the Fifty-fourth and Fifty-fifth Massachusetts Regiments, beginning in early 1864 with Sergeant Stephen A. Swails, an educated mulatto with an exemplary military record.[125] While the War Department delayed in discharging Swails and other black men so that they could take up their commissions, pressure on the government was clearly intensifying. Enlisted men were not unique in condemning the delay. Northern free blacks and sympathetic Republican politicians all demanded that the black candidates be awarded their commissions. In January 1865, after Lincoln had called for an additional 300,000 volunteers, Abbott, Rapier and other contract surgeons added their voices to the protest. With some non-commissioned officers in the black regiment, including two of Frederick Douglass's sons, they petitioned the secretary of war "to raise a number of *colored regiments,* to be officered *exclusively* by *colored men.*" They argued that this step would encourage recruitment, reward loyalty, and recognize the capacity already demonstrated by hundreds of brave and qualified black non-commissioned officers.[126] At almost the same time, Rapier petitioned Tennessee governor Andrew Johnson to commission black officers in his state's regiments. As he explained to Johnson, he had made the suggestion due to the "liberality that has ever distinguished your political career, with which, as a Tennessean, I am familiar."[127] Johnson's response is not recorded, but unlike Governor Andrew, he made little or no attempt to appoint black officers.

All the lobbying produced only limited results. In the first half of 1865, the War Department commissioned approximately ten black officers, many of whom received their commissions only after the war had ended. Most had earned their promotion as effective and courageous non-commissioned officers in black regiments, but some, such as Martin Delany, the former frustrated physician who received a commission in the 104th USCT, were appointed to assist in recruiting new units, not to serve in regiments.[128] No black doctors, however, were offered new commissions as regimental surgeons or assistant surgeons. Nevertheless, months after the war ended, Alexander Augusta was promoted to lieutenant colonel by brevet, a symbolic recognition of his contribution.[129]

The end of the war raised new questions for the black doctors about their future careers and their place in the world, both geographical and personal. In a new era, where much seemed possible, each had to choose where he would live and work, decisions that were being made throughout the black communities. Their post-war careers reflect their very differing identification with the North American black communities and illustrate the interconnection between the communities themselves. John Rapier, the wanderer whose attitude toward the United States was the most ambivalent, had the shortest time in which to make any life choices. He continued to work at the Freedmen's Hospital until his sudden death in May 1866.[130] By that time, his beliefs about white intransigency may have begun to change, for he was "pleasantly surprised by the cordial treatment accorded black army officers, even by white enlisted men."[131] In a letter to his uncle, written late in the war, Rapier explained that "coloured men in the U.S. Uniform are much respected here, and in visiting the various Departments if the dress is that of an Officer, you receive the military salute from the ground as promptly as if your blood was a Howard or a Plantagenet instead of a Pompey or Cuffee's."[132]

For Alexander Augusta, the question of where to practise medicine was apparently straightforward. As he told Lincoln, his move to Canada West had been impelled by professional necessity alone. Now that slavery was ended and African Americans had proven their worth to the Union, he saw great potential in the United States. Moreover, like many educated black professionals, he felt an obligation to help freedmen create a new position in American society. Life as a civilian would be delayed. In May 1865, while still in the army, he was detailed for work with the Freedmen's Bureau, first in South Carolina and then in Georgia. While in Georgia, he was notified that he had been brevetted lieutenant colonel.[133] In September, he moved to the Lincoln Hospital in Savannah, Georgia, where he remained, after being mustered out of service on 13 November 1866, as a contract surgeon. He did not retire from the Freedmen's Bureau until March 1867, when he finally moved back to Washington.[134]

In September 1868, Augusta became a founding member of the Howard University Medical Department, where he taught anatomy until 1877. Over the next few years, he received two honorary degrees from the university. Old prejudices had not vanished, however. Despite his professional accomplishments, both he and Dr. Robert W. Purvis, another African American, were repeatedly refused membership in the Medical Society of the District of Columbia.[135] Although the medical society had issued their licences, this did not enrol them in the society itself, a step that was necessary before they could consult with its members.[136] In the summer of 1869, they applied for membership, meeting "every rule and regulation demanded," only to be refused. In that vote, Purvis was "rejected by 55 nays to 11 yeas, and Dr. Augusta, 57 nays to 12 yeas." The *Medical and Surgical Reporter* noted that this result had "excited considerable comment from the daily press, and some very bitter expressions."[137] The denial of membership sprang from the American Medical Association's conviction that rejecting racial equality was a key component in remaining the national voice of the medical profession.[138] Like national reconciliation, unity in the national medical association came at the cost of black aspirations. As a result of their rejection, Augusta, Purvis, and others established the National Medical Society of the District of Columbia, with Augusta as one of its first vice-presidents.[139]

Augusta faced further difficulties. In early September 1877, the Howard medical faculty approved a resolution to transfer him from the chair of anatomy to that of materia medica and to give the anatomy chair to Daniel Smith Lamb. Refusing to cooperate with the exchange, Augusta left Howard University.[140] In May 1879, he appealed to the board of trustees for reinstatement as chair of anatomy but was turned down. The trustees explained that they did not want to reopen the issue after two years, although they emphasized that they saw him "as a learned and able physician and anatomist."[141] Despite these setbacks to his professional career, Augusta remained in Washington, and there is no indication that he considered moving back to Toronto. The military was more enlightened than the medical profession in its attitude toward Augusta's accomplishments. Fittingly, when he died in December 1890, he was buried with full military honours at Arlington National Cemetery.

Life in the United States, especially in areas with a large black population, greater economic opportunities, and a chance for national citizenship, was a powerful attraction for black men who were raised in the British colonies. Like Augusta, Jerome Riley also chose not to return to Canada West. He moved initially to Pine Bluff, Arkansas, where he practised medicine and served as the county coroner.[142] He may have selected Pine Bluff because of its economic prospects and the quality of black education there, an issue to which his family had always been committed.[143] His interests soon expanded beyond medicine, and he was increasingly drawn into politics, although not to the Republican Party, as he was critical of its Reconstruction policies. Instead, he joined the Democratic Party and cooperated with Southern white politicians, perhaps because Democratic leaders in Arkansas tended to ignore the white-supremacist elements in their party and followed moderate racial policies.[144] Some authors have accused him of being an accommodationist and of supporting the Democratic Party for reasons of expediency. Riley argued, perhaps incorrectly, that African Americans had fared better under a Democratic administration than under the former Republican one.[145] By temperament, he was most comfortable in a society dominated by prominent and well-educated elites, for he cited his earlier life "residing in Western Canada with my parents, many years ago" as an example of a successful community based on manual labour, hard work, and white oversight.[146] Certainly, Riley's criticism of black Republican officeholders in Arkansas became increasingly vocal.[147] In the 1870s, after he had left Arkansas, Riley defended his support of the Democratic Party by pointing out that under the

This photograph of Dr. Jerome R. Riley appeared as the frontispiece of his 1895 publication, *Philosophy of Negro Suffrage* (Hartford, CT: American Publishing).

new Democratic administration, "more colored men were elected and are commissioned to offices of trust and pay" than under the Republicans.[148]

By 1869, Riley had moved to Chicago, where he studied at the Chicago Medical College for a year before transferring to Howard University to complete his medical degree.[149] There he attended "sessions 3 to 5, 1870-3" and graduated in 1873 with a medical degree. He practised medicine in Chicago for some years, and by 1880 he had married a younger woman, Agnes, whose parents were from Virginia. By 1900, he had moved once again and was "said to be now living in Hartford, Connecticut."[150] Riley was clearly a transient by nature, for near the end of the century one source gave his residence as Seattle, although he is listed in the 1900 US census as a lodger and a widower living in Brooklyn, New York.[151]

For much of his political if not professional life, Riley existed on the margins. In the 1870s and 1880s, he supported John M. Palmer, helping to establish the John M. Palmer Colored Democratic Club. However, when Palmer challenged William Jennings Bryan and his free-silver platform as the Democratic presidential candidate in 1896, Riley supported Bryan, and the Palmer

Club became the William Jennings Bryan Club.[152] By 1898, his opposition to American imperialism in the wake of the Spanish American War had motivated him to help found the Colored National Anti-Imperialist League, which Republicans would deride as an auxiliary to the Anti-Imperialist League. Like many African American intellectuals, Riley believed that American policy in Cuba, Puerto Rico, and the Philippines reflected a paternalistic attitude that denied agency to those who were being liberated.[153] Whereas most Southern African Americans shunned Riley and his league, he had more success when he acted with both white and black Democrats. Along with Colonel William Scott of East St. Louis, Louisiana senator T.B. Stamps, and other Democrats, he helped form the National Negro Anti-Expansion, Anti-Imperialist, Anti-Trust, Anti-Lynching League, which tried to combine African American issues with the Democratic platform.[154] The organization was better known for the length of its name than the importance of its members. It had relatively little influence and was largely ineffectual in advancing its causes. It did, however, offer a choice to those black activists who felt alienated from the Republican Party.

By the turn of the century, Riley had published at least three books, including one, *Philosophy of Negro Suffrage*, that went through three editions.[155] In *Philosophy*, Riley argued that the mass enfranchisement of illiterate ex-slaves during Reconstruction, their manipulation by the Republican Party, and the poor quality of many of their candidates had laid the basis for the forcible removal of blacks from politics in the 1890s. He cited one particular unqualified black Republican candidate, Ned Hill, who could neither read nor write but whose "fighting weight was two hundred pounds, drunk or sober."[156]

If Jerome Riley believed that the United States offered greater opportunities for a Canadian black doctor, Anderson Abbott did not. Despite the appeal of life in Washington, he decided to return home to Toronto when his contract expired in April 1866, because his family had significant assets there and because he wished to complete his medical degree. When he left Washington, he took a remarkable symbol of his contacts with Abraham Lincoln's family. Following Lincoln's death, Abbott received a black-and-white houndstooth shawl that the president had frequently worn. He later claimed that "Mrs. Lincoln sent me, as a memento, the plaid Shawl worn by the president on his way to his first inauguration."[157] In an article that he wrote for the *Anglo-American Magazine* decades after Lincoln's death, he professed to have formed a friendship with the president, stating that "the shepherds plaid shawl which Mr. Lincoln wore during the mild weather ...

was given to Dr. Abbott, of Canada, who had been one of his warmest friends."[158] Dalyce Newby suggests that Abbott may have exaggerated the depth of the relationship and that Elizabeth Keckley, seamstress and confidante to Mary Todd Lincoln, was probably his connection with the Lincoln family. Certainly, Mrs. Lincoln was distraught after the assassination, and Keckley did play a large part in distributing many of Lincoln's possessions.[159] Some historians have also claimed that Abbott participated in Lincoln's death watch, but they have confused him with Dr. Ezra W. Abbott of Concord, New Hampshire, who was present during the vigil.[160]

Abbott did return home with impressive testimonies from the senior doctors with whom he had worked, recommendations that he valued highly. Dr. R.O. Abbott, the medical director for the Department of Washington, noted that he had been "efficient and zealous in the discharge of his duties" at the Freedmen's Hospital from 1863 to the summer of 1864. Caleb W. Hornor, chief medical officer of the Freedmen's Bureau, for whom Abbott worked after August 1865, took "great pleasure in bearing witness to the good and faithful service" he had rendered. Even before Abbott had joined the bureau, Hornor's "attention was directed to Dr. Abbott then Executive Officer of Contraband Camp and Freedmen's Hospital where his efficiency soon gained for him the promotion of Surgeon in Charge since which time he has continued to discharge with credit to himself and the entire satisfaction of his Superior Officers duties involving professional and administrative duties."[161]

Once he was in Toronto, Abbott re-entered medical school and may have received his bachelor's degree in medicine from the University of Toronto in 1867.[162] During the next four years, he worked in Toronto, became a member of the College of Physicians and Surgeons, and was the acting resident physician for the Toronto General Hospital.[163] In 1871, Abbott married Mary Ann Casey, the eighteen-year-old daughter of a successful black barber, and they moved to Chatham, where he established a medical practice.[164] Here, as elsewhere, he played an active part in local society. He became the coroner for the County of Kent, president of the Chatham Medical Society in 1878, and president of the Wilberforce Educational Institute. His personal records show that he did not see Canadian society as free of racism, but his post-war professional life in Ontario offers a stark contrast to that of Augusta in the American capital.

After a decade in Chatham, the Abbotts spent eight years in Dundas, where Abbott served a contentious term as chair of the Internal Management Committee (the board of education). The family relocated to Oakville and eventually returned to Toronto, where he became a member of the

James S. Knowlton Post, No. 532, Grand Army of the Republic (GAR).[165] As so often throughout his life, he soon became a prominent force in the organization. In November 1892, he was appointed aide-de-camp "on the Staff of the Commanding Officers Dept." of New York.[166] Perhaps in connection with joining the GAR, or perhaps because he wanted the same recognition that his mentor, Alexander Augusta, had received, Abbott petitioned the secretary of war in early 1891, asking for an "honorary or brevet rank in the United States Military Service."[167] His request was denied.

Late in his life, the attraction of the United States drew Abbott across the border, and in 1891 he moved his family to Chicago.[168] In 1894, he accepted an appointment as surgeon-in-chief at Provident Hospital in Chicago, the first training hospital for black nurses in the United States, and then became its medical superintendent. The *Chicago Conservator* noted that he had retired from "active practice," welcomed his appointment, and added that he was "well-known and universally recognized as one of the ablest colored surgeons in this country."[169] Citing business matters, Abbott resigned in 1897, but the family remained in Chicago for several years and subsequently returned to Toronto, where Abbott died in 1913.[170]

The black doctors who worked together in Washington were not representative of the hundreds of black British North Americans who served in the Civil War. Rather, they were exceptionally accomplished and ambitious individuals, part of the small black elite of their day. Their careers delineated both the limits and possibilities for black professionals in North America but also revealed the ways in which events from 1861 to 1865 created new opportunities for black men. Their frustrations, and the constraints on their goals, were a measure of how far there was to go. However, the doctors were also excellent symbols of the black communities. Their diverse goals, self-identification, and world views reflected the complexity and variety of the black communities across North America.

CHAPTER SEVEN

POST-WAR LIFE

CONTINUITY AND CHANGE

TRACKING THE POST-WAR lives of black veterans from British North America is every bit as challenging as researching their pre-war lives. A few of them, such as the black doctors, enjoyed successful professional careers that left a wealth of public records for the diligent researcher, but they were the exceptions. Most veterans left few records that allow a detailed assessment of their adjustment to civilian life, all too often a hardscrabble existence, or the degree to which their military experiences influenced their later lives. Occasionally, the records do provide brief glimpses that hint at broader social patterns. Some veterans returned to their pre-war lives with little apparent change, whereas others pursued entirely new trajectories. Nevertheless, the end of slavery in the United States had permanently changed the landscape for all black North Americans and ushered in a new if brief sense of optimism.

The black veterans were not alone in facing complex decisions about how to spend the remainder of their lives. The war and American emancipation had transformed the way in which many black North Americans viewed their world. African Americans who had sought sanctuary in the British colonies before the war now had new reasons to return to their country of birth. Those who remained in the United States no longer conceived of British North America as a preferable society. Before the Civil War, black migrants had flowed north, but emancipation reversed that trend and enticed them south. For black British North Americans, the post-war United States opened up attractive new economic and professional opportunities. The Fourteenth Amendment, ratified in 1868, not only ensured national citizenship for all African Americans but also enabled African Canadians to become naturalized American citizens.

The transformative social changes unleashed by the war altered the lives of thousands of black North Americans in multiple ways. They reversed the long pattern of northward black migration, as is indicated by the Canadian and US censuses of the post-war decades, which chronicle an extended restructuring in the new Dominion of Canada's black population. African Americans ceased moving north in significant numbers, and African Canadians increasingly explored life in the United States. The resultant demographic changes in the black communities are most evident in Ontario, although they also occurred in the Maritimes. In 1861, the official enumerated black population of Nova Scotia and New Brunswick had stood at 5,927 and 1,581 respectively.[1] Ten years later, and five years after the Civil War, the figure for Nova Scotia had edged up to 6,212, an increase of just over 5 percent. In New Brunswick, it had reached 1,701, reflecting a 7 percent rise from the previous census. The number who gave the United States as their birthplace remained small – 196 in Nova Scotia and only 60 in New Brunswick.[2] By contrast, the general population of the two provinces had grown by approximately 17 percent for Nova Scotia and 13 percent for New Brunswick. Ten years later, in 1881, the black population of Nova Scotia totalled 7,062, an increase of over 13 percent, whereas in New Brunswick it declined by almost 4 percent to 1,638.[3]

Harvey Amani Whitfield has identified three critical developments in the black community, at least for Nova Scotia, that became evident by the late 1860s. The black population had become increasingly isolated from mainstream society, in part because of a long history of racial snubs and insults. At the same time, it received diminishing government attention. The second development involved the religious life of the black community. After the death of Richard Preston in 1861, the African Baptist Association endured a schism of almost two decades, when James Thomas, a white minister, became its head. The third trend, which was clearly influenced by the other two, was an increased migration of black Nova Scotians to the northeastern United States.[4] At the end of the century, Rufus Lewis Perry explained why some black residents left Halifax: "The United States with her faults, which are many, has done much for the elevation of the coloured race. She has given to the race Professors in Colleges, Senators, Engineers, Doctors,

Lawyers, Mechanics of every description. Sad and sorry are we to say that is more than we can boast of here in Nova Scotia." Perry believed that even ambitious mechanics had "to go to the United States to prosecute their mechanical skills."[5]

Farther west, Anderson Abbott saw the same pattern of migration, and for many of the same reasons. "The younger generation saw few opportunities for advancement open to them," he reflected late in the century, "and they naturally sought more favorable environments across the border."[6] He stressed, however, that young white residents were also migrating. In Ontario, the decades after the Civil War saw a significant decline in the black population, although scholars disagree regarding its magnitude. Their stance depends on which population number is accepted for 1861. The 1861 census enumerators identified 17,053 black residents, whereas the published figure gave only 11,223; as the former total seems most accurate, using it in comparison with other census returns seems logical.[7] The published returns for Ontario's 1871 census recorded a black population of just 13,435, but this time, as current research indicates, virtually all the individuals whom the enumerators listed were included in the official figure. Of that figure, only 5,824, or 43 percent of the black population enumerated, claimed "origin" in the United States.[8] The number of US-born black residents had diminished by 14 percent.[9] A decade later, the official census tally of black residents had dropped to 12,097. Thus, between 1861 and 1871, Ontario's black population declined by more than 22 percent and dropped a further 11 percent during the next decade, a pattern that stands in sharp contrast with the slow growth of its counterpart in the Maritimes. Moreover, other evidence supports the argument that black out-migration from Ontario, though not an "exodus," was significant, spanning several decades and involving Canadian-born individuals as well as African Americans who were returning to the United States.

The key factor driving the demographic change was not so much that African Americans were returning south, for some had done so almost as soon as they reached British North America. Rather, it was the fact that after 1865, there was virtually no influx of African Americans while the out-migration of African Canadians grew. Of course, other Americans were reluctant to move north after the Civil War. Between 1871 and 1881, Ontario added only two thousand residents, white or black, who claimed to have been born in the United States. For the rest of the century, few blacks entered Canada, a fact partly due to government policy. From 1870 to 1939, only about 5,000 of the 1.8 million new immigrants who came to Canada were African Americans or West Indians.[10]

Developments at Buxton, the most successful of the pre-war black communities, afford a good example of the demographic changes following the war. From 1861 to 1871, its black population dropped slightly, from 700 to just under 650. The decline accelerated through the 1870s and 1880s, as residents left, most for cities in the United States but some for other places in Canada.[11] Some of Buxton's black veterans were part of this move. After being discharged from the army, Lorenzo Rann returned to Buxton, married, and relocated to Michigan during the 1870s. Kincheon Brooks also returned to Buxton, only to leave for the United States following the death of his wife. In 1890, he was living in Richmond, Indiana. By contrast, his Canadian-born brother, Benjamin, remained in the United States and only occasionally visited his birthplace.[12]

Other immigrants, both white and black, left British North America, or the Dominion of Canada as it became in 1867, to explore new opportunities in the United States. For many black residents, the end of slavery and the repeal of much discriminatory state legislation eliminated the factors that had forced them to move north. At the same time, a brief period of greater optimism among all black North Americans fuelled hopes that race relations in the United States had entered a new and better era. The prospect of a brighter future and greater economic opportunities encouraged hundreds of African Canadians to move south. As a result, the number of black Canadian-born residents in the United States increased from approximately 1,200 in 1860 to about 3,600, as reported in the 1870 census.

Among this group were many black soldiers and sailors who had left British North America to fight in the war. As they mustered out of service, they made a series of crucial choices. Should they remain in the United States and create new lives, or should they go home? To get a sense of their decisions, the 1870 United States and 1871 Canadian censuses were searched for references to them.[13] Experienced researchers know that attempting to link specific individuals across censuses is a difficult and time-consuming task. The effort to link the black veterans to the two censuses yielded limited but nonetheless useful results. Among the navy veterans, only 10 percent could be identified in either census, perhaps because of the nature of their occupation. Men born in the Maritimes were more likely to have returned home than those from Ontario. Over 16 percent of sailors from Nova Scotia and 6 percent of those from New Brunswick could be identified; virtually all were living in their home provinces. Among the 7 percent of Canada West sailors who could be positively identified in the censuses, slightly more than half had returned home. The remainder were scattered across the United

States, from Brooklyn and Chicago to Brownsville, Texas, and Oakland, California. A common pattern among almost all naval veterans was that they had taken up non-maritime occupations. Only two were still working on the water – Thomas Smith as a "fisherman" in Guysborough, Nova Scotia, and William Thomas as a "sailor" in Dunnville, Ontario, at the head of a Welland "feeder" canal. In neither case did their occupation entail extended maritime voyages.

A larger number of the soldiers who survived the war, some 213 individuals, could be linked with a high degree of certainty to the later censuses.[14] Only 27.5 percent of all veterans could be found, but the percentage from the Maritimes was higher than that from the Canadas. Indeed, almost 60 percent of the Nova Scotian soldiers who mustered out at the end of the war were found in the censuses, and of these 28 men, all but 5 had returned to their province of birth. Approximately 20 percent of the New Brunswickers were listed in the censuses, and only 3 of the 9 were living in the United States. Locating the Canadian-born veterans was more difficult, and they were far more likely to remain in the United States. About 25 percent of them were found in the censuses; of these, 45 percent had stayed in the United States, whereas 55 percent had returned to their province of birth.

Many men who remained in the United States were scattered widely. W. Henry Williams, a sailor from "Canada" who joined the Third United States Colored Troops (USCT) in January 1865, was living in Lafayette, Louisiana, in 1870, where he was teaching school.[15] John Talbot had been a cook when he left Canada West in December 1863 to enlist in the Twentieth USCT. He was a sergeant by the time he was mustered out but was working as a labourer in Stockdale, California, in 1870.[16] George Caples, a naval veteran from Canada West, was also living in California by the 1880s.[17] Thomas Brooks left Canada West in October 1864 and enlisted in the 102nd USCT. In 1870, he was residing in Savannah, Georgia, where he earned his living as a fisherman.[18] These men had relocated farther from home than most. A majority of the veterans who remained in the United States were living in states adjacent to Canada. Wherever they ended up, however, few had significantly improved their occupational level. Most were labourers, farmers, or farm hands, or were engaged in the traditional service industries as waiters, servants, cooks, and barbers.[19]

Although many white residents of the British colonies, like many Americans, either never knew of or quickly forgot the black veterans' contribution to the Union victory, the veterans themselves and senior American military leadership did not. The soldiers had proved both their worth to the

This photograph (date unknown) of George Caples was submitted as part of his veteran's pension application in the 1890s, when he was living in California.
Courtesy of the National Archives and Records Administration.

Union army and their commitment to the cause of emancipation, equality, and the preservation of the republic. Shortly after the Civil War, as testament to their now accepted value, the War Department created four black regiments as part of the regular army's permanent establishment – the Ninth and Tenth Cavalry Regiments and the Twenty-fourth and Twenty-fifth Infantry Regiments.[20] During the subsequent decades, the army would offer black recruits a work environment that, though harsh and undervalued by the standards of civilian society, provided a greater degree of equality than most forms of civilian employment. Some Civil War veterans from British North America, such as George H. Brown of Halifax and Isaac Maynard of "Canada," took advantage of that opportunity and became buffalo soldiers.[21]

Wartime service had also created strong emotional bonds between the men who served together. Many veterans, especially those who joined the Grand Army of the Republic (GAR), the largest post-war veterans' organization, found these ties to be an important part of their lives long after the war was over. Whether they remained in the United States or returned to their home provinces, many Canadian veterans, black and white, joined the GAR. Founded in 1866 by Civil War veterans, it was open to everyone who had served in the Union army or navy during the war.[22] Reaching a peak membership in 1890, the GAR, whose cardinal principles were fraternity, charity, and loyalty, became an effective advocate for a more expansive and generous pension policy for Union veterans.[23] Local posts, the basic unit of the GAR, reported to a department commander who generally represented one state and who reported to a national body. During its existence, the GAR created thousands of posts, some of which were international.[24] Although GAR membership was open to all Union army and navy veterans, whether black or white, earlier studies have argued that most blacks had to join all-black posts.[25] In a new study of black and white comradeship in the GAR, Barbara Gannon persuasively demonstrates that although black veterans still dealt with racial prejudice, the GAR treated its black comrades with a degree of equality uncommon elsewhere in white society. Far from being the exception in the GAR, as Gannon found, the integrated posts (467) more than doubled the all-black posts (222).[26]

British North American veterans established at least eight GAR posts in Quebec, Manitoba, and Ontario, several of which became integrated.[27] It is difficult to know how many of their members were black because, unlike most other organizations at the time, the GAR was officially colour-blind in its record keeping. As well, the records for many Canadian posts no longer exist. However, membership in the GAR, perhaps the most racially progressive fraternal society in nineteenth-century North America, provides another insight into the lives of a few black veterans. There is convincing evidence that the Ontario posts were not only integrated but also willing to appoint black members to prominent leadership roles. Toronto's James S. Knowlton Post, No. 532, which was chartered under the Department of New York, was integrated, and in 1892 at least three of its forty-three members were black, two of whom held major offices.

Albert R. Garrison was appointed chaplain of the James S. Knowlton Post, and Anderson Abbott was its surgeon.[28] Garrison, an African American who had moved to Toronto before the war, served in the Union navy for four years and subsequently returned to Toronto, where he worked as a barber and lived on Queen Street West. He remained active in the GAR until his death in 1904.[29] Abbott's influence extended beyond his Toronto post. His 1892 appointment as aide-de-camp to the commander of the Department of New York spoke to the willingness of the GAR to include black veterans in meaningful positions. All new members, both black and white, had to be elected, which meant that a handful of racists could block the acceptance of a black candidate.[30] Moreover, had the GAR been prejudiced against Abbott due to his colour, it could very easily have denied him membership because, as a contract surgeon, he was not technically a Union army veteran. Nevertheless, he was given full membership in the post and its white veterans valued his presence. Abbott claimed that in the 1890s, probably 150 veterans lived in Toronto alone but that "a good many veterans are deterred from joining these posts from the fear that, in some way, they may compromise their citizenship."[31] Unfortunately, Abbott provided only limited information concerning the workings of his post or about its third black member, "Corporal Brown, 7th USCT."[32]

The William W. Cooke Post, No. 472, one of the two GAR posts in Hamilton, was also integrated. By 1891, when the *Hamilton Spectator* began to cover its Decoration Day ceremonies, its membership had dwindled to twenty-six. On 30 May, the veterans marched to the Burlington cemetery and, after prayers and an address from the post commander, laid flowers on the graves of their former comrades. One veteran thus honoured in 1891 and later years was Nelson Stevens, a private in the Twenty-fifth USCT who had died in 1890.[33] Originally from Virginia, he had settled in Hamilton, where he worked as a labourer before enlisting in Buffalo on 23 February 1865. After being discharged from the army, he spent the rest of his life in Hamilton.[34]

Many British North American veterans chose to stay in the United States after the war and frequently joined GAR posts there. Glimpses of their participation in the GAR appear occasionally in the records that they left behind. John W. Price, a sailor who was born in Halifax and who had served three years in the Union navy, was one such veteran. Working as a barber in Boston when he enlisted, he remained in Massachusetts after the war. For many years he was a member of the integrated C.C. Phillips Post in Hopkinton, Massachusetts, where he lived. In 1904, when Price applied for a pension, post commander John T. Wilson provided a testimony on his behalf: "I was well acquainted with the said John W. Price, he being Quartermaster of my post No. 14 G.A.R. (C.C. Phillips Post) and amongst the best whoever filled the office. He was very nearly white in appearance and in speech fully so. But we all knew he belonged to and was looked upon as one of the colored race."[35]

Although the number of black veterans in the Canadian GAR posts was never high, their mere presence was an important indicator of how their white comrades perceived them. Their visibility in the various posts, especially during public activities, and the speeches they gave to larger GAR meetings, helped shape the collective memory of contemporary Canadians and Americans to at least partially recognize black contributions and sacrifices in the Civil War.

Canadian black veterans received more than just the psychological benefits of shared comradeship in the GAR. They were also eligible for US government pension benefits that expanded over the years, in part because the GAR lobbied long and vigorously on behalf of all Union veterans.[36] In implementing the various pension acts, the government understood that white and black veterans held equal claim to benefits. Unfortunately, although the pension legislation used racially neutral language, its actual implementation often worked against black applicants. A sample study of pension applications across the United States revealed that white veterans (92 percent) were more likely than black veterans (74 percent) to be granted a pension.[37] This discrepancy was even larger for black dependants who applied for pensions. Many black applicants were illiterate and very poor, and had less access to the necessary documents, facts that partially explain why fewer managed to obtain a pension. In one case, William Gibson, a former slave from Kentucky who was resident in Canada West when he enlisted in the Fifty-fourth Massachusetts, explained the difficulty of establishing his date of birth. "There is no public, church or bible record of my birth," he testified.[38] Moreover, the bureaucratic problems were exacerbated by the tendency of pension officials to let racial attitudes determine the disposition of cases.[39] If an applicant were to succeed, both he and his witnesses had to be accepted by the officials as trustworthy and honest, a key factor that could be influenced by subtle biases.

Nevertheless, in the decades after the war, any veteran who had been wounded or incapacitated in various ways by his military service could apply for a federal pension. The first pension laws, passed in 1862, granted pensions to disabled soldiers based on the nature and severity of their war-related wounds, whereas subsequent legislation broadened the qualifications. In 1873, a new act accepted disabilities caused by conditions and diseases contracted during military service but that only later produced impairment. GAR lobbying led to a major change in the pension laws of 1890, which now encompassed many more veterans who were deemed incapable of manual labour. The Disability Pension Act of that year "allowed veterans to claim for disabilities unrelated to military service so long as they were not the product of vicious habits or gross carelessness" and reduced the necessary service time to just ninety days.[40] Veterans who had never requested a pension now took action. When pension officials asked Augustus Anderson, a sailor from "British America," why he had not applied before, he replied, "Because I considered I was not entitled to it," and added, "While I had what I considered rheumatism in the Navy, I cannot prove it so I never applied."[41] Anderson's attitude was common. However, in 1904, the system was effectively turned into an old age pension system for all Union soldiers, when President Theodore Roosevelt issued Executive Order No. 78, which declared that old age itself was a disability as defined by the 1890 act. Three years later, Congress sustained his argument and incorporated the applicant's age as a factor in determining pension rates.[42]

The constantly evolving pension system, with new acts and new interpretations of existing laws, meant that the terms and conditions for receiving a pension were continually altering while the benefits grew significantly. The changes and the large sums involved spawned a plethora of US claims agents and lawyers who sought out potential pensioners and promised to handle their applications on a contingency fee basis. The result, by the turn of the century, was a dramatic increase in applications from men who asserted their eligibility and a growing popular concern that the system was rife with corruption and fraudulent claims.[43] Verifying the claims of applicants, assessing the veracity of supporting testimonies, and reaching medical consensus regarding how a disability should be rated meant that the process was highly subjective.[44] Not surprisingly, the skepticism directed at many applicants who were seen as pawns of unscrupulous agents mirrored contemporary assumptions about class and race. Perhaps as a result, pension officials were predisposed to distrust a black veteran such as Spencer Watts, who served in the 102nd USCT, because they questioned the ethics of his lawyer.[45]

By 1890, all veterans, regardless of the reasons for their infirmities, who had served honourably in the Union army or navy for ninety days were equally eligible for pensions, and thus many British North American–born veterans applied for and received them. The application process and that for obtaining a periodic increase generated extensive files of diverse information about the service, health, and marital status of veterans and their families. The files offer tantalizing glances into their post-war lives but should not be seen as representing all black veterans. Successful applicants had their own particular characteristics, and the picture that they presented of themselves should be viewed cautiously. For one thing, creating a sympathetic narrative for the

Pension Office led many to exaggerate their disabilities and destitution. Perhaps on the advice of agents, they employed the strategy of emphasizing their poverty and the extent of their injuries and illnesses, giving the impression that all or most veterans were desperately poor and physically infirm.

Moreover, though many British North American–born veterans, both black and white, received pensions, the successful applicants were drawn most heavily from those who had remained in the United States after the war and who applied for their benefits through local agents. Information about their pension rights was more readily available to them, knowledgeable attorneys were eager to help, and they had easier access to the medical boards that reviewed their health.[46] Those who had returned home could encounter significant obstacles, as was true of Joseph D. Crowell, a sailor from Windsor, Nova Scotia, who was required to submit testimony on his behalf from former shipmates. In his affidavit, he claimed, "I have been quite unable to learn the whereabouts or address of any of them. In the prosecution of my inquiries, I expended considerable sums of money and spent six days in the city of Boston." Despite all his efforts, Crowell managed to find just one shipmate.[47]

Other applicants had to explain apparent contradictions in their military records. William H. Hardy, who was born in St. Catharines but who moved to New York as a child, experienced difficulty in establishing that he had indeed served on the USS *Anacostia* for a year. His height was a problem. When he enlisted as a landsman in June 1864, he was five foot six, but when he applied for a pension in the late 1890s, he was five foot eight. Hardy had to persuade the Pension Office that, despite what his enlistment form said, he had been younger than nineteen when he joined up and thus had not stopped growing. His application did not succeed until 1909. He was receiving twelve dollars a month when he died at the Buffalo Emergency Hospital in May 1916.[48]

Even after they secured their pensions, veterans living in Canada sometimes had trouble getting the increased benefits offered by new legislation. Albert R. Garrison was a four-year veteran of the Union navy who had travelled to England after the war and returned permanently to Toronto in 1869. He began receiving his pension in 1890 and managed to have his monthly benefits increased from twelve dollars to twenty-four dollars in 1901. However, when he applied for another increase in 1903, he was told that he would have to appear before a board of physicians in Buffalo. In a letter to the Pension Office, Garrison explained his predicament:

I send you this letter it is imposbull for me to go to Buffalo as I am to week and not able to be trusted from home instead of getting better I am getting worse all the time So I will let it drop as I feel to sick to bother with it any more I will do the best I can without it.

Following the advice of pension officials, Garrison was able to get local physicians to testify before the US consul in Toronto concerning his physical state. In March 1904, his pension was increased to thirty dollars a month, but he died in Toronto only five months later.[49]

Often the pension records provide only fragmentary images of complex lives. Such is the case for Joel Monroe (or Munroe), who joined the Twenty-ninth Connecticut Regiment in September 1864 at the age of thirty-seven or thirty-four. At his enlistment, he gave his birthplace simply as "Canada."[50] In fact, he was born in Oro Township, Simcoe County, Canada West.[51] His brother, Nelson Monroe, testified that Joel had been married in Oro before the Civil War but that his wife and child had died about a year after the wedding.[52] Perhaps the loss of his family prompted Monroe to leave Oro and join the Union army, but he was silent on his motives. He received the first installment of the standard three-hundred-dollar bounty when he enlisted, but since he was also credited as a "voluntary recruit for Middletown, 2nd Congressional District, Conn.," he may have been paid additional local bounties. He was with his regiment in October 1864 for the battles of Darbytown Road and Kell House in Virginia, but there is no record that he suffered injury. Then, after General Robert E. Lee surrendered his army, the Twenty-ninth Connecticut, as part of the all-black Twenty-fifth Corps, was transferred west to the Texas–Mexico border.

Although Monroe had avoided injury, he endured a serious illness in Texas and spent more than a month in the Brownsville hospital.[53] After being discharged from the army in October 1865, he stayed in the United States, married Matilda Robinson, and lived in New Haven, Connecticut. Years later, however, he returned to Collingwood by himself, where he died in his brother's house on 13 April 1890. We can only speculate as to why he returned to Ontario. The pension that he applied for was never officially approved, although his wife, who remained in Connecticut, received one after his death.[54]

Many black veterans who returned to British North America may never have known that they were eligible for benefits. Those who did apply dealt with many other bureaucratic obstacles beyond the higher cost of submitting their applications. Indeed, the fact that they obtained a pension is a testament to their perseverance. Only about 10 percent of black sailors applied for a pension and only two of the successful applicants lived in Canada.[55] A larger number of soldiers applied, perhaps because more of them were either living in the United States or had closer ties with people there. Such factors ensured that the vast majority of successful applications submitted by British North American–born veterans came from men who remained in the United States.

Those who lived in the United States had certain obvious advantages. They had the best chance of learning about the pension laws and their subsequent revisions, information that would have been relayed by newspapers, politicians, GAR members and posts, and a network of fellow veterans.[56] Numerous attorneys and agents were keen to help them draft applications in ways that would maximize their likelihood of success. Such was not the case for most veterans who returned to Canada. Of course, we cannot know whether their failure to apply reflects lack of knowledge or a decision to refrain from doing so.

The efforts of Augustus Anderson, a veteran who remained in the United States, illustrate how much time and assistance were needed to submit a successful pension application. After the new pension legislation was passed in 1890, Anderson, who was living in New York, heard about the revisions and went to the office of A.P. Lloyd, a lawyer, to have him file a claim. As Anderson noted, in addition to Lloyd and his two clerks, the office retained a "squire who swore me also several col'd men. I can't recall the names of any one I met there except Lloyd." After asking Anderson about his service and his health, Lloyd wrote out the claim, indicating that the veteran was suffering from "rheumatism, dis. of lungs, throat, eyes and ears, and affliction of right arm and dizziness."[57] Anderson was then told to find two of his old navy shipmates and obtain their testimony, a task that would have been somewhat easier in a major American seaport. Although he eventually managed to achieve this, it took him "some months after the application."

Once the paperwork was submitted, Lloyd kept Anderson informed of developments. In early 1891, the lawyer told him to appear before the Pension Examination Board of Surgeons at the Customs House, which would evaluate his physical condition and rate his alleged disabilities. Examination boards were established in various US cities, and veterans were required to appear before the closest one for assessment. For veterans outside the United States, this requirement caused considerable difficulty and increased costs.

Anderson made a series of visits to Lloyd's office during the next few months, including one to complete an affidavit regarding his naval service, although he was vague about exactly who was in the office at the time and who had co-signed his various forms. In the winter of 1893-94, he again appeared before the examination board. "I think I made one or two visits to Lloyd's office after that and was sworn to papers by the same squire" whose office was a few doors from Lloyd's. During these years, Anderson contacted at least six people who knew him and had them appear at Lloyd's office to give formal statements about his service, background, health, and marriage. A special investigator from the Pension Office interviewed Anderson in 1894 about his application process and some of the inconsistencies in his file. If the process was difficult, time consuming, and expensive for Anderson in New York, it was much more so in Canada. Shortly after Anderson initiated it, and as many veterans tried to take advantage of the 1890 pension act, Congress took steps to limit who could apply. A March 1893 act approved by Congress provided "that from and after July 1st, 1895, no pension shall be paid to a non-resident, who is not a citizen of the United States, except for actual disabilities occurred in the service."[58] The act, later repealed, disqualified many Canadians who had returned home but who might otherwise have applied for benefits in the 1890s.

With the aid of pension attorneys, successful applicants crafted their claims in a formulaic way to satisfy what were seen as the expectations of officials. Very quickly, ailments that were difficult to disprove and that officials generally accepted became suspiciously common on applications. Financial destitution and the severity of disabilities were accentuated, or inflated. Moreover, judging the health of a veteran or the extent to which his disabilities impaired his capacity to work was highly subjective. When it came to rating degree of disability, doctors often radically disagreed, as was the case for Samuel Duncan. He left London, Canada West, to join the Fifty-fourth Massachusetts in late April 1863 and was wounded by a Confederate sharpshooter at the Battle of Honey Hill, during "which action he displayed great bravery." His record indicates that "the ball entered the left side of the neck passed downward to the right & was cut out below the right scapula." One surgeon judged that his ability to perform manual labour had been reduced by one-third. A second surgeon reported that Duncan could "raise right arm no higher than shoulder" and rated his disability at one-half. A third surgeon claimed that "the right arm is almost useless. He cannot raise it from the shoulder, it hanging by his side."[59] For all these reasons, statements about a veteran's deteriorating health or inability to work had to be assessed carefully.

The wives and mothers of black servicemen often had an even more difficult time in obtaining pensions than the veterans themselves. Under most pension regulations, a female dependant was eligible to claim benefits only if she "was without any other means of support than her daily labor."[60] Establishing dependency could be problematic, as the story of Hannah Weeks demonstrates. Her son, John Weeks, had given up his job as a cook in Chatham to join the Union army, and when he enlisted in Company E, Fifty-fourth Massachusetts, on 14 April 1863, he was among the company's first recruits. He was nineteen. Three months later, following the Fifty-fourth's famous and bloody 18 July assault on Fort Wagner, he was reported missing.[61] He was never seen again. Hannah Weeks did not apply for a mother's pension until November 1871, when she was sixty-five, although her reasons for delay are not specified.

Initially, as a resident of Chatham, she tried to apply under the pension act of July 1862 by submitting to the Pension Office a document sworn before the clerk for the County of Kent.[62] She did, however, indicate that she had retained Eugene Fecht of Detroit as her American attorney "to prosecute this her Claim before the proper Department." Having heard nothing by early 1872, she wrote the commissioner of pensions to inquire about her submission and to emphasize that she was "entirely destitute of support from anyone, and was dependent on support from my late son John." Aware of the difficulty of applying from Chatham, she then travelled to Detroit and signed an article of agreement with Fecht, who would, for a fee of twenty-five dollars, handle her subsequent application. In May, she heard back from the Pension Office, which rejected her original supporting evidence as unsatisfactory and listed the material that required re-submission. To prove her claim that John had supported her financially, she had to obtain "the testimony of persons by whom he was employed or to whom he made payments for rent, fuel, provisions and clothing." She also had to submit testimony from people who had seen her receive money from John after he had enlisted. Alternatively, she could include letters from John to the same effect. These statements, which were to be explicit as to dates and amounts, must "detail minutely all the particulars."

The requirements of the Pension Office were extensive and specific. The testimony of the family physician, outlining the father's previous and current disabilities, was also necessary. Furthermore, the Pension Office added, the "credibility and professional standing of the physician must be certified by an examining surgeon of this office." The expectation that the Weeks family and other very poor families could afford a regular physician may not have been reasonable. Certainly, how these demands were to be satisfied and who would pay the costs were not clear to Hannah Weeks. There were two final requirements. "The celibacy of the son must be shown," and Weeks and two witnesses had to testify if John had been seen since the Fort Wagner assault. Whether Hannah Weeks was able to submit the required paperwork is unknown. She died before the Pension Office made its final decision.[63]

The application of a widow, Mary E. Bailey, illustrates a different range of problems facing some women. Her husband, Gideon H. Stump, was a twenty-six-year-old sailor from Kent County, Canada West, who enlisted at Lockport, New York, on 15 September 1864 and served in the Sixth USCT. He apparently was a good soldier, for he was promoted to corporal in January 1865. After he was mustered out in Wilmington, North Carolina, in September 1865, he remained in the United States, moving to Ypsilanti, Michigan, and then to Braidwood, Illinois.[64] By the time he reached Braidwood, he had changed his surname to Bailey and married Mary E. Cook – the second marriage for both of them. After several unsuccessful applications, he received a pension of four dollars a month in 1884. He subsequently applied for pension increases and was receiving twelve dollars a month when he died in Seattle in 1905. Mary E. Bailey had considerable difficulty in generating the necessary evidence to support her subsequent pension claim. Like many widows who married veterans well after the war, she was vague about his military service and knew nothing about his early life. Moreover, she herself had been a slave before the war and could neither read nor write; as she testified, she had "always depended on her husband to do the writing and correspondence." Although she had "tried to find some one that could testify to the death of her husband's first wife," she had been unable to do so. As was sometimes the case with African American applicants who had difficulty providing documentation, the Pension Office displayed some flexibility.[65] It accepted the testimony of her minister, and she was able to obtain a pension. When she died in 1922, she was receiving twenty dollars a month.

Nettie Going also had great difficulty in finding credible witnesses to prove the legitimacy of her marriage to a veteran. Her husband, Samuel H. Going, was born in Chatham in 1845 and was working as a carpenter when he enlisted in the 102nd USCT late in the war. After he was mustered out in September 1865, he stayed in the United States and moved west. He and Nettie, who was part Sioux, were married in Cheyenne, Wyoming, in May 1870, and they lived in Fort Robinson, Nebraska, and at the Pine Ridge Indian Agency in South Dakota. Long after Samuel died in 1884, Nettie Going began an application for a widow's pension under the act of 19 April 1908.[66] Four years later, her submission was still incomplete as she tried to find the necessary witnesses and answer all the Pension Office's questions. She never received a pension.

Hattie White, who was married to a Brantford man, encountered a different problem with the Pension Office. John White, her husband, was born in Brantford in 1844, where he worked as a shoemaker. In late 1863, he left Canada West and enlisted in the Fifty-fourth Massachusetts. When the war ended and the regiment was mustered out, he returned home to Brantford.[67] In 1880, his first wife died, and he married Hattie in Windsor four years later. When he died in October 1894 of an "apoplectic fit," he and Hattie were living in Detroit, and he was receiving a small pension for "disease of eyes and rheumatism." Hattie then applied for and received a widow's pension of twelve dollars a month, based in part on the fact that John had owned no property at the time of his death. A decade later, however, the Pension Office dropped her from its roll of widow pensioners due to her "open and notorious violation" of the pension act. It had acquired evidence that Hattie was living with another man, Jim Farrell. A neighbour, William Spencer, testified that "it was generally known they were living together as man and wife but I never saw them in bed together." However, he had heard Farrell boast that "he didn't have to work unless he wanted to as his woman Hattie White got a pension." Spencer also testified that when "Mrs. White gets her pension money, Farrell usually gets drunk." Although the file contained no evidence that Farrell was supporting Hattie financially, pension officials believed that she was probably living in a "sporting house." Hattie White lost her pension in May 1904.[68]

Only a few children of black soldiers applied for pensions, but they too had trouble with the Pension Office. Joseph Robinson was a twenty-five-year-old farmer from Lachute, Canada East, who enlisted in March 1864 and was assigned to Company A, Eleventh United States Colored Heavy Artillery.[69] At the time, he received sixty dollars from his three-hundred-dollar bounty and a one-month advance on his pay, perhaps indicating that he wanted to leave money with his wife.[70] A few months later, he joined the regiment in Louisiana and served with it for the remainder of the war. Once he was discharged, he returned to Lachute and his wife. They had two sons, in 1871 and 1875. Five years later, in March 1880, Robinson died of complications following a surgical procedure in Boston. He had undergone an operation for piles, only to contract tetanus as a result. A subsequent pension application in 1887 on behalf of his two sons argued that because he had contracted the piles as a result of being in the army, his death was a direct result of his military service.

Records of his time in New Orleans show that he was often sick but that the diagnosis, when entered in the regimental records, was only for "remit. fever" or "Anemia."[71] Although the mayor of Lachute, James Fish, supported the young boys' application, the pension officials ultimately rejected it without explaining why.

By the turn of the century, the sums paid to pensioners generally ranged from two to twelve dollars a month, with the severely injured being allotted thirty dollars.[72] Although the money would have been crucial for the truly destitute, veterans of modest means may have seen it as insufficient motivation to embark on the extended and onerous application process, especially if they lived outside the United States. Thus, the pension files create the image of men who were prematurely aging, desperately poor, and seriously infirm, an image that may not accurately depict the spectrum of black veterans. The same can be said for the women who appear in the files. No doubt most of the widows were poverty stricken, although some were accused of concealing adequate sources of income. Some veterans or their dependants who were eligible for a pension but comfortably off may have chosen not to bother applying. Others who were just scraping by did not do so until necessity forced them to act. Terry Ford, a sailor from Toronto, applied for a pension only in 1896, under the terms of the 1890 law. The Pension Office's special examiner interviewed Ford's attorney and relayed his statement "that he has known the claimant since 1880[,] that the latter has failed fast in recent years, is much disabled for labor, and the Claim't is a man of unusual correct life and habits."[73] Evidently, Ford did not consider applying for government money until his health began to fail badly and he could not support himself.

At the end of their military service, the vast majority of black veterans returned to lives that were largely anonymous. Few left personal records of their post-war experiences that would provide a sense of their world and the texture of their lives. However, the pension and other records do chronicle significant parts of a few careers; thus the four following vignettes could be created. These accounts do not pretend to be a representative sample or a full depiction of the average lives of most veterans but will hopefully give some indication of the diversity of their post-war experience.

Of all the black British North Americans examined, George H. Brown could perhaps make the best claim for being a dual citizen. Although he most frequently gave Halifax as his place of origin, as he did when he enlisted in the navy, he cited Boston when he dealt with the Metropolitan Life Insurance Company in the 1890s. He explained this apparent contradiction in a form filled out for the National Soldiers Home in Dunville, Illinois. He had in fact been born at sea while his mother was travelling between Boston and Halifax.[74] It is significant, therefore, that he chose to name Halifax as his birthplace, perhaps because that was where he grew up. Unlike many Maritimers who joined the Union navy (and despite the happenstance of his birth), Brown seems to have had little marine experience. If he was living in Massachusetts when he enlisted, the census enumerators missed him. Of course, they missed many British North American–born blacks who lived in the United States. On 25 November 1861, Brown signed up at the Boston rendezvous for three years and was rated a landsman. He gave his occupation as "waiter," although at other times in his life he said he was a barber. He was only seventeen when he went off to war.[75]

While in the navy, Brown served primarily on the USS *Sagamore*, a wooden screw steam gunboat attached to the East Gulf Blockading Squadron. Part of a blockade that stretched from Florida to Mississippi, the *Sagamore* participated in raids along the Gulf shore, targeting Confederate salt works, shipping, and stores of cotton. In April 1862, its crew captured Apalachicola, a Florida town, although what role Brown played is unknown. An active blockader, the *Sagamore* helped capture or destroy at least twenty sailing vessels as they attempted to avoid the blockade.[76] Brown would have been eligible for some prize money from the captured vessels, although his file is quiet on this topic. On 30 July 1864, he was mustered out of the navy, just a few months before the *Sagamore* was decommissioned.

By the start of 1865, Brown had decided to re-enter the war but this time as a soldier. He enlisted in Boston on 26 January and was mustered into Company A, Fifty-fifth Massachusetts, on 12 March 1865. At the time of his enlistment, he again gave his birthplace as Halifax and his occupation as waiter.[77] He was credited to the Massachusetts Sixth Congressional District and received an initial bounty payment of a hundred dollars, with the remaining two hundred due when he was mustered out of the army.[78] When he joined Company A in March, it was on duty just outside of Charleston, South Carolina. The city had surrendered to Union forces several weeks earlier, and though there were reports of enemy cavalry in the area, their target was rumoured to be African Americans who were trying to reach Union lines.[79] Over the next few weeks, the regiment skirmished sporadically with isolated Confederate cavalry units until the surrender of General Robert E. Lee's forces marked the end of most fighting in the East. After that, men of the regiment served as provost guards and garrison troops when they were not repairing railroads and protecting the newly freed African Americans, whereas many of its officers were detailed to help draft labour contracts between planters and freed slaves.[80] During this period, the men speculated whether they would be retained for their full three-year term or be discharged with the white Massachusetts troops. By August, they had learned that they were going home. On 29 August 1865, the regiment was mustered out in Charleston and then shipped back to Boston, where the men were formally discharged from the service before crowds of friendly supporters.[81]

After his discharge, Brown lived in Boston for two years. Apparently unsatisfied with civilian life, however, he re-entered the army in 1867. In the summer of 1866, Congress had created a number of permanent all-black regiments in the regular army. When they began recruiting in the fall of 1867, more than half of their volunteers were USCT veterans. Brown enlisted as one of the "original members" of the Tenth Cavalry Regiment and served in it for the next nine years as one of its famous buffalo soldiers.[82] His commanding officer described him as "a good and efficient soldier." By the time of his 1876 discharge, he had served five years as the quartermaster sergeant, a rank just below that of regimental sergeant major.[83] In his pension application, Brown indicated that after leaving the army he stayed in the Indian Territories for ten years before he moved back east in 1886, first to Kansas City and then to other eastern towns.[84]

Like many veterans, Brown married several times. A year after his discharge from the Fifty-fifth Massachusetts, he married Lucinda Hodge (née Johnson), and for a brief period the couple lived in Boston. In part, her premature death may have prompted his enlistment in the Tenth Cavalry. Years afterward, in 1896, he married Elisa E. Brom (née Thomas) in Burlington. At that time, he was about fifty-three years old and was receiving a pension. He married a final time in September 1907 to Lucy Mildred Brown, who had already married twice. They lived for three years in Milwaukee, where he apparently owned the barbershop in the National Soldiers Home. Their marriage was exceptionally unhappy. On 12 April 1911, he informed Lucy that he was going to visit a daughter in Chicago. He never returned.

Lucy Brown subsequently applied to the Pension Office for half of his twelve-dollar pension on the grounds that he had deserted her. A year later, the office informed her that George Brown had filed his own statement, which included a complete list of her shortcomings. During their marriage, Brown testified, she "did not do a day's work" and "began to accumulate flesh" shortly after their wedding, although he admitted this was due to an illness. More importantly, as he had told his wife, she was "a woman of ungovernable temper and if you could not find someone else to quarrel with, you would quarrel with the dog." His home had been a torment for two years, and his wife asserted that she was the boss and that he could do nothing around the house without her permission. He claimed that she would not cook his breakfast, that she withheld sex, and that when angry with him, she said she could do without him. The Pension Office concluded by noting "that if he [Brown] had stood this life longer, he would have gone insane; that if the day comes that you are willing to act like a wife, he will try you again; that you drove him away; and that you have roomers enough to make a living."[85] Pension officials gave Lucy Brown thirty days to submit a rebuttal. They also explained to her that "one cannot be deserted within the meaning of the said act while she or he consents to the separation, but the one who intentionally drives the other away is the deserter." In May 1913, only six months before George Brown's death, she submitted a form specifying that he had deserted her and seeking the amount of $37.50, or half of what he was to receive in 1913. The records do not reveal the outcome.[86]

Unlike George Brown, Benjamin Jackson remained bound to his Nova Scotia home throughout his life.[87] His brief service in the Union navy altered neither the general pattern of his life nor his self-identification. Jackson was born on 2 January 1835 in a log house at Horton Township, Nova Scotia, in an area later known as Lockhartville.[88] In 1851, when he was sixteen, he shipped out from Horton on the brig *Chalerodonia*.[89] Described as "a strong, stalwart young man," Jackson apparently enjoyed the life of a sailor, and he crewed on several voyages with Captain George King, a shipowner in Horton.[90] During the late 1850s, he stopped sailing for several years and married Rachel Carter of Windsor in January 1858.[91] Just a few years later, however, he returned to the sea. After several short voyages, in December 1863, he signed on as ship's cook with the captain of the *Marlborough*, based in Saint John, for a return voyage to Liverpool and New York.[92] In May 1864, while in New York, Jackson enlisted in the Union navy, although how or why he joined is the subject of dispute.

His obituary of 1915 claimed that his navy service was not voluntary. Instead, the writer alleged, "Benjamin was in a sailing vessel in New York, and while ashore one night was taken by force or conscription on board one of the U. S. battleships. Here he went under the assumed name of Lewis Saunders."[93] Stories of Canadian lads who were unwillingly pressed into navy service by predatory enlistment agents recurred during the twentieth century, but in Jackson's case, the tale was almost certainly not true. He himself supplied a different account on a pension form that he submitted in May 1879, as he explained to the Pension Office why he was cashing cheques made out to Lewis Saunders. He said that he had "enlisted as a substitute, and was enrolled as Lewis Saunders, for whom he was a substitute, instead of Benjamin Jackson, his own name."[94] During his time in the navy, he served under the name of Saunders.[95] Moreover, an auditor's report written in 1879 and included in Jackson's file verified that he had enlisted for three years as a substitute for Saunders.

In the pension records, Jackson did not indicate how much Saunders had paid him to act as a substitute, but he should have received at least three hundred dollars and probably more, plus local bounties.[96] He sent his bounty money to a justice of the peace in King's County, Nova Scotia, who later testified that "at the time that he enlisted and received his Bounty, he sent it to me and I gave it to his wife."[97] Jackson was able to sell his services as a substitute and to receive the local bounties because Congress had amended the Enrollment Act in February 1864 to allow "navy and marine enlistments to be credited to the locality of enrollment as part of the draft quota."[98]

Although Jackson had enlisted for three years, he was discharged from the navy in June 1865 due to his "chronic bronchitis of uncertain duration."[99] For several days in September 1864, he had joined a salvage crew, working in difficult conditions on the wreck of a blockade-runner. Shortly afterward, he developed bronchitis and was admitted to hospital. A month later, he was back in hospital after injuring his right hand and arm in an accident. Over time, this injury, or at least his description of it, became increasingly severe. In 1879, the Bureau of Medicine and Surgery reported that on 17 October 1864, "while mooring the 1st cutter astern, his fingers were caught between the side of the ship and the boat. The skin of the fingers broken and the flesh contused, no bones broken." On a surgeon's certificate of 1887, Jackson indicated that "he was wounded in hand (right) and right arm at battle of Fort Morgan." Three years later, he stated, "While assisting in raising a torpedo shell in the Mississippi river [I] was caught between towing boat and vessel severely crushing the right hand and arm and wounding the head – was unconscious for days." In 1892, he explained that his injury resulted from "the premature bursting of a torpedo, serious injury was done the right arm and hand, also contused wound of head." In 1898, his description was even more dramatic: "the right hand was dreadfully lacerated – portions of loose bone coming out – the forearm was much injured at the time, small pieces of bone coming out of it during the healing process."[100]

Although Jackson repeatedly revised his testimony, he may nonetheless have been seriously hurt. After all, he was discharged for disability before his term of service ended, and he later received a pension of four dollars a month,

After the war, Ben Jackson returned to Nova Scotia, where he worked as a sailor and then a purveyor of fresh fish and homegrown vegetables. A familiar sight around Lockhartville, Jackson is shown here with his horse, Jack. *Courtesy of the West Hants Historical Society.*

going back to his discharge of 1865. In effect, his pension was equivalent to losing half the use of his hand.[101] However, even the surgeons who examined him throughout the years differed significantly regarding the ranking of his injury. Some testified that his right arm was almost totally disabled, whereas others rated him as only partially incapacitated. This disagreement speaks to the highly subjective, and perhaps adversarial, nature of the disability rating system.

The very fact that Jackson was able to receive his pension from the United States government and get it periodically increased was due as much to his determination and perseverance as to his injuries and ailments. After leaving the navy, Jackson returned to Lockhartville and began crewing on Nova Scotia ships a few months later, often for voyages to Britain or the Mediterranean.[102] He continued going to sea until he was about forty, when he retired from work as a sailor and began a small business as a peddler.[103] In 1879, Jackson applied for an invalid pension, citing the injury to his right hand and arm. Under the Arrears Act of 25 January 1879, a veteran who was eligible for a pension could collect a lump sum payment dating back to the time of his discharge. For Jackson, whose pension was four dollars a month, the sum would have been more than six hundred dollars.

Before he could receive it, however, he had to convince the Pension Office that Benjamin Jackson of Nova Scotia was the Lewis Saunders who had served in the Union navy. Not only were his enlistment and discharge papers made out in the name of Lewis Saunders, but also the Pension Office records indicated that he had received prize money as Saunders and that while in the navy he had always been known by that name. Therefore, Jackson included in his May application a deposition from Daniel Crowell, a childhood friend and a sailor who had visited him on USS *Richmond*, that he was known there as Lewis Saunders. Despite the auditor's report, which indicated that he had signed on as a substitute for Saunders, the issue was raised virtually every time he made a new application for a pension increase. Jackson finally resolved all the Pension Office's doubts only in 1887, after he personally appeared before the American consul in Halifax, who ultimately notified the office that Saunders and Jackson were the same person and that Jackson was "a worthy man instead of a nuisance whenever he comes to town."[104]

Jackson was not the only Canadian pension applicant who was obliged to appear before the consul. Other veterans experienced difficulty getting the Pension Office to accept their documents, "which should be sworn before some officer authorized to administer oaths for general purposes." In fact, the office rejected some of Jackson's first testimonies; his paperwork was not "accepted as a valid declaration for the reason that it purports execution before a justice of the peace for the province of Nova Scotia, Canada – an officer who does not appear to have authority to administer oaths for general purposes." The solution, though time-consuming and costly, was to have the witnesses and justices of the peace appear before the consul in Halifax. One justice of the peace, W.H. Whitman of Hantsport, went to Halifax in 1911, where the consul gave him the following note: "I am pleased to hand you herewith, properly certified, the form sent you by the Bureau of Pensions regarding your official character as a justice of the peace." For Jackson, having the consul verify his paperwork was not the final hurdle; he still had to employ a pension agent in Washington, V.W. Tierney, to formally submit his application and charge him ten dollars.[105]

Canadian applicants had the further problem of satisfying the Pension Office requirement for medical examinations to determine their level of disability. The office had established boards of surgeons across the various states whose task was to assess pensioners and rate their disabilities according to a scale fixed by the Pension Office. In questionable cases, the board was to provide its opinion regarding the validity of the claim. After 1873, all pensioners were required to take a biennial exam unless exempted by a pension certificate.[106] For veterans who lived in Canada, where there were no boards, this stipulation created problems.

Jackson no doubt emphasized the extent to which his disability hampered his capacity to earn a living, but his description of his occupation in 1907, "Do some peddling in a small way, am partially blind," was probably accurate.[107] For Jackson and his family, the pension money made a critical difference. Thus, whenever a new law increased the benefits, he submitted an application. In 1888, his pension rose to $8 a month and to $10 in 1890. Two years later, he was allocated $14 a month. For more than a decade, he would receive at least $168 a year. Jackson's military service illustrates the opportunities and risks involved in joining the Civil War. In return for his navy service, he gained a substitute fee, prize money, and pension payments spanning almost fifty years that would have amounted to well over $5,000, if he received it all. On the other hand, he had risked death and incurred an injury that, at the very least, left him partially disabled for much of his eighty years.

In May 1913, Rachel Jackson, Ben's wife of fifty-five years, died. Fourteen months later, he married Mary Eliza Martin, a forty-nine-year-old widow whose husband had died at sea. Their union may have been one of convenience, as many aging pensioners married for that reason, trading the possibility of a widow's pension for assistance in their later lives.[108] If Mary Martin went to the altar in hopes of a pension, she was destined for disappointment. When Ben died in 1915, he was receiving twenty-four dollars a month. However, when Mary applied for a widow's pension, her submission was rejected. They wrote, "You were not married to the sailor prior to June 27, 1890, and have, therefore, no pensionable status under said act."[109] In a final indignity that further minimized Mary's role, Ben Jackson stipulated that he was to be buried beside Rachel, his wife of so many years.

For Isaiah F. Wilson, wartime service opened a new world. He was born in Brantford in 1842, where he was working as a labourer when the Union army began recruiting black soldiers. In April 1863, he travelled to Boston and joined the Fifty-fourth Massachusetts. He was with the regiment when it attacked Fort Wagner, but there is no indication that he was wounded during the assault. Less than a month later, he was selected for detached service as a "boatman" on the steamer *Planter*, a job that he held for several months. Though seemingly unimportant, his work on the boat helped shape his future. The rest of his military career was uneventful, at least according to his service records. Before his regiment mustered out in Charleston and sailed back to Boston for discharge, he spent some months in the smallpox hospital of the South Carolina city.[110]

Wilson's account of his subsequent life, submitted when he applied for a pension, is a fascinating tale of world travel and chronic pain. Whether other ailments besides smallpox put Wilson in the Charleston hospital is unknown, but he stated that after his discharge he suffered from "the Intermitten fever which struck me all winter, in the spring the fever left, but I was subject to pains in the thyes and between the shoulders." He would complain of these pains for most of his life. Instead of returning to Brantford after being mustered out of the army, he signed on for "a voyage in a merchant ship around to Panama and back," perhaps because of his shipboard experience in South Carolina. He spent much of the next two decades on various vessels, and most frequently, as he recounted, in considerable pain. After his second trip, from New York to Cuba and back, he was admitted to the Seamen's Retreat Hospital on Staten Island because, as he remembered, he "was full of pain from head to foot." In March 1869, feeling a little improved, he travelled to Boston, where he "applied to a herb Dr., on Cambridge St. ... who did me no good."

By the fall he was feeling somewhat better, and he "footed it from Boston to Providence where [he] took steamer to N. York joined ship as cook went to N. Orleans." By the time he reached New Orleans, the pain had returned and he "was forced to go to the Sisters Charity Hospital." After a time working as a cook and a steward in a coffee house, he returned to New York, a series of hospitals, and "the old folks collor'd home." Finally, in March or April 1871, he headed back to Brantford, although he did not reach it until early May. He may have been visiting his family in Brantford but did not stay long. Soon he was off to Buffalo, where he signed on as a deckhand on a trip to Detroit, but he left the steamer because of "excruciating pains" and went to an almshouse, "where [he] was kindly treated & sent back to N. York." By October 1872, he was back on the water, this time working as a cook on a barquentine bound for San Francisco. By 1874, Wilson's travels had taken him to Liverpool, where he again received medical treatment.

In May of that year, now an able-bodied seaman, he shipped out for Calcutta, where he spent a month in hospital, because, he said, his "pains were at all times Internal as well as External." After returning to Liverpool, he went to London and found a berth as an experienced sailor on a vessel bound for Georgetown in South Africa's Cape Colony. There, in 1877, he found a young doctor who gave him "two half ounce bottles of medicine which cured me for the time." Apparently, Wilson was relatively pain-free until 1886, when he was about forty-four years old and living in Philadelphia. He consulted several new doctors but with little result other than being told that "there was no cure." Finally, he found a physician, Dr. Fox of Frankford, who "gave me a remedy which cured me in a few days (he is long since dead) now before rain or in cloudy weather I feel very uncomfortable."[111] He continued to experience chronic pain until his death in early 1890.

The experiences of one woman who married a Civil War soldier capture many of the themes suggested by this study. Harriet A. Mulder was born in January 1846 in South Colchester Township, Essex County, and grew up there. In 1856, Benjamin Drew wrote that Colchester, a "beautiful farming town, on the north shore of Lake Erie, contains a population not far from 1,500, of whom about 450 are colored persons." However, few of them lived in the well-cleared farms along the lakeshore. Most were located farthest from the lake, where much of the land was uncultivated. Attractive though the town may have been, Drew feared that its black residents had "but few friends among the white settlers." What they did have was economic opportunity, for after talking with the black farmers, Drew concluded that "there is not one who cannot find work within a few hours after he gets here."[112]

Some time after 1845, John Nelson, a slave who had escaped from his owner in Louisville, Kentucky, when he was about fifteen, arrived in Canada West and had found employment in the town of Colchester by the 1850s. For parts of two winters, he attended school.[113] He worked in the neighbourhood of the Mulder home and got to know Harriet. Before 1859, he left Colchester and moved to Ypsilanti, a town just west of Detroit. He and Isaac Hardy, who was born and raised in South Colchester, had earlier gone to Ann Arbor to cut wood for two or three months during the winter. Like many other black migrants, they used the short work experience to explore the possibilities of a permanent move. They must have discovered opportunities in the region, for both subsequently moved to Ypsilanti. Members of the Mulder family had been considering a similar move, for in 1859, Harriet, who was only thirteen, "made a visit to my sister Rachel Bradford who was living at Ypsilanti, Mich."[114] Although Harriet did not say that the point of her visit was to be closer to John, she married him in Ann Arbor on 20 May 1860. Significantly, many of the wedding guests were originally from Colchester. John and Harriet were married in the home of Sarah Henderson, Harriet's former teacher in Colchester.[115] Also present were Emily Miller from Ann Arbor and Isaac Hardy, whom, Harriet testified, had been "raised with me."[116] Another guest, Ypsilanti resident Levi Simpson, had also known Harriet as a child.

Ypsilanti attracted black migrants from Chatham as well. George Bartlett, who worked as a teamster and labourer, was born in Chatham in 1840, where he lived until he moved to Ypsilanti in 1863. Shortly afterward, he met an old friend, Elias Rouse, and recorded, "I have known him since we were boys."[117]

After their marriage, Harriet and John Nelson lived in Ypsilanti for the next few years and had two children. Early in 1865, John enlisted in the Sixth USCT at Lockport, New York, and was credited to the Twenty-ninth Congressional District of New York. He may have chosen Lockport because its local bounty was $875. He enlisted under the name Alexander Carter and gave his place of birth as Canada. Why he did so is unclear. As a volunteer, he received no special benefit by claiming to be an alien. Of course, he may have feared that if he were captured by Confederate soldiers and his true background was discovered, he could be the target of reprisals and perhaps re-enslaved.

By enlisting as he did, his family could be provided for financially. The military service records indicate that when he signed up he received a hundred dollars, the first installment of his bounty, and was able to deposit eight hundred dollars with the paymaster.[118] Financial considerations aside, Nelson had an additional motive for joining the army. In 1909, Robert Hughbanks, then eighty years old, testified that in early 1865 John "was in prison, I believe in Ann Arbor as he lived in Ypsilanti, on account of some sheep and I think that the custom at that time was to liberate a certain class of prisoners who would enlist."[119]

After John left for the army, Harriet and her children moved back to Colchester to stay with her parents. A friend remembered that her father, John Mulder, had come to Ypsilanti and taken "John Nelson's team and brought her and two or three of their children to his home in Canada."[120] After Nelson was discharged from the army, he returned to Colchester, where he and his family lived for perhaps a decade.[121] Then, in the late 1870s, they moved back to the Ypsilanti area and remained there until his death in 1906. In June 1890, Nelson had applied for and ultimately received a pension. After his death, Harriet also submitted an application and was subsequently allocated a widow's pension. Many who testified on her behalf for her pension application, such as Margaret A. Crosby and James and Enoch Dennis, were all living in Detroit at the time but had grown up in Colchester and had known Harriet there.

The four individuals discussed above are not representative of black British North Americans, but the diversity of their experiences does give a sense of the complexity of the black community. For Benjamin Jackson, a year of navy service little altered the trajectory of his personal and occupational life, although it left him with extra finances and a physical disability. He remained closely rooted to the place where he was born and raised. For Isaiah Wilson, wartime service seems to have disengaged him from wider society. He never married and apparently spent much of his life searching for something that he never found, be it freedom from chronic pain or a place to belong. George Brown and Harriet Nelson offer two very different examples of British North Americans who were drawn into the larger American society. For Brown, unlike Jackson, Nova Scotia did not pull him home, and by the end of his career he was virtually indistinguishable from the African Americans around him. By contrast, Harriet Nelson and many of her relatives and friends became true transmigrants, mobile people who both created and sustained multiple social relations that crossed borders and served to connect their societies of origin and of residence.

Conclusion

From the late 1890s until his death in 1913, Anderson Abbott was an active Grand Army of the Republic (GAR) member, participating in the life of his post and giving speeches and toasts at a range of GAR gatherings. He took part in the national encampment at Buffalo, New York, in 1897, where the black residents of the city had erected an arch to welcome the GAR members, decorating it with the words, "They fought for the liberty we now enjoy."[1] This was a sentiment that Abbott and other black veterans would endorse. Throughout the years, his public addresses remained remarkably consistent, with only minor variations on what was essentially the same speech. His retrospective assessment of the causes of the war and the contributions made by Canadians reflected the attitude of a man near the end of his career who embraced the values of most Union veterans. He and his comrades saw themselves as a generation that had come of age, and come alive, during the bloody convulsions of the war. They had shared not only a common purpose but also a common set of values – courage, duty, service, a belief in the importance of the Union as a symbol of liberty, and a commitment to human rights. The issues underpinning their fight had been greater than the prevention of secession. In 1891, Abbott expressed feelings that many black veterans would have shared: "I am now an old man and as I grow older I appreciate more highly the part (though humble) I took in those troublous times and which resulted in the emancipation of my race in the United States."[2]

When Abbott addressed his comrades on the 22 May 1907 Decoration Day to commemorate the fallen and to keep alive their memory, his recollections of the war would have resonated with other black veterans. Men who had taken part in any battle, he believed, understood the full horrors and hardships of combat. But, he argued, if ever there were a righteous and justifiable conflict, it was the American Civil War. "It was not a war for conquest or territorial aggrandizement, racial, social or political supremacy," he told his audience. Rather, it "was a war for humanity," for the cause of the Union was "freedom, individual liberty and national greatness." The veterans had been part of something larger than themselves, something with international implications. As Abbott put it,

> We have been the agents, the unconscious agents it may be, in securing to the humblest citizen of the Commonwealth whether he lives under the protecting folds of the red cross of St. George, or the glorious star spangled banner, the blessings of peace, civil and religious liberty and in giving to the world a higher conception of the value of human liberty.[3]

He believed that this held true even if the soldiers were unaware of it at the time. In this and other speeches, Abbott distinguished between what he felt was an individual soldier's decision making and the role of divine influence. "We were too near the scene of the conflict 45 years ago," he repeated, "to see the magnitude of the problem. Whatever may have been our motives as Canadians in engaging in that conflict of the American Civil War, we can now recognize that there was a great problem being worked out by the God Almighty and that we were the instruments, the unconscious instruments perhaps, of his Divine purpose."[4]

Whereas Abbott's listeners may have agreed with his mythologized presentation of the war, his simplistic dichotomy of the conflict "between Beautiful Right and Ugly Wrong, between civilization and barbarism" would have struck many black soldiers serving in 1863 as misleading, given their unequal treatment when they first enlisted. Men such as Sergeant Samuel Robinson may have shared Abbott's belief that they had joined a fight for liberty, justice, and equality, but as late as January 1864 he felt compelled to complain about the ways that black soldiers were being mistreated.[5] The Toronto-born sergeant had come to believe that not everyone who wore Union blue was his ally, and he paid a personal price for his criticism of the army.

In this photograph, taken late in his life, Anderson Abbott wears academic robes. During this period, he wrote extensively of his reminiscences of the war. *Courtesy of Toronto Reference Library.*

Of course, Abbott and the other doctors who had been forced to serve as contract surgeons rather than commissioned officers, despite their credentials and the desperate need for army surgeons, fully understood the frustration, anger, and humiliation felt by many black soldiers. As a group, the doctors were among the most talented and educated black men who aided the war effort, and they expected justice and equal treatment in return. What they received instead demonstrated the intolerance of Northern society, and it left its mark on them. Although Jerome Riley spent his post-war years working for the interests of African Americans as he saw them, he did so as a Democrat, not a Republican. Abbott, later in his life, behaved as if he had been a commissioned officer, although he knew he was not. He joined the GAR, an organization open only to Union veterans who had been honourably discharged, requested a brevet rank from the US Army, and did little to correct impressions, such as that in the *Chicago Conservator,* that he had been "commissioned a surgeon in the United States Army."[6] Abbott would seek equality in memory, for he had not received it in wartime.

Given the barriers, biases, and prejudice that confronted black recruits who wanted to fight against slavery, it is remarkable that almost 2,500 black British North American residents, men from every colony, volunteered for the Union army and navy. Sympathy for the emancipation struggle was widespread in British North American black communities, but the extent to which their residents were willing to risk their lives in support of it depended on where they lived and on the strength of their cross-border ties. Of course, even those who lacked close links to African American communities often felt emotional and intellectual connections to the issues facing them. The ideology of emancipation may have resonated across all the British colonies, but its impact differed from area to area. The willingness to enlist in the Union war effort, thus risking serious wounds, death, and Confederate atrocities, provides the best measurement of the extent to which blacks in British North America believed that they had a stake in the conflict. The quantity of volunteers who came from Canada West reveals that its black residents felt the greatest need to participate in the struggle for emancipation.

Obviously, their numbers were never large enough to alter battles or influence campaigns, and they were generally subsumed in the greater mass of African American volunteers. Nevertheless, given the relatively small size of British North America's black population, they constituted a remarkably large group, and their involvement demonstrates the extent to which the Emancipation Proclamation and the Union's use of black combat troops gave the war a new international dimension. Their participation is all the more striking because they acted of their own free will. No black British North American was compelled to volunteer in the Union army or navy by the threat of conscription. Indeed, many signed up despite their knowledge that they could be prosecuted under the British Foreign Enlistment Act. Perhaps the best way to measure their commitment to the war effort is to contrast their enlistment rates to those of African Americans in the Northern states. By that standard, their response matched or exceeded the black turnout in New York and New Jersey, and was not much lower than the overall rate for all Northern African Americans.[7]

Nevertheless, their willingness to serve in the struggle against slavery was conditional on fair dealing by the Northern government. A study of the timing of black enlistment from the British colonies is valuable because it highlights the dilemma that challenged many potential black recruits in

1863. They had to weigh their desire to fight for "freedom, individual liberty and national greatness," as Abbott would term it, against being treated as second-class soldiers by a biased military. Of course, no simplistic generalization fully explains the individual motivations that inspired thousands to volunteer. At one level, a spectrum of factors, such as ideological commitment, youthful romanticism, financial desperation, or avoidance of criminal prosecution, drove men to join up. Yet, enlistment patterns show that most black men from British North America entered the war only after a change in government policy accorded them reasonably comparable status with white troops. Although some did come forward when the first black regiments were being organized, many more held back, especially when 1863 demonstrated that, as far as pay, pensions, and service in the field were concerned, they would not be treated equally. Only after the resolution of the pay issue in the summer of 1864 and after the Lincoln administration and senior military officers proclaimed that Confederate atrocities would incur retaliation, did the majority of black enlistment take place. Of course, it was in this latter stage of the war that the greatest financial offers were made to entice new enlistees, a fact that poses a difficult question for researchers. When a poor man enlists and receives significant economic benefit, is the money his primary goal, or is it a means to an end, a tool that enables him to act on his principles? During the early summer of 1864, significant money was being offered to substitutes and volunteers, but few black recruits from the British colonies responded to the inducement. For black British North Americans, the dramatic correlation between the settlement of the pay issue and the surge in enlistment suggests that equal treatment trumped financial benefits.

Historians such as Michael Bennett have argued that the sailors who enlisted in the Union navy were generally less motivated by ideology than were the soldiers and that though they wanted the ready money offered by the navy, they "did not want to die or suffer for their country if they could avoid it."[8] This was true, at least in part, for the black British North American naval recruits. They tended to choose shorter periods of service than the soldiers, and many viewed the Union navy as just one more employer in their maritime career. However, the fact that their numbers dramatically increased after the Final Emancipation Proclamation of 1 January 1863 suggests that for many, their motivation was at least partially grounded in opposition to slavery and support for emancipation. Black British colonists were willing to put aside their civilian life and serve in the Union war effort, but on their own terms. They chose whether to join the army or the navy and for how long.

Fewer than a third of those who selected the navy had enough maritime experience to be rated as more than landsman. For many, naval service entailed their first time afloat. The reverse was that many men who entered the army, such as William Gardner from St. Andrews, New Brunswick, James Harris from Halifax, and Thomas Thompson from Hamilton, had all worked as sailors before they enlisted as soldiers.[9]

After the soldiers and sailors were mustered out, their obvious first task was deciding what to do next. Should they start a new life in the United States or go home? Many soldiers had formed new attachments to places or persons in the various states, which complicated their long-term plans. Not surprisingly, men who served afloat and who seldom spent time ashore came out of the war with fewer ties to the United States. Most Maritimers went home soon after being mustered out of the military. By contrast, the veterans from Canada West and Canada East were almost as likely to stay in the United States as to return to their former residences.

Nevertheless, emancipation in the United States permanently altered the social landscape for all black North Americans. Those who moved south across the international border enjoyed more enticements and fewer restrictions. A physician such as Abbott would not have been surprised by the greater black mobility, for the black surgeons who served in the war were among the most mobile of the black volunteers, both geographically and socially. Despite the lure of the United States, the out-migration of black residents from the new Dominion of Canada, though significant, was more limited than many writers have suggested, and it spanned several decades. There was no quick exit "en masse." Many former slaves, as Abbott suggested, "drifted back to the South in search of relatives."[10] In doing so, the African American sojourners were increasingly joined by black Canadians who, like the small number of black British North Americans who had moved south before the Civil War, were hoping for a better life in the United States.[11] During the post-1865 period, the greatest demographic factor that changed the structure of Canada's black population, especially in Ontario, was the sudden end of new black immigration from the United States, as African Americans adjusted to emancipation there.

In all his speeches to his GAR comrades, Abbott described himself simply as a "Canadian." This did not mean that he was not also an African Canadian and a transnational any more than his knowledge that men enlisted for diverse reasons, not all of them honourable, meant that they were not fighting for a noble cause. He felt the need, he said, to congratulate "ourselves as Canadians that our lives have not been a failure but that we have done something to ameliorate the conditions of our fellow men and have helped to give to other nations a higher conception of the value of human liberty and that righteousness which exalteth a nation."[12] When addressing GAR meetings at the start of the twentieth century, Abbott worried that "the present generations do not fully realize the importance and value of the work that was accomplished in the war" or the sacrifice of the British North Americans who had "poured out their blood on the battlefield as libation upon the alter [sic] of freedom."[13] He would have been disappointed had he known how few twenty-first-century Canadians understand the full measure of the contribution made by black British North Americans in the Civil War.

Appendix

Establishing the location of black British North American veterans, 1865-75

To locate the place of residence for black British North American veterans during the immediate post-war years, the author employed a data linkage methodology. Military recruitment information drawn from military records was connected to that for individuals who were enumerated in the 1870 United States and 1871 Canadian censuses. The goal was to use the censuses to discover where the veterans had settled after 1865.

The veterans were divided into separate categories depending on their enlistment record details and whether they had served in the navy or the army. The first data set to be examined was the naval enlistment records from the Civil War Soldiers and Sailors System. A database was created to document the name, enlistment date, approximate age at enlistment, occupation, complexion, birthplace, and place of enlistment. Individuals in this database were alphabetized by surname and grouped according to place of birth. The birthplaces were Canada West, Canada East, Nova Scotia, New Brunswick, and Prince Edward Island. All who gave "Canada" as their birthplace were added to the Canada West category. Not surprisingly, this was the largest subset. A second similar data set was drawn from the information logged in the regimental descriptive books of the black regiments.

To link the enlistment record data to the 1870 United States and 1871 Canadian censuses, www.ancestry.ca was used as a searching tool. Both censuses were simultaneously searched for every veteran. In each query, in the advanced search format for the "given" and "surname" fields, the search options of exact, soundex, phonetic match, and matches of names with similar meanings were selected to catch names whose spelling varied from one database to the other. (The soundex function matches names of similar pronunciation.) Next, information for year of birth was entered, and here the search parameters were set to a five-year range to encompass men who either lied about their age at enlistment or were unsure of their exact date of birth. For place of birth, the search function was set to the broad geographic region "Canada," which captures all men who were recorded as born in any region of Canada and excludes foreign-born men with the corresponding search terms. Next, the gender field was set to male.

Finally, and very importantly, the men's complexion data were entered into the origin/race fields. In the 1871 Canadian census, the first of the new dominion, residents were asked to specify their "origin." This language had been adopted so that census officials could distinguish between francophones and anglophones, an issue of importance to Canadians, or at least to Canadian politicians, at the time. However, the term "origin" created some uncertainty, because respondents could interpret it as applying to place of birth, race, or ethnicity. The initial search field was set to "African," the term that most enumerators used to record residents of African descent. Ancestry.ca also filters the men of African descent, placing them in a higher match position in the search results. However, it became evident that there were a few cases of possible linkage where the census had recorded "origin" as "American." These were all scrutinized more closely. Examining the image of the original enumeration revealed that the origin field of some individuals had initially stated "African," but this had been crossed out and replaced with "American." Given the ambiguousness of the term "origin" and the fact that some African Canadians may have been passing as white, some potential links will have been missed.

For the United States 1870 census, searches were completed with the race field set to "black" and "mulatto," which was comparable to inputting "African" in the Canadian census. Once all the search terms were set in the query engine, the results were consulted to find the most appropriate match. Ancestry.ca uses a five-star system to rate the strength of matches in its results. The greater the number of stars, the more likely the match is correct.

Selecting the right match was the most time-consuming part of the research. This was because the information from the enlistment records was limited and because the most important fields that affected selection of the match, such as race/origin and age, all had an element of imprecision. The two men listed below illustrate the difficulties. Both were found in the 1871 Canadian census and both share the same name and virtually the same age with an identified black veteran who is also listed:

Thomas Johnson, born 1841, "Canada," complexion "brown"
Thomas Johnson, born 1842, Canada West, Scottish/white
Thomas Johnson, born 1843, Canada West, African/black

Plainly, there were many possible matches for many of the veterans who were being tracked across time and space – men with the exact same names and the same date of birth. For most linkages, the information in the race/origin field was deemed the most critical, except in the few instances where a recorded physical description allowed the possibility that a veteran might pass as white in subsequent censuses. Of course, possible linkages were also affected by the fact that a few soldiers had enlisted under an alias or changed their name after the war. Some obvious linkage problems were associated with place of birth. In the United States census, most black individuals who were born north of the border gave "Canada" as their place of birth, but whether this refers to the United Province of Canada or the Dominion of Canada is not clear. An additional problem is the fact that, for various reasons, some enlisting soldiers lied about their place of birth. Next, in cases of very similar individuals, the original enumeration documents were examined to determine occupation. Finally, on occasion, ancestry.ca automatically links matches to military records. This affords crucial information for the linkage process because the records provided by ancestry.ca could be compared with those in the Civil War Soldiers and Sailors System and the regimental descriptive books. The information was noted, and a snapshot was taken of the document.

Once a possible match was found, it was ranked according to the strength of the linkage.

Rank	Description
High	Given and surnames correct. Age within four years. Place of birth accurate with the given information. Occupation match (where applicable), military records (including pension)
Medium	Given and surnames reasonably close. Age within four years. Place of birth not within the given province

Low   Given and surnames moderate match. Age off by five years. Place of birth not matching

In most cases, the high-ranked linkages were accepted, and virtually all the low-ranked linkages were rejected. All linkages with a medium ranking were examined more closely and checked against other record sources, where possible.

NOTES

INTRODUCTION

1 "Samuel J. Robinson," Compiled Military Service Records (CMSR), RG 94, National Archives and Records Administration (NARA), Washington, DC.
2 The first sergeant was the senior sergeant in a company, and the sergeant major was the senior sergeant in the regiment. The quartermaster sergeant assisted the regimental quartermaster in handling the ordnance and supplies for the men in the regiment.
3 "Samuel J. Robinson," Civil War Pension File (CWPF), RG 15, NARA.
4 These black regiments, all of which retained their state designations, were normally referred to as the Fifty-fourth and Fifty-fifth Massachusetts and the Twenty-ninth Connecticut Regiments.
5 "Joel Monroe," CMSR, RG 94, NARA; "Joel Monroe," CWPF, RG 15, NARA.
6 "William Jones," CMSR, RG 94, NARA. Boyd, whose name had been pulled in the draft, was able to avoid military service by hiring a substitute.
7 "William Jones," CWPF, RG 15, NARA.
8 Eric Foner, *Reconstruction: America's Unfinished Revolution, 1863-1877* (New York: Harper and Row, 1988), 471.
9 For an analysis of the changing ways in which historians have conceptualized "borderlands," see John Nieto-Phillips, "Margins to Mainstream: The Brave New World of Borderland History, an Introduction," *Journal of American History* 98, 2 (September 2011): 337-61.
10 This stood in sharp contrast to white British North Americans, who moved south in the tens of thousands during the decades leading up to 1860.
11 Although Canada West and Canada East were legally just administrative districts, they functioned as separate provinces in many ways. The union formed by Confederation on 1 July 1867 quickly expanded to include Manitoba and the North-West Territory (15 July 1870), British Columbia (20 July 1871), Prince Edward Island (1 July 1873), and

finally Newfoundland (31 March 1949). In this work, the term "African Canadian" is used in two contexts. When applied to the period before 1867, it refers to persons of African descent who were born in the United Province of Canada. When used for the period after 1867, it refers to persons of African descent who were born anywhere in the new Dominion of Canada.

12 Sharon A. Roger Hepburn, *Crossing the Border: A Free Black Community in Canada* (Urbana: University of Illinois Press, 2007); Harvey Amani Whitfield, *Blacks on the Border: The Black Refugees in British North America, 1815-1860* (Burlington: University of Vermont Press, 2006).

13 Gustavo Cano, *Organizing Immigrant Communities in American Cities: Is This Transnationalism, or What?* Working Paper 103 (La Jolla: Center for Comparative Immigration Studies, 2004), 8. http://www.ime.gob.mx/investigaciones/bibliografias/Cano2.pdf.

14 The reason for confining the analysis to native-born black British North Americans is more fully discussed in Chapter 2.

15 Bell Wiley cites a Southern historian whom he does not name as claiming in 1951 that "the majority of Yankee soldiers were foreign hirelings." Bell Irvin Wiley, *The Life of Billy Yank: The Common Soldier of the Union* (Indianapolis: Bobbs-Merrill, 1962), 428n51.

16 *The War of the Rebellion: A Compilation of the Official Records of the Union and Confederate Armies*, 128 vols. (Washington, DC: Government Printing Office, 1880-1901), ser. 3, 5:688; James McPherson, *Ordeal by Fire: The Civil War and Reconstruction* (New York: Alfred A. Knopf, 1982), 468; David Herbert Donald, Jean Harvey Baker, and Michael F. Holt, *The Civil War and Reconstruction* (New York: W.W. Norton, 2001), 239.

17 Tyler Anbinder, "Which Poor Man's Fight? Immigrants and the Federal Conscription of 1863," *Civil War History* 52, 4 (December 2006): 344-47; Christian B. Keller, "Flying Dutchmen and Drunken Irishmen: The Myths and Realities of Ethnic Civil War Soldiers," *Journal of Military History* 73, 1 (January 2009): 119-30.

18 A sample of this literature would include William Burton, *Melting Pot Soldiers: The Union's Ethnic Regiments*, 2nd ed. (New York: Fordham University Press, 1998); David L. Valuska and Christian B. Keller, *Damn Dutch: Pennsylvania Germans at Gettysburg* (Mechanicsville, PA: Stackpole Books, 2004); and Susannah U. Bruce, *The Harp and the Eagle: Irish-American Volunteers and the Union Army, 1861-1865* (New York: New York University Press, 2006).

Chapter 1: British North America

1 A few black slaves were held in New France during the 1600s, although slavery was not legalized there until 1709. Among the first black inhabitants of New France were Olivier Le Jeune and Mathieu Da Costa. Marcel Trudel, "Le Jeune, Olivier," *Dictionary of Canadian Biography Online*, http://www.biographi.ca/; Linda Brown-Kubisch, *The Queen's Bush Settlement: Black Pioneers, 1839-1865* (Toronto: Natural Heritage Books, 2004), 1. For an overview of slavery in New France and the post-Conquest era, see Afua Cooper, *The Hanging of Angelique: The Untold Story of Canadian Slavery and the Burning of Old Montreal* (Athens: University of Georgia Press, 2007), 68-107.

2 David Herbert Donald, Jean Harvey Baker, and Michael F. Holt, *The Civil War and Reconstruction* (New York: W.W. Norton, 2001), 104-5; Chandra Manning, *What This Cruel War Was Over: Soldiers, Slavery and the Civil War* (New York: Alfred A. Knopf, 2007), 17. In *Dred Scott v. Sanford*, Chief Justice Roger B. Taney ruled that though an African American might be a citizen of a state, that did not make him a citizen of the United States. Taney was challenged by other justices in this momentous case, but fears

remained strong that the court, or at least Taney, would one day rule that state laws prohibiting slavery were unconstitutional.

3 Sharon A. Roger Hepburn, *Crossing the Border: A Free Black Community in Canada* (Urbana: University of Illinois Press, 2007), 21.

4 Barrington Walker, *Race on Trial: Black Defendants in Ontario's Criminal Courts, 1858-1958* (Toronto: Osgoode Society for Canadian Legal History/University of Toronto Press, 2010), 3.

5 Chris Apap, "'Let No Man of Us Budge One Step': David Walker and the Rhetoric of African Emplacement," *Early American Literature* 46, 2 (June 2011): 340.

6 Before Nova Scotia was partitioned in 1784, it encompassed all of what is now Nova Scotia and New Brunswick. For a discussion of slavery in this region under the French regime, see Harvey Amani Whitfield, *Blacks on the Border: The Black Refugees in British North America, 1815-1860* (Burlington: University of Vermont Press, 2006), 10-14.

7 The Constitutional Act of 1791 authorized the division of Quebec into the colonies of Upper and Lower Canada, with territories corresponding to the southern parts of today's Ontario and Quebec. In 1840, the British government reacted to colonial discontent by passing the Act of Union to create the United Province of Canada, composed of Canada West and Canada East. Many residents, however, continued to use the old names.

8 The first significant black migration into the Far West did not occur until 1858, when James Douglas, the governor of British Columbia, invited a group of almost eight hundred African Americans to come from California to Vancouver Island. Given the timing of their arrival, it is not surprising that no blacks born in the province served in the Union army or navy.

9 Prior to the influx of American refugees during the 1780s, there were about five hundred black residents, slave and free, in Nova Scotia. J.M. Bumsted, "1763-1783: Resettlement and Rebellion," in *The Atlantic Region to Confederation: A History*, ed. Phillip A. Buckner and John G. Reid (Toronto: University of Toronto Press, 1994), 182.

10 Maya Jasanoff, *Liberty's Exiles: American Loyalists in the Revolutionary World* (New York: Alfred A. Knopf, 2011), 6.

11 The exact number of loyalists who went to the various British colonies may never be known. Overall estimates for the total number vary from forty-five thousand to thirty-seven thousand. Elizabeth Mancke, "The American Revolution in Canada," in *A Companion to the American Revolution*, ed. Jack P. Greene and J.R. Pole (Oxford: Blackwell, 2000), 508-9; Barnet Schecter, *The Battle for New York: The City at the Heart of the American Revolution* (New York: Walker, 2002), 374; John G. Reid, *Six Crucial Decades: Times of Change in the History of the Maritimes* (Halifax: Nimbus, 1987), 64.

12 Greg Marquis, *In Armageddon's Shadow: The Civil War and Canada's Maritime Provinces* (Montreal and Kingston: McGill-Queen's University Press, 1998), 60.

13 James W. St. G. Walker, "African Canadians: Migration," *Encyclopedia of Canada's Peoples*, Multicultural Canada, http://www.multiculturalcanada.ca/.

14 The best and most perceptive analysis of the contested nature of Maritime slavery is Harvey Amani Whitfield, "The Struggle over Slavery in the Maritime Colonies," *Acadiensis* 41, 2 (Summer-Autumn 2012): 17-44.

15 Whitfield, *Blacks on the Border*, 18.

16 Reid, *Six Crucial Decades*, 70-71.

17 Quoted in Jasanoff, *Liberty's Exiles*, 175.

18 Margaret Conrad and Alvin Finkel, *History of the Canadian Peoples*, vol. 1, *Beginnings to 1867* (Toronto: Addison Wesley Longman, 2002), 188.

19 James W. St. G. Walker, *The Black Loyalists: The Search for a Promised Land in Nova Scotia and Sierra Leone, 1788-1870* (New York: Africana, 1976), 137: Marquis, *In Armageddon's Shadow*, 60; Jasanoff, *Liberty's Exiles*, 175.

20 Whitfield, *Blacks on the Border*, 22-23; Allister Hinds, "'Deportees in Nova Scotia': The Jamaican Maroons, 1796-1800," in *Working Slavery, Pricing Freedom: Perspectives from the Caribbean, Africa and the African Diaspora*, ed. Verene Shepherd (New York: Palgrave, 2002), 206-22; Marquis, *In Armageddon's Shadow*, 60.
21 W.A. Spray, *The Blacks in New Brunswick* (Fredericton, NB: Brunswick Press, 1972), 16-17.
22 Mancke, "The American Revolution in Canada," 510.
23 Spray, *The Blacks in New Brunswick*, 23-27; Jennifer Harris, "Black Life in a Nineteenth-Century New Brunswick Town," *Journal of Canadian Studies/Revue d'études canadiennes* 46, 1 (Winter 2012): 146. According to Harris, oral testimony indicates that some people were held as slaves until 1834.
24 For men such as Peters and Henry, this move was only one of many. Both subsequently immigrated to Sierra Leone, although they spent some time in England. Cassandra Pybus, *Epic Journeys of Freedom: Runaway Slaves of the American Revolution and Their Global Quest for Liberty* (Boston: Beacon Press, 2006), 145, 212, 215-16.
25 Jasanoff, *Liberty's Exiles*, 184.
26 Robin Winks, *The Blacks in Canada: A History*, 2nd ed. (Montreal and Kingston: McGill-Queen's University Press, 1997), 150.
27 Robin Winks argues that this influx of "Refugee Negroes" marked "the real beginnings of racism in Canada." Ibid., 113.
28 D.A. Sutherland, "1810-1820: War and Peace," in Buckner and Reid, *The Atlantic Region*, 256; Whitfield, *Blacks on the Border*, 32.
29 Whitfield, *Blacks on the* Border, 89. The colonial press consistently depicted the black population as lacking in honesty, intelligence, and industry but was quite willing to use the same black population to highlight the benefits of living in the British Empire. Ibid., 85-89.
30 The Prince Edward Island censuses for both 1848 and 1855 do not include a category for race or ethnic origin. However, of the 74,496 inhabitants in 1855, only 316 were born elsewhere than England, Scotland, Ireland, Prince Edward Island, or a British colony. *Abstract of the Census of the Population, and Other Statistical Returns of Prince Edward Island: Taken in the Year 1855, by Virtue of an Act of the General Assembly* (Charlottetown: E. Whelan, 1855).
31 Reid, *Six Crucial Decades*, 66; Jim Hornby, *Black Islanders: Prince Edward Island's Historical Black Community* (Charlottetown: Institute of Island Studies, 1991), 2-3.
32 Harvey Amani Whitfield and Barry Cahill, "Slave Life and Slave Law in Colonial Prince Edward Island, 1769-1825," *Acadiensis* 38, 2 (Summer-Autumn 2009): 29-51.
33 The province's Supreme Court recognized the validity of a slave sale in 1802. Marquis, *In Armageddon's Shadow*, 62.
34 Hornby, *Black Islanders*, xv, 4-9.
35 Canada, *Census of Canada, 1881* (Ottawa: MacLean, Roger and Co., 1882), 208.
36 The large body of research on the accuracy and undercounts of the Canadian and American censuses of the nineteenth century reveals that virtually all censuses undercounted the population, particularly among the economically marginalized, the young, and the transient. The underenumeration of black residents was particularly marked, at least 15 or even 20 percent in some places and some censuses. However, despite their inaccuracies, the censuses are not necessarily less reliable than anecdotal evidence provided by contemporaries, who often had an agenda. For this study, it is assumed that most colonial censuses undercounted by about 20 percent. For further analysis of underenumeration, see Donald H. Parkerson, "Comments on the Underenumeration of the U.S. Census, 1850-1880," *Social Science History* 15, 4 (Winter 1991): 509-15; Miriam L. King and Diana L. Magnuson, "Perspectives on Historical U.S. Census Undercounts," *Social Science History* 19, 4 (Winter 1995): 455-66; Richard M. Reid, "The 1870 United States

Census and Black Underenumeration: A Test Case from North Carolina," *Histoire sociale/Social History* 28, 56 (November 1995): 487-99; Patrick A. Dunae, "Making the 1891 Census in British Columbia," *Histoire sociale/Social History* 31, 62 (1998): 223-39; and Bruce Curtis, *The Politics of Population: State Formation, Statistics, and the Census of Canada, 1840-1875* (Toronto: University of Toronto Press, 2000).

37 Phillip A. Buckner, "The 1860s: An End and a Beginning," in Buckner and Reid, *The Atlantic Region*, 363.

38 The black population ranged from about 1,500 to 1,700 in the censuses of 1824 (1,513), 1834 (1,623), 1840 (1,711), and 1861 (1,581). Only in 1851 (1,058) was the enumerated figure outside this range.

39 Census officials criticized enumerators for having omitted large numbers of black residents in the 1851 census for Canada West. This underenumeration may also have occurred in New Brunswick.

40 For New Brunswick, the percentage of black females edged upward from 51.1 in 1824 to 53.4 in 1834, 51.6 in 1840, 52.3 in 1851, and 53.8 in 1861. In Nova Scotia, black females made up 52.7 percent of the black population in 1851.

41 Of course, in a maritime colony, the enumeration may have missed at least some (male) sailors.

42 Recent work has revealed the extent to which fugitive slaves took advantage of maritime networks to gain their freedom. For examples, see David Cecelski, "The Shores of Freedom: The Maritime Underground Railroad in North Carolina, 1800-1861," *North Carolina Historical Review* 71, 2 (1994): 174-206; W. Jeffrey Bolster, *Black Jacks: African American Seamen in the Age of Sail* (Cambridge, MA: Harvard University Press, 1997); and John Michael Vlach, "Above Ground on the Underground Railroad: Places of Flight and Refuge," in *Passages to Freedom: The Underground Railroad in History and Memory*, ed. David W. Blight (Washington, DC: Smithsonian Books, 2004), 103-5.

43 Marquis, *In Armageddon's Shadow*, 67.

44 Fugitives were reported leaving Boston for Saint John, "driven from the Northern States by the operation of" the Fugitive Slave Act. *Halifax British Colonist*, 13 March 1851.

45 Tom Calarco, *People of the Underground Railroad: A Biographical Dictionary* (Westport, CT: Greenwood Press, 2008), 18.

46 Marquis, *In Armageddon's Shadow*, 67-68.

47 William Arthur Spray, "Patterson, Robert J.," *Dictionary of Canadian Biography Online*, http://www.biographi.ca/.

48 Marquis, *In Armageddon's Shadow*, 68-69.

49 The total number of slaves held over a two-hundred-year period in what is now Quebec is estimated at 4,092, of whom 1,400 were of African descent and almost 2,700 were panis, or Amerindian slaves. Dorothy W. Williams, *The Road to Now: A History of Blacks in Montreal* (Montreal: Véhicule Press, 1997), 25.

50 Winks, *The Blacks in Canada*, 35.

51 Daniel G. Hill suggests that there were as many as seven hundred. Daniel G. Hill, *The Freedom-Seekers: Blacks in Early Canada* (Agincourt: Book Society of Canada, 1981), 118.

52 John Butler was a New York loyalist who raised a provincial regiment called Butler's Rangers, a unit that contained some black soldiers. For part of the war, it was based at Niagara-on-the-Lake. John Johnson, second baronet of New York, organized the core of the King's Royal Regiment of New York for service in the American Revolution.

53 Joseph Brant was an important military and political figure whose support for the British led him to relocate after the war to the newly created Mohawk reserve on the Grand River.

54 Hill, *The Freedom-Seekers*, 12-13, 15; Winks, *The Blacks in Canada*, 30.

55 Both the Northwest Ordinance of 1787 and the gradual emancipation act passed in 1793 in Upper Canada forbade the introduction of new slaves into their respective territories.

Slaves in both the United States and Canada soon understood that they could claim their freedom by crossing the border. As American-British relations deteriorated during the years prior to 1812, American authorities reacted unfavourably to the legal attempt to reclaim slaves who had escaped from Upper Canada. Gregory Wigmore, "Before the Railroad: From Slavery to Freedom in the Canadian-American Borderland," *Journal of American History* 98, 2 (September 2011): 438, 447-53; Winks, *The Blacks in Canada*, 99.

56 The legislation, "An Act to prevent the future introduction of Slaves, and to limit the terms of contracts for servitude within this Province," freed no slave; nor did it forbid their sale. Indeed, it actually made manumission more difficult by forcing owners to provide security to local authorities in case the manumitted slave became a ward of the state. Michael Power and Nancy Butler, *Slavery and Freedom in Niagara* (Niagara-on-the-Lake: Niagara Historical Society, 1993), 9, 25-26.

57 When the bill went into effect on 1 April 1834, the last two slaves in Upper Canada demanded and received their freedom. Spray, *The Blacks in New Brunswick*, 28.

58 The black volunteers made up the Colored Corps, sometimes referred to as Captain Robert Runchey's Company of Colored Men. Blacks served in the armies and navies of both sides during the conflict. Garth Newfield, "Upper Canada's Black Defenders? Re-evaluating the War of 1812 Coloured Corps," *Canadian Military History* 18, 3 (2009): 31-40.

59 Robert Malcomson, *A Very Brilliant Affair: The Battle of Queenston Heights, 1812* (Toronto: Robin Brass Studio, 2003), 179, 186, 269: John R. Elting, *Amateurs, to Arms! A Military History of the War of 1812* (Chapel Hill: Algonquin Books of Chapel Hill, 1991), 47, 122; Hill, *The Freedom-Seekers*, 114-17.

60 Hill, *The Freedom-Seekers*, 114.

61 Sharon A. Roger Hepburn, "Following the North Star: Canada as a Haven for Nineteenth-Century American Blacks," *Michigan Historical Review* 25, 2 (Fall 1999): 104.

62 For a debate on the nature of black loyalism in the Maritimes, see Barry Cahill, "The Black Loyalist Myth in Atlantic Canada," *Acadiensis* 29, 1 (Autumn 1999): 76-87; and James W. St. G. Walker, "Myth, History, and Revisionism: The Black Loyalists Revisited," *Acadiensis* 29, 1 (Autumn 1999): 88-105.

63 Quoted in Colin Read and Ronald J. Stagg, *The Rebellion of 1837 in Upper Canada: A Collection of Documents* (Ottawa: Carleton University Press, 1985), lxv, 123; Hill, *The Freedom-Seekers*, 118.

64 The historical debate over the makeup and effectiveness of the Underground Railroad continues to grow. Whereas scholars such as Larry Gara and John Hope Franklin and Loren Schweninger question whether many fugitives reached freedom via the Railroad, others such as Stanley Harrold and Fergus Bordewich argue that it developed a sophisticated system of routes to move large numbers of escaping slaves. All, however, accept the importance of black agency. See Larry Gara, *The Liberty Line: The Legend of the Underground Railroad* (Lexington: University of Kentucky Press, 1961); John Hope Franklin and Loren Schweninger, *Runaway Slaves: Slaves on the Plantation* (New York: Oxford University Press, 1999); Stanley Harrold, *Subversives: Antislavery Community in Washington, D.C., 1828-1865* (Baton Rouge: Louisiana State University Press, 2003); and Fergus Bordewich, *Bound for Canaan: The Epic Story of the Underground Railroad, America's First Civil Rights Movement* (New York: Amistad, 2005).

65 "Transmigrants" refers to transitory individuals who create and sustain multiple social relations and personal ties across nation-state boundaries by linking together their societies of origin and of current residence. Nina Glick Schiller has been particularly influential in developing this concept. Nina Glick Schiller, *Nations Unbound: Transnational Projects, Postcolonial Predicaments and Deterritorialized Nation-States* (New York: Gordon and Breach, 1994).

66 Government support for the scheme was motivated as much by the area's strategic importance as by humanitarianism. Jason H. Silverman, *Unwelcome Guests: Canada West's Response to American Fugitive Slaves, 1800-1865* (Millwood, NY: Associated Faculty Press, 1985), 24-26.
67 These attempts were part of a broader phenomenon. During the nineteenth century, African Americans and sympathetic white supporters organized a number of black settlements across the northern United States and British North America, with mixed results. Hepburn, *Crossing the Border*, 2.
68 Ibid., 43.
69 The history of Wilberforce illustrates the danger of assuming that all African Americans who were reported as setting out for a British colony actually arrived there. Norman N. Feltes, *This Side of Heaven: Determining the Donnelly Murders, 1880* (Toronto: University of Toronto Press, 1999), 33-34.
70 Peter Baskerville, *Ontario: Image, Identity, and Power* (New York: Oxford University Press, 2002), 69.
71 Donald G. Simpson, *Under the North Star: Black Communities in Upper Canada* (Trenton, NJ: Africa World Press, 2005), 178-79; Silverman, *Unwelcome Guests*, 29-33.
72 The act, itself a part of the Compromise of 1850, was designed to make it easier for Southern slaveholders to seize escaped slaves. It established federal commissioners to enforce the law and paid them a higher fee if they found for Southern claimants. The law also provided severe penalties for state officials or civilians who obstructed their efforts. Accused runaways were denied jury trials or the right to testify on their own behalf. The act led to resistance, riots, rescues, and recaptures across the North. Stanley W. Campbell, *Slave Catchers: Enforcement of the Fugitive Slave Law, 1850-1860* (Chapel Hill: University of North Carolina Press, 1968), 23-25.
73 Brown-Kubisch, *The Queen's Bush Settlement*, 120, 130.
74 Janice Martz Kimmel, "Break Your Chains and Fly for Freedom," *Michigan History Magazine*, January 1996, 27.
75 Simpson, *Under the North Star*, 10, 289-91.
76 Kimmel, "Break Your Chains," 27.
77 Originally named the Elgin Settlement in honour of the governor general of Canada, it soon became known simply as the Buxton settlement.
78 Hepburn, *Crossing the Border*, 27-40; Jason H. Silverman, "King, William," *Dictionary of Canadian Biography Online*, http://www.biographi.ca/.
79 Whereas Hepburn links the failures of other settlements to white hostility, a lack of religious and social institutions, and an isolated setting, Fergus Bordewich argues that Buxton was successful because, under the leadership of William King, it was exceptionally paternalistic. His strict regulations left little to chance. Bordewich, *Bound for Canaan*, 39.
80 David Murray, *Colonial Justice: Justice, Morality, and Crime in the Niagara District, 1791-1849* (Toronto: University of Toronto Press, 2002), 196.
81 Anyone who was charged by the executive of a foreign nation with "Murder, Forgery, Larceny or other crimes which if committed within the province would have been punished with death, corporal punishment, the pillory, whipping, or confinement at hard labour" could be seized and returned at the discretion of the lieutenant governor and his council. Silverman, *Unwelcome Guests*, 37.
82 Karolyn Smardz Frost, *I've Got a Home in Glory Land: A Lost Tale of the Underground Railroad* (New York: Farrar, Straus and Giroux, 2007), 162-81, 198-204, 252-53.
83 Silverman, *Unwelcome Guests*, 37-40; Murray, *Colonial Justice*, 198-204; Winks, *The Blacks in Canada*, 170. Murray emphasizes the important role played by black women in freeing Moseby.
84 Murray, *Colonial Justice*, 201-2, 210; Silverman, *Unwelcome Guests*, 37-42.

85 Hepburn, *Crossing the Border*, 20.
86 Roman J. Zorn, "An Arkansas Fugitive Slave Incident and Its International Repercussions," *Arkansas Historical Quarterly* 16, 2 (Summer 1957): 148; Elizabeth Abbott-Namphy, "Hackett, Nelson," *Dictionary of Canadian Biography Online*, http://www.biographi.ca/.
87 Walker, *Race on Trial*, 34; Fred Landon, "The Anderson Fugitive Case," *Journal of Negro History* 7, 3 (July 1922): 242; Calarco, *People of the Underground Railroad*, 10; Smardz Frost, *I've Got a Home in Glory Land*, 251. For a full discussion of the case, see Patrick Brode, *The Odyssey of John Anderson* (Toronto: University of Toronto Press, 1989).
88 Robert C. Reinders, "Anderson, John," *Dictionary of Canadian Biography Online*, http://www.biographi.ca/.
89 Abolitionist groups were especially eager to hear the testimonies of African Americans who had experienced slavery personally. *Kingston Chronicle and Gazette*, 5 July 1837; *Toronto Christian Guardian*, 17 January 1838; *Kingston Chronicle and Gazette*, 12 January 1843; *Kingston Chronicle and Gazette*, issues 19 and 23, August 1843.
90 *Kingston British Whig*, 12 May 1837.
91 *Montreal Gazette*, 13 January 1855.
92 *Montreal Gazette*, 3 February 1855.
93 *Kingston Chronicle and Gazette*, 17 April 1841.
94 Gary Lee Collison, *Shadrach Minkins: From Fugitive Slave to Citizen* (Boston: Harvard University Press, 1997), 180-82. Butler would later claim that he had given $7.50 to one fugitive who had not told the other four.
95 *Halifax British Colonist*, 19 October 1850.
96 Collison, *Shadrach Minkins*, 221.
97 Ibid., 198, 221.
98 James M. McPherson, *Battle Cry of Freedom: The Civil War Era* (New York: Oxford University Press, 1988), 86; Calarco, *People of the Underground Railroad*, 159-62.
99 For an extended discussion of this incident, see Thomas P. Slaughter, *Bloody Dawn: The Christiana Riot and Racial Violence in the Antebellum North* (New York: Oxford University Press, 1991); and Ella Forbes, "'By My Own Right Arm': Redemptive Violence and the 1851 Christiana, Pennsylvania Resistance," *Journal of Negro History* 83, 2 (Summer 1998): 159-68.
100 William Parker, "The Freedman's Story," *Atlantic Magazine*, February 1866, 152-66.
101 McPherson, *Battle Cry of Freedom*, 85.
102 Darlene Clark Hine, William C. Hine, and Stanley Harrold, *The African-American Odyssey* (Upper Saddle River, NJ: Prentice Hall, 2000), 1:211.
103 James McPherson, *Ordeal by Fire: The Civil War and Reconstruction* (New York: Alfred A. Knopf, 1982), 79-80; Calarco, *People of the Underground* Railroad, 57-62; Simpson, *Under the North Star*, 8-9. The most detailed account of the Burns affair is Albert J. Von Frank, *The Trials of Anthony Burns: Freedom and Slavery in Emerson's Boston* (Cambridge, MA: Harvard University Press, 1998).
104 Burns was buried in the Victoria Lawn Cemetery at St. Catharines. Fred Landon, "Anthony Burns in Canada," *Ontario Historical Society, Papers and Records* 22 (1925): 164; Roger Riendeau, *An Enduring Heritage: Black Contributions to Early Ontario* (Toronto: Dundurn Press, 1984), 44.
105 Frederick Douglass, *Life and Times of Frederick Douglass* (1881; repr., New York: Macmillan, 1962), 279.
106 Hepburn, "Following the North Star," 100.
107 Under most of these laws, the state appointed attorneys to defend fugitives and paid their defence costs. The legislation also stringently disallowed kidnapping, forbid the use of public buildings for the detention of accused ex-slaves, and guaranteed jury trials in state courts. McPherson, *Ordeal by Fire*, 79.

108 In total almost three hundred escapees were returned under the provisions of the Fugitive Slave Act. Pease and Pease claim that no slave was legally returned after 1858, although Campbell gives several examples of fugitives who were arrested and returned in Ohio, Pennsylvania, and New York. In April 1856, one runaway, Archy Lanton, was illegally arrested in Canada West as a horse thief and handed over to his alleged owner. The two magistrates involved were subsequently dismissed. Jane H. Pease and William H. Pease, *The Fugitive Slave Law and Anthony Burns: A Problem of Law Enforcement* (Philadelphia: J.B. Lippincott, 1975), 59; Lois E. Horton, "Kidnapping and Resistance: Antislavery Direct Action in the 1850s," in *Passages to Freedom*, ed. David W. Blight (Washington, DC: Smithsonian Books, 2006), 166; Campbell, *Slave Catchers*, 134-36: McPherson, *Ordeal by Fire*, 80; Richard J. Gwyne, *John A: The Man Who Made Us* (Toronto: Random House, 2007), 151.

109 Hepburn, "Following the North Star," 97.

110 One influential account of the fugitive slave experience, written by Samuel Ringgold Ward, argued that there were "some 35,000 to 40,000 coloured people in the colony, of whom, if the children of the fugitives were excluded, only 3,000 were free-born." Samuel Ringgold Ward, *Autobiography of a Fugitive Negro; His Anti-Slavery Labours in the United States, Canada, and England* (London: John Snow, 1855), 154.

111 Indications of the continuing strength of this sentiment are the 2008 Governor General's Award for Non-Fiction given to Karolyn Smardz Frost's *I've Got a Home in Glory Land* and the popular reaction to the book.

112 Fred Landon, "The Negro Migration to Canada after the Passing of the Fugitive Slave Act," *Journal of Negro History* 5, 1 (January 1920): 22.

113 In one characteristic example, he cited Hiram Walker, a St. Catharines missionary, who claimed in the 13 December 1851 edition of the *Boston Liberator* that "probably not less than 3,000 have taken refuge in this country since the first of September." Quoted in ibid., 23.

114 Adrienne Shadd, Afua Cooper, and Karolyn Smardz Frost, *The Underground Railroad: Next Stop Toronto!* (Toronto: Natural Heritage Books, 2002), 25.

115 Although forty thousand is the most frequently cited figure, one that Robin Winks suggests is reasonably accurate, some recent works have estimated a higher number. In a recent overview of African American history, Hine, Hine, and Harrold contend that between 1851 and 1860, the number of "black Americans in Canada rose from approximately eight thousand to about sixty thousand." Hine, Hine, and Harrold, *The African-American Odyssey*, 1:196. Authors of a popular Canadian survey text claim that "30,000 to 40,000 had arrived by 1861," half of whom returned to the United States at war's end. R. Douglas Francis, Richard Jones, and Donald B. Smith, *Origins: Canadian History to Confederation* (Toronto: Nelson Thomson, 2004), 314-15. Nora Faires suggests that "between twenty and thirty thousand African Americans fled to Canada for refuge" and that they "joined a black population of some ten thousand already resident in Ontario." Nora Faires, "Leaving the 'Land of Second Chance': Migration from Ontario to the Upper Midwest in the Nineteenth and Early Twentieth Centuries," in John Bukowczyk et al., *Permeable Border: The Great Lakes Basin as Transnational Region, 1650-1990* (Pittsburg: University of Pittsburg Press, 2005), 105.

116 Silverman, *Unwelcome Guests*, 159. Silverman cites a high of forty thousand just before the war, which dropped to fewer than fifteen thousand by 1871.

117 *Census of the Canadas, 1860-1861*, personal census (Quebec: S.B. Foote, 1863), 1:78-79; *Census of Canada, 1871* (Ottawa: I.B. Taylor, 1873), 280. The reliability issue was intensified by the 1871 census, which recapitulated earlier census findings and gave the 1861 number of blacks as 13,566.

118 Winks, *The Blacks in Canada*, 233.

119 Ibid., 240.

120 In column 13 of their schedules, enumerators were to "mark a figure (1) after every *Colored* person's name, i.e., Negro or Negress." As their instructions pointed out, "This was much neglected last Census and the number of colored persons was not ascertained." Apparently, enumerators were more diligent than the officials who tabulated the data for publication. Quoted in Michael Wayne, "The Black Population of Canada West on the Eve of the American Civil War: A Reassessment Based on the Manuscript Census of 1861," *Histoire sociale/Social History* 28, 56 (November 1995): 467; David P. Gagan, "Enumerator's Instruction for the Census of Canada 1852 and 1861," *Histoire sociale/Social History* 7, 14 (November 1974): 364.

121 Collison, *Shadrach Minkins*, 206.

122 Wayne, "The Black Population of Canada West," 470.

123 The Anti-Slavery Society of Canada claimed that there were thirty thousand blacks in Canada West in 1852, whereas the *Boston Liberator* reported twenty-five thousand in the same year. By 1860, the Anti-Slavery Society had increased its estimate to sixty thousand. Demographers generally distrust numbers that end with three zeros. Benjamin Drew, *A North-Side View of Slavery. The Refugee: Or, The Narratives of Fugitive Slaves in Canada, Related by Themselves, with an Account of the History and Condition of the Colored Population of Upper Canada* (1856; repr., New York: Negro Universities Press, 1968), v; *Boston Liberator*, 30 July 1852.

124 Matthew Furrow, "Samuel Gridley Howe, the Black Population of Canada West, and the Racial Ideology of the 'Blueprint for Radical Reconstruction,'" *Journal of American History* 97, 2 (September 2010): 349-50, 353, 358.

125 Robin Winks lists a series of ways in which the numbers of fugitives who entered British North America may have been significantly inflated. Winks, *The Blacks in Canada*, 234-40.

126 William W. Freehling, *The Road to Disunion: Secessionists at Bay, 1776-1854* (New York: Oxford University Press, 1990), 503; McPherson, *Ordeal by Fire*, 76.

127 The very term "fugitive" creates some confusion. Although it is often used to designate a recent escapee, there was no statute of limitations for a runaway. A fugitive slave was always a fugitive, at least in the eyes of the law, and if the escaped slave were female, all of her children were legally the property of her "former" owner, regardless of where they were born.

128 Some black nationalists, such as Paul Cuffee, had supported emigration to Africa even before the founding of the white-dominated American Colonization Society. The society was established in 1816 to support the return of free African Americans to Africa. Many African Americans believed that the white motive was part of a racist desire to remove as many black residents from the United States as possible. During the 1820s, thousands of African Americans migrated to Haiti, although probably a third had returned to the United States by the end of the decade, disillusioned with what they had found. A majority of blacks, however, opposed colonization. People such as Samuel Cornish, publisher of the first African American newspaper, *Freedom's Journal*, saw themselves as Americans, not Africans, and worked to improve conditions in the United States. Hine, Hine, and Harrold, *The African-American Odyssey*, 1:172.

129 There had been talk among African Americans of emigration, but not colonization, in the late 1820s and during the 1830s, but interest increased dramatically after 1850. Floyd J. Miller, *The Search for a Black Nationality: Black Colonization and Emigration, 1787-1863* (Urbana: University of Illinois Press, 1975), 93-103, 109-11.

130 Quoted in Collison, *Shadrach Minkins*, 81.

131 At this conference, Delany was ambivalent about the prospects of African Americans who settled in an overwhelmingly white society. *Voice of the Fugitive* (Windsor), 24 September 1852, 2, 3; Miller, *The Search for a Black Nationality*, 125-26.

132 The two boys lived with Thomas so that they could attend Buxton's excellent school and so that he could keep an eye on them. Others, such as Henry Johnson, a black businessman from Massillon, Ohio, moved his family to Buxton because of the school. Hepburn, *Crossing the Border*, 166.
133 Quoted in Ian Radforth, *Royal Spectacle: The 1860 Visit of the Prince of Wales to Canada and the United States* (Toronto: University of Toronto Press, 2004), 73, 74.
134 Delany voiced his pessimism about conditions facing blacks in America in his book, *The Condition, Elevation, Emigration, and Destiny of the Colored People of the United States, Politically Considered*. While in Chatham, Delany was a principal canvasser in the Riding of Kent, and he "belonged to the private caucus of A. McKellers, Esq., member of the Provincial Parliament." Frank A. Rollins, *Life and Public Service of Martin R. Delany* (Boston: Lee and Shepard, 1883), 83-84; Cyril E. Griffith, *The African Dream: Martin R. Delany and the Emergence of Pan-African Thought* (University Park: Pennsylvania State University Press, 1975), 31-32.
135 Griffith, *The African Dream*, 34, 70.
136 R.J.M. Blackett, *Beating against the Barriers: Biographical Essays in Nineteenth-Century Afro-American History* (Baton Rouge: Louisiana State University Press, 1986), 310.
137 An active publicist in New York, he was selected in 1867 as inspector-general of schools in Maryland and Delaware, and was editor of *Our National Progress*. In 1878, he was elected school director in Harrisburg, Pennsylvania. Ibid., 315-86.
138 Ward, *Autobiography of a Fugitive Negro*, 126.
139 William S. McFeely, *Frederick Douglass* (New York: W.W. Norton, 1991), 200, 202. The Secret Six were six wealthy, white abolitionists who secretly funded John Brown prior to his raid on Harper's Ferry.
140 Winks, *The Blacks in Canada*, 395-96.
141 Quoted in Collison, *Shadrach Minkins*, 185.
142 Collison argues that they "had substantially greater occupational success in Montreal than blacks typically experienced in Northern U.S. cities." Collison, *Shadrach Minkins*, 208.
143 Thomas Bayne to William Sill, 23 June 1855, quoted in William Sill, *The Underground Railroad* (Philadelphia: Porter and Coates, 1872), 258.
144 In 1852, Jonathan Lemmon, his family, and eight slaves arrived in New York from Virginia to catch a steamship to Texas. Before they could leave, however, the slaves were freed under an 1841 statute that banned slavery in the state. Hepburn, *Crossing the Border*, 10.
145 Robin Winks refers to "a rising tide of prejudice" in the 1850s. Winks, *The Blacks in Canada*, 250.
146 Tracey Adams, "Making a Living: African Canadian Workers in London, Ontario, 1861-1901," *Labour/Le travail* 67 (Spring 2011): 11.
147 James Oliver Horton, *Free People of Color: Inside the African American Community* (Washington, DC: Smithsonian Institution Press, 1993), 27, 28. Horton does not give figures for the separate colonies.
148 All information drawn from the 1860 United States census comes from HeritageQuest Online, www.heritagequestonline.com, and was kindly provided to me by Dr. Adam Arenson of the University of Texas at El Paso. The entire 1860 census was searched, using the categories of race (in the column "Color, Race and Ethnicity," enumerators entered either "B" for black or "M" for mulatto) and place of birth. Unfortunately, HeritageQuest has apparently recoded the birthplace for all the British colonies under one heading, "Canada." The underenumeration for black residents is high in virtually all censuses, but the rates may well be even higher for foreign-born short-term sojourners.

149 Enumerators identified 128 black British North Americans in Boston and another 30 in Lynn.
150 The confusion regarding Hardy's age created difficulties when he applied for a pension. "William H. Hardy," Civil War Pension Files (CWPF), RG 15, National Archives and Records Administration (NARA), Washington, DC.
151 "Henry Brown," Compiled Military Service Records (CMSR), RG 94, NARA. There was perhaps a certain bitter irony about this oath. St. Louis was the point of origin of the *Dred Scott* case, in which Chief Justice Taney, though not all the justices, had ruled that no blacks, either slave or free, could be citizens of the United States. Brown was promoted to corporal before he was mustered out with the rest of his regiment in February 1866.
152 The 1860 census information is from Albert P. Marshall, *Unconquered Souls: The History of the African American in Ypsilanti* (Ypsilanti, MI: Marlan, 1993). Marshall cites "Canada" in discussing the birthplace of the children. Given the context, it is assumed that this refers to Canada West.
153 Ibid., 35-41. It is not known when he married Amanda, a native of Canada West.
154 Louis Haber, *Black Pioneers of Science* (New York: Odyssey Books, 1970), 51-59; Beverley Tallon, "Steam Engine Lubricator," *Canada's History* 92, 1 (2012): 7. Fans of single malt whiskey will know that the term has most frequently been attributed to a corruption of the phrase "a drappie o' the real McKay," an advertising slogan of the Scottish G. McKay & Co., Ltd.
155 "James M. Harrison," CWPF, RG 15, NARA.
156 His deposition is in the file "Harriet A. Nelson, Widow of John Nelson," CWPF, RG 15, NARA.
157 "Thomas W. Brown," CWPF, RG 15, NARA.

Chapter 2: The Black Response

1 These include Enrico Dal Lago, David Brion Davis, Don H. Doyle, Andre Fleche, Eric Foner, Peter Kolchin, Paul Quigley, Edward Bartlett Rugemer, Rebecca J. Scott, and Jay Sexton, several of whom presented papers at a conference titled "The Transnational Significance of the American Civil War," held in Jena, Germany, in September 2011. Their work is part of the trend that places slavery and the Civil War era in a larger international context.
2 James M. McPherson, *Abraham Lincoln and the Second American Revolution* (1991; repr., New York: Oxford University Press, 1992), 28.
3 Quoted in Oliver Carlson, *The Man Who Made News: James Gordon Bennett* (New York: Duell, Sloan and Pearce, 1942), 317.
4 Quoted in R.J.M. Blackett, *Divided Hearts: Britain and the American Civil War* (Baton Rouge: Louisiana State University Press, 2001), 29.
5 Quoted in Duncan Andrew Campbell, *English Public Opinion and the American Civil War* (Rochester, NY: Boydell Press, 2003), 132.
6 *Halifax Morning Journal*, 10 October 1862; *New Brunswick Reporter*, 23 January 1863.
7 *Hamilton Evening Times*, 5 January 1863.
8 *Saint John Morning Freeman*, 3 January 1863; *Kingston Daily News*, 29 December 1862.
9 *Kingston Daily News*, 3 February 1863.
10 *Toronto Globe*, 3 January 1863.
11 "Abbott, A.R.," Medical Officers' Files, Personal Papers of Medical Officers and Physicians, RG 94, National Archives and Records Administration (NARA), Washington, DC.
12 Adele Logan Alexander, *Homelands and Waterways: The American Journey of the Bond Family, 1846-1926* (New York: Vintage Books, 1999), 46.

13 Quoted in Edwin S. Redkey, ed., *A Grand Army of Black Men: Letters from African-American Soldiers in the Union Army, 1861-1865* (New York: Cambridge University Press, 1992), 214. Singer's language is reminiscent of John Winthrop's 1630 sermon "A City upon a Hill." Both men espoused the belief that America had a special instructional role to play in the world.

14 Black communities in British North America were quite different from their counterparts in the Caribbean. At most, they were only a few generations removed from living in the United States. In addition, their proximity to the Northern states facilitated easier enlistment. Nevertheless, black sailors from the West Indies made up a large part of the foreign contingent in the Union navy.

15 James Robertson, *Soldiers Blue and Gray* (Columbia: University of South Carolina Press, 1988), 28, claims that 15,000 "Canadians" joined the federal army, whereas Benjamin Gould, *Investigations in the Military and Anthropological Statistics of the American Soldiers* (1869; repr., New York: Arno Press, 1979), 27, puts the figure at 53,532. The most common estimates range from 40,000 to 50,000. In a widely used survey text, Margaret Conrad and Alvin Finkel estimate that 40,000 to 50,000 British North American men, many who had previously migrated to the United States, served in the war, primarily on the Northern side. Margaret Conrad and Alvin Finkel, *History of the Canadian Peoples*, vol. 1, *Beginnings to 1867* (Toronto: Addison Wesley Longman, 2002), 396. By contrast, David J. Bercuson et al. claim that "35,000 British North Americans enlisted in the northern army, including many black fugitives who had crossed the border to escape from slavery." David J. Bercuson et al., *Colonies: Canada to 1867* (Toronto: McGraw-Hill, 1992), 426. In *The Civil War Years: Canada and the United States* (Montreal and Kingston: McGill-Queen's University Press, 1998), 178-88, Robin Winks explores the origins of the "mythical forty thousand" as well as the methodology of Benjamin Gould and concludes that the true number was much lower. In *The Blacks in Canada*, Winks suggests that Canadian self-interest exaggerated the figure: "The flow of some eighteen thousand British North American recruits into the Northern armies, and the subsequent inflation of that figure into a myth of over forty thousand Canadian enlistments in the cause of anti-slavery, fed the Canadian sense of moral superiority." Robin Winks, *The Blacks in Canada: A History*, 2nd ed. (Montreal and Kingston: McGill-Queen's University Press, 1997), 288.

16 Greg Marquis, *In Armageddon's Shadow: The Civil War and Canada's Maritime Provinces* (Montreal and Kingston: McGill-Queen's University Press, 1998), 80, 96-101.

17 Winks, *The Blacks in Canada*, 152.

18 Marquis, *In Armageddon's Shadow*, 80.

19 R. Douglas Francis, Richard Jones, and Donald B. Smith, *Origins: Canadian History to Confederation* (Toronto: Thomson Nelson, 2004), 315. Ken Alexander and Avis Glaze make the wildly inflated claim that "some 30,000 [black Canadians] took the Underground Railroad in reverse to join the Union army." Ken Alexander and Avis Glaze, *Towards Freedom: The African-Canadian Experience* (Toronto: Umbrella Press, 1996), 79.

20 Historical works frequently apply the term "Canadian" to persons living anywhere in British North America, although, of course, the Dominion of Canada was not formed until 1867. Although the United Province of Canada did exist, the term "Canadian" is and was used by some to include Maritimers.

21 From the 1840s onward, the British North American colonies experienced a large population outflow to various Northern states. By 1860, almost 250,000 British North Americans had joined this movement, a number that would almost double during the next decade. Randy William Widdis, *With Scarcely a Ripple: Anglo-Canadian Migration into the United States and Western Canada, 1880-1920* (Montreal and Kingston: McGill-Queen's University Press, 1998), 65; William Marr and Donald Patterson, *Canada: An Economic History* (Toronto: Gage, 1980), 179.

22 Aliens who claimed exemption from the draft despite long-term residence and voting participation were an ongoing problem for most draft officials. Eugene C. Murdock, *One Million Men: The Civil War Draft in the North* (Madison: State Historical Society of Wisconsin, 1971), 305-14.
23 Winks, *The Civil War Years*, 187.
24 Sharon Roger Hepburn, as one example, suggests that young black men in Canada West volunteered to show their support for both the United States and their brethren in bondage. Sharon A. Roger Hepburn, *Crossing the Border: A Free Black Community in Canada* (Urbana: University of Illinois Press, 2007), 177.
25 Less than a quarter of the nearly 180,000 black soldiers who enrolled in the Union army were credited to the Northern free states, where the literacy level was similar to that of British North American blacks.
26 For an insightful discussion of this problem, see Jennifer Harris, "Black Life in a Nineteenth-Century New Brunswick Town," *Journal of Canadian Studies/Revue d'études canadiennes* 46, 1 (Winter 2012): 144-45.
27 In some regiments, especially those organized in Southern states where few recruits were literate, a handful of white senior non-commissioned officers with combat experience were appointed to help train the black soldiers. An equally small number of black officers, chaplains or surgeons, were appointed in the early months before the War Department changed its policy. Not until near the end of the war were some of the most competent black sergeants commissioned as line officers.
28 The exceptions were the Fifty-fourth and Fifty-fifth Massachusetts Regiments, the Fifth Massachusetts Cavalry, and the Twenty-ninth Connecticut Regiment. Black regiments first organized with a state designation, such as the First Kansas or the First North Carolina Colored Volunteers, were given a numbered USCT designation in early 1864.
29 For a full description of the project and its methodology, see Joseph P. Reidy, "Black Jack: African American Sailors in the Civil War," in *New Interpretations in Naval History: Selected Papers from the Twelfth Naval History Symposium*, ed. William B. Cogar (Annapolis: Naval Institute Press, 1997), 213-20. The results of the project's research can be found at http://www.itd.nps.gov/cwss/ by searching under the category "sailors." The information provided for most recruits includes place of birth, age, complexion (a signifier of race), occupation, height, place of enlistment, term of enlistment, and rating. Most sailors also have a muster record, listing dates and ships. As with virtually all Civil War records, the data contain a degree of error but nonetheless provide the most complete information available.
30 Despite any possible omissions, the project's research provides the most complete database that we have on black Civil War sailors. In this chapter, all general demographic and recruitment data plus the service records of individual sailors are drawn from the project unless otherwise indicated.
31 Benjamin Jackson, a black sailor from Nova Scotia, appeared in the naval records under the name of the white man who hired him as a substitute. Three additional sailors are mentioned in David L. Valuska, *The African American in the Union Navy, 1861-1865* (New York: Garland, 1993), 313. Two other likely black sailors have been identified via ship's rosters, but they have not been included because their race could not be established absolutely.
32 Michael J. Bennett, *Union Jacks: Yankee Sailors in the Civil War* (Chapel Hill: University of North Carolina Press, 2004), 9.
33 Experienced sailors could expect three months' advance salary, and even landsmen, recruits with no maritime skills, received two months' pay. Ibid., 13-19.
34 About 162 black regiments were organized during the Civil War (7 numbered cavalry regiments, 14 numbered artillery regiments, and 141 numbered infantry regiments). The

regimental descriptive books are part of Record Group 94 in the National Archives and Records Administration, Washington, DC.
35 Thomas Kennedy, who was described as having a "fair" complexion, "blue" eyes, and "light" hair, is one of the exceptional cases, a white non-commissioned officer in this Southern regiment. Regimental Descriptive Books, Third USCHA, RG 94, NARA.
36 "John Littlefield," http://www.nps.gov/civilwar/search-sailors.htm.
37 If no British North Americans were found in a sample of regiments raised in Louisiana, Mississippi, North Carolina, and South Carolina, the remainder of these regiments were not examined.
38 In the late 1880s, the War Department began to create compiled military service records for all soldiers by collecting data from descriptive rolls, muster and pay rolls, hospital records, and even some court martial proceedings. The information regarding each soldier was entered on cards, which were stored in a jacket-envelope bearing his name.
39 The recording officer wrote "Canada" into the regimental descriptive book but crossed it out and wrote "Kentucky." Regimental Descriptive Books, Fifth Massachusetts Cavalry, RG 94, NARA. James Finley, who had left Chatham to serve in the 102nd USCT, did much the same thing. "James Finley," Civil War Pension Files (CWPF), RG 15, NARA.
40 "Silas Garrison," Compiled Military Service Records (CMSR), RG 94, NARA.
41 Harris, "Black Life," 155.
42 Just at war's end, Lucien Boyd was convicted of a breach of the Foreign Enlistment Act and sentenced to two years in Kingston Penitentiary. Lucien Boyd File, Buxton National Historic Site and Museum, North Buxton, Ontario.
43 His pension file was recorded under his alias, but his compiled military service record, which contains information under the name "Therman," was corrected after the war, showing his true name to be Benjamin F. Talbot. "William Thurman," CWPF, RG 15, NARA; "Benjamin F. Talbot," CMSR, RG 94, NARA. Ben Jackson, a sailor from Lockhartville, Nova Scotia, enlisted in the Union navy under the alias Lewis Saunders. Marquis, *In Armageddon's Shadow*, 80.
44 "Franklin Howard," CWPF, RG 15, NARA.
45 "Harriet A. Nelson, Widow of John Nelson," CWPF, RG 15, NARA.
46 Canada, *Correspondence Relating to the Fenian Invasion and the Rebellion of the Southern States* (Ottawa: Hunter, Rose and Co., 1869), 9.
47 The forms that give differing birthplaces include a declaration for pension form, a War Department form, and a death certificate for the State of Michigan. "Luke Fizer," CWPF, RG 15, NARA.
48 Michael Wayne, "The Black Population of Canada West on the Eve of the American Civil War: A Reassessment Based on the Manuscript Census of 1861," *Histoire sociale/ Social History* 28, 56 (November 1995): 472, 473.
49 The act was originally passed to prevent mercenary service in South America in the aftermath of the Napoleonic Wars. Dean B. Mahin, *One War at a Time: The International Dimensions of the American Civil War* (Washington, DC: Brassey's, 1999), 48; Amanda Foreman, *A World on Fire: Britain's Crucial Role in the American Civil War* (New York: Random House, 2010), 93.
50 For a discussion of the ways in which Confederate agents tried to evade the British ban on a direct sale of warships to the Confederacy, see Mahin, *One War at a Time*, 142-60, 174-84.
51 Indeed, it was especially ironic, given the American response when Britain explored the possibility of enlisting willing American volunteers for the Crimean War. For a full discussion, see William F. Liebler, "John Bull's American Legion: Britain's Ill-Starred Recruiting Attempt in the United States during the Crimean War," *Pennsylvanian Magazine of History and Biography* 99, 3 (July 1975): 309-35.

52 Quoted in James J. Barnes and Patience P. Barnes, eds., *The American Civil War through British Eyes: Dispatches from British Diplomats*, vol. 1, *November 1860–April 1862* (Kent, OH: Kent State University Press, 2003), 28-29.
53 Ibid., 188, 197-99, 248.
54 *The War of the Rebellion: A Compilation of the Official Records of the Union and Confederate Armies*, 128 vols.(Washington, DC: Government Printing Office, 1880-1901), ser. 3, 1:137, 175, 176 (hereafter *Official Records Army*).
55 Senior American officers were concerned that this could "wilfully endanger the peace between the United States and Great Britain." Ibid., ser. 3, 1:734.
56 Patrick Brode, "Rankin, Arthur," *Dictionary of Canadian Biography Online*, http://www.biographi.ca/; Winks, *The Civil War Years*, 189-90. He was released, the press explained, because his alleged crime had transgressed an imperial statute and was committed in a foreign country. Thus, he could be tried only in the Court of Queen's Bench in England.
57 *Official Records Army*, ser. 3, 1:750.
58 Josiah Henson, *An Autobiography of the Rev. Josiah Henson, from 1789 to 1876* (London: Christian Age Office, 1876), 177.
59 Ibid.
60 Ibid.
61 Ibid., 180-82.
62 Ibid., 183-84.
63 Diary of Reverend Thomas Hughes, 9 April 1865, Diocese of Huron Archives, London, Ontario.
64 *Hamilton Evening Times*, 19 September 1863; *Hamilton Evening Times*, 10 October 1863.
65 *Hamilton Evening Times*, 21 July 1864.
66 Canada, *Correspondence Relating to the Fenian Invasion*, 14, 21, 26.
67 Ibid., 21, 26.
68 *Hamilton Evening Times*, 20 March 1865.
69 Lucien Boyd File, Buxton National Historic Site and Museum.
70 In October 1865, a man named Tuttle was convicted at the Hamilton fall assizes and sentenced to "six months hard labor in common jail," the length of time specified in the new law. *Hamilton Evening Times*, 19 October 1865.
71 Because the Canadian census, unlike its American counterpart, does not include an age breakdown for the population that lists males of "military age," or between eighteen and forty-five years, the rate of volunteering has to be measured against the total black population.
72 By contrast, in Massachusetts, when Governor John Andrew was estimating the potential black recruits for his regiment, he used the white rate of volunteering, which was approximately 20 percent of the men of military age in the state. Unfortunately, the various British North American censuses do not break down the age of subgroups in the population. Richard F. Miller, "For His Wife, His Widow, and His Orphan: Massachusetts and Family Aid during the Civil War," *Massachusetts Historical Review* 6 (2004): 100.
73 Some historians have ignored regional differences. Ella Lonn, who wrote a very influential book on foreigners in the Union military, and for whom the local apparently did not matter, is a case in point. Her lack of understanding was evident in her comment concerning Canada that the "insistence of its citizens on the geographical subdivisions fascinates the modern reader. Not British America, as the whole of Canada was then termed, but rather New Brunswick or Nova Scotia was the place of origin commonly given by the Canadian soldier." Ella Lonn, *Foreigners in the Union Army and Navy* (New York: Greenwood Press, 1951), 150.
74 Horne was referring to the 1860 comments of Reverend W.M. Mitchell. Gerald Horne, *Negro Comrades of the Crown: African Americans and the British Empire Fight the U.S. before Emancipation* (New York: New York University Press, 2012), 191.

75 An original purpose of the US census was to provide Congress with the number of military-aged men in the country. As a result, all censuses include a breakdown of adult males who were aged eighteen to forty-five. Canadian censuses did not include such a category in the nineteenth century. As a result, any comparisons must be based on total population size.
76 Certain states, such as Massachusetts and Connecticut, which had small black populations but a large number of black volunteers who came from elsewhere, do not provide a good basis for comparison.
77 The number of black soldiers credited to any given state is taken from the 1865 report of the Bureau of Colored Troops. It should be noted that soldiers who were "credited" to a state were not necessarily born there but rather had been enrolled in one of its regiments. *Official Records Army*, ser. 3, 5:138.
78 As Harvey Amani Whitfield notes, works that deal with the Maritimes have concentrated on Nova Scotia. The differing response rates in Nova Scotia and New Brunswick may suggest new areas for comparison. Harvey Amani Whitfield, "Reviewing Blackness in Atlantic Canada and the African Atlantic Canadian Diaspora," *Acadiensis* 37, 2 (Summer-Autumn 2008): 138.

CHAPTER 3: BLACKS IN THE NAVY

1 This information is drawn from the entry for John Anderson at http://www.itd.nps.gov/cwaa/. Information on Anderson can be found by following the link to the sailor database.
2 Robin Winks, *The Civil War Years: Canada and the United States* (Montreal and Kingston: McGill-Queen's University Press, 1998), 198-99; Greg Marquis, *In Armageddon's Shadow: The Civil War and Canada's Maritime Provinces* (Montreal and Kingston: McGill-Queen's University Press, 1998), 79-81, 109. Popular works also neglect the involvement of sailors. See Claire Hoy, *Canadians in the Civil War* (Toronto: McArthur, 2004), 124-25, 145.
3 Judith Fingard describes a career sailor as one whose goal "was to ascend the seafaring hierarchy as rapidly as possible." Casual sailors, who signed for short terms, sometimes repeatedly, included men whose employment at sea was "either as an escape from the pressures of society or as a short-term prospect for adventure or employment." Enlistment records for the Civil War indicate that a significant number of black men were short-term sailors. Judith Fingard, *Jack in Port: Sailortowns of Eastern Canada* (Toronto: University of Toronto Press, 1982), 47, 56.
4 Hall served in the Crimean War and later, during the Indian Mutiny, he was part of a naval brigade sent to the relief of Lucknow. For his part in the fighting around the city, Hall was awarded the Victoria Cross in 1859, "the first black, the first Nova Scotian, and the first Canadian sailor to receive the decoration." Bridglal Pachai, "Hall, William," *Dictionary of Canadian Biography Online*, http://www.biographi.ca/.
5 The fate of the ship was never known, but it was assumed to have sunk during a violent hurricane that struck the North Pacific. Some months afterward, a small bottle containing a card was recovered on Cape Sable Island, Nova Scotia, that seemed to be a message from the last of the crew. Thomas Willett of Pubnico, Nova Scotia, whose son had been on the *Levant*, was given the card. *Yarmouth Herald*, 30 January 1862.
6 In periods of national crisis, of course, the law was sometimes ignored. Although the Battalion of Free Men of Color that served under General Andrew Jackson at New Orleans in 1814 did so under that state's special exemption, there is evidence that black soldiers served where some regiments desperately needed manpower, including the Twenty-sixth United States Infantry Regiment.

7. Steven J. Ramold, *Slaves, Sailors, Citizens: African Americans in the Union Navy* (DeKalb: Northern Illinois University Press, 2002), 8, 16.
8. David L. Valuska, *The African American in the Union Navy, 1861-1865* (New York: Garland, 1993), 10.
9. Ramold, *Slaves, Sailors, Citizens*, 21.
10. Michael J. Bennett, *Union Jacks: Yankee Sailors in the Civil War* (Chapel Hill: University of North Carolina Press, 2004), 9.
11. Quoted in James E. Valle, *Rocks and Shoals: Order and Discipline in the Old Navy, 1880-1861* (Annapolis: Naval Institute Press, 1980), 19.
12. During the Civil War, most foreign black soldiers came from the Caribbean islands and British North America, but many African and Asian countries were also represented. Only some of the fifty-eight sailors from Cape Verde Islands had anglicized names, but the eight who came from India, Ceylon, and Borneo all had "American" names.
13. Robert M. Browning, *From Cape Charles to Cape Fear: The North Atlantic Blockading Squadron during the Civil War* (Tuscaloosa: University of Alabama Press, 1993), 202.
14. Ramold, *Slaves, Sailors, Citizens*, 11-20.
15. Valle, *Rocks and Shoals*, 20.
16. Ramold, *Slaves, Sailors, Citizens*, 16-23; Valuska, *The African American*, 11. In the 1840s, Captain Matthew C. Perry obtained permission to hire a number of black sailors for the ships of his Africa Squadron. Donald L. Canney, *Africa Squadron: The U.S. Navy and the Slave Trade* (Washington, DC: Potomac Books, 2006), 55.
17. Basing his estimate on sampling, Michael J. Bennett concludes that British North American–born sailors made up 4.7 percent of the wartime Union navy, or approximately 5,500 men. Bennett, *Union Jacks*, 10.
18. Herbert Aptheker accepted and popularized this number after randomly checking the muster rolls for several ships that served in 1863 and 1864. His findings generally agreed with the official assessment. Herbert Aptheker, "The Negro in the Union Navy," *Journal of Negro History* 32, 2 (April 1947): 179.
19. Valuska lists thirty from "Canada," eighty from Nova Scotia, and one from Cape Breton (none came from New Brunswick or Prince Edward Island). This research, done for his 1973 dissertation, was slightly modified for his monograph. Valuska, *The African American*, 25, 38, 53, 58, 62, 83-84.
20. For information on the Civil War Sailors Project, see Joseph P. Reidy, "Black Jack: African American Sailors in the Civil War," in *New Interpretations in Naval History: Selected Papers from the Twelfth Naval History Symposium*, ed. William B. Cogar (Annapolis: Naval Institute Press, 1997), 213-20. Unless otherwise indicated, the general demographic and recruitment data for this chapter come from the project. Most sailors had a muster record that listed dates and ships, and the information for most recruits includes place of birth, age, complexion (a signifier of race), occupation, height, place of enlistment, term of enlistment, and rating.
21. Individuals who were recorded as "Negro," "Colored," or "Mulatto" were considered to be black. Others, such as those whose complexion is listed as "Yellow," are more difficult to classify. The project chose to err on the side of inclusion.
22. The three men are Adam Willis from "Canada," Edward Berrion from Halifax, and William A. Dehart from Nova Scotia. Valuska, *The African American*, 122, 125, 126, 313.
23. Marquis, *In Armageddon's Shadow*, 80-81; "Benjamin Jackson, alias Lewis Saunders," Civil War Pension Files (CWPF), RG 15, National Archives and Records Administration (NARA), Washington, DC.
24. Because the evidence does not clearly establish that Crowell was black, he has been omitted from this study. "Benjamin Jackson, alias Lewis Saunders," CWPF, RG 15, NARA.

25 Because naval records omit place of residence, they cannot be used to identify African Americans who had moved to the British colonies. Nor do we know how many of these transplanted individuals would have self-identified as British North American. Anecdotal evidence indicates that some did join the navy. Tom Henson, the son of Josiah Henson, a well-known black abolitionist and minister who had escaped to Upper Canada in the 1830s, did so, and his family lost track of him. Joseph Hayden, who had escaped from Kentucky as a child and lived for a while in Canada West, enlisted and served in the Gulf Coast Squadron before his death in 1865. Fergus Bordewich, *Bound for Canaan: The Epic Story of the Underground Railroad; America's First Civil Rights Movement* (New York: Amistad, 2005), 431.

26 There is some dispute over the exact number in commission. Paul Silverstone and Samuel Negus put the number at forty-two in March 1861. Gary D. Joiner calculates it at thirty-nine. He identifies twelve that were attached to the Home Squadron, six in the East Indies Squadron, three in the Mediterranean Squadron, three in the Brazilian Squadron, eight in the African Squadron, and seven in the Pacific Squadron. Paul H. Silverstone, *Civil War Navies, 1855-1883* (Annapolis: Naval Institute Press, 2001), ix; Samuel Negus, "A Notorious Nest of Offence: Neutrals, Belligerents, and Union Jails in Civil War Blockade Running," *Civil War History* 56, 4 (December 2010): 354; Gary D. Joiner, *Mr. Lincoln's Brown Water Navy: The Mississippi Squadron* (New York: Rowman and Littlefield, 2007), 4.

27 As soon as Lincoln took office, Congress voted censure against Toucey. William M. Fowler Jr., *Under Two Flags: The American Navy in the Civil War* (New York: W.W. Norton, 1990), 34.

28 Dean B. Mahin, *One War at a Time: The International Dimensions of the American Civil War* (Washington, DC: Brassey's, 1999), 45.

29 A naval academy was actually created in 1845, then reorganized and given its current name in 1850. For more on the establishment of the academy, see Mark C. Hunter, *A Society of Gentlemen: Midshipmen at the U.S. Naval Academy, 1845-1861* (Annapolis: Naval Institute Press, 2010).

30 Silverstone, *Civil War Navies*, 13; Joiner, *Mr. Lincoln's Brown Water Navy*, 1-3.

31 Joiner, *Mr. Lincoln's Brown Water Navy*, 3.

32 Although Admiral David G. Farragut had used both the *Hartford* and the *Brooklyn* to force his way past the forts guarding New Orleans and took them as far as Vicksburg, he had serious misgivings about using them on the Mississippi. Fowler, *Under Two Flags*, 116-22, 129-30, 193, 219.

33 General Benjamin Butler first used the term "contrabands" in May 1861. Three Virginian slaves had escaped to Union lines, only to have their owner, a Confederate officer, arrive the next day under a flag of truce, cite the Fugitive Slave Act, and demand their return. Butler avoided a legal dilemma by declaring that the slaves were "contraband of war" and that, as the confiscated property of a belligerent, they were not liable for return. Soon all escaped slaves were referred to as contrabands.

34 The lowest rating in the Union navy, based on the combined factor of age and skills, was "boy," first, second, or third class. Before the war, this rating was assigned to recruits who were younger than eighteen. All ex-slaves, regardless of age, were initially rated boy. The ranking, placing them at the bottom of the naval hierarchy, fed racial stereotypes and limited ex-slaves to the lowest pay rate. Bennett, *Union Jacks*, 163-64.

35 David Herbert Donald, Jean Harvey Baker, and Michael F. Holt, *The Civil War and Reconstruction* (New York: W.W. Norton, 2001), 398.

36 James M. McPherson, *Battle Cry of Freedom: The Civil War Era* (New York: Oxford University Press, 1988), 313.

37 Joseph P. Reidy, "Black Men in Navy Blue during the Civil War," *Prologue: Quarterly of the National Archives and Records Administration* 33, 3 (Fall 2001): 157-58.

38 Bennett puts the figure at 4.7 percent of all Union sailors. By contrast, British North Americans in the Union army made up only 2.6 percent of all soldiers. Bennett, *Union Jacks*, 10-11.
39 Reidy, "Black Men in Navy Blue," 158-59.
40 Ramold, *Slaves, Sailors, Citizens*, 56.
41 Previously, port towns had discouraged naval enlistment because recruits were not added to their draft quotas. In fact, these towns had provided bounties to five thousand seamen to join the army. Ari Hoogenboom, *Gustavus Vasa Fox of the Union Navy* (Baltimore: Johns Hopkins University Press, 2008), 216; Ramold, *Slaves, Sailors, Citizens*, 66.
42 The act also enabled trained seamen to transfer from the army to the navy. Some British North Americans who had joined the army even though they were mariners by occupation took advantage of this provision. Since black regiments had just started to be formed in 1863, few black seamen in infantry regiments transferred. However, William Martin of Pictou, Nova Scotia, who transferred to the USS *Minnesota*, may have been a black seaman. His files give the colour of his eyes, hair, and complexion as "black, black, dark." James W. Geary, *We Need Men: The Union Draft in the Civil War* (DeKalb: Northern Illinois University Press, 1991), 12-13, 66-67; http://www.tfoenander.com/minnesota.htm.
43 Department of the Navy, Naval Historical Center, "Mohongo," *Dictionary of American Naval Fighting Ships*, http://www.history.navy.mil/.
44 Ramold, *Slaves, Sailors, Citizens*, 75-76.
45 Ibid., 60.
46 Valuska, *The African American*, 31; Reidy, "Black Men in Navy Blue," 156. In 1864, the pay for most ratings was raised by two dollars a month. Ramold, *Slaves, Sailors, Citizens*, 85.
47 Training on a steam-powered vessel for this rating took quite some time, so it is not surprising that only one black British North American, Samuel Smith of Canada West, enlisted as a fireman. More surprising is the fact that, when he signed up at Cincinnati in December 1862, he gave his occupation as farmer. Within a few weeks, he was serving on the USS *Silver Lake*, a wooden stern-wheel gunboat attached to the Mississippi Squadron.
48 Only one British North American sailor, James Ingraham, signed on as a coal heaver. Ironically, Ingraham, a twenty-five-year-old Nova Scotian, had been a fireman before the war.
49 Many may have been what W. Jeffrey Bolster calls "transient" seamen – sailors who signed on for one or two terms because of unemployment on land or in hopes of adventure. Bolster suggests that many were familiar with a range of occupations on both land and sea, which is confirmed by the occupational listings for recruits. W. Jeffrey Bolster, *Black Jacks: African American Seamen in the Age of Sail* (Cambridge, MA: Harvard University Press, 1997), 178-79.
50 Bennett, *Union Jacks*, 19.
51 Ibid., 28.
52 *Official Records of the Union and Confederate Navies in the War of the Rebellion* (Washington, DC: Government Printing Office, 1894-1927), ser. 1, 2:417, 467-68, 567-71 (*Official Records Navy*).
53 Silverstone, *Civil War Navies*, 54-55, 122.
54 Hundreds of new recruits, along with sailors whose vessels were undergoing long-term repairs, were quartered in receiving ships, old and obsolete sailing ships, before being forwarded to their new assignments. Browning, *From Cape Charles to Cape Fear*, 200-1.
55 Quoted in Bennett, *Union Jacks*, 2-3.
56 Fingard, *Jack in Port*, 5, 194-241. Fingard describes in detail how crimps worked in Quebec City, Halifax, and Saint John.

57 Canada, *Correspondence Relating to the Fenian Invasion and the Rebellion of the Southern States* (Ottawa: Hunter, Rose and Co., 1869), 15-6, 20, 22. Although the British sailors claimed that they had been "sold like slaves," officials believed that their anger was fuelled by the loss of their bounty money.
58 Marquis, *In Armageddon's Shadow*, 98.
59 Canada, *Correspondence Relating to the Fenian Invasion*, 11-12. Adam Mayers, "Stolen Soldiers," *Civil War Times Illustrated* 34, 2 (June 1995): 56.
60 David Valuska records Adam Willis of "Canada" as having enlisted in Buffalo in late July 1864, although Willis is not in the Civil War Sailors Project data bank. Valuska, *The African American*, 313.
61 Ramold, *Slaves, Sailors, Citizens*, 65-66.
62 For a case study that illustrates the complexities and conflicts generated by the settlement of a prize, see Frederick C. Leiner, "The Squadron Commander's Share: *Decatur vs Chew* and the Prize Money for the *Chesapeake*'s First War of 1812 Cruise," *Journal of Military History* 73, 1 (January 2009): 69-82.
63 In New York, the court costs to process prizes were almost three times higher than in Boston. Browning, *From Cape Charles to Cape Fear*, 262.
64 Hoogenboom, *Gustavus Vasa Fox*, 99.
65 "Benjamin Jackson, Civil War Veteran Passes Away," *Windsor Journal*, 1 September 1915.
66 The *Lady Sterling* was one of the many fully loaded ships that cleared Halifax, theoretically bound for Nassau or Bermuda, only to dash for Wilmington. *Official Records Navy*, ser. 1, 10:469, 476, 12:529, 543; Browning, *From Cape Charles to Cape Fear*, 263; David D. Porter, *The Naval History of the Civil War* (New York: Sherman, 1886), 838, 839; David G. Surdam, *Northern Naval Superiority and the Economics of the American Civil War* (Columbia: University of South Carolina Press, 2001), 85.
67 *Official Records Navy*, ser. 1, 17:550-54; Porter, *The Naval History*, 837.
68 By August 1864, Secretary Welles was forcefully reminding his admirals that sinking and destroying blockade-runners took precedence over capturing them as prizes. *Official Records Navy*, ser. 1, 10:402-3.
69 The *San Jacinto*'s captain, Richard W. Meade, was subsequently court-martialled for negligence. *Official Records Navy*, ser.1, 17:790-91, 793-95.
70 In October 1864, however, sailors in the Mississippi Squadron benefitted from Admiral David Porter's general order that all enemy property, particularly cotton, could be seized as a legitimate prize of war and sent to Cairo for adjudication. The potential profits were immense. In one case, adjudicated in early 1865, more than $450,000 was distributed to the crews of twenty-one vessels. Porter, *The Naval History*, 835; Craig L. Symonds, *Lincoln and His Admirals: Abraham Lincoln, the U.S. Navy, and the Civil War* (Oxford: Oxford University Press, 2008), 284.
71 Negus, "A Notorious Nest," 355.
72 Quoted in Robert W. Daly, ed., *Aboard the USS Florida, 1863-65: The Letters of Acting Paymaster William Frederick Keeler, U.S. Navy, to His Wife, Anna* (Annapolis: Naval Institute Press, 1964), 210.
73 Bennett, *Union Jacks*, 8; Valle, *Rocks and Shoals*, 4.
74 Sullivan served on the USS *Rachel Seaman*, re-enlisted, and was assigned to the USS *Monadnock*, a twin-turret monitor commissioned in October 1864. He was aboard when the *Monadnock* left Philadelphia for California by way of the Straits of Magellan. Hoogenboom, *Gustavus Vasa Fox*, 270-71; "James Sullivan," CWPF, RG 15, NARA; Department of the Navy, Naval Historical Center, "Monadnock," *Dictionary of American Naval Fighting Ships*, http://www.history.navy.mil/.
75 Joseph P. Reidy argues that the navy frequently discounted the skills of black mariners and cites the case of James Forten Dunbar, the nephew of a prominent sail maker in Philadelphia, as illustration. Reidy, "Black Men in Navy Blue," 160.

76 Ibid., 161.
77 Ramold, *Slaves, Sailors, Citizens*, 77.
78 Bennett, *Union Jacks*, x.
79 Eric W. Sager, *Seafaring Labour: The Merchant Marine of Atlantic Canada, 1820-1914* (Montreal and Kingston: McGill-Queen's University Press, 1989), 3, 199.
80 The obvious exception occurred when black soldiers were transferred from the US army to the navy in 1864.
81 Thompson and Trust were both in their early twenties when they enlisted at Portsmouth, New Hampshire, on 9 September 1864 for three years. Both served on the USS *Mohongo*. Bushlaw and Johnson, both born in Saint John, joined together at New York on 22 December 1864 for a similar two-year term. They served out their enlistment on the USS *Spirea*.
82 *Official Records Navy*, ser. 1, 10:244, 326.
83 The attack cost the ship thirty-three crewmen, but it is not clear how many, if any, were from British North America. Chris E. Fonvielle, Jr., *The Wilmington Campaign: Last Rays of Departing Hope* (Mechanicsburg, PA: Stackpole Books, 1997), 258.
84 Barbara Brooks Tomblin, *Bluejackets and Contrabands: African Americans and the Union Navy* (Lexington: University Press of Kentucky, 2009), 258.
85 Two of these, William Martin of Nova Scotia and Francis Peters from Montreal, both of whom were missed by the Civil War Sailors Project, may well have been black. The descriptive books give their eyes, hair, and complexion as "black" or "dark," a common listing for African Americans. Ibid., 329-30; USS *Minnesota* Muster Roll, http://www.tfoenander.com/minnesota.htm. The site now requires researchers to go through "Naval Records."
86 *Official Records Navy*, ser. 1, vol. 11:193, 400.
87 Ramold, *Slaves, Sailors, Citizens*, 96.
88 Browning, *From Cape Charles to Cape Fear*, 176.
89 Silverstone, *Civil War Navies*, 104.
90 *Official Records Navy*, ser. 1, 3:217. Aspinwall, the name given by the American émigré community to the town of Colon, was the eastern terminus of the Panama Railroad.
91 Even in the summer of 1864, crewmembers from the *Potomac* were being transferred to more efficient steam-powered vessels. Ibid., ser. 1, 21:171; Silverstone, *Civil War Navies*, 96; Porter, *The Naval History*, 835.
92 Quoted in Daly, *Aboard the USS Florida*, 11 (emphasis in original).
93 Quoted in Craig L. Symonds, ed., *Charleston Blockade: The Journals of John B. Marchand, U.S. Navy, 1861-1862* (Newport, RI: Naval War College Press, 1976), 75.
94 The *Virginia* was built from the hull of the USS *Merrimack*, a Union frigate that had been scuttled when the Norfolk Navy Yard fell into Confederate hands. The day after its first attack on the Union fleet, the *Virginia* engaged the USS *Monitor* in one of the most famous Civil War naval battles. Northerners continued to refer to the ship as the *Merrimack*.
95 "John Anderson," CWPF, RG 15, NARA.
96 When the *Mackinaw*'s captain signalled that he was in a disabled and defenceless condition, Admiral David Porter responded, "Remain where you are and fight." John W. Grattan, *Under the Blue Pennant or Notes of a Naval Officer, 1863-1865*, ed. Robert J. Schneller (New York: John Wiley and Sons, 1999), 153.
97 Whether any black British North Americans were among the injured is unknown. The records give the numbers of injured but not their names. Fonvielle, *The Wilmington Campaign*, 136-37; Grattan, *Under the Blue Pennant*, 152.
98 David F. Riggs, "Sailors of the *U.S.S. Cairo*: Anatomy of a Gunboat Crew," *Civil War History* 28, 3 (September 1982): 270.
99 Joiner, *Mr. Lincoln's Brown Water Navy*, 100-1.

100 Although Joiner believes that the explosion was detonated electrically, Timothy S. Wolters, in an extensive article tracing the early advocates of electric torpedoes (or mines), argues that the first warship sunk in this manner was the USS *Commodore Jones* in May 1864 in the James River. Wolters, however, focuses most of his attention on actions in the eastern seaboard. Joiner, *Mr. Lincoln's Brown Water Navy*, 101; Timothy S. Wolters, "Electric Torpedoes in the Confederacy: Reconciling Conflicting Histories," *Journal of Military History* 72, 3 (July 2008): 756.
101 John D. Milligan, *Gunboats Down the Mississippi* (Annapolis: United States Naval Institute, 1965), 104-5; Valle, *Rocks and Shoals*, 165; Bennett, *Union Jacks*, 97.
102 *Official Records Navy*, ser. 1, 11:647.
103 Ramold, *Slaves, Sailors, Citizens*, 129.
104 Symonds, *Charleston Blockade*, 150.
105 *Official Records Navy*, ser. 1, 3:195, 424-25.
106 As late as May 1864, the captain of the CSS *Alabama*, Raphael Semmes, was still hoping that the *Agrippa* would arrive, although he admitted that he feared "some disaster has befallen her." *Official Records Navy*, ser. 1, 2:743; *Civil War Naval Chronology* (Washington, DC: Naval History Division, 1971), 6:190; Silverstone, *Civil War Navies*, 103.
107 The USS *Niagara* and its consort, the USS *Sacramento*, wanted to engage the ram when the weather was blowing and the seas rough. A smooth sea, they felt, gave too great an advantage to the armoured Confederate cruiser.
108 William B. Gould IV, *Diary of a Contraband: The Civil War Passage of a Black Sailor* (Stanford: Stanford University Press, 2002), 220, 225.
109 Ibid., 75.
110 Conway W. Henderson, "The Anglo-American Treaty of 1862 in Civil War Diplomacy," *Civil War History* 15, 4 (1969): 311; Valuska, *The African American*, 68. For Rear Admiral S.F. Du Pont, the twenty-four ships were the maximum "which in all possibility can ever be used for the purpose set forth in the treaty." *Official Records Navy*, ser. 1, 14:229-30.
111 The seven ships were the USS *Wabash*, USS *Paul Jones*, USS *Powhatan*, USS *Unadilla*, USS *Flag*, USS *South Carolina*, and USS *Flambeau*. Although they were to be available to interdict the trade, they spent most of their time in American waters.
112 A. Taylor Milne, "The Lyons-Seward Treaty of 1862," *American Historical Review* 38, 3 (April 1933): 515.
113 http://www.hazegray.org/danfs/steamers/powhatan.htm. *The Dictionary of American Fighting Ships Online* can be used to find the Civil War vessels mentioned here.
114 Ramold, *Slaves, Sailors, Citizens*, 5.
115 Bennett, *Union Jacks*, 180.
116 Quoted in Tomblin, *Bluejackets and Contrabands*, 14.
117 "A Personal Reminiscence by Edward W. Hammond, Boatswain, U.S. Navy, of an Incident on Board the U.S. Ship St. Mary's in Valparaiso Harbor 1865," quoted in Reidy, "Black Men in Navy Blue," 154-55.
118 Daly, *Aboard the USS Florida*, 70.
119 Donald R. Shaffer, *After the Glory: The Struggles of Black Civil War Veterans* (Lawrence: University Press of Kansas, 2004), 122.
120 Establishing their number, or that of their dependants, is a difficult task. Naval pension files are indexed alphabetically by sailors' names, unlike army files, which are also indexed by unit. Thus, to determine whether the William Johnson who enlisted as a twenty-one-year-old farmer from "Canada" applied for a pension, a researcher must scrutinize the documents in thirty-one separate files, each for a different William Johnson. A full search of the files revealed that only about 10 percent of British North American sailors applied for a pension.

Chapter 4: Promises Deferred

1. J.L. Stevens to Salmon P. Chase, 10 August 1861, quoted in Ira Berlin, Joseph P. Reidy, and Leslie S. Rowlands, eds., *The Black Military Experience*, ser. 2 of *Freedom: A Documentary History of Emancipation, 1861-1867* (Cambridge: Cambridge University Press, 1982), 78-79 (emphasis in original).
2. W.T. Boyd and J.T. Alston to Salmon P. Chase, 15 November 1861, quoted in Berlin, Reidy, and Rowlands, *The Black Military Experience*, 80. Similar claims came from groups in Michigan, New York, and Pennsylvania.
3. William A. Jones to Hon. S. Cameron, 27 November 1861, quoted in Berlin, Reidy, and Rowlands, *The Black Military Experience*, 81 (emphasis in original).
4. Quoted in Noah Andre Trudeau, *Like Men of War: Black Troops in the Civil War* (Boston: Little, Brown, 1998), 8.
5. Black men in Pittsburgh had organized the Fort Pitt Cadets at the start of the war and continued to train until black soldiers were finally able to enter the Union army. Berlin, Reidy, and Rowlands, *The Black Military Experience*, 83-84.
6. Quoted in ibid., 82 (emphasis in original). White apologized for his poor writing "as I never went to School a day in my life." Ibid.; Edward A. Miller Jr., "Garland H. White, Black Army Chaplain," *Civil War History* 43, 3 (September 1997): 204.
7. George Hendrick and Willene Hendrick, *Black Refugees in Canada: Accounts of Escape during the Era of Slavery* (Jefferson, NC: McFarland, 2010), 98.
8. Quoted in Berlin, Reidy, and Rowlands, *The Black Military Experience*, 82.
9. The A.M.E. organization, which had been active in Upper Canada since 1826, had churches in Amherstburg, St. Catharines, Queen's Bush, Malden, Hamilton, Brantford, and Toronto by the late 1830s. However, a number of Canadian churches came together in 1856 to create a new denomination, the British Methodist Episcopal Church, which absorbed most A.M.E. congregations in the Canadas. Robin Winks discerns two key factors in the movement out of the A.M.E.: "The impulse behind this separatist movement came from fugitives who would be safer from the effects of the Fugitive Slave Act if they became British citizens and were protected by an entirely Canadian-based organization." Second, a number of fugitives had married black Canadians, and they objected to the inclusion of "African" in the name of the church. Robin Winks, *The Blacks in Canada: A History*, 2nd ed. (Montreal and Kingston: McGill-Queen's University Press, 1997), 355-57; Hendrick and Hendrick, *Black Refugees in Canada*, 98.
10. The "loyal" slave states that remained in the Union were Kentucky, Maryland, Missouri, and Delaware. John David Smith, "Let Us All Be Grateful That We Have Colored Troops That Will Fight," in *Black Soldiers in Blue: African American Troops in the Civil War Era*, ed. John David Smith (Chapel Hill: University of North Carolina Press, 2002), 10.
11. Smith, *Black Soldiers in Blue*, 14. Because the Militia Act assumed that blacks would perform menial tasks, it authorized a lower rate of pay for blacks employed under its auspices than was received by soldiers. Historians have debated the motives behind and the importance of these acts. See Benjamin P. Thomas and Harold M. Hyman, *Stanton: The Life and Times of Lincoln's Secretary of War* (New York: Knopf, 1962), 233, 237, 238; Mary Frances Berry, *Military Necessity and Civil Rights Policy: Black Citizenship and the Constitution, 1861-1868* (Port Washington, NY: Kennikat Press, 1977), 42; Mark E. Neely Jr., "Confiscation Act of July 17, 1862," in *The Abraham Lincoln Encyclopaedia* (New York: McGraw-Hill, 1982), 67-68.
12. Samuel J. Kirkwood to General Henry W. Halleck, 5 August 1862, quoted in Berlin, Reidy, and Rowlands, *The Black Military Experience*, 85-86.
13. The Preliminary Emancipation Proclamation, which Lincoln released on 22 September 1862, did not specifically mention using African Americans in the military.

14 The disappointing results of the 2 July 1862 call for more troops forced the government to enact a draft of state militia in August 1862. At the same time, it began to increase the traditional hundred-dollar bounty paid to soldiers who were honourably discharged. James M. McPherson, *Battle Cry of Freedom: The Civil War Era* (New York: Oxford University Press, 1988), 492-94; David Herbert Donald, Jean Harvey Baker, and Michael F. Holt, *The Civil War and Reconstruction* (New York: W.W. Norton, 2001), 227-29.

15 These consisted of thirty-six regiments that had signed on for two years in 1861 and ninety-two nine-month militia regiments that were organized in 1862, all expecting to be mustered out during the summer. McPherson, *Battle Cry of Freedom*, 600; Iver Bernstein, *The New York City Draft Riots: Their Significance for American Society and Politics in the Age of the Civil War* (New York: Oxford University Press, 1990), 7.

16 He could claim an exemption if he were at least thirty-five and married, was the sole supporter of either a widow or infirm parents, or was the father of motherless children. Exemptions were not made for occupations. Tyler Anbinder, "Which Poor Man's Fight? Immigrants and the Federal Conscription of 1863," *Civil War History* 52, 4 (December 2006): 347, 352.

17 Both substitutes and commutation payments were legacies of the old militia system. The pool of substitutes was filled primarily by eighteen- and nineteen-year-olds and by aliens who resided in either the United States or another country, such as British North America.

18 Quoted in Roy P. Basler, ed., *Collected Works of Abraham Lincoln* (New Brunswick, NJ: Rutgers University Press, 1954), 6:30. The Preliminary Emancipation Proclamation of 22 September 1862 did not contain this clause.

19 *Toronto Globe*, 3 January 1863.

20 Berlin, Reidy, and Rowlands, *The Black Military Experience*, 75; Richard M. Reid, *Freedom for Themselves: North Carolina's Black Soldiers in the Civil War Era* (Chapel Hill: University of North Carolina Press, 2008), 13.

21 Edwin S. Redkey, "Brave Black Volunteers: A Profile of the Fifty-Fourth Massachusetts Regiment," in *Hope and Glory: Essays on the Legacy of the 54th Massachusetts Regiment*, ed. Martin H. Blatt, Thomas J. Brown, and Donald Yacovone (Amherst: University of Massachusetts Press, 2000), 22.

22 A measure of Andrew's accomplishments was that, by the end of the war, Massachusetts was credited with having enlisted 3,966 black recruits. Berlin, Reidy, and Rowlands, *The Black Military Experience*, 12.

23 Luis F. Emilio, *A Brave Black Regiment: History of the Fifty-Fourth Regiment of Massachusetts Volunteer Infantry, 1863-1865* (1891; repr., New York: Arno Press, 1969), 6-7.

24 A wealthy businessman from Medford, Massachusetts, Stearns had been a supporter of John Brown and a member of the Secret Six, which had funded Brown's activities. Fearing arrest in the wake of the Harper's Ferry raid, Stearns and Six members Samuel Gridley Howe and Franklin Benjamin Sanborn fled to Quebec City and then Niagara Falls. Russell Duncan, ed., *Blue-Eyed Child of Fortune: The Civil War Letters of Colonel Robert Gould Shaw* (Athens: University of Georgia Press, 1992), 26-27; Charles E. Heller, *Portrait of an Abolitionist: A Biography of George Luther Stearns, 1809-1867* (Westport, CT: Greenwood Press, 1996), 106-8.

25 Emilio, *A Brave Black Regiment*, 11.

26 In addition to using his influential *Douglass' Monthly* to publicize the need for black recruits, Douglass also canvassed western New York, encouraging black men to enlist. Duncan, *Blue-Eyed Child of Fortune*, 28.

27 Noah Andre Trudeau, *Voices of the 55th: Letters from the 55th Massachusetts Volunteers, 1861-1865* (Dayton, OH: Morningside, 1996), 10; Redkey, "Brave Black Volunteers," 22.

28 Some volunteers claimed that they had been promised much larger bounties. Certainly, just a few months later, the state offered recruits one "up-front" payment of $325 or a slightly larger amount on an instalment plan. Charles Barnard Fox, *Record of the Service of the Fifty-Fifth Regiment of Massachusetts Volunteer Infantry* (Cambridge, MA: John Wilson and Son, 1868), 17; Richard F. Miller, "For His Wife, His Widow, and His Orphan: Massachusetts and Family Aid during the Civil War," *Massachusetts Historical Review* 6 (2004): 94.
29 Miller, "For His Wife, His Widow," 95; Duncan, *Blue-Eyed Child of Fortune*, 28.
30 Quoted in Duncan, *Blue-Eyed Child of Fortune*, 298.
31 "Why Should a Colored Man Enlist?" *Douglass' Monthly*, April 1863, 1.
32 Private Alfred E. Pellett in the Fifty-fifth Massachusetts later claimed that he "had no hope of anything, but enlisted for fear of being drafted." Diary of Burt Green Wilder, 22 December 1863, Cornell University, Ithaca, New York. Few blacks who enlisted in 1863 had to fear the Enrollment Act of March 1863. Whereas free blacks were apparently eligible for the draft under the act, which required the enrolment of every male citizen between the ages of twenty and forty-five, very few were actually enrolled and drafted. Not until February 1864, when the legislation was amended, did it specifically include the enrolment of all blacks in the target age group. Eugene C. Murdock, *One Million Men: The Civil War Draft in the North* (Madison: State Historical Society of Wisconsin, 1971), 180; James W. Geary, *We Need Men: The Union Draft in the Civil War* (DeKalb: Northern Illinois University Press, 1991), 67-68.
33 R.J.M. Blackett, ed., *Thomas Morris Chester: Black Civil War Correspondent; His Dispatches from the Virginia Front* (New York: Da Capo Press, 1989), 34-35.
34 Frank P. Stearns, *The Life and Public Service of George Luther Stearns* (Philadelphia: J.P. Lippincott, 1907), 286.
35 Heller, *Portrait of an Abolitionist*, 147.
36 Not only was there anecdotal evidence for this, but the practice was also identified in the United States. Senator Henry Wilson protested in Congress about the drugging and involuntary enlistment of a "man of character" in his district, and Major General John A. Dix claimed that several "boys" had died because they had been "so badly drugged." Michael Thomas Smith, "The Most Desperate Scoundrels Unhung: Bounty Jumpers and Recruitment Fraud in the Civil War North," *American Nineteenth Century History* 6, 2 (June 2005): 156.
37 When Josiah Henson encouraged young black men in Canada West to join the Union army, and when he accepted money from Alexander Pool for helping Pool's son and brother-in-law to enlist, his behaviour satisfied the definition of a bounty broker and crimp. Because he was clearly motivated by a desire to end slavery and the sense that black North Americans had a religious duty to support the war, Henson challenges the common perception of brokers and crimps. Josiah Henson, *An Autobiography of the Rev. Josiah Henson, from 1789 to 1876* (London: Christian Age Office, 1876), 183-85.
38 For specific cases, see Robin Winks, *The Civil War Years: Canada and the United States* (Montreal and Kingston: McGill-Queen's University Press, 1998), 195-97.
39 George L. Stearns to Gerrit Smith, 13 March 1863, Gerrit Smith Collection, Syracuse University Library, Syracuse, New York.
40 Dudley T. Cornish, *The Sable Arm: Negro Troops in the Union Army, 1861-1865* (New York: Longmans Green, 1965), 159.
41 Quoted in Lonnie R. Speer, *Portals to Hell: Military Prisons in the Civil War* (Mechanicsburg, PA: Stackpole Books, 1997), 108, 9.
42 James G. Hollandsworth, "The Execution of White Officers from Black Units by Confederate Forces during the Civil War," in *Black Flag over Dixie: Racial Atrocities and*

Reprisals in the Civil War Gregory, ed. J.W. Urwin (Carbondale: Southern Illinois University Press, 2004), 52.
43 *Hamilton Evening Times*, 27 May 1863.
44 Quoted in Dorothy Wickenden, "Dismantling the Peculiar Institution," *Wilson Quarterly* 14, 4 (1990): 107.
45 General Order No. 252, 31 July 1863, in *The War of the Rebellion: A Compilation of the Official Records of the Union and Confederate Armies*, 128 vols. (Washington, DC: Government Printing Office, 1880-1901), ser. 2, 6:163 (hereafter *Official Records Army*).
46 The extent of atrocities experienced by black troops is well covered in Gregory J.W. Urwin, ed., *Black Flag over Dixie: Racial Atrocities and Reprisals in the Civil War* (Carbondale: Southern Illinois University Press, 2004).
47 *Toronto Globe*, 29 and 31 July 1863.
48 Quoted in John Dwight Warner Jr., "Crossed Sabres: A History of the Fifth Massachusetts Volunteer Cavalry, an African American Regiment in the Civil War" (PhD diss., Boston College, 1997), 56.
49 Duncan, *Blue-Eyed Child of Fortune*, 298.
50 This did not stop individual states and local municipalities from offering a range of bounties to encourage enlistments; increasingly as the war progressed, black recruits in Northern states received many of these bounties. Richard M. Reid, "Government Policy, Prejudice, and the Experience of Black Civil War Soldiers and Their Families," *Journal of Family History* 27, 4 (October 2002): 388.
51 The changing laws that covered the payment of bounties to black soldiers are outlined in "Report of the Provost Marshall General," 17 March 1866, *Official Records Army*, ser. 3, 5:654-62.
52 The agents did not leave until 25 February. Duncan, *Blue-Eyed Child of Fortune*, 296, 298.
53 Moore was discharged for disabilities in June 1864. Some military records give his birthplace as Ontario County, New York, although the regimental descriptive books give his place of origin as "Canada." Regimental Descriptive Books, Fifty-fourth Massachusetts Regiment, RG 94, National Archives and Records Administration (NARA), Washington, DC.
54 "John W. Moore," Compiled Military Service Records (CMSR), RG 94, NARA.
55 Quoted in Duncan, *Blue-Eyed Child of Fortune*, 309, 10.
56 The regimental descriptive book gives Robinson's birthplace as Halifax, whereas his compiled military service records put it in the West Indies. Regimental Descriptive Books, Fifty-fourth Massachusetts Regiment, RG 94, NARA; "John Robinson," CMSR, RG 94, NARA.
57 Five were born in Canada West and one in Montreal. The number may be higher because the place of residence was not given for some men. Fox, *Record of the Service*, 114-44.
58 The Third United States Colored Troops (USCT), which was being raised in Camp William Penn just outside of Philadelphia, had twenty-nine British North American recruits among its ranks, and the Fourteenth Rhode Island Heavy Artillery, later the Eleventh United States Colored Heavy Artillery, had begun recruiting in July; it attracted almost twenty British North Americans.
59 John F. Marszalek, *Sherman: A Soldier's Passion for Order* (New York: Free Press, 1993), 270-71.
60 Reid, *Freedom for Themselves*, 56-57, 68-72.
61 *Philadelphia Christian Recorder*, 23 October 1863.
62 Quoted in Harold Holzer, ed., *The Lincoln Mailbag: America Writes to the President, 1861-1865* (Carbondale: Southern Illinois University Press, 1998), 166-67.

63 Virginia M. Adams, ed., *On the Altar of Freedom: A Black Soldier's Civil War Letters from the Front* (Amherst: University of Massachusetts Press, 1991), xxviii.
64 *New York Weekly Anglo-African*, 14 March 1863. For a full discussion of this, see James G. Hollandsworth Jr., *The Louisiana Native Guards: The Black Military Experience during the Civil War* (Baton Rouge: Louisiana State University Press, 1995).
65 Edwin S. Redkey, ed., *A Grand Army of Black Men: Letters from African-American Soldiers in the Union Army, 1861-1865* (New York: Cambridge University Press, 1992), 252-56.
66 The drafters of the bill had assumed that any blacks who were employed by the army would be used as labourers. Warner, "Crossed Sabres," 60; *Official Records Army*, ser. 3, 3:420.
67 Berlin, Reidy, and Rowlands, *The Black Military Experience*, 20-21, 375-76.
68 Emilio, *A Brave Black Regiment*, 137.
69 Joseph T. Glatthaar, *Forged in Battle: The Civil War Alliance of Black Soldiers and White Officers* (New York: Free Press, 1990), 170.
70 Emilio, *A Brave Black Regiment*, 109, 130, 135-36, 142.
71 When Solicitor Whiting ruled on the pay issue, the Third South Carolina had already been paid at the rate of white soldiers. Moreover, civilian labourers were then receiving more than ten dollars a month. Howard C. Westwood, "The Cause and Consequence of a Union Black Soldier's Mutiny and Execution," *Civil War History* 31, 2 (September 1985): 224-29.
72 Quoted in Glatthaar, *Forged in Battle*, 173.
73 Quoted in Richard M. Reid, ed., *Practicing Medicine in a Black Regiment: The Civil War Diary of Burt G. Wilder, 55th Massachusetts* (Amherst: University of Massachusetts Press, 2010), 27.
74 J.A. Andrew to J.M. Forbes, 20 November 1863, John Albion Andrew Papers, Letters Official, vol. 39, 321-25, 443-46, Massachusetts State Archives, Boston, quoted in Warner, "Crossed Sabres," 37, 38.
75 On his volunteer enlistment form, Williams indicated "no Parent or Guardian," perhaps because he had left his parents in Prince Edward Island when he moved to Boston as a student. "Nathaniel Williams," CMSR, RG 94, NARA; Regimental Descriptive Books, Fifth Massachusetts Cavalry, RG 94, NARA.
76 A wealthy Republican, James Y. Smith was elected in early 1863. Determined to avoid imposing the draft in his state, he used large state bounties and recruiting agents as a way of meeting its quota. His wartime popularity was largely due to his avoidance of a draft. Stewart Sifakis, *Who Was Who in the Civil War* (New York: Facts on File, 1988), 604; William H. Chenery, *The Fourteenth Regiment Rhode Island Heavy Artillery (Colored) in the War to Preserve the Union, 1861-1865* (Providence: Snow and Farnham, 1898), 7.
77 Unlike infantry regiments, which had ten companies, heavy artillery regiments had twelve companies. The three battalions in each regiment consisted of four companies, which often operated independently. While they trained on the heavy guns, artillerymen were also drilled as infantrymen.
78 Joshua M. Addeman, *Reminiscences of Two Years with the Colored Troops: Personal Narratives of Events in the War of the Rebellion* (Providence: N. Bangs Williams, 1880), 5.
79 Ibid., 5-6.
80 "Charles L. Clayton," CMSR, RG 94, NARA.
81 Addeman, *Reminiscences*, 7.
82 "Charles L. Clayton," CMSR, RG 94, NARA. Clayton probably died of tuberculosis. Because the water table was so high, the regiment was forced to bury its dead on the levees.
83 "Thomas C. Skanks" and "David Jones," CMSR, RG 94, NARA.
84 *New York Weekly Anglo-African*, 15 October 1864.

85 Ibid.
86 "Henry A. Berryman," CMSR, RG 94, NARA.
87 "John Jackson," CMSR, RG 94, NARA; Chenery, *The Fourteenth Regiment*, 233.
88 "Nelson Dunkerson," CMSR, RG 94, NARA.
89 The records of a court martial case usually hide as much as they reveal, and they seldom indicate the context in which the court made its decision.
90 "Nelson Dunkerson," CMSR, RG 94, NARA.
91 "John Jackson," CMSR, RG 94, NARA. Unfortunately, most of the records from this trial are illegible.
92 Chenery, *The Fourteenth Regiment*, 134.
93 In 1866, two Chatham residents, Amelia Robinson and Sarah Finer Pearson, testified that they had witnessed the marriage in Ripley. Priscilla Atwood died a resident of Chatham in 1912. "Priscilla Atwood, Widow of Alexander Atwood," CMSR, RG 94, NARA.
94 "Alfred McIntosh," CMSR, RG 94, NARA.
95 "William Anderson," CMSR, RG 94, NARA.
96 "James A. Myers," CMSR, RG 94, NARA.
97 Canada, *Correspondence Relating to the Fenian Invasion and the Rebellion of the Southern States* (Ottawa: Hunter, Rose and Co., 1869), 12. Donohoe did not specify the newspaper.
98 James M. Paradis, *Strike the Blow for Freedom: The 6th United States Colored Infantry in the Civil War* (Shippensburg, PA: White Main Books, 2000), 34, 115.
99 Ibid., 28.
100 Quoted in Miller, "Garland H. White," 205; Hendrick and Hendrick, *Black Refugees in Canada*, 99.
101 "Garland White," CMSR, RG 94, NARA.
102 Under army regulations established in early 1864, a chaplain could not be appointed until the regiment was completely formed. Ibid.
103 Miller, "Garland H. White," 206, 210.
104 Hendrick and Hendrick, *Black Refugees in Canada*, 99; Regimental Descriptive Books, Twenty-eighth USCT, RG 94, NARA.
105 "Jerry Marks," CMSR, RG 94, NARA.
106 "James Peak," CMSR, RG 94, NARA. Like some compiled military service records, the one for Peak briefly documents the court martial proceedings.
107 "Thomas Kennedy," CMSR, RG 94, NARA.
108 Michael O. Smith, "Raising a Black Regiment in Michigan: Adversity and Triumph," *Michigan Historical Review* 16, 2 (March 1990): 26, 28.
109 Hondon Hargrove, "Their Greatest Battle Was Getting into the Fight," *Michigan History Magazine* 75, 1 (January 1991): 26.
110 Quoted in George M. Blackburn, "The Negro Viewed by a Michigan Civil War Soldier: Letters of John C. Buchanan," *Michigan History Magazine* 47, 1 (March 1963): 81.
111 *Detroit Free Press*, 8 May 1863.
112 Sheryl James's suggestion that over two hundred had enlisted in the Fifty-fourth Massachusetts is certainly too high. Sheryl James, "A Small Community Stands Tall," *Michigan History Magazine* 82, 4 (July 1998): 45.
113 Smith, "Raising a Black Regiment," 28.
114 Quoted in Randal Maurice Jelks, *African Americans in the Furniture City: The Struggle for Civil Rights in Grand Rapids* (Urbana: University of Illinois Press, 2006), 12.
115 The explanation, of course, is that many Americans who ardently opposed the institution of slavery had little sympathy or concern for the dire situation of many African Americans, whom they did not see as fellow citizens deserving of equal treatment.
116 Smith, "Raising a Black Regiment," 30-31.

117 Regimental Descriptive Books, 102nd USCT, RG 94, NARA.
118 Sharon A. Roger Hepburn, *Crossing the Border: A Free Black Community in Canada* (Urbana: University of Illinois Press, 2007), 177-78.
119 Robin Winks, *The Civil War Years: Canada and the United States* (Montreal and Kingston: McGill-Queen's University Press, 1998), 199.
120 Smith, "Raising a Black Regiment," 32-33.
121 *Detroit Advertiser and Tribune*, 16 September 1863; *Detroit Advertiser and Tribune*, 18 September 1863.
122 Quoted in Berlin, Reidy, and Rowlands, *The Black Military Experience*, 81, 379. Assessing who was more reliable in this exchange is made difficult both by the fact that Freeman seems to have led his regiment's opposition to the unequal pay offered to black soldiers and by the captain's anger that Freeman had contracted "a very loathsome type of Syphilis" (381).
123 Smith, "Raising a Black Regiment," 33.
124 Ibid., 34-35.
125 *Detroit Advertiser and Tribune*, 18 December 1863; *Detroit Advertiser and Tribune*, 23 December 1863; *Detroit Advertiser and Tribune*, 2 January 1864; *Detroit Advertiser and Tribune*, 4 January 1864.
126 Hargrove, "Their Greatest Battle," 28.
127 "Why Should a Colored Man Enlist?" *Douglass' Monthly*, April 1863, 1.
128 *Detroit Free Press*, 29 October 1863; *Detroit Free Press*, 15 January 1864; *Detroit Advertiser and Tribune*, 21 February 1864; *Detroit Advertiser and Tribune*, 24 March 1864.
129 Quoted in Hargrove, "Their Greatest Battle," 29; Smith, "Raising a Black Regiment," 35-36.
130 Smith, "Raising a Black Regiment," 36.
131 Ibid., 35; Regimental Descriptive Books, 102nd USCT, RG 94, NARA.
132 Regimental Descriptive Books, 102nd USCT, RG 94, NARA.
133 Smith, "Raising a Black Regiment," 37.
134 Lt. Edward Cahill to Hon. Chas. S. May, Lt. Gov. of Michigan, 13 July 1864 (emphasis in original), 102nd USCT, Report of Wounds, Letters, box 137, folder 10, State Archives of Michigan, Lansing. I wish to thank Dr. Sharon Roger Hepburn for sharing this research document with me.
135 Hepburn, *Crossing the Border*, 178; Regimental Descriptive Books, 102nd USCT, RG 94, NARA.
136 *Official Records Army*, ser. 3, 4:164, 214.
137 Glatthaar, *Forged in Battle*, 10, 38.
138 Hollandsworth, *The Louisiana Native Guards*, 96; *Official Records Army*, ser. 3, 3:215-16, 4:215; *Official Records Army*, ser. 1, 34:pt. 3, 221.
139 *Official Records Army*, ser. 1, 35:pt. 2, 212, 215, 230-32, 240.
140 *Detroit Advertiser and Tribune*, 27 December 1864; Smith, "Raising a Black Regiment," 39-41.
141 Quoted in Adams, *On the Altar of Freedom*, 47.
142 Walter H. Wild to Burt Green Wilder, 31 March 1914, Burt Green Wilder Papers, Cornell University.
143 The black soldiers were trapped in a Catch-22 situation, where the poor condition of their clothes and equipment, the result of heavy fatigue duties, reinforced existing prejudices, causing many white commanders to see them as unfit for combat and useful only as labourers. Berlin, Reidy, and Rowlands, *The Black Military Experience*, 504.
144 Quoted in ibid., 501-2.
145 Quoted in Glatthaar, *Forged in Battle*, 185.

Chapter 5: Promises Fulfilled

1 *The War of the Rebellion: A Compilation of the Official Records of the Union and Confederate Armies*, 128 vols.(Washington, DC: Government Printing Office, 1880-1901), ser. 3, 3:576 (hereafter *Official Records Army*).
2 Ibid., ser. 3, 3:983.
3 Ibid., ser. 3, 3:1102.
4 Quoted in Richard M. Reid, ed., *Practicing Medicine in a Black Regiment: The Civil War Diary of Burt G. Wilder, 55th Massachusetts* (Amherst: University of Massachusetts Press, 2010), 111.
5 Quoted in Christian G. Samito, "The Intersection between Military Justice and Equal Rights: Mutinies, Court-Martial, and Black Civil War Soldiers," *Civil War History* 53, 2 (June 2007): 187-90; Donald Yacovone, *A Voice of Thunder: The Letters of George E. Stephens* (Urbana: University of Illinois Press, 1997), 274-75.
6 "Sampson Goliah," Compiled Military Service Records (CMSR), RG 94, National Archives and Records Administration (NARA), Washington, DC.
7 Eric Foner, *Fiery Trial: Abraham Lincoln and American Slavery* (New York: W.W. Norton, 2010), 255.
8 *New York Weekly Anglo-African*, 14 November 1863.
9 "Report of the Secretary of War," 5 December 1863, in *Message of the President of the United States, and Accompanying Documents, to the Two Houses of Congress, at the Commencement of the First Session of the Thirty-Eighth Congress* (Washington, DC: Government Printing Office, 1863), 8.
10 *Official Records Army*, ser. 3, 4:271-74.
11 Diary of Burt Green Wilder, 23 April 1864, Cornell University, Ithaca, New York.
12 Richard M. Reid, *Freedom for Themselves: North Carolina's Black Soldiers in the Civil War Era* (Chapel Hill: University of North Carolina Press, 2008), 17.
13 *Official Records Army*, ser. 3, 5:659.
14 Ibid., ser. 3, 4:518.
15 Quoted in Ira Berlin, Joseph P. Reidy, and Leslie S. Rowlands, eds., The *Black Military Experience*, ser. 2 of *Freedom: A Documentary History of Emancipation, 1861-1867* (Cambridge: Cambridge University Press, 1982), 401, 402; Noah Andre Trudeau, *Voices of the 55th: Letters from the 55th Massachusetts Volunteers, 1861-1865* (Dayton, OH: Morningside, 1996), 116-18.
16 Reid, *Practicing Medicine*, 178.
17 Charles Barnard Fox, *Record of the Service of the Fifty-Fifth Regiment of Massachusetts Volunteer Infantry* (Cambridge, MA: John Wilson and Son, 1868), 34-35.
18 In fact, some of the first black units to be formally organized had black officers.
19 Samuel Robinson, letter to the editor, *Boston Liberator*, 29 January 1863, quoted in Trudeau, *Voices of the 55th*, 62.
20 "Samuel J. Robinson," CMSR, RG 94, NARA.
21 Reid, *Practicing Medicine*, 32.
22 *New York Weekly Anglo-African*, 13 August 1864 (emphasis in original).
23 For details on many of the incidents, see Gregory J.W. Urwin, ed., *Black Flag over Dixie: Racial Atrocities and Racial Reprisals in the Civil War* (Carbondale: Southern Illinois University Press, 2004).
24 *Toronto Daily Globe*, 16 April 1864; *Toronto Daily Globe*, 27 April 1864; *Toronto Daily Globe*, 28 April 1864; *Toronto Daily Globe*, 13 May 1864; "The Massacre at Fort Pillow," *Toronto Daily Globe*, 20 May 1864.
25 "The Massacre at Fort Pillow," *Toronto Daily Globe*, 20 May 1864.

26 *Perth Courier*, 22 April 1864; *Perth Courier*, 29 April 1864.
27 *Saint John Morning Freeman*, 21 April 1864.
28 "Fort Pillow Massacre Re-enacted," *Toronto Daily Globe*, 28 April 1864.
29 *Saint John Morning Freeman*, 28 April 1864.
30 Letter to the editor, *Weekly Anglo-African*, 30 April 1864.
31 Joshua M. Addeman, *Reminiscences of Two Years with the Colored Troops: Personal Narratives of Events in the War of the Rebellion* (Providence: N. Bangs Williams, 1880), 22-23.
32 At the start of the war, the federal government could only request that the various states provide troops. The states themselves raised, trained, equipped, and officered their own regiments, who were then accepted into federal service. The Militia Act of July 1862 gave Washington greater power, allowing it to draft militia if a state had not filled its quota of three-year volunteers.
33 In theory, the act did apply to African Americans, but many Northerners disagreed. Residents of Kentucky vehemently objected when Congress took steps to authorize the enrolment and drafting of African Americans in February 1864. The colonel of the First Kentucky Cavalry, Frank Wolford, even counselled "forcible resistance to the enrollment of negroes." Eugene C. Murdock, *One Million Men: The Civil War Draft in the North* (Madison: State Historical Society of Wisconsin, 1971), 88, 180.
34 *Official Records Army*, ser. 3, 5:657.
35 The last call for new recruits was made only after the presidential election was safely over.
36 James W. Geary, *We Need Men: The Union Draft in the Civil War* (DeKalb: Northern Illinois University Press, 1991), 70, 80-81.
37 Peter Levine, "Draft Evasion in the North during the Civil War, 1863-1865," *Journal of American History* 67, 4 (March 1981): 821.
38 Geary, *We Need Men*, 132.
39 Murdock, *One Million Men*, 154-55.
40 *Official Records Army*, ser. 3, 5:740.
41 James M. McPherson, *Battle Cry of Freedom: The Civil War Era* (New York: Oxford University Press, 1988), 605-6.
42 Robert E. Mitchell, "Civil War Recruiting and Recruits from Ever-Changing Labor Pools: Midland County, Michigan, as a Case Study," *Michigan Historical Review* 35, 1 (Spring 2009): 40.
43 Nevertheless, many writers have emphasized the importance of the bounties and the ways in which bounty brokers and complicit recruiting officers defrauded men of much of their bounties and encouraged others to enlist and desert. Eugene C. Murdock, "New York's Civil War Bounty Brokers," *Journal of American History* 54, 2 (September 1966): 259-64, 268-70; Robin Winks, *The Civil War Years: Canada and the United States* (Montreal and Kingston: McGill-Queen's University Press, 1998), 184-87.
44 "James Robinson," "William E. Stratton," and "Paul Western," CMSR, RG 94, NARA.
45 "Francis Warren," and "Alexander Carter," CMSR, RG 94, NARA.
46 "Major Rose," CMSR, RG 94, NARA.
47 An assumption is made here that the quality of penmanship is an indicator of a recruit's literacy level.
48 Josiah Henson, *An Autobiography of the Rev. Josiah Henson, from 1789 to 1876* (London: Christian Age Office, 1876), 177.
49 Ibid., 182, 84. Alexander Pool apparently claimed that he had never received the money, and the men tried unsuccessfully to get it from Henson.
50 By the end of the war, more than 161,000 men had failed to report after their names were drawn. Geary, *We Need Men*, 83.

51 Tyler Anbinder found that 55 percent of all exemptions in 1863 were for physical disabilities. Tyler Anbinder, "Which Poor Man's Fight? Immigrants and the Federal Conscription of 1863," *Civil War History* 52, 4 (December 2006): 352.
52 Geary, *We Need Men*, 83.
53 Ibid., 74.
54 Quoted in Anbinder, "Which Poor Man's Fight?" 344.
55 Quoted in Roy P. Basler, ed., *Collected Works of Abraham Lincoln* (New Brunswick, NJ: Rutgers University Press, 1953-55), 6:447, 48.
56 *Quebec Mercury*, 1 November 1862.
57 Geary, *We Need Men*, 144.
58 *St. Catharines Constitutional*, 25 August 1864.
59 As commander in chief of the military, Lincoln was exempt from the draft laws, but he wished to set an example, so on 30 September 1864 he had James B. Fry find him a substitute. Fry persuaded John Summerfield Staples to take on the task, for which the president paid Staples five hundred dollars. John M. Taylor, "Representative Recruit for Abraham Lincoln," *Civil War Times Illustrated* 13, 3 (March 1978): 34-35.
60 "John Brown," "Alexander Turner," "Moses Joiner," "Ervin Butler," "Thomas H. Jackson," and "Andrew Johnson," CMSR, RG 94, NARA.
61 A recent study of Confederate substitution sees the issue as more complex than has previously been assumed. Substitution was just one possible avenue that was available to men of military age, and it was sometimes supported by the local community. John Sacher, "The Loyal Draft Dodger? A Re-examination of Confederate Substitution," *Civil War History* 58, 2 (June 2011): 153-78.
62 Anbinder, "Which Poor Man's Fight?" 351; Geary, *We Need Men*, 113; *Quebec Mercury*, 20 August 1864.
63 Geary, *We Need Men*, 78.
64 *Official Records Army*, ser. 3, 3:548.
65 Ibid., ser. 3, 3:474, 475.
66 *Detroit Free Press*, 19 July 1864.
67 *Official Records Army*, ser. 3, 3:549.
68 In some military records, his name is given as Samuel Silvey. "Samuel Sylvia," CMSR, RG 94, NARA.
69 "Horace S. Moody," personal census manuscript, United States Census, 1860, accessed using Ancestry.com. Moody is an example of a man of modest means who was nonetheless able to obtain a substitute.
70 Geary, *We Need Men*, 113.
71 "Samuel Sylvia," CMSR, RG 94, NARA.
72 Ibid.
73 *Official Records Army*, ser. 3, 4:499.
74 The Twenty-fifth Corps was removed from Virginia because Confederate resistance did not end until late May, there were concerns about events along the US-Mexico border, and Virginians were lobbying for its relocation. Reid, *Freedom for Themselves*, 260-62.
75 For a discussion of the impact of disease on the black soldiers along the Rio Grande, see Margaret Humphreys, *Intensely Human: The Health of the Black Soldier in the American Civil War* (Baltimore: Johns Hopkins University Press, 2008), 119-41.
76 "William H. Miner," CMSR, RG 94, NARA.
77 "William S. Boyd," CMSR, RG 94, NARA.
78 Murdock, *One Million Men*, 7.
79 After an extensive analysis of implementation of the draft, Tyler Anbinder concludes that "Native-born citizens on the bottom rungs of the North's socioeconomic ladder, especially unskilled workers living in the countryside, were the only ones driven

disproportionally into military service by the Conscription Act of 1863." Anbinder, "Which Poor Man's Fight?" 372.
80 Winks, *The Civil War Years*, 184-85, 192-27.
81 Quoted in Brooks D. Simpson, *Ulysses S. Grant: Triumph over Adversity, 1822-1865* (New York: Houghton Mifflin, 2000), 375.
82 Fletcher Pratt, *Stanton: Lincoln's Secretary of War* (New York: W.W. Norton, 1953), 379.
83 Murdock, *One Million Men*, 186.
84 *Toronto Daily Globe*, 11 December 1865.
85 "The News Condenser," *Moore's Rural New Yorker*, 10 September 1864, 298, http://www.libraryweb.org/~digitized/newspapers/moores_rural_new_yorker/vol.XV,no.37.pdf.
86 "Henry Williams" and "Richard Williams," CMSR, RG 94, NARA.
87 Canada, *Correspondence Relating to the Fenian Invasion and the Rebellion in the Southern States* (Ottawa: Hunter, Rose and Co., 1869), 8-10, 12-13.
88 "Henry Williams" and "Richard Williams," CMSR, RG 94, NARA. Both men would also apply for a veteran's pension in 1890, although only Richard was successful. "Henry Williams" and "Richard F. Williams," Civil War Pension Files (CWPF), RG 15, NARA.
89 Diary of Reverend Thomas Hughes, 9 April 1865, Diocese of Huron Archives, London, Ontario.
90 Edwin S. Redkey, "Brave Black Volunteers: A Profile of the Fifty-Fourth Massachusetts Regiment," in *Hope and Glory: Essays on the Legacy of the 54th Massachusetts Regiment*, ed. Martin H. Blatt, Thomas J. Brown, and Donald Yacovone (Amherst: University of Massachusetts Press, 2000), 24.
91 Some of the thirty men who reported themselves as barbers may have been self-employed entrepreneurs who owned their own establishment.
92 Ward's information might be suspect. In December 1864, he enlisted as a substitute in the Sixth USCT and "deserted on route to reg't." "Thomas Ward," CMSR, RG 94, NARA.
93 "Hannah Weeks" and "John Weeks," personal census, Census of Canada, 1861, Enumeration District 2, Town of Chatham, County of Kent, 46, 47, Library and Archives Canada, http://www.bac-lac.gc.ca/eng/census/1861.
94 "John Weeks," CMSR, RG 94, NARA. Three other Canadians – Silas Garrison (a printer from Chatham), Franklin Willis (a farmer from Chatham), and Thomas Peter Riggs (an upholsterer from Georgetown) – died at Fort Wagner. Their bodies were never found, but they are presumed to be in the mass grave. "Silas Garrison," "Franklin Willis," and "Thomas Peter Riggs," CMSR, RG 94, NARA.
95 Hannah Weeks's unsuccessful attempt to obtain a mother's pension is detailed in Chapter 7.
96 Murdock, *One Million Men*, 182-83.
97 "George Crosby," CMSR, RG 94, NARA.
98 "John Brown," CMSR, RG 94, NARA.
99 Maynard must have enjoyed military life, for he later served in the Twenty-fifth US Infantry Regiment, one of the "buffalo soldier" units. "Isaac Maynard," CMSR, RG 94, NARA.
100 Murdock, *One Million Men*, 184-85.
101 Timothy J. Perri, "The Economics of US Civil War Conscription," *American Law and Economic Review* 10, 2 (January 2008): 433.
102 "James Brown" and "George Kennedy," CMSR, RG 94, NARA.
103 "James Blackman," CMSR, RG 94, NARA.
104 "John Hope," CMSR, RG 94, NARA.
105 "Andrew Johnson," CMSR, RG 94, NARA.
106 Other British North Americans who deposited money with the paymaster included Thomas H. Jackson ($603.43), Moses Joiner ($166.67), Samuel Porter ($542.50), and

107 Ervin Butler ($412.00). "Thomas H. Jackson," "Moses Joiner," "Samuel Porter," and "Ervin Butler," CMSR, RG 94, NARA.
107 Diary of Reverend Thomas Hughes, 10 April 1865, Diocese of Huron Archives.
108 Quoted in James M. McPherson, *For Cause and Comrades: Why Men Fought in the Civil War* (New York: Oxford University Press, 1997), 9 (emphasis in original).
109 "William H. Miner," CMSR, RG 94, NARA.
110 "Henry Allen," CMSR, RG 94, NARA. Allen was one of the substitutes who enlisted for just a year.
111 Edward A. Miller Jr., *The Black Civil War Soldiers of Illinois: The Story of the Twenty-Ninth U.S. Colored Infantry* (Columbia: University of South Carolina Press, 1998), 131; "John Benson," CMSR, RG 94, NARA.
112 "John A. Benson," CWPF, RG 15, NARA.
113 "Stephen Ray," CMSR, RG 94, NARA.
114 "John Lewis," "William Jackson," and "William Unpleasant," CMSR, RG 94, NARA.
115 It is not clear from individual cases exactly how the term "deserter" was used in the regimental descriptive book. In some cases, it described men who left their regiment but returned voluntarily, while in other cases it was used only for men who had deliberately tried to escape the army.
116 Mark Mayo Boatner III, *The Civil War Dictionary* (New York: David McKay, 1959), 858.
117 Officials at the time associated desertion with large cities, large bounties, and foreigners. It was "probable," they claimed, that close examination would reveal "that desertion is a crime of foreign rather than native birth." *Official Records Army*, ser. 3, 5:688; James McPherson, *Ordeal by Fire: The Civil War and Reconstruction* (New York: Alfred A. Knopf, 1982), 468; David Herbert Donald, Jean Harvey Baker, and Michael F. Holt, *The Civil War and Reconstruction* (New York: W.W. Norton, 2001), 239.
118 For anyone who had crewed on a ship before joining the Union navy, the ritual of signing on, the disciplinary powers of the captain, the pattern of shipboard life and work, and the often integrated relations while at sea would have seemed familiar.
119 Quoted in Fox, *Record of the Service*, 86.
120 Reid, *Practicing Medicine*, 134, 145, 167.
121 Quoted in Berlin, Reidy, and Rowlands, *The Black Military Experience*, 384.
122 Trudeau, *Voices of the 55th*, 156.
123 Ibid.
124 Fox, *Record of the Service*, 106, 119; "Gabriel P. Iverson," CMSR, RG 94, NARA. In Canada, Iverson was apparently known as Harry Lee Gordon.
125 Regimental Descriptive Books, 102nd USCT, RG 94, NARA.
126 "Peter Jackson," CMSR, RG 94, NARA.
127 "Thomas Leslie," CMSR, RG 94, NARA.
128 Joseph T. Glatthaar, *Forged in Battle: The Civil War Alliance of Black Soldiers and White Officers* (New York: Free Press, 1990), 112.
129 "James Jones," CMSR, RG 94, NARA.
130 Ibid. James Jones Jr. was the son of the well-known blacksmith and gunsmith in Chatham, James Munroe "Gunsmith" Jones.
131 "William H. Noble," CMSR, RG 94, NARA.
132 Bryce A. Suderow, "The Battle of the Crater: The Civil War's Worst Massacre," in Urwin, *Black Flag over Dixie*, 203-9.
133 Glatthaar, *Forged in Battle*, 150.
134 Miller, *The Black Civil War Soldiers*, 32, 99; "James L. Williams," CMSR, RG 94, NARA.
135 "William E. Howard," CMSR, RG 94, NARA.
136 "John Simons," CMSR, RG 94, NARA.
137 "Holman Singleton," CMSR, RG 94, NARA.

Chapter 6: Black Doctors

1 One of the best-known regimental surgeons from Canada West is Francis M. Wafer, who was a student at the Medical College of Queen's University when he enlisted in the Union army. He was commissioned an assistant surgeon in the 108th New York Infantry. Cheryl A. Wells, ed., *A Surgeon in the Army of the Potomac* (Montreal and Kingston: McGill-Queen's University Press, 2008), xxxii, xli. The most prominent British North American doctor in the Confederate service was Solomon Secord from Kincardine. Dr. John L. Bray, an 1863 graduate of the Medical College of Queen's University, also served in the Confederate medical system. White British North American–born doctors serving in United States Colored Troops included William Clunie of Toronto and William Naden of Hampton in the Tenth USCT, Charles M. Wright of Canada West and Anselm Achim from Montreal in the Thirty-second USCT, and William S. Tremaine from Prince Edward Island in the Thirty-first USCT. Tremaine, who had graduated from the University of Pennsylvania, had previously served as assistant surgeon in the Twenty-fourth Massachusetts Regiment. "William S. Tremaine," CMSR, RG 94, NARA. This list is probably not a complete record of British North American doctors who served in the war.
2 Canada West was the only source of black British North American doctors who served in the war. Robert G. Slawson, *Prologue to Change: African Americans in Medicine in the Civil War Era* (Frederick, MD: National Museum of Civil War Medicine Press, 2006), 31, 35.
3 Riley may have been born in Detroit in 1844, but he reported his place of birth as Canada to the 1870 and 1880 US census enumerator.
4 David Rosner, "Medicine," in *The Reader's Companion to American History*, ed. Eric Foner and John A. Garraty (Boston: Houghton Mifflin, 1991), 717.
5 William Mervale Smith, *Swamp Doctor: The Diary of a Union Surgeon in the Virginia and North Carolina Swamps* (Mechanicsburg, PA: Stackpole Books, 2001), xxii.
6 Joseph F. Kett, "American and Canadian Medical Institutions, 1800-1870," *Journal of the History of Medicine and Allied Sciences* 22, 4 (October 1967): 348-50; Ira Rutkow, *Seeking the Cure: A History of Medicine in America* (New York: Scribner, 2010), 40-41. A very few schools, including the Medical School of Maine and the Medical School at Dartmouth College, had more than one black graduate. Slawson, *Prologue to Change*, 10.
7 Toby A. Appel, "The Thomsonian Movement, the Regular Profession, and the State in Antebellum Connecticut: A Case Study of the Repeal of Early Medical Licensing Laws," *Journal of the History of Medicine and Allied Sciences* 65, 2 (April 2010): 153.
8 R.D. Gidney and W.P.J. Millar, "The Origins of Organized Medicine in Ontario, 1850-1869," in *Health, Disease and Medicine in Canadian History*, ed. Charles G. Roland (Toronto: Hannah Institute for the History of Medicine, 1984), 71, 75.
9 William G. Rothstein, *American Physicians in the Nineteenth Century: From Sects to Science* (Baltimore: Johns Hopkins University Press, 1972), 98; Slawson, *Prologue to Change*, 10.
10 Rainer Baehre, "The Medical Profession in Upper Canada Reconsidered: Politics, Medical Reform, and Law in a Colonial Society," *Canadian Bulletin of Medical History* 12 (1995): 103.
11 Ibid., 104-5.
12 Ibid., 109.
13 Bernard Blishen, *Doctors in Canada: The Changing World of Medical Practice* (Toronto: University of Toronto Press, 1991), 10. In some states and colonies, the only limit on unlicensed practitioners was the restriction that they could not use the courts to pursue defaulting patients who would not pay their bills.
14 Gidney and Millar, "The Origins of Organized Medicine," 65.

15 Quoted in Marian A. Patterson, "The Life and Times of the Hon. John Rolph, M.D. (1793-1870)," *Medical History* 5 (January 1961): 27; G.M. Craig, "Rolph, John," *Dictionary of Canadian Biography Online*, http://www.biographi.ca/.
16 *Christian Guardian*, 6 October 1852.
17 Michael Bliss, *William Osler: A Life in Medicine* (Toronto: University of Toronto Press, 1999), 54. For a discussion of the entrance requirements and the educational program offered at McGill, see Joseph Hanaway and Richard Cruess, *McGill Medicine*, vol. 1, *The First Half Century, 1829-1885* (Montreal and Kingston: McGill-Queen's University Press, 1996), 36-64.
18 M. Dalyce Newby, *Anderson Ruffin Abbott: First Afro-Canadian Doctor* (Markham, ON: Fitzhenry and Whiteside, 1998), 22; Bliss, *William Osler*, 59-60.
19 Hanaway and Cruess, *McGill Medicine*, 34-35, 157-58.
20 B. Aldren, "Life in Upper Canada in 1837," *Canadian Medical Association Journal* 20 (January 1929): 66. Aldren wrote the letter to C.B. Rose, a surgeon living in Norfolk, England.
21 Regimental Descriptive Books, Twenty-ninth Connecticut Regiment, RG 94, National Archives and Records Administration (NARA), Washington, DC.
22 "Moses Jackson," Compiled Military Service Records (CMSR), RG 94, NARA. Despite whatever medical knowledge Jackson possessed, he was never given detached duties with the regimental surgeon.
23 He also worked with two other doctors, F. Julius LeMoyne and Joseph P. Gazzam. Victor Ullman, *Martin R. Delany: The Beginnings of Black Nationalism* (Boston: Beacon Press, 1971), 28, 32-33.
24 Laing and Snowden had been accepted largely because they were sponsored by the American Colonization Society and were planning to practise medicine in Liberia. As discussed below, neither were permitted to finish their studies at Harvard Medical School. Had they been its only black students, they would probably have completed their training and left for Liberia. Delany clearly planned to practise in the United States after graduating, and this appears to be the flashpoint for the subsequent uproar. Nora N. Nercessian, "Nineteenth-Century Black Graduates of Harvard Medical School," *Journal of Blacks in Higher Education* 47 (Spring 2005): 88.
25 The woman, Harriot Kezia Hunt, had already been rejected in 1847. Her 1850 application was no more successful. The male students objected to "having the company of any female forced upon us, who is disposed to unsex herself, and to sacrifice her modesty, by appearing with men in the medical lecture room." Quoted in Harriot K. Hunt, *Glances and Glimpses; Or, Fifty Years Social, Including Twenty Years Professional Life* (Boston: John P. Jewett, 1856), 270.
26 Quoted in Nercessian, "Nineteenth-Century Black Graduates," 88; Ullman, *Martin R. Delany*, 116. Harvard's five British North American medical students split on the issue of black enrolment. Two from Canada West, including Richard Gundy of Simcoe, supported it, and a third was neutral. The two white students from Nova Scotia and New Brunswick signed the majority petition asking for expulsion. Werner Sollors, Caldwell Titcomb, and Thomas H. Underwood, eds., *Blacks at Harvard: A Documentary History of African-American Experience at Harvard and Radcliffe* (New York: New York University Press, 1993), 26-27.
27 Quoted in Ullman, *Martin R. Delany*, 121.
28 Quoted in Sollors, Titcomb, and Underwood, *Blacks at Harvard*, xix.
29 Laing managed to complete a medical degree. After studying at the Royal College of Physicians and Surgeons in London, he took his MD at Medical School at Dartmouth College. Snowden, on the other hand, was again rejected by Harvard Medical School despite the fact that he had garnered support from a majority of the white students.
30 *Provincial Freeman*, 5 July 1856.

31 Dorothy Sterling, *The Making of an Afro-American: Martin Robinson Delany, 1812-1885* (New York: Da Capo Press, 1971), 281.
32 George Hendrick and Willene Hendrick, *Black Refugees in Canada: Accounts of Escape during the Era of Slavery* (Jefferson, NC: McFarland, 2010), 107.
33 James Haskins, *Black Stars of Civil War Times* (Hoboken, NJ: John Wiley and Sons, 2003), 43.
34 Henry S. Robinson, "Alexander Thomas Augusta," *Journal of the National Medical Association* 44, 4 (July 1952): 327.
35 In 1850, a group of doctors who had just created the Upper Canada School of Medicine suggested that it become the faculty of medicine in the Anglican college, Trinity College, which was in the process of being incorporated. Their offer was accepted and medical lectures commenced that fall. A royal charter for the University of Trinity College was granted in 1852, and the college federated with the University of Toronto in 1904. Martin L. Friedland, *The University of Toronto: A History* (Toronto: University of Toronto Press, 2002), 30, 104. During the 1850s, Toronto had two other medical schools, the University of Toronto Medical Faculty (formerly the Medical Faculty of King's College) and the Toronto School of Medicine (affiliated with the University of Toronto and Victoria University).
36 George W. Spragge, "The Trinity Medical College," *Ontario History* 58, 2 (June 1966): 67.
37 Although James Haskins gives his graduation date as 1856, Robert G. Slawson incorrectly claims that he graduated in 1860. The Trinity College medical faculty resigned en masse in the summer of 1856, and the school would not resume operations for another fifteen years. Haskins, *Black Stars*, 43; Spragge, "The Trinity Medical College," 74-75, 97; Slawson, *Prologue to Change*, 16.
38 Samuel Gridley Howe, *Report to the Freedmen's Inquiry Commission, 1864* (Boston: Wright and Potter, 1864), 79.
39 Bliss, *William Osler*, 54. Mid-nineteenth-century North American hospitals tended to be welfare institutions whose patients were largely marginalized, generally poor, and often the newest to the city. Morris J. Vogel, "The Transformation of the American Hospital, 1850-1920," in *Health Care in America: Essays in Social History*, ed. Susan Reverby and David Rosner (Philadelphia: Temple University Press, 1979), 105.
40 Herbert M. Morais, *International Library of Negro Life and History: The History of the Negro in Medicine* (New York: Publishers Company, 1967), 36.
41 Sharon A. Roger Hepburn, *Crossing the Border: A Free Black Community in Canada* (Urbana: University of Illinois Press, 2007), 158.
42 Hendrick and Hendrick, *Black Refugees in Canada*, 110.
43 By 1871, Wilson Abbott owned forty-two houses, five lots, and a warehouse as well as property in Hamilton and Owen Sound. Newby, *Anderson Ruffin Abbott*, 16-18.
44 Hepburn, *Crossing the Border*, 48, 158; Catherine Slaney, *Family Secrets: Crossing the Colour Line* (Toronto: Natural Heritage Books, 2003), 39-40, 42.
45 Anderson Ruffin Abbott Papers, Toronto Reference Library (TRL), Toronto.
46 Slaney, *Family Secrets*, 48-49.
47 Historian Daniel G. Hill states that Abbott graduated from the Toronto School of Medicine in 1857, but Abbott's own papers do not support this claim. Also, Abbott would not have later applied for the position of "medical cadet," which was open to medical students who had one year of medical lectures, if he had graduated. Owen Thomas, "Abbott, Anderson Ruffin," *Dictionary of Canadian Biography Online*, http://www.biographi.ca/.
48 Howe, *Report to the Freedmen's Inquiry*, 79.
49 Thomas, "Abbott, Anderson Ruffin"; Robin Winks, *The Blacks in Canada: A History*, 2nd ed. (Montreal and Kingston: McGill-Queen's University Press, 1997), 329.

50 Hepburn, *Crossing the Border*, 1, 166.
51 Arlie C. Robbins, *Legacy to Buxton* (Chatham: Ideal Printing, 1983), 74; Daniel G. Hill, *The Freedom-Seekers: Blacks in Early Canada* (Agincourt: Book Society of Canada, 1981), 84-85.
52 His eldest son, John, also graduated from Knox College and eventually served as a minister in Louisville. Hepburn, *Crossing the Border*, 183.
53 Robbins, *Legacy to Buxton*, 62; Victor Ullman, *Look to the North Star: A Life of William King* (Boston: Beacon Press, 1969), 151-53.
54 Ullman, *Look to the North Star*, 235.
55 Newby, *Anderson Ruffin Abbott*, 92.
56 Philip N. Alexander, "John H. Rapier, Jr., and the Medical Profession in Jamaica, 1861-1862," part 1, *Jamaica Journal* 24 (February 1993): 38.
57 Southern law assigned the status of the mother, free or slave, to her children. After Susan and two of her children died in 1841, John started a second family with his slave, Lucretia, and these children, under Alabama law, were not free.
58 James T. Rapier to John H. Rapier Jr., 28 September 1858, Rapier Papers, Howard University Moorland Spingarn Research Center, Howard University Library, Washington, DC.
59 John H. Rapier Jr. to William McLain, 28 December 1854, 5 March 1855, American Colonization Society Papers, Library of Congress, Washington, DC.
60 Thomas was an acquaintance of William Walker, the filibuster who had just organized a temporary confederation of states (Nicaragua, Honduras, El Salvador, and Costa Rica), where, reportedly, blacks could hold positions of authority.
61 Alexander, "John H. Rapier, Jr.," 38.
62 Loren Schweninger, *James T. Rapier and Reconstruction* (Chicago: University of Chicago Press, 1978), 27-28.
63 Rapier told his uncle that, while attending a "Musical Soiree," he had seen that one of the ladies was appalled and "shocked almost speechless" by the presence of a dentist among the dancers. It is possible that he misunderstood the cause of her distress. Philip N. Alexander, "John H. Rapier, Jr., and the Medical Profession in Jamaica, 1861-1862," part 2, *Jamaica Journal* 25 (October 1993): 58-59.
64 Ibid., 57-59.
65 However, Robert Sutherland, a native of Jamaica, attended Queen's from 1849 to 1852, graduating with honours in classics and mathematics. He then studied law and qualified for practise in 1855.
66 Quoted in Schweninger, *James T. Rapier*, 28.
67 J.H. Rapier to Surgeon General, 21 April 1864, "Rapier, J.H., Jr.," Medical Officers' Files, Personal Papers of Medical Officers and Physicians, RG 94, NARA.
68 J.H. Rapier to Medical Director's Office, 23 June 1864, "Rapier, J.H., Jr.," Medical Officers' Files, Personal Papers of Medical Officers and Physicians, RG 94, NARA.
69 Schweninger, *James T. Rapier*, 28; Slawson, *Prologue to Change*, 10, 15.
70 In the Anglo-American military tradition, officers were assumed to be gentlemen.
71 When James H. Lane organized the First Kansas Colored Volunteers in the summer of 1862, he used blacks as recruiters and subsequently commissioned them as company officers. After a long delay, the War Department finally mustered the regiment into service, but it refused to recognize the black commissions. Although the Louisiana Native Guards entered service in December 1862 with black officers, General Nathaniel P. Banks quickly took steps to purge them. Ira Berlin, Joseph P. Reidy, and Leslie S. Rowlands, eds., *The Black Military Experience*, ser. 2 of *Freedom: A Documentary History of Emancipation, 1861-1867* (Cambridge: Cambridge University Press, 1982), 303-9.

72 Because chaplains and surgeons did not "command" men, potential conflicts of authority with white officers, primarily in time of combat, could be avoided.
73 Margaret Humphreys, *Intensely Human: The Health of the Black Soldier in the American Civil War* (Baltimore: Johns Hopkins University Press, 2008), 62.
74 The Preliminary Emancipation Proclamation of 22 September 1862 had freed "all persons held as slaves" in any state that was in rebellion against the United States, whereas the Final Emancipation Proclamation specified, "And I further declare and make known, that such persons of suitable condition, will be received into the armed service of the United States to garrison forts, positions, stations, and other places, and to man vessels of all sorts in said service." *Preliminary Emancipation Proclamation*, 22 September 1862, http://www.archives.gov/; *Final Emancipation Proclamation*, 1 January 1863, http://www.archives.gov/.
75 A.T. Augusta to President Abraham Lincoln, 7 January 1863, service record of Alexander T. Augusta, Seventh USCT, Carded Records, Volunteer Organizations, Civil War, ser. 519, RG 94, NARA (Augusta service record, NARA).
76 A.T. Augusta to Secretary of War Edwin M. Stanton, 7 January 1863, Augusta service record, NARA.
77 When the assistant secretary of war replied to Augusta, his letter was addressed to Trinity College. P.H. Watson to A.T. Augusta, 14 January 1863, Augusta service record, NARA.
78 C. Clymer to W.A. Hammond, 23 March 1863, Augusta service record, NARA.
79 P.H. Watson to W.A. Hammond, 26 March 1863; A.T. Augusta to C. Clymer, 30 March 1863, Augusta service record, NARA; "Alexander T. Augusta," CMSR, RG 94, NARA. Augusta's tactful letter to the medical board was written a few days after the assistant secretary of war ordered the examination.
80 W.A. Hammond to R.C. Abbott, 20 May 1863; J.R. Smith to R.C. Abbott, 23 May 1863, Augusta service record, NARA. Hammond wanted the white assistant surgeon in the camp to be re-assigned when Augusta arrived, presumably so that he would not be subordinate to a black doctor.
81 Quoted in Edwin S. Redkey, ed., *A Grand Army of Black Men: Letters from African-American Soldiers in the Union Army, 1861-1865* (New York: Cambridge University Press, 1992), 254.
82 Ibid., 255-56 (emphasis in original); Joseph T. Glatthaar, *Forged in Battle: The Civil War Alliance of Black Soldiers and White Officers* (New York: Free Press, 1990), 197.
83 Humphreys, *Intensely Human*, 63; Kate Masur, *An Example for All the Land: Emancipation and the Struggle over Equality in Washington, D.C.* (Chapel Hill: University of North Carolina Press, 2010), 101.
84 For details on this extended struggle, see Masur, *An Example for All the Land*, 101-12.
85 Previously a surgeon in the Fifty-second Ohio Volunteer Infantry, Morse had been pressured to resign by its officers. At age forty, he may have felt that his opportunities for advancement were fading. In a letter to Senator John Sherman, a moderate Republican, he described his "surprise and indignation" when he learned that his superior officer was an African American. He asked the surgeon general for a transfer, but the War Department disallowed his request. Shortly afterward, Augusta was placed on detached duty. J. Morse to J. Sherman, 14 May 1864, Augusta service record, NARA; "Joel Morse," CMSR, RG 94, NARA.
86 Quoted in Berlin, Reidy, and Rowlands, *The Black Military Experience*, 356, 357 (emphasis in original). In language and phraseology, this letter is remarkably similar to the one that Morse sent to Senator Sherman, suggesting the identity of its main author.
87 Augusta had been mustered into the Seventh USCT on 2 October 1863 but was reassigned on 17 October as the examining surgeon for colored troops at Baltimore.

Although he never rejoined his regiment, he was brevetted lieutenant colonel in 1865, becoming the highest-ranking black officer of the Civil War era. "Alexander Augusta," CMSR, RG 94, NARA; Berlin, Reidy, and Rowlands, *The Black Military Experience*, 357-58.

88 Quoted in Berlin, Reidy, and Rowlands, *The Black Military Experience*, 357. Morse claimed that he would resign on principle if Augusta returned to the regiment. Although he did not object to Augusta holding a surgeon's commission, he felt that his position "should be an independent one, for instance, the one he was first appointed to last year in Washington, as Surgeon of Volunteers, in charge of Contraband Camp, or as Surgeon of Some General Hospital for Colored Troops." Ibid.

89 "Case of Joel Morse, June 4, 1864," Augusta service record, NARA; "Joel Morse," CMSR, RG 94, NARA. In March 1865, Morse was finally appointed surgeon in the 117th USCT.

90 This decision was in keeping with the War Department policy that black non-commissioned officers, unlike white corporals and sergeants, would receive the same wages as black privates.

91 Robinson, "Alexander Thomas Augusta," 327.

92 In addition to Augusta, African American surgeons John V. Degrasse (Thirty-fifth USCT), David O. McCord (Sixty-third USCT), Cortlandt van Rensselaer Creed (Thirtieth Connecticut), and William C. Powell (127th USCT) served with their regiments, at least for part of their enlistment.

93 The best-known example of this policy reversal involved the black officers in the Louisiana Native Guards. For an insightful discussion of this case, see James G. Hollandsworth Jr., *The Louisiana Native Guards: The Black Military Experience during the Civil War* (Baton Rouge: Louisiana State University Press, 1995), 25-28, 71-78.

94 George Bliss Jr. to Col. C.W. Foster, Ass. Adj. Gen., 14 December 1863; Foster to Bliss, 15 December 1863; Bliss to Foster, 17 December 1863; and Foster to Bliss, 19 December 1863, Letters Received, Division of Colored Troops, RG 94, NARA.

95 In April 1863, Augusta used the *Anglo-African* in New York City to appeal to black doctors to join the army, but his public call to service ended after he was treated poorly by white officers and civilians. *New York Anglo-African*, 13 April 1863.

96 Quoted in Newby, *Anderson Ruffin Abbott*, 54.

97 Guy R. Hasegawa, "The Civil War Medical Cadets: Medical Students Serving the Union," *Journal of the American College of Surgeons* 193, 1 (2001): 81-89.

98 Although Abbott must have understood the distinction between an army surgeon and a contract surgeon, after the war he would behave and write as if he had been a commissioned officer.

99 Stewart Brooks claims that "some were undoubtedly conscientious and helpful, but most came to the battlefield and hospitals to see the sights or test their mettle at cutting and carving." George Worthington Adams hesitates to dismiss the majority of contract surgeons as bad, but he believes that "they averaged lower in quality than the profession at large." Stewart Brooks, *Civil War Medicine* (Springfield: Charles C. Thomas, 1966), 26; George Worthington Adams, *Doctors in Blue: The Medical History of the Union Army in the Civil War* (Baton Rouge: Louisiana State University Press, 1952), 175.

100 James W. Wengert, "The Contract Surgeon," *Journal of the West* 36, 1 (1997): 67.

101 Adams, *Doctors in Blue*, 175.

102 Quoted in Newby, *Anderson Ruffin Abbott*, 64.

103 Laurence M. Hauptman, "John E. Wool and the New York City Draft Riots of 1863: A Reassessment," *Civil War History* 49, 4 (November 2003): 372.

104 Anderson Ruffin Abbott Papers, TRL.

105 For more on the riot, see Iver Bernstein, *The New York City Draft Riots: Their Significance for American Society and Politics in the Age of the Civil War* (New York: Oxford University

Press, 1990); and Edward K. Spann, *Gotham at War: New York City, 1860-1865* (Wilmington, DE: Scholarly Resources, 2002).

106 Divided into four quadrants, Washington was laid out on a grid pattern that centred on the Capitol. Streets that ran north-south were numbered, whereas those that ran east-west were designated with a letter. The camp was in the northwest quadrant.

107 Quoted in Jim Downs, *Sick from Freedom: African-American Illness and Suffering during the Civil War and Reconstruction* (New York: Oxford University Press, 2012), 31.

108 Daniel Smith Lamb claims that Augusta remained in charge until the spring of 1864, but Augusta's military records note that he was transferred to Birney Barracks in Baltimore at the end of October 1863. Daniel Smith Lamb, *Howard University Medical Department, Washington, DC: A Historical, Biological and Statistical Souvenir* (Washington, DC: R. Bereford, 1900), pt. 3:10-11.

109 W. Montague Cobb, "A Short History of the Freedmen's Hospital," *Journal of the National Medical Association* 54 (May 1962): 277-78, 281.

110 Anderson Ruffin Abbott Papers, TRL.

111 Cobb, "A Short History," 280.

112 Under the new contract, Abbott's salary was a hundred dollars a month. Anderson Ruffin Abbott Papers, TRL.

113 Lamb, *Howard University*, 11.

114 Schweninger, *James P. Rapier and Reconstruction*, 28.

115 Newby, *Anderson Ruffin Abbott*, 66.

116 John H. Rapier to James P. Thomas, 19 August 1864, Records of Adjutant General's Office, Medical Officer's File of John Rapier, RG 94, NARA.

117 Ullman, *Look to the North Star*, 289, 296; Newby, *Anderson Ruffin Abbott*, 92.

118 Anderson Ruffin Abbott Papers, TRL.

119 Rapier to Thomas, 19 August 1864, NARA.

120 Anderson Ruffin Abbott Papers, TRL. Abbott's account of their experience, written many years later, does not indicate how they obtained an invitation. Elizabeth Keckley may have been the intermediate. Lincoln frequently held levees, often twice a week, a number that increased during the first four months of 1864.

121 Anderson Ruffin Abbott Papers, TRL. Although contract doctors did not hold a commission, they were allowed to wear a military uniform. In many of his manuscripts, written well after the war was over, Abbott implies that he was a commissioned officer.

122 J.H. Rapier to Dr. Hornor, 28 November 1864, "Rapier, J.H., Jr.," Medical Officers' Files, Personal Papers of Medical Officers and Physicians, RG 94, NARA.

123 Whatever Abbott submitted is not in his folder in the Medical Officers' Files.

124 Rapier to Hornor, 28 November 1864, NARA.

125 Glatthaar, *Forged in Battle*, 179-80; Redkey, *A Grand Army of Black Men*, 282.

126 Quoted in Berlin, Reidy, and Rowlands, *The Black Military Experience*, 340-41 (emphasis in original).

127 Quoted in Schweninger, *James T. Rapier and Reconstruction*, 29. If, in fact, Rapier actually was familiar with Johnson's political nature, his comment is either exceptionally diplomatic or deliberately dishonest, as was his claim to be a Tennessean.

128 Glatthaar, *Forged in Battle*, 179; Berlin, Reidy, and Rowlands, *The Black Military Experience*, 311, 342-45, 741.

129 A brevet rank, for practical purposes, was regarded as an honorary title given for courageous or meritorious service. It carried none of the authority, precedence, or pay of a similar regular rank. General Order No. 67, 16 July 1865, "Alexander T. Augusta," CMSR, RG 94, NARA.

130 Hepburn, *Crossing the Border*, 184.

131 Schweninger, *James T. Rapier and Reconstruction*, 28. Although they were not commissioned officers, acting assistant surgeons could wear uniforms and thus received military salutes and other honours.
132 Dr. John H. Rapier to James P. Thomas, 19 August 1864, Rapier Papers, Moorland-Springarn Research Center, Howard University. "Pompey" and "Cuffee" were two common slave names.
133 General Order No. 67, 16 July 1865, "Alexander T. Augusta," CMSR, RG 94, NARA.
134 Summary of Surgeon General J.K. Barnes, 17 June 1881, "Alexander T. Augusta," CMSR, RG 94, NARA.
135 Due to the society's discriminatory treatment of Augusta and other black doctors, Senator Charles Sumner introduced a bill to repeal its charter. Robinson, "Alexander Thomas Augusta," 328.
136 Masur, *An Example for All the Land*, 164.
137 "Colored Physicians in the District of Columbia," *Medical and Surgical Reporter*, 3 July 1869, 19.
138 Douglas M. Hayes, "Policing the Social Boundaries of the American Medical Association, 1847-70," *Journal of the History of Medicine and Allied Sciences* 60, 2 (April 2005): 170.
139 Lamb, *Howard University*, 21.
140 Robinson, "Alexander Thomas Augusta," 329.
141 Lamb, *Howard University*, 36.
142 Ullman, *Look to the North Star*, 298.
143 The American Missionary Society established a school in Pine Bluff before the end of the war, and only a few years later the state legislature chartered the Branch Normal College for Negroes (now the University of Arkansas at Pine Bluff) to serve black students. Thomas A. DeBlack, *With Fire and Sword: Arkansas, 1861-1874* (Fayetteville: University of Arkansas Press, 2003), 201, 207, 209; John William Graves, *Town and Country: Race Relations in an Urban-Rural Context, Arkansas, 1865-1905* (Fayetteville: University of Arkansas Press, 1990), 34.
144 Graves, *Town and Country*, 52.
145 John Michael Giggie, *After Redemption: Jim Crow and the Transformation of African American Religion in the Delta, 1875-1915* (New York: Oxford University Press, 2007), 81.
146 Jerome R. Riley, *Philosophy of Negro Suffrage* (Hartford, CT: American Publishing, 1895), 77-78.
147 Blake J. Wintory, "African-American Legislators in the Arkansas General Assembly, 1868-1893," *Arkansas Historical Quarterly* 65 (Winter 2006): 389-90.
148 Graves, *Town and Country*, 54.
149 While in Chicago, he lived in the Third Ward. Personal census manuscript, Third Ward, City of Chicago, US Census 1870. Ascessed using Ancestry.com.
150 Lamb, *Howard University*, 210.
151 Bruce L. Mouser, *For Labor, Race, and Liberty: George Edwin Taylor, His Historic Rule for the White House and the Making of Independent Black Politics* (Madison: University of Wisconsin Press, 2011), 191; US Census 1900.
152 Riley claimed to have received private correspondence from Bryan that "complimented and commended" both him and other "intelligent and thoughtful colored advocates of bimetallism." Jerome R. Riley, *Philosophy of Negro Suffrage*, 125-26.
153 Mouser, *For Labor, Race, and Liberty*, 96.
154 Randall B. Woods, "C.H.J. Taylor and the Movement for Black Political Independence, 1882-1896," *Journal of Negro History* 67 (Summer 1982): 127-28.
155 The books included Riley, *Philosophy of Negro Suffrage*; Riley, *Evolution or Racial Development* (New York: J.S. Ogilvie, 1901); and Jerome Riley, *Reach the Reached Negro* (Atlanta: Byrd Printing, 1903).

156 Riley, *Philosophy of Negro Suffrage*, 197.
157 A.R. Abbott to the Surgeon General's Office, 18 February 1891, "Abbott, A.R.," Medical Officers' Files, Personal Papers of Medical Officers and Physicians, RG 94, NARA.
158 "Some Recollections of Lincoln's Assassination," *Anglo-American Magazine*, May 1901, 401.
159 Keckley's memoir lists many items that were given away but does not mention the gift to Abbott, although she claimed that "all of the presents passed through my hands." Elizabeth Keckley, *Behind the Scenes: Thirty Years a Slave and Four Years in the White House* (New York: Arno Press, 1968), 202-3. However, Catherine Clinton suggests that Mrs. Lincoln played a greater role in the distribution of Lincoln's personal effects than was earlier believed. Catherine Clinton, *Mrs. Lincoln: A Life* (New York: Harper Collins, 2009), 262.
160 In the *Dictionary of Canadian Biography*, Owen Thomas claims that Abbott was "among the select group who stood vigil over the dying President Abraham Lincoln." Owen Thomas, "Abbott, Anderson Ruffin," *Dictionary of Canadian Biography Online*, http://www.biographi.ca/. However, Dr. Charles A. Leale, who was at Ford's Theatre and who acted as the primary physician while Lincoln lay dying in the Petersen House, listed all the doctors who took part "in the physical, mental or spiritual welfare of the President" but does not name Abbott. He did say that "during the night several other physicians unknown to me called, and through courtesy I permitted some to feel the President's pulse, but none of them tended the wound." Charles A. Leale, *Lincoln's Last Hours: Address Delivered before the Commandery of the State of New York Military Order of the Loyal Legion of the United States* (New York: privately printed, 1909), 14. Although Leale makes no mention of Dr. Ezra W. Abbott, who claimed to have been with the president when he was carried to the Petersen House and to have kept the record of his respiration and pulse, the *New York Times* identified Abbott as present. David Herbert Donald and Harold Holzer, *Lincoln in the Times: The Life of Abraham Lincoln as Originally Reported in the New York Times* (New York: St. Martin's Press, 2005), 252-53.
161 Anderson Ruffin Abbott Papers, TRL.
162 Owen Thomas claims that Abbott attended primary medical classes in 1867, "although he would never graduate." Catherine Slaney, in contrast, states that he "graduated with a Bachelor's Degree in Medicine." Abbott's obituary noted that he had graduated from the Toronto School of Medicine. Thomas, "Abbott, Anderson Ruffin"; Slaney, *Family Secrets*, 81.
163 Newby, *Anderson Ruffin Abbott*, 90-91; *Toronto Globe*, 29 December 1913.
164 Thomas, "Abbott, Anderson Ruffin."
165 In the years after the Civil War, the GAR became the Union army's largest veteran organization. In addition to the Toronto post, there were two in Hamilton (William W. Cooke Post, No. 472, and William Winer Post, No. 77) and one in London (Hannibal Hamlin Post, No. 652), all part of the New York Department. Winnipeg had a post and the province of Quebec had posts in Coaticook, Montreal, and Quebec City.
166 Barbara A. Gannon, *The Won Cause: Black and White Comradeship in the Grand Army of the Republic* (Chapel Hill: University of North Carolina Press, 2011), 26. Thomas, "Abbott, Anderson Ruffin," argues that this was "the highest military honour ever bestowed to that time on a person of African descent in Canada or the United States." It was certainly a symbol of respect for Abbott, but it was not the highest rank achieved by a black veteran. For example, James Wolff served in the Massachusetts Department as junior vice-commander, second in command, and finally as department commander.
167 Anderson Ruffin Abbott Papers, TRL.
168 Slaney, *Family Secrets*, 122.

169 "Miscellaneous file," Anderson Ruffin Abbott Collection, TRL.
170 *Toronto Evening Telegraph,* 30 December 1913, Anderson Ruffin Abbott Collection, TRL.

CHAPTER 7: POST-WAR LIFE

1 Canada, *Censuses of Canada, 1665-1861, Statistics of Canada Volume IV* (Ottawa: I.B. Taylor, 1876), 333, 350. The published census figures are used for the purposes of comparison. The assumption is that the actual number of black residents is probably 15 or 20 percent higher. The assumption is also made that the undercount of black inhabitants was generally the same in all censuses, except in certain specific situations where the data on black households were significantly more accurate or inaccurate.
2 *Census of Canada, 1871,* vol. 1 (Ottawa: I.B. Taylor), 322, 332.
3 *Census of Canada, 1881* (Ottawa: MacLean, Roger and Co., 1882), 208, 220.
4 Harvey Amani Whitfield, *Blacks on the Border: The Black Refugees in British North America, 1815-1860* (Burlington: University of Vermont Press, 2006), 116-17.
5 Quoted in Peter McKerrow, *A Brief History of the Coloured Baptists of Nova Scotia, 1783-1895,* ed. Frank S. Boyd Jr. (1895; repr., Halifax: Afro Nova Scotian Enterprises, 1976), 101.
6 Anderson Ruffin Abbott Collection, Toronto Reference Library (TRL), Toronto. At the same time, Abbott also believed that "a great many of the fugitives drifted back to the South in search of relatives." Ibid.
7 It is, however, assumed that the 17,053 black residents represent a significant undercount by the enumerators, as was typical of most North American censuses.
8 As mentioned in Chapter 1, the 1861 census has been described as particularly unreliable, whereas the published figures for 1871 are accepted with little criticism, especially by authors who emphasize the numbers of African Americans returning to the United States. Nevertheless, two factors mitigate against this scenario. Enumerators in 1861 were instructed to make an accurate return for black residents because this had been poorly done in the 1851 census. In addition, whereas the 1861 census employed the terms "black" and "mulatto" to identify residents, the 1871 census used the more uninformative "origin" instead. For a discussion of the factors and problems behind this change, see N.B. Ryder, "The Interpretation of Origin Statistics," *Canadian Journal of Economics and Political Science/Revue canadienne d'économique et de science politique* 21, 4 (November 1955): 466-79.
9 In 1861, African Americans made up 57 percent of the province's black population.
10 Sarah-Jane Mathieu, *North of the Color Line: Migration and Black Resistance in Canada, 1870-1955* (Chapel Hill: University of North Carolina Press, 2010), 12.
11 Sharon A. Roger Hepburn, *Crossing the Border: A Free Black Community in Canada* (Urbana: University of Illinois Press, 2007), 185-86.
12 Ibid., 186.
13 The methodology used to identify the veterans in later censuses is described in the Appendix.
14 At least 51 of the 835 men who enlisted died before their regiments were mustered out. Probably as many men received an early discharge due to physical disabilities and prolonged illness. Some would have died prior to the censuses.
15 "W. Henry Williams," Compiled Military Service Records (CMSR), RG 94, National Archives and Records Administration (NARA).
16 "John Talbot," CMSR, RG 94, NARA; United States Census 1870.
17 "George Caples," Civil War Pension Files (CWPF), RG 15, NARA.
18 "Thomas Brooks," CMSR, RG 94, NARA; United States Census 1870.

19 Of course, some barbers may have owned their establishments. It is less clear how to categorize James B. Johnson, a resident of Kingston in 1871, who gave his occupation as "hair dresser." Johnson enlisted in the 102nd USCT in January 1864, but a month later he became one of the many who deserted that regiment.

20 The act to increase and fix the Military Peace Establishment of 28 July 1866 authorized the regular army to expand its forces to forty-five infantry regiments, of which four were segregated black units. The act also established two black cavalry regiments. Almost three years later, in March 1869, Congress reduced the total number of infantry regiments to twenty-five, and the four black infantry regiments were consolidated into two. The two cavalry regiments remained unaffected.

21 "George H. Brown" and "Isaac Maynard," CWPF, RG 15, NARA.

22 The GAR was initially a partisan organization with close links to the Republican Party. After a sharp decline in membership during the early 1870s, it was reinvented as a lobby group that sought better federal pensions for veterans.

23 Barbara A. Gannon, *The Won Cause: Black and White Comradeship in the Grand Army of the Republic* (Chapel Hill: University of North Carolina Press, 2011), 21, 35-36.

24 The Grand Army of the Republic Records Project has documented more than 8,600 community-level posts, including the ones in Canada. For specific listings, especially for the Canadian posts, see Grand Army of the Republic (GAR) Records Project, http://suvcw.org/.

25 Stuart McConnell suggests that black veterans "were admitted to the GAR on terms of formal equality accompanied by informal discrimination." David Blight concludes that by the 1880s, virtually all GAR posts were segregated. Stuart McConnell, *Glorious Contentment: The Grand Army of the Republic, 1865-1900* (Chapel Hill: University of North Carolina Press, 1992), 218; David Blight, *Race and Reunion: The Civil War in American Memory* (Cambridge, MA: Harvard University Press, 2001), 194.

26 Gannon, *The Won Cause*, 201-20.

27 Quebec had three posts, at Montreal, Quebec City, and Coaticook, Winnipeg had one, and Ontario had four. Interestingly, no posts are recorded for the Maritimes.

28 Anderson Ruffin Abbott Collection, TRL.

29 "Albert R. Garrison," CWPF, RG 15, NARA.

30 All post members voted on the acceptance of each new "recruit," and if 10 percent (later 20 percent) voted negative, the "recruit" was rejected. In posts where only two out of ten white members disliked the idea of integration, black members would be refused. In addition, recruits had to pass further votes to become a "soldier" and then a "veteran." As a result, if five white veterans in the Knowlton Post had dissented, they could easily have excluded black members. Gannon, *The Won Cause*, 86, 94; McConnell, *Glorious Contentment*, 31.

31 Anderson Ruffin Abbott Collection, TRL.

32 Ibid. This was probably Corporal Alexander Brown, Company C, who had been a slave in Maryland prior to the Civil War.

33 *Hamilton Spectator*, 1 June 1891, 31 May 1892, 30 May 1896, 29 May 1897, 31 May 1898, 30 May 1900, and 30 May 1904.

34 Adrienne Shadd, *The Journey from Tollgate to Parkway: African Canadians in Hamilton* (Hamilton: Dundurn Press, 2010), 160; "Nelson Stevens," CMSR, RG 94, NARA.

35 "John W. Price," CWPF, RG 15, NARA.

36 During the war and into the 1920s, Congress passed a series of acts that continually altered the pension regulations. For a good overview, see Claudia Linares, *The Civil War Pension Law* (Chicago: Center for Population Economics, 2001).

37 Donald R. Shaffer, *After the Glory: The Struggles of Black Civil War Veterans* (Lawrence: University Press of Kansas, 2004), 122, 209.

38 "William Gibson, alias John Sunders," CWPF, RG 15, NARA. Gibson, whose application succeeded, was receiving thirty-eight dollars a month in June 1918.
39 For a detailed discussion of the factors that worked against black applicants, see Shaffer, *After the Glory*, 122-33. In addition, pension officials tended to be less sympathetic to black veterans who claimed that an ailment, especially diminished mental competence, was the result of military service. Richard M. Reid, *Freedom for Themselves: North Carolina's Black Soldiers in the Civil War Era* (Chapel Hill: University of North Carolina Press, 2008), 316.
40 Peter David Blanck and Michael Millender, "Before Disability Civil Rights: Civil War Pensions and the Politics of Disability in America," *Alabama Law Review* 52, 1 (Fall 2000): 9.
41 "Augustus Anderson," CWPF, RG 15, NARA.
42 Blanck and Millender, "Before Disability Civil Rights," 9.
43 Not surprisingly, many aging black veterans who were illiterate and desperately poor fell prey to unscrupulous agents who advanced loans against the claims at exorbitant interest rates or who waited until the claims were paid and then extorted money well beyond the 10 percent allowed to them under the law. Shaffer, *After the Glory*, 120-21.
44 For a contemporary discussion of the difficulties in handling applications, see Gaillard Hunt, "The United States Pension Office," *Atlantic Monthly*, January 1890, 18-22.
45 Watts ultimately received his pension. "Spencer Watts," CWPF, RG 15, NARA.
46 Whereas many agents behaved ethically, many more were the late-nineteenth-century equivalent of ambulance chasers. For more on agents, see Shaffer, *After the Glory*, 123-28.
47 "Joseph D. Crowell," CWPF, RG 15, NARA.
48 Prior to his death, Hardy lived in the Soldier's and Sailor's Home at Bath, New York. "William H. Hardy," CWPF, RG 15, NARA.
49 Garrison's death certificate noted that he was born in the United States but did not indicate when he first moved to Canada West. "Albert R. Garrison," CWPF, RG 15, NARA.
50 The records list his age as thirty-seven and thirty-four. Soldiers who gave conflicting ages at different times might later have difficulty persuading pension officials that they were who they claimed to be. "Joel Monroe," CMSR, RG 94, NARA.
51 In 1861, enumerators counted ninety-seven black inhabitants in Oro Township. Michael Wayne, "The Black Population of Canada West on the Eve of the American Civil War: A Reassessment Based on the Manuscript Census of 1861," *Histoire sociale/Social History* 28, 56 (November 1995): 484.
52 "Joel Monroe," CWPF, RG 15, NARA.
53 Ibid. He was probably suffering from scurvy, a major problem for the black soldiers when they first arrived in Texas.
54 Ibid.
55 Of the 352 black sailors examined in this study, only about 36 could be identified as having received a pension.
56 By 1890, the GAR had over four hundred thousand members in thousands of posts across the United States, and it functioned as a powerful lobby group to ensure that most veterans would receive pensions. Gannon, *The Won Cause*, 21.
57 "Augustus Anderson," CWPF, RG 15, NARA. Most of the forms completed by pension lawyers cited a wide range of non-specific ailments that were difficult to disprove. As a result, lawyers such as Lloyd were viewed with suspicion.
58 "Priscilla Atwood, Widow of Alexander Atwood," CWPF, RG 15, NARA.
59 "Samuel Duncan," CWPF, RG 15, NARA.
60 Linares, *The Civil War Pension Law*, 16; William H. Glasson, *Federal Military Pensions in the United States* (New York: Oxford University Press, 1918), 230-37. Well after 1890, more liberal rules were adopted without this limitation.

61 "John Weeks," CMSR, RG 94, NARA.
62 Both Hannah Weeks and her two witnesses, John Henry and Robert Woods, were presumably illiterate, for all signed with a mark.
63 "Hannah Weeks, Mother of John Weeks," CWPF, RG 15, NARA.
64 "Gideon Stump," CMSR, RG 94, NARA; "Gideon Bailey, alias Gideon Stump," CWPF, RG 15, NARA.
65 In fact, Congress had established a more lenient standard of proof for African American widows, in part because slave marriages were so difficult to properly document. Shaffer, *After the Glory*, 122, 232n6.
66 "Nettie Going, Wid. of Samuel H. Going," CWPF, RG 15, NARA.
67 "John White," CMSR, RG 94, NARA.
68 "Hattie White, Widow of John White," CWPF, RG 15, NARA.
69 As was the case for many soldiers who signed up in 1864, his enlistment was credited to a congressional district, specifically Maine's Second Congressional District, to help it meet its draft quota.
70 "Joseph Robinson," CMSR, RG 94, NARA.
71 "Joseph Robinson," CWPF, RG 15, NARA.
72 Linares, *The Civil War Pension Law*, 14.
73 "Terry Ford," CWPF, RG 15, NARA.
74 "George H. Brown," CWPF, RG 15, NARA.
75 National Park Service, "The Civil War: Soldiers and Sailors Database," http://www.itd.nps.gov/.
76 Unfortunately for Brown, the prize money for most of the vessels was less than $1,000. The richest prize taken by the *Sagamore* was the schooner *New Year*, which was worth $15,906.18, and the total for all the captured vessels would have been under $50,000. David D. Porter, *The Naval History of the Civil War* (New York: Sherman, 1886), 833-43; Department of the Navy, Naval Historical Center, "Sagamore," *Dictionary of American Naval Fighting Ships*, http://www.history.navy.mil/.
77 Charles Barnard Fox, *Record of the Service of the Fifty-Fifth Regiment of Massachusetts Volunteer Infantry* (Cambridge, MA: John Wilson and Son, 1868), 116.
78 It appears that he also received eighty dollars from Middlesex County, the district in which he enlisted. "George H. Brown," CMSR, RG 94, NARA.
79 Fox, *Record of the Service*, 68-70.
80 Ibid., 80.
81 "George H. Brown," CMSR, RG 94, NARA; Fox, *Record of the Service*, 83-84.
82 Elizabeth D. Leonard, *Men of Color to Arms! Black Soldiers, Indian Wars, and the Quest for Equality* (New York: W.W. Norton, 2010), 40-41, 53.
83 Quartermaster sergeants are responsible for obtaining, storing, and distributing all regimental property, including clothing and garrison and camp equipage. As such, they should be men of integrity who can keep accurate records of their transactions. Frank N. Schubert, ed., *On the Trail of the Buffalo Soldier: Biographies of the African Americans in the U.S. Army, 1866-1917* (Wilmington, DE: Scholarly Resources, 1995), 59.
84 "George H. Brown," CWPF, RG 15, NARA.
85 Ibid. Under the pension act of 1890, widows could claim a pension only if they were unable to support themselves.
86 Ibid. Because her marriage to Brown was postdated 27 June 1890, she was ineligible for a pension, and it is highly unlikely that the Pension Office would have accepted her application.
87 The author wishes to thank St. Clair Patterson for sharing his extensive knowledge of Jackson's life, especially his career in Lockhartville after the war.
88 As with many veterans, there is some uncertainty regarding the exact date of his birth.

89 Greg Marquis, *In Armageddon's Shadow: The Civil War and Canada's Maritime Provinces* (Montreal and Kingston: McGill-Queen's University Press, 1998), 80.
90 "Benjamin Jackson, Civil War Veteran, Passes Away," *Hants Journal* (Windsor, Nova Scotia), 1 September 1915.
91 "Benjamin Jackson, alias Lewis Saunders," CWPF, RG 15, NARA.
92 "Benjamin Jackson, Civil War Veteran," manuscript in the possession of St. Clair Patterson.
93 "Benjamin Jackson," *Hants Journal*, 1 September 1915.
94 "Benjamin Jackson, alias Lewis Saunders," CWPF, RG 15, NARA.
95 It seems reasonable to assume that if he were pressed into the navy, he would have used his own name.
96 Because Jackson enlisted before Congress repealed the three-hundred-dollar commutation fee, the price offered to substitutes was much less than it would be by late 1864. Of course, agents who acted honestly (or dishonestly) in obtaining substitutes for draftees often ended up with much of this money.
97 "Benjamin Jackson, alias Lewis Saunders," CWPF, RG 15, NARA.
98 Roy P. Basler, ed., *Collected Works of Abraham Lincoln* (New Brunswick, NJ: Rutgers University Press, 1954), 7:45.
99 "Benjamin Jackson," CWPF, RG 15, NARA. Bronchitis and other respiratory diseases were much more common among sailors than among soldiers, who all too often suffered from chronic diarrhea.
100 "Benjamin Jackson," CWPF, RG 15, NARA.
101 Linares, *The Civil War Pension Law*, 26.
102 At least in the first years, Jackson apparently crewed for the Windsor shipowner Shubael Dimock. "Benjamin Jackson, Civil War Veteran."
103 "Benjamin Jackson," *Hants Journal*, 1 September 1915.
104 "Benjamin Jackson, alias Lewis Saunders," CWPF, RG 15, NARA.
105 Ibid.
106 Linares, *The Civil War Pension Law*, 21.
107 "Benjamin Jackson, alias Lewis Saunders," CWPF, RG 15, NARA.
108 Contemporary critics often described the young women who married much older pensioners as "frauds." Jennifer L. Gross, "Civil War Pensions," in *Encyclopedia of the American Civil War* (New York: W.W. Norton, 2000), 267.
109 "Benjamin Jackson, alias Lewis Saunders," CWPF, RG 15, NARA.
110 "Isaiah Wilson," CMSR, RG 94, NARA
111 "Isaiah Wilson," CWPF, RG 15, NARA.
112 Benjamin Drew, *A North-Side View of Slavery: The Refugee, Or, The Narratives of Fugitive Slaves in Canada, Related by Themselves, with an Account of the History and Condition of the Colored Population of Upper Canada* (1856; repr., New York: Negro Universities Press, 1968), 367, 69. Robin Winks believes that the black settlers made up about "33 percent of Colchester's" total population. Robin Winks, *The Blacks in Canada: A History*, 2nd ed. (Montreal and Kingston: McGill-Queen's University Press, 1997), 493.
113 He attended school with another Kentucky fugitive who also found sanctuary in Colchester, Robert W. Hughbanks, who farmed in South Colchester for fifty years until 1907, when he moved to Ann Arbor to live with his daughter. "Harriet A. Nelson, Widow of John Nelson," CWPF, RG 15, NARA; "Alexander Carter," CMSR, RG 94, NARA.
114 "Harriet A. Nelson, Widow of John Nelson," CWPF, RG 15, NARA.
115 Sarah and her husband, Joe Henderson, had previously lived in Amherstburg, Canada West, where Joe worked as a blacksmith.
116 "Harriet A. Nelson, Widow of John Nelson," CWPF, RG 15, NARA.

117 "Mary A. Rouse, Widow of Elias S. Rouse," CWPF, RG 15, NARA.
118 "Alexander Carter," CMSR, RG 94, NARA.
119 "Harriet A. Nelson, Widow of John Nelson," CWPF, RG 15, NARA.
120 Ibid.
121 James W. Dennis remembered that John Nelson brought his gun and uniform home. Soldiers on discharge could purchase their guns from the army for $4.50.

Conclusion

1 Barbara A. Gannon, *The Won Cause: Black and White Comradeship in the Grand Army of the Republic* (Chapel Hill: University of North Carolina Press, 2011), 66-67.
2 A.R. Abbott to the Surgeon General's Office, 18 February 1891, "Abbott, A.R.," Medical Officers' Files, Personal Papers of Medical Officers and Physicians, RG 94, National Archives and Records Administration (NARA), Washington, DC.
3 Anderson Ruffin Abbott Collection, Toronto Reference Library (TRL), Toronto.
4 Ibid.
5 Ibid.; Noah Andre Trudeau, *Voices of the 55th: Letters from the 55th Massachusetts Volunteers, 1861-1865* (Dayton, OH: Morningside, 1996), 61-62.
6 *Chicago Conservator*, 8 December 1896.
7 Indeed, because they were credited to Northern states when they enlisted, as were many Southern black Americans, the differences between the enrolment rates of Northern African Americans and those of black British North Americans are even less than they first appear.
8 Michael J. Bennett, *Union Jacks: Yankee Sailors in the Civil War* (Chapel Hill: University of North Carolina Press, 2004), 19. Sailors may have been less motivated ideologically, but Bennett's comment raises the question of how many soldiers wished to die or suffer.
9 "William Gardner," "James Harris," "Thomas Thompson," CMSR, RG 94, NARA.
10 Anderson Ruffin Abbott Collection, TRL.
11 By 1870, there were about 3,600 African Canadians in the United States, up from about 1,200 in 1860.
12 Anderson Ruffin Abbott Collection, TRL.
13 Ibid.

Selected Bibliography

Archival Sources

Buxton National Historic Site and Museum, North Buxton, Ontario
Lucien Boyd File
Rapier Brothers File

Cornell University, Ithaca, New York
Burt Green Wilder Papers
Diary of Burt Green Wilder

Diocese of Huron Archives, London, Ontario
Diary of Reverend Thomas Hughes

Howard University Library, Washington, DC
Rapier Papers, Moreland-Springarn Research Center

Library of Congress, Washington, DC
American Colonization Society Papers

Massachusetts State Archives, Boston
John Albion Andrew Papers

National Archives and Records Administration (NARA), Washington, DC
Record Group 15 (RG 15)
    Civil War Pension Files (CWPF)
Record Group 94 (RG 94)
    Carded Records, Volunteer Organizations, Civil War
    Compiled Military Service Records (CMSR)

Letters Received, Division of Colored Troops
Personal Papers of Medical Officers and Physicians
Records of Adjutant General's Office
Regimental Descriptive Books

State Archives of Michigan, Lansing
102nd USCT, Report of Wounds, Letters

Syracuse University Library, Syracuse, New York
Gerrit Smith Collection

Toronto Reference Library (TRL), Toronto
Anderson Ruffin Abbott Collection

Newspapers and Magazines

Atlantic Magazine
Boston Liberator
British Whig
Christian Guardian
Christian Recorder
Detroit Advertiser and Tribune
Detroit Free Press
Douglass' Monthly
Halifax British Colonist
Halifax Morning Journal
Hamilton Evening Times
Hamilton Spectator
Hants Journal (Windsor, Nova Scotia)
Kingston Chronicle and Gazette
Kingston Daily News
Medical and Surgical Reporter
Montreal Gazette
Moore's Rural New Yorker
New Brunswick Reporter
New York Weekly Anglo-African
Perth Courier
Provincial Freeman
Quebec Mercury
Saint John Morning Freeman
St. Catharines Constitutional
Toronto Christian Guardian
Toronto Globe
Voice of the Fugitive (Windsor)
Windsor Journal
Yarmouth Herald

Published Primary Sources

Government Publications

Canada. *Censuses of Canada, 1665-1871, Statistics Canada, Vol. IV.* Ottawa: I.B. Taylor, 1876.
–. *Correspondence Relating to the Fenian Invasion and the Rebellion of the Southern States.* Ottawa: Hunter, Rose and Co., 1869.
The Medical and Surgical History of the War of the Rebellion. 6 vols. Washington, DC: Government Printing Office, 1870-88.
Message of the President of the United States, and Accompanying Documents, to the Two Houses of Congress, at the Commencement of the First Session of the Thirty-Eighth Congress. Washington, DC: Government Printing Office, 1863.
Official Records of the Union and Confederate Navies in the War of the Rebellion. 31 vols. Washington, DC: Government Printing Office, 1894-1927.
The War of the Rebellion: A Compilation of the Official Records of the Union and Confederate Armies. 128 vols. Washington, DC: Government Printing Office, 1880-1901.

Books and Articles

Adams, Virginia M., ed. *On the Altar of Freedom: A Black Soldier's Civil War Letters from the Front*. Amherst: University of Massachusetts Press, 1991.

Addeman, Joshua M. *Reminiscences of Two Years with the Colored Troops: Personal Narratives of Events in the War of the Rebellion*. Providence: N. Bangs Williams, 1880.

Aldren, B. "Life in Upper Canada in 1837." *Canadian Medical Association Journal* 20 (January 1929): 65-66.

Barnes, James J., and Patience P. Barnes, eds. *The American Civil War through British Eyes: Dispatches from British Diplomats*. Vol. 1, *November 1860–April 1862*. Kent, OH: Kent State University Press, 2003.

Basler, Roy P., ed. *Collected Works of Abraham Lincoln*. 9 vols. New Brunswick, NJ: Rutgers University Press, 1953-55.

Berlin, Ira, Joseph P. Reidy, and Leslie S. Rowlands, eds. *The Black Military Experience*. Ser. 2 of *Freedom: A Documentary History of Emancipation, 1861-1867*. Cambridge: Cambridge University Press, 1982.

Blackburn, George M. "The Negro Viewed by a Michigan Civil War Soldier: Letters of John C. Buchanan." *Michigan History Magazine* 47, 1 (March 1963): 75-84.

Blackett, R.J.M., ed. *Thomas Morris Chester: Black Civil War Correspondent; His Dispatches from the Virginia Front*. New York: Da Capo Press, 1989.

Chenery, William H. *The Fourteenth Regiment Rhode Island Heavy Artillery (Colored) in the War to Preserve the Union, 1861-1865*. Providence: Snow and Farnham, 1898.

Daly, Robert W., ed. *Aboard the USS Florida, 1863-65: The Letters of Acting Paymaster William Frederick Keeler, U. S. Navy to His Wife, Anna*. Annapolis: Naval Institute Press, 1964.

Donald, David Herbert, and Harold Holzer. *Lincoln in the Times: The Life of Abraham Lincoln as Originally Reported in the New York Times*. New York: St. Martin's Press, 2005.

Drew, Benjamin. *A North-Side View of Slavery: The Refugee, Or, The Narratives of Fugitive Slaves in Canada, Related by Themselves, with an Account of the History and Condition of the Colored Population of Upper Canada*. 1856. Reprint, New York: Negro Universities Press, 1968.

Duncan, Russell, ed. *Blue-Eyed Child of Fortune: The Civil War Letters of Colonel Robert Gould Shaw*. Athens: University of Georgia Press, 1992.

Emilio, Luis F. *A Brave Black Regiment: History of the Fifty-Fourth Regiment of Massachusetts Volunteer Infantry, 1863-1865*. 1891. Reprint, New York: Arno Press, 1969.

Fox, Charles Barnard. *Record of the Service of the Fifty-Fifth Regiment of Massachusetts Volunteer Infantry*. Cambridge, MA: John Wilson and Son, 1868.

Gould, Benjamin. *Investigations in the Military and Anthropological Statistics of the American Soldiers*. 1869. Reprint, New York: Arno Press, 1979.

Gould, William B., IV. *Diary of a Contraband: The Civil War Passage of a Black Sailor*. Stanford: Stanford University Press, 2002.

Grattan, John W. *Under the Blue Pennant, Or Notes of a Naval Officer, 1863-1865*. Ed. Robert J. Schneller. New York: John Wiley and Sons, 1999.

Henson, Josiah. *An Autobiography of the Rev. Josiah Henson, from 1789 to 1876*. London: Christian Age Office, 1876.

Holzer, Harold, ed. *The Lincoln Mailbag: America Writes to the President, 1861-1865*. Carbondale: Southern Illinois University Press, 1998.

Howe, Samuel Gridley. *Report to the Freedmen's Inquiry Commission, 1864*. Boston: Wright and Potter, 1864.

Hunt, Harriot K. *Glances and Glimpses; Or, Fifty Years Social, Including Twenty Years Professional Life*. Boston: John P. Jewett, 1856.

Keckley, Elizabeth. *Behind the Scenes: Thirty Years a Slave and Four Years in the White House*. New York: Arno Press, 1968.
McKerrow, Peter. *A Brief History of the Coloured Baptists of Nova Scotia, 1783-1895*. Ed. Frank S. Boyd Jr. 1895. Reprint, Halifax: Afro Nova Scotian Enterprises, 1976.
Read, Colin, and Ronald J. Stagg. *The Rebellion of 1837 in Upper Canada: A Collection of Documents*. Ottawa: Carleton University Press, 1985.
Redkey, Edwin S., ed. *A Grand Army of Black Men: Letters from African-American Soldiers in the Union Army, 1861-1865*. New York: Cambridge University Press, 1992.
Reid, Richard M., ed. *Practicing Medicine in a Black Regiment: The Civil War Diary of Burt G. Wilder, 55th Massachusetts*. Amherst: University of Massachusetts Press, 2010.
Riley, Jerome R. *Philosophy of Negro Suffrage*. Hartford, CT: American Publishing, 1895.
Sill, William. *The Underground Railroad*. Philadelphia: Porter and Coates, 1872.
Smith, William Mervale. *Swamp Doctor: The Diary of a Union Surgeon in the Virginia and North Carolina Swamps*. Mechanicsburg, PA: Stackpole Books, 2001.
Sollors, Werner, Caldwell Titcomb, and Thomas H. Underwood, eds. *Blacks at Harvard: A Documentary History of African-American Experience at Harvard and Radcliffe*. New York: New York University Press, 1993.
Symonds, Craig L., ed. *Charleston Blockade: The Journals of John B. Marchand, U.S. Navy, 1861-1862*. Newport, RI: Naval War College Press, 1976.
Ward, Samuel Ringgold. *Autobiography of a Fugitive Negro; His Anti-Slavery Labours in the United States, Canada, and England*. London: John Snow, 1855.
Wells, Cheryl A., ed. *A Surgeon in the Army of the Potomac*. Montreal and Kingston: McGill-Queen's University Press, 2008.
Yacovone, Donald. *A Voice of Thunder: The Civil War Letters of George E. Stephens*. Urbana: University of Illinois Press, 1997.

Secondary Sources

Adams, George Worthington. *Doctors in Blue: The Medical History of the Union Army in the Civil War*. Baton Rouge: Louisiana State University Press, 1952.
Adams, Tracey. "Making a Living: African Canadian Workers in London, Ontario, 1861-1901." *Labour/Le travail* 67 (Spring 2011): 9-43.
Alexander, Adele Logan. *Homelands and Waterways: The American Journey of the Bond Family, 1846-1926*. New York: Vintage Books, 1999.
Alexander, Philip N. "John H. Rapier, Jr., and the Medical Profession in Jamaica, 1861-1862." Part 1. *Jamaica Journal* 24 (February 1993): 37-46.
–. "John H. Rapier, Jr., and the Medical Profession in Jamaica, 1861-1862." Part 2. *Jamaica Journal* 25 (October 1993): 52-64.
Anbinder, Tyler. "Which Poor Man's Fight? Immigrants and the Federal Conscription of 1863." *Civil War History* 52, 4 (December 2006): 344-72.
Apap, Chris. "'Let No Man of Us Budge One Step': David Walker and the Rhetoric of African Emplacement." *Early American Literature* 46, 2 (June 2011): 319-50.
Appel, Toby A. "The Thomsonian Movement, the Regular Profession, and the State in Antebellum Connecticut: A Case Study of the Repeal of Early Medical Licensing Laws." *Journal of the History of Medicine and Allied Sciences* 65, 2 (April 2010): 153-86.
Aptheker, Herbert. "The Negro in the Union Navy." *Journal of Negro History* 32, 2 (April 1947): 169-200.
Baehre, Rainer. "The Medical Profession in Upper Canada Reconsidered: Politics, Medical Reform, and Law in a Colonial Society." *Canadian Bulletin of Medical History* 12 (1995): 101-24.

Baskerville, Peter. *Ontario: Image, Identity, and Power.* New York: Oxford University Press, 2002.
Bennett, Michael J. *Union Jacks: Yankee Sailors in the Civil War.* Chapel Hill: University of North Carolina Press, 2004.
Bernstein, Iver. *The New York City Draft Riots: Their Significance for American Society and Politics in the Age of the Civil War.* New York: Oxford University Press, 1990.
Berry, Mary Frances. *Military Necessity and Civil Rights Policy: Black Citizenship and the Constitution, 1861-1868.* Port Washington, NY: Kennikat Press, 1977.
Blackett, R.J.M. *Beating against the Barriers: Biographical Essays in Nineteenth-Century Afro-American History.* Baton Rouge: Louisiana State University Press, 1986.
–. *Divided Hearts: Britain and the American Civil War.* Baton Rouge: Louisiana State University Press, 2001.
Blanck, Peter David, and Michael Millender. "Before Disability Civil Rights: Civil War Pensions and the Politics of Disability in America." *Alabama Law Review* 52, 1 (Fall 2000): 1-50.
Blight, David. *Race and Reunion: The Civil War in American Memory.* Cambridge, MA: Harvard University Press, 2001.
Blishen, Bernard. *Doctors in Canada: The Changing World of Medical Practice.* Toronto: University of Toronto Press, 1991.
Bolster, W. Jeffrey. *Black Jacks: African American Seamen in the Age of Sail.* Cambridge, MA: Harvard University Press, 1997.
Bordewich, Fergus. *Bound for Canaan: The Epic Story of the Underground Railroad; America's First Civil Rights Movement.* New York: Amistad, 2005.
Brode, Patrick. *The Odyssey of John Anderson.* Toronto: University of Toronto Press, 1989.
Brooks, Stewart. *Civil War Medicine.* Springfield: Charles C. Thomas, 1966.
Brown-Kubisch, Linda. *The Queen's Bush Settlement: Black Pioneers, 1839-1865.* Toronto: Natural Heritage Books, 2004.
Browning, Robert M. *From Cape Charles to Cape Fear: The North Atlantic Blockading Squadron during the Civil War.* Tuscaloosa: University of Alabama Press, 1993.
Buckner, Phillip A., and John G. Reid, eds. *The Atlantic Region to Confederation: A History.* Toronto: University of Toronto Press, 1994.
Buker, George E. *Blockaders, Refugees, and Contrabands: Civil War on Florida's Gulf Coast, 1861-1865.* Tuscaloosa: University of Alabama Press, 1993.
Bukowczyk, John, Nora Faires, David Smith, and Randy Widdis. *Permeable Border: The Great Lakes Basin as Transnational Region, 1650-1990.* Pittsburg: University of Pittsburg Press, 2005.
Cahill, Barry. "The Black Loyalist Myth in Atlantic Canada." *Acadiensis* 29, 1 (Autumn 1999): 76-87.
Calarco, Tom. *People of the Underground Railroad: A Biographical Dictionary.* Westport, CT: Greenwood Press, 2008.
Campbell, Duncan Andrew. *English Public Opinion and the American Civil War.* Rochester, NY: Boydell Press, 2003.
Campbell, Stanley W. *Slave Catchers: Enforcement of the Fugitive Slave Law, 1850-1860.* Chapel Hill: University of North Carolina Press, 1968.
Canney, Donald L. *Africa Squadron: The U.S. Navy and the Slave Trade, 1842-1861.* Washington, DC: Potomac Books, 2006.
Cecelski, David. "The Shores of Freedom: The Maritime Underground Railroad in North Carolina, 1800-1861." *North Carolina Historical Review* 71, 2 (1994): 174-206.
Clinton, Catherine. *Mrs. Lincoln: A Life.* New York: Harper Collins, 2009.
Cobb, W. Montague. "A Short History of the Freedmen's Hospital." *Journal of the National Medical Association* 54 (May 1962): 273-89.

Collison, Gary Lee. *Shadrach Minkins: From Fugitive Slave to Citizen*. Boston: Harvard University Press, 1997.
Cooper, Afua. *The Hanging of Angelique: The Untold Story of Canadian Slavery and the Burning of Old Montreal*. Athens: University of Georgia Press, 2007.
Cornish, Dudley T. *The Sable Arm: Negro Troops in the Union Army, 1861-1865*. New York: Longmans Green, 1965.
Curtis, Bruce. *The Politics of Population: State Formation, Statistics, and the Census of Canada, 1840-1875*. Toronto: University of Toronto Press, 2000.
DeBlack, Thomas A. *With Fire and Sword: Arkansas, 1861-1874*. Fayetteville: University of Arkansas Press, 2003.
Donald, David Herbert, Jean Harvey Baker, and Michael F. Holt. *The Civil War and Reconstruction*. New York: W.W. Norton, 2001.
Downs, Jim. *Sick from Freedom: African-American Illness and Suffering during the Civil War and Reconstruction*. New York: Oxford University Press, 2012.
Dunae, Patrick A. "Making the 1891 Census in British Columbia." *Histoire sociale/Social History* 31, 62 (May 1998): 223-39.
Egerton, Douglas R. "Rethinking Atlantic Historiography in a Postcolonial Era: The Civil War in a Global Perspective." *Journal of the Civil War Era* 1, 1 (March 2011): 79-95.
Elting, John R. *Amateurs, to Arms! A Military History of the War of 1812*. Chapel Hill: Algonquin Books of Chapel Hill, 1991.
Faires, Nora. "Leaving the 'Land of Second Chance': Migration from Ontario to the Upper Midwest in the Nineteenth and Early Twentieth Centuries." In John Bukowczyk, Nora Faires, David Smith, and Randy Widdis, *Permeable Border: The Great Lakes Basin as Transnational Region, 1650-1990*, 78-119. Pittsburg: University of Pittsburg Press, 2005.
Feltes, Norman N. *This Side of Heaven: Determining the Donnelly Murders, 1880*. Toronto: University of Toronto Press, 1999.
Fingard, Judith. *Jack in Port: Sailortowns of Eastern Canada*. Toronto: University of Toronto Press, 1982.
Fleche, Andre M. *The Revolution of 1861: The American Civil War in the Age of Nationalistic Conflict*. Chapel Hill: University of North Carolina Press, 2012.
Foner, Eric. *Fiery Trial: Abraham Lincoln and American Slavery*. New York: W.W. Norton, 2010.
–. *Reconstruction: America's Unfinished Revolution, 1863-1877*. New York: Harper and Row, 1988.
Fonvielle, Chris E., Jr. *The Wilmington Campaign: Last Rays of Departing Hope*. Mechanicsburg, PA: Stackpole Books, 1997.
Forbes, Ella. "'By My Own Right Arm': Redemptive Violence and the 1851 Christiana, Pennsylvania Resistance." *Journal of Negro History* 83, 2 (Summer 1998): 159-68.
Foreman, Amanda. *A World on Fire: Britain's Crucial Role in the American Civil War*. New York: Random House, 2010.
Fowler, William M., Jr. *Under Two Flags: The American Navy in the Civil War*. New York: W.W. Norton, 1990.
Franklin, John Hope, and Loren Schweninger. *Runaway Slaves: Slaves on the Plantation*. New York: Oxford University Press, 1999.
Freehling, William W. *The Road to Disunion: Secessionists at Bay, 1776-1854*. New York: Oxford University Press, 1990.
Furrow, Matthew. "Samuel Gridley Howe, the Black Population of Canada West, and the Racial Ideology of the 'Blueprint for Radical Reconstruction.'" *Journal of American History* 97, 2 (September 2010): 344-70.

Gagan, David P. "Enumerator's Instruction for the Census of Canada 1852 and 1861." *Histoire sociale/Social History* 8, 14 (November 1974): 355-65.
Gannon, Barbara A. *The Won Cause: Black and White Comradeship in the Grand Army of the Republic.* Chapel Hill: University of North Carolina Press, 2011.
Gara, Larry. *The Liberty Line: The Legend of the Underground Railroad.* Lexington: University of Kentucky Press, 1961.
Geary, James W. *We Need Men: The Union Draft in the Civil War.* DeKalb: Northern Illinois University Press, 1991.
Giggie, John Michael. *After Redemption: Jim Crow and the Transformation of African American Religion in the Delta, 1875-1915.* New York: Oxford University Press, 2007.
Glatthaar, Joseph T. *Forged in Battle: The Civil War Alliance of Black Soldiers and White Officers.* New York: Free Press, 1990.
Graves, John William. *Town and Country: Race Relations in an Urban-Rural Context, Arkansas, 1865-1905.* Fayetteville: University of Arkansas Press, 1990.
Griffith, Cyril E. *The African Dream: Martin R. Delany and the Emergence of Pan-African Thought.* University Park: Pennsylvania State University Press, 1975.
Hanaway, Joseph, and Richard Cruess. *McGill Medicine.* Vol. 1, *The First Half Century, 1829-1885.* Montreal and Kingston: McGill-Queen's University Press, 1996.
Hargrove, Hondon. "Their Greatest Battle Was Getting into the Fight." *Michigan History Magazine,* January 1991, 24-30.
Harris, Jennifer. "Black Life in a Nineteenth-Century New Brunswick Town." *Journal of Canadian Studies/Revue d'études canadiennes* 46, 1 (Winter 2012): 138-66.
Harrold, Stanley. *Subversives: Antislavery Community in Washington, D.C., 1828-1865.* Baton Rouge: Louisiana State University Press, 2003.
Hasegawa, Guy R. "The Civil War Medical Cadets: Medical Students Serving the Union." *Journal of the American College of Surgeons* 193, 1 (2001): 81-89.
Hayes, Douglas M. "Policing the Social Boundaries of the American Medical Association, 1847-70." *Journal of the History of Medicine and Allied Sciences* 60, 2 (April 2005): 170-95.
Henderson, Conway W. "The Anglo-American Treaty of 1862 in Civil War Diplomacy." *Civil War History* 15, 4 (1969): 308-19.
Hendrick, George, and Willene Hendrick. *Black Refugees in Canada: Accounts of Escape during the Era of Slavery.* Jefferson, NC: McFarland, 2010.
Hepburn, Sharon A. Roger. *Crossing the Border: A Free Black Community in Canada.* Urbana: University of Illinois Press, 2007.
–. "Following the North Star: Canada as a Haven for Nineteenth-Century American Blacks." *Michigan Historical Review* 25, 2 (Fall 1999): 91-126.
Hill, Daniel G. *The Freedom-Seekers: Blacks in Early Canada.* Agincourt: Book Society of Canada, 1981.
Hinds, Allister. "'Deportees in Nova Scotia': The Jamaican Maroons, 1796-1800." In *Working Slavery, Pricing Freedom: Perspectives from the Caribbean, Africa and the African Diaspora,* ed. Verene Shepherd, 206-22. New York: Palgrave, 2002.
Hine, Darlene Clark, William C. Hine, and Stanley Harrold. *The African-American Odyssey.* Vol. 1. Upper Saddle River, NJ: Prentice Hall, 2000.
Hollandsworth, James G., Jr. *The Louisiana Native Guards: The Black Military Experience during the Civil War.* Baton Rouge: Louisiana State University Press, 1995.
Hoogenboom, Ari. *Gustavus Vasa Fox of the Union Navy.* Baltimore: Johns Hopkins University Press, 2008.
Hornby, Jim. *Black Islanders: Prince Edward Island's Historical Black Community.* Charlottetown: Institute of Island Studies, 1991.

Horton, James Oliver. *Free People of Color: Inside the African American Community.* Washington, DC: Smithsonian Institution Press, 1993.
Horton, Lois E. "Kidnapping and Resistance: Antislavery Direct Action in the 1850s." In *Passages to Freedom*, ed. David W. Blight, 149-73. Washington, DC: Smithsonian Books, 2006.
Hoy, Claire. *Canadians in the Civil War.* Toronto: McArthur, 2004.
Humphreys, Margaret. *Intensely Human: The Health of the Black Soldier in the American Civil War.* Baltimore: Johns Hopkins University Press, 2008.
Hunter, Mark C. *A Society of Gentlemen: Midshipmen at the U.S. Naval Academy, 1845-1861.* Annapolis: Naval Institute Press, 2010.
James, Sheryl. "A Small Community Stands Tall." *Michigan History Magazine*, July 1998, 43-46.
Jasanoff, Maya. *Liberty's Exiles: American Loyalists in the Revolutionary World.* New York: Alfred A. Knopf, 2011.
Jelks, Randal Maurice. *African Americans in the Furniture City: The Struggle for Civil Rights in Grand Rapids.* Urbana: University of Illinois Press, 2006.
Joiner, Gary D. *Mr. Lincoln's Brown Water Navy: The Mississippi Squadron.* New York: Rowman and Littlefield, 2007.
Kett, Joseph F. "American and Canadian Medical Institutions, 1800-1870." *Journal of the History of Medicine and Allied Sciences* 22, 4 (October 1967): 343-56.
Kimmel, Janice Martz. "Break Your Chains and Fly for Freedom." *Michigan History Magazine*, January 1996, 20-27.
King, Miriam L., and Diana L. Magnuson. "Perspectives on Historical U.S. Census Undercounts." *Social Science History* 19, 4 (Winter 1995): 455-66.
Lamb, Daniel Smith. *Howard University Medical Department, Washington, DC: A Historical, Biological and Statistical Souvenir.* Part 3. Washington, DC: Howard University Medical Department, 1900.
Landon, Fred. "The Anderson Fugitive Case." *Journal of Negro History* 7, 3 (July 1922): 233-42.
–. "Anthony Burns in Canada." *Ontario Historical Society, Papers and Records* 22 (1924): 162-66.
–. "The Negro Migration to Canada after the Passing of the Fugitive Slave Act." *Journal of Negro History* 5, 1 (January 1920): 22-36.
Leiner, Frederick C. "The Squadron Commander's Share: *Decatur vs Chew* and the Prize Money for the *Chesapeake*'s First War of 1812 Cruise." *Journal of Military History* 73, 1 (January 2009): 69-82.
Leonard, Elizabeth D. *Men of Color to Arms! Black Soldiers, Indian Wars, and the Quest for Equality.* New York: W.W. Norton, 2010.
Levine, Peter. "Draft Evasion in the North during the Civil War, 1863-1865." *Journal of American History* 67, 4 (March 1981): 816-34.
Liebler, William F. "John Bull's American Legion: Britain's Ill-Starred Recruiting Attempt in the United States during the Crimean War." *Pennsylvanian Magazine of History and Biography* 99, 3 (July 1975): 309-35.
Lonn, Ella. *Foreigners in the Union Army and Navy.* New York: Greenwood Press, 1951.
Mahin, Dean B. *One War at a Time: The International Dimensions of the American Civil War.* Washington, DC: Brassey's, 1999.
Malcomson, Robert. *A Very Brilliant Affair: The Battle of Queenston Heights, 1812.* Toronto: Robin Brass Studio, 2003.
Mancke, Elizabeth. "The American Revolution in Canada." In *A Companion to the American Revolution*, ed. Jack P. Greene and J.R. Pole, 521-28. Oxford: Blackwell, 2000.

Manning, Chandra. *What This Cruel War Was Over: Soldiers, Slavery and the Civil War.* New York: Alfred A. Knopf, 2007.
Marquis, Greg. *In Armageddon's Shadow: The Civil War and Canada's Maritime Provinces.* Montreal and Kingston: McGill-Queen's University Press, 1998.
Marr, William, and Donald Patterson. *Canada: An Economic History.* Toronto: Gage, 1980.
Marshall, Albert P. *Unconquered Souls: The History of the African American in Ypsilanti.* Ypsilanti, MI: Marlan, 1993.
Masur, Kate. *An Example for All the Land: Emancipation and the Struggle over Equality in Washington, D.C.* Chapel Hill: University of North Carolina Press, 2010.
Mathieu, Sarah-Jane. *North of the Color Line: Migration and Black Resistance in Canada, 1870-1955.* Chapel Hill: University of North Carolina Press, 2010.
Mayers, Adam. *Dixie and the Dominion: Canada, the Confederacy, and the War for the Union.* Toronto: Dundurn Press, 2003.
–. "Stolen Soldiers." *Civil War Times Illustrated* 34, 2 (June 1995): 56-60.
McConnell, Stuart. *Glorious Contentment: The Grand Army of the Republic, 1865-1900.* Chapel Hill: University of North Carolina Press, 1992.
McFeely, William S. *Frederick Douglass.* New York: W.W. Norton, 1991.
McPherson, James M. *Abraham Lincoln and the Second American Revolution.* 1991. Reprint, New York: Oxford University Press, 1992.
–. *Battle Cry of Freedom: The Civil War Era.* New York: Oxford University Press, 1988.
–. *For Cause and Comrades: Why Men Fought in the Civil War.* New York: Oxford University Press, 1997.
Miller, Edward A., Jr. *The Black Civil War Soldiers of Illinois: The Story of the Twenty-Ninth U.S. Colored Infantry.* Columbia: University of South Carolina Press, 1998.
–. "Garland H. White, Black Army Chaplain." *Civil War History* 43, 3 (September 1997): 201-20.
Miller, Floyd J. *The Search for a Black Nationality: Black Colonization and Emigration, 1787-1863.* Urbana: University of Illinois Press, 1975.
Miller, Richard F. "For His Wife, His Widow, and His Orphan: Massachusetts and Family Aid during the Civil War." *Massachusetts Historical Review* 6 (2004): 70-106.
Milligan, John D. *Gunboats Down the Mississippi.* Annapolis: United States Naval Institute, 1965.
Milne, A. Taylor. "The Lyons-Seward Treaty of 1862." *American Historical Review* 38, 3 (April 1933): 511-25.
Mitchell, Robert E. "Civil War Recruiting and Recruits from Ever-Changing Labor Pools: Midland County, Michigan, as a Case Study." *Michigan Historical Review* 35, 1 (Spring 2009): 29-60.
Morais, Herbert M. *International Library of Negro Life and History: The History of the Negro in Medicine.* New York: Publishers Company, 1967.
Mouser, Bruce L. *For Labor, Race, and Liberty: George Edwin Taylor, His Historic Rule for the White House and the Making of Independent Black Politics.* Madison: University of Wisconsin Press, 2011.
Murdock, Eugene C. "New York's Civil War Bounty Brokers." *Journal of American History* 54, 2 (September 1966): 254-78.
–. *One Million Men: The Civil War Draft in the North.* Madison: State Historical Society of Wisconsin, 1971.
Murray, David. *Colonial Justice: Justice, Morality, and Crime in the Niagara District, 1791-1849.* Toronto: University of Toronto Press, 2002.
Negus, Samuel. "A Notorious Nest of Offence: Neutrals, Belligerents, and Union Jails in Civil War Blockade Running." *Civil War History* 56, 4 (December 2010): 350-85.

Nercessian, Nora N. "Nineteenth-Century Black Graduates of Harvard Medical School." *Journal of Blacks in Higher Education* 47 (Spring 2005): 88-92.

Newby, M. Dalyce. *Anderson Ruffin Abbott: First Afro-Canadian Doctor*. Markham, ON: Fitzhenry and Whiteside, 1998.

Nieto-Phillips, John. "Margins to Mainstream: The Brave New World of Borderland History, an Introduction." *Journal of American History* 98, 2 (September 2011): 337-61.

Paradis, James M. *Strike the Blow for Freedom: The 6th United States Colored Infantry in the Civil War*. Shippensburg, PA: White Main Books, 2000.

Parkerson, Donald H. "Comments on the Underenumeration of the U.S. Census, 1850-1880." *Social Science History* 15, 4 (Winter 1991): 509-15.

Pease, Jane H., and William H. Pease. *The Fugitive Slave Law and Anthony Burns: A Problem of Law Enforcement*. Philadelphia: J.B. Lippincott, 1975.

Perri, Timothy J. "The Economics of US Civil War Conscription." *American Law and Economic Review* 10, 2 (January 2008): 424-53.

Porter, David D. *The Naval History of the Civil War*. New York: Sherman, 1886.

Power, Michael, and Nancy Butler. *Slavery and Freedom in Niagara*. Niagara-on-the-Lake: Niagara Historical Society, 1993.

Pratt, Fletcher. *Stanton: Lincoln's Secretary of War*. New York: W.W. Norton, 1953.

Pybus, Cassandra. *Epic Journeys of Freedom: Runaway Slaves of the American Revolution and Their Global Quest for Liberty*. Boston: Beacon Press, 2006.

Radforth, Ian. *Royal Spectacle: The 1860 Visit of the Prince of Wales to Canada and the United States*. Toronto: University of Toronto Press, 2004.

Ramold, Steven J. *Slaves, Sailors, Citizens: African Americans in the Union Navy*. DeKalb: Northern Illinois University Press, 2002.

Raney, William F. "Recruiting and Crimping in Canada for the Northern Forces, 1861-1865." *Mississippi Valley Historical Review* 10, 1 (June 1923): 21-33.

Redkey, Edwin S. "Brave Black Volunteers: A Profile of the Fifty-Fourth Massachusetts Regiment." In *Hope and Glory: Essays on the Legacy of the 54th Massachusetts Regiment*, ed. Martin H. Blatt, Thomas J. Brown, and Donald Yacovone, 21-34. Amherst: University of Massachusetts Press, 2000.

Reid, John G. *Six Crucial Decades: Times of Change in the History of the Maritimes*. Halifax: Nimbus, 1987.

Reid, Richard M. *Freedom for Themselves: North Carolina's Black Soldiers in the Civil War Era*. Chapel Hill: University of North Carolina Press, 2008.

–. "Government Policy, Prejudice, and the Experience of Black Civil War Soldiers and Their Families." *Journal of Family History* 27, 4 (October 2002): 374-99.

–. "The 1870 United States Census and Black Underenumeration: A Test Case from North Carolina." *Histoire sociale/Social History* 28, 56 (November 1995): 487-99.

Reidy, Joseph P. "Black Jack: African American Sailors in the Civil War." In *New Interpretations in Naval History: Selected Papers from the Twelfth Naval History Symposium*, ed. William B. Cogar, 213-20. Annapolis: Naval Institute Press, 1997.

–. "Black Men in Navy Blue during the Civil War." *Prologue: Quarterly of the National Archives and Records Administration* 33, 3 (Fall 2001): 155-67.

Riendeau, Roger. *An Enduring Heritage: Black Contributions to Early Ontario*. Toronto: Dundurn Press, 1984.

Riggs, David F. "Sailors of the *U.S.S. Cairo*: Anatomy of a Gunboat Crew." *Civil War History* 28, 3 (September 1982): 266-73.

Robbins, Arlie C. *Legacy to Buxton*. Chatham: Ideal Printing, 1983.

Robertson, James. *Soldiers Blue and Gray*. Columbia: University of South Carolina Press, 1988.

Robinson, Henry S. "Alexander Thomas Augusta." *Journal of the National Medical Association* 44, 4 (July 1952): 325-29.
Roland, Charles G., ed. *Health, Disease and Medicine in Canadian History*. Toronto: Hannah Institute for the History of Medicine, 1984.
Rothstein, William G. *American Physicians in the Nineteenth Century: From Sects to Science*. Baltimore: Johns Hopkins University Press, 1972.
Rutkow, Ira. *Seeking the Cure: A History of Medicine in America*. New York: Scribner, 2010.
Ryder, N.B. "The Interpretation of Origin Statistics." *Canadian Journal of Economics and Political Science/Revue canadienne d'économique et de science politique* 21, 4 (November 1955): 466-79.
Sacher, John. "The Loyal Draft Dodger? A Re-examination of Confederate Substitution." *Civil War History* 58, 2 (June 2011): 153-78.
Sager, Eric W. *Seafaring Labour: The Merchant Marine of Atlantic Canada, 1820-1914*. Montreal and Kingston: McGill-Queen's University Press, 1989.
Samito, Christian G. "The Intersection between Military Justice and Equal Rights: Mutinies, Court-Martial, and Black Civil War Soldiers." *Civil War History* 53, 2 (June 2007): 170-202.
Schecter, Barnet. *The Battle for New York: The City at the Heart of the American Revolution*. New York: Walker, 2002.
Schiller, Nina Glick. *Nations Unbound: Transnational Projects, Postcolonial Predicaments and Deterritorialized Nation-States*. New York: Gordon and Breach, 1994.
Schubert, Frank N., ed. *On the Trail of the Buffalo Soldier: Biographies of the African Americans in the U.S. Army, 1866-1917*. Wilmington, DE: Scholarly Resources, 1995.
Schweninger, Loren. *James T. Rapier and Reconstruction*. Chicago: University of Chicago Press, 1978.
Shadd, Adrienne. *The Journey from Tollgate to Parkway: African Canadians in Hamilton*. Hamilton: Dundurn Press, 2010.
Shaffer, Donald R. *After the Glory: The Struggles of Black Civil War Veterans*. Lawrence: University Press of Kansas, 2004.
Silverman, Jason H. *Unwelcome Guests: Canada West's Response to American Fugitive Slaves, 1800-1865*. Millwood, NY: Associated Faculty Press, 1985.
Silverstone, Paul H. *Civil War Navies, 1855-1883*. Annapolis: Naval Institute Press, 2001.
Simpson, Brooks D. *Ulysses S. Grant: Triumph over Adversity, 1822-1865*. New York: Houghton Mifflin, 2000.
Simpson, Donald G. *Under the North Star: Black Communities in Upper Canada*. Trenton, NJ: Africa World Press, 2005.
Slaney, Catherine. *Family Secrets: Crossing the Colour Line*. Toronto: Natural Heritage Books, 2003.
Slaughter, Thomas P. *Bloody Dawn: The Christiana Riot and Racial Violence in the Antebellum North*. New York: Oxford University Press, 1991.
Slawson, Robert G. *Prologue to Change: African Americans in Medicine in the Civil War Era*. Frederick, MD: National Museum of Civil War Medicine Press, 2006.
Smardz Frost, Karolyn. *I've Got a Home in Glory Land: A Lost Tale of the Underground Railroad*. New York: Farrar, Straus and Giroux, 2007.
Smith, John David, ed. *Black Soldiers in Blue: African American Troops in the Civil War Era*. Chapel Hill: University of North Carolina Press, 2002.
Smith, Michael O. "Raising a Black Regiment in Michigan: Adversity and Triumph." *Michigan Historical Review*, March 1990, 22-41.

Smith, Michael Thomas. "The Most Desperate Scoundrels Unhung: Bounty Jumpers and Recruitment Fraud in the Civil War North." *American Nineteenth Century History* 6, 2 (June 2005): 149-72.

Spann, Edward K. *Gotham at War: New York City, 1860-1865*. Wilmington, DE: Scholarly Resources, 2002.

Speer, Lonnie R. *Portals to Hell: Military Prisons in the Civil War.* Mechanicsburg, PA: Stackpole Books, 1997.

Spragge, George W. "The Trinity Medical College." *Ontario History* 58, 2 (June 1966): 63-98.

Spray, W.A. *The Blacks in New Brunswick.* Fredericton, NB: Brunswick Press, 1972.

Stearns, Frank P. *The Life and Public Service of George Luther Stearns.* Philadelphia: J.P. Lippincott, 1907.

Sterling, Dorothy. *The Making of an Afro-American: Martin Robinson Delany, 1812-1885.* New York: Da Capo Press, 1971.

Stouffer, Allan P. *In the Light of Nature and the Law of God: Antislavery in Ontario, 1833-1877.* Montreal and Kingston: McGill-Queen's University Press, 1992.

Surdam, David G. *Northern Naval Superiority and the Economics of the American Civil War.* Columbia: University of South Carolina Press, 2001.

Symonds, Craig L. *Lincoln and His Admirals: Abraham Lincoln, the U.S. Navy, and the Civil War.* Oxford: Oxford University Press, 2008.

Taylor, John M. "Representative Recruit for Abraham Lincoln." *Civil War Times Illustrated* 13, 3 (March 1978): 34-35.

Thomas, Benjamin P., and Harold M. Hyman. *Stanton: The Life and Times of Lincoln's Secretary of War.* New York: Knopf, 1962.

Tomblin, Barbara Brooks. *Bluejackets and Contrabands: African Americans and the Union Navy.* Lexington: University Press of Kentucky, 2009.

Trudeau, Noah Andre. *Like Men of War: Black Troops in the Civil War.* Boston: Little, Brown, 1998.

–. *Voices of the 55th: Letters from the 55th Massachusetts Volunteers, 1861-1865.* Dayton, OH: Morningside, 1996.

Ullman, Victor. *Look to the North Star: A Life of William King.* Boston: Beacon Press, 1969.

–. *Martin R. Delany: The Beginnings of Black Nationalism.* Boston: Beacon Press, 1971.

Urwin, Gregory J.W., ed. *Black Flag over Dixie: Racial Atrocities and Reprisals in the Civil War.* Carbondale: Southern Illinois University Press, 2004.

Valle, James E. *Rocks and Shoals: Order and Discipline in the Old Navy, 1880-1861.* Annapolis: Naval Institute Press, 1980.

Valuska, David L. *The African American in the Union Navy, 1861-1865.* New York: Garland, 1993.

Vlach, John Michael. "Above Ground on the Underground Railroad: Places of Flight and Refuge." In *Passages to Freedom: The Underground Railroad in History and Memory*, ed. David W. Blight, 95-115. Washington, DC: Smithsonian Books, 2004.

Von Frank, Albert J. *The Trials of Anthony Burns: Freedom and Slavery in Emerson's Boston.* Cambridge, MA: Harvard University Press, 1998.

Walker, Barrington. *Race on Trial: Black Defendants in Ontario's Criminal Courts, 1858-1958.* Toronto: Osgoode Society for Canadian Legal History/University of Toronto Press, 2010.

Walker, James W. St. G. *The Black Loyalists: The Search for a Promised Land in Nova Scotia and Sierra Leone, 1788-1870.* New York: Africana, 1976.

–. "African Canadians: Migration." *Encyclopedia of Canada's Peoples.* Multicultural Canada. http://www.multiculturalcanada.ca/.

–. "Myth, History, and Revisionism: The Black Loyalists Revisited." *Acadiensis* 29, 1 (Autumn 1999): 88-105.
Warner, John Dwight, Jr. "Crossed Sabres: A History of the Fifth Massachusetts Volunteer Cavalry, an African American Regiment in the Civil War." PhD diss., Boston College, 1997.
Wayne, Michael. "The Black Population of Canada West on the Eve of the American Civil War: A Reassessment Based on the Manuscript Census of 1861." *Histoire sociale/Social History* 28, 56 (November 1995): 465-85.
Wengert, James W. "The Contract Surgeon." *Journal of the West* 36, 1 (1997): 67-76.
Westwood, Howard C. "The Cause and Consequence of a Union Black Soldier's Mutiny and Execution." *Civil War History* 31, 2 (September 1985): 222-36.
Whitfield, Harvey Amani. *Blacks on the Border: The Black Refugees in British North America, 1815-1860*. Burlington: University of Vermont Press, 2006.
–. "Reviewing Blackness in Atlantic Canada and the African Atlantic Canadian Diaspora." *Acadiensis* 37, 2 (Summer-Autumn 2008): 130-39.
–. "The Struggle over Slavery in the Maritime Colonies." *Acadiensis* 41, 2 (Summer-Autumn 2012): 17-44.
Whitfield, Harvey Amani, and Barry Cahill. "Slave Life and Slave Law in Colonial Prince Edward Island, 1769-1825." *Acadiensis* 38, 2 (Summer-Autumn 2009): 29-51.
Wickenden, Dorothy. "Dismantling the Peculiar Institution." *Wilson Quarterly* 14, 4 (Autumn 1990): 102-13.
Widdis, Randy William. *With Scarcely a Ripple: Anglo-Canadian Migration into the United States and Western Canada, 1880-1920*. Montreal and Kingston: McGill-Queen's University Press, 1998.
Wigmore, Gregory. "Before the Railroad: From Slavery to Freedom in the Canadian-American Borderland." *Journal of American History* 98, 2 (September 2011): 437-54.
Williams, Dorothy W. *The Road to Now: A History of Blacks in Montreal*. Montreal: Véhicule Press, 1997.
Winks, Robin. *The Blacks in Canada: A History*. 2nd ed. Montreal and Kingston: McGill-Queen's University Press, 1997.
–. *The Civil War Years: Canada and the United States*. Montreal and Kingston: McGill-Queen's University Press, 1998.
Wolters, Timothy S. "Electric Torpedoes in the Confederacy: Reconciling Conflicting Histories." *Journal of Military History* 72, 3 (July 2008): 755-83.
Zorn, Roman J. "An Arkansas Fugitive Slave Incident and Its International Repercussions." *Arkansas Historical Quarterly* 16, 2 (Summer 1957): 139-49.

INDEX

Note: "(i)" after a page number indicates an illustration; "(m)" after a page number indicates a map.

Abbott, Anderson Ruffin, 147, 148, 164(i), 208(i): accosted in New York, 165-66; accused of misusing alcohol, 169; applies for commission, 163; applies as medical cadet, 163-64; apprentices with Augusta, 155; attends Buxton Mission School, 155; attends Lincoln's Levee, 168-69; on black emigration, 179; calls for black officers, 170; as contract surgeon, 164-65, 166; County of Kent coroner, 175; decision to enlist, 38, 206-7; early life, 155; in Grand Army of the Republic, 176, 183-84, 206-7, 208, 211-12; gift from the Lincolns, 174-75; licenced to practise, 155; married, 175; postwar life, 174-76, 206-8; president of Chatham Medical Society, 175; at Provident Hospital, 176; as transnationalist, 211; view of the war's importance, 168, 206-7
Abbott, Ellen, 155
Abbott, Ezra W., 175, 260n160
Abbott, Mary Ann (née Casey), 175
Abbott, Wilson, 155, 254n43

Achim, Anselm, 252n1
Act of Union, 219n7
Addeman, Joshua, 99, 120
African Americans: discriminatory treatment in Northern states, 26; immigration north, 29-30, 221n44, 227n132; oppose American Colonization Society efforts, 226n128; return migration, 33, 177-78, 179. *See also* doctors (black); regiments; sailors (black); soldiers (black)
African Baptist Association (Nova Scotia), 178
African Methodist Episcopal Church (London), 84
agency, 9-10, 29, 89-90, 114, 119, 132, 138, 209, 210-11, 222n64
Agrippa, CSS, 78, 239n106
Alabama, CSS, 78, 79, 239n106
Aldren, B., 151
Alexander, John, 51-52
Allen, Henry, 138
Allinson, John Bland, 67
Alston, J.T., 83

280

INDEX • 281

Amendatory Act (1864), 64
American Colonization Society, 152, 156, 226n128
American Freedmen's Inquiry Committee, 28
American Medical Association, 171
American Revolution, 11, 12: and black refugees, 13,
Anacostia, USS, 187
Anderson, Augustus, 186, 189-90
Anderson, John, 23, 56, 65, 66, 75-76
Anderson, William, 102
Andrew, John, 90, 92, 98-99, 111-12, 232n72: commissions black officers, 118-19, 142, 169; demands equal treatment of black soldiers, 97, 141; forms black regiments, 87-89
Anglo-American (magazine), 174
Anti-Slavery Society of Canada, 20, 31, 226n123
Appomattox, 130, 142
Arletta, USS, 74, 75
Arlington National Cemetery, 172
Association for the Education and Elevation of the Colored People, 154
Atlantic Magazine, 25
atrocities, 92: alleged killings of black soldiers, 119-20; reported in Canadian press, 91-92, 119-20; threats by Confederate officials, 91-92, 210. *See also* Fort Pillow; Plymouth (NC)
Atwood, Alexander, 101
Atwood, Pricilla, 245n93. *See also* Hartsill, Pricilla
Augusta, Alexander T., 147, 148, 154(i), 176: accused of misusing alcohol, 169; applies for commission, 159-60; attacked in Baltimore, 97, 160-61; attends Lincoln's Levee, 168-69; breveted lieutenant colonel, 170, 171; death, 172; denied membership in Medical Society, 171; early life, 153; and Freedmen's Hospital, 166; at Howard University, 171-72; moves to Toronto, 153; paid as private, 162; passes army medical board, 160; receives medical degree, 153-54; rejected by American medical schools, 153; and segregated Washington street cars, 161; and 7th USCT, 161-62
Augusta, Mary (née Burgoin), 153, 165-66

Autobiography of a Fugitive Negro (Ward), 31
Autobiography of the Rev. Josiah Henson, 50, 59

Backus, John, 70
Bailey, Gideon, 192
Bailey, James, 46
Bailey (née Cook), Mary E., 192
Banks, Nathaniel P., 255n71
Bankster, Abraham, 64
Barker, Ellen, 101
Barnes, Henry, 105-6, 107, 108
Bartlett, George, 204
Bates, Edward, 116
Baynard, Levine T., 75
Bennett, Michael J., 45, 66, 73, 80, 81, 210
Benson, John A., 138-39
Berrion, Edward, 234n22
Berryman, Henry A., 34, 100
Bibb, Henry, 21,
Bibb, Mary, 21
Birney, William, 161
"Black Committee," 87, 95
Blackburn, Benjamin, 109, 110(i)
Blackburn, Thornton, 22
Blackman, James, 138
Blacks in Canada (Winks), 27
Blair, Austin, 106, 111
Bliss, Michael, 150
blockade runner, 69, 237n68
Bond, John Robert, 39
Boston Daily Evening Traveler, 30
Boston Liberator, 27, 33, 117, 119, 225n113, 226n123
bounties, 41, 64, 86: "big bounty" men, 138; delayed payment, 137; federal bounties, 115, 116, 126, 188, 193, 204; initially denied to black soldiers, 93, 97-98, 124; local bounties, 106-7, 124-27, 132, 188, 204; perception of abuse of, 131, 138, 248n43
bounty-jumpers, 41, 131, 132, 137, 140
bounty broker, 91, 131, 242n37
Boyd, Lucien, 53, 231n42
Boyd, William S., 130-31
Boyd, W.T., 83
Bradford (née Mulder), Rachael, 203
Branch, John, 58, 81
Brant, Joseph, 18, 19, 221n53
Bray, John L., 252n1

British American Institute, 21
British Methodist Episcopal Church, 240n9
British North America, 12(m): Civil War doctors from, 146-47, 252n1; emigration from, 33-35, 40, 217n10, 229n21; volunteers from, 39-40, 41, 42, 131, 229n15
Brom (née Thomas), Elisa E., 196
Brooklyn, USS, 60, 66, 235n32
Brooks, Benjamin, 180
Brooks, Kincheon, 180
Brooks, Thomas, 181
Brown, Aaron, 75
Brown, Abraham F., 94(i)
Brown, Alexander, 107, 262n32
Brown, George H., 205: early life, 194-95; in Civil War army, 195-96; joins postwar army, 182, 196; leaves his third wife, 196-97; in navy, 195; occupation, 195, 196; quartermaster sergeant, 196
Brown, Henry, 34
Brown, James, 138
Brown, John (abolitionist), 32, 54, 241n24
Brown, John (private), 136
Brown, Lucy Mildred, 196-97, 264n86
Brown, Thomas W., 36
Brown, William, 69-70
Bryan, William Jennings, 173-74
Bryant, Thomas, 63, 72
Buchanan, John C., 106
"buffalo soldiers," 182, 196
Bureau of Colored Troops, 111
Bureau of Medicine and Surgery, 198
Bureau of Refugees, Freedmen, and Abandoned Lands, 166. *See also* Freedmen's Bureau
Burgoin, Mary. *See* Augusta, Mary (née Burgoin)
Burns, Anthony, 25, 224n104
Bushlaw, Philip, 73, 238n81
Butler, Benjamin F., 104, 115, 141, 235n33
Butler, Ervin, 250n106
Butler, John, 18, 221n52
Butler's Real Ethiopian Serenaders, 24
Buxton Mission School, 22, 30, 155-56
Buxton settlement 20, 25, 41, 159: establishment of, 21-22; postwar population decline, 180; recruits from, 107, 111; successful establishment of, 21-22, 155-56, 223n79, 227n132. *See also* Elgin Settlement

Cahill, Edward, 110-11
Cairo, USS, 76, 77(i)
Calypso, USS, 69
Cameron, Simon, 49
Campbell, David, 66
Camp Barker, 166. *See also* Freedmen's Hospital
Camp Stanton, 161
Camp Ward, 108, 109, 110, 142
Camp William Penn, 103, 143
Canada, Dominion of: black emigration from, 178-80, 211; creation of, 5-6, 217n11; reasons for emigration, 178-79, 180
Canada, United Province of, 5, 219n7
Canada East, 6, 217n11: black emigration from, 36; black population, 18; black volunteers from, 48-49, 54, 53; creation of, 219n7, fugitive slaves in, 23-24, illegal recruiting, 53
Canada West, 6, 217n11: American recruiters in, 87, 90-91; black emigration from, 29, 33; black gender balance, 28; black immigration, 26, 30; black volunteers from, 48-49, 53; censuses, 27, 27, 221n39; creation of, 219n7; disputed black population of 1861, 26-29, 225n115; fugitive slaves in, 22-23, 24-25, 28, 29; popular perception of black population, 26. *See also* Ontario
Cape Breton, 13, 45
Caples, George, 181, 182(i)
Carter, Alexander, 126. *See also* Nelson, John
Carter, Rachel. *See* Jackson (née Carter), Rachael
Cary, Isaac, 155
Casey, Mary Ann. *See* Abbott, Mary Ann (née Casey)
C.C. Phillips Post (Hopkinton), 184
censuses: Canada, 18, 27, 135, 213-16; Canada East, 18, 28; Canada West, 27, 41, 48-49; linking veterans across censuses; 180-81, 213-16; Lower Canada, 18; New Brunswick, 16; Nova Scotia, 16; Ontario, 27, 179;

Prince Edward Island, 16; underenumeration, 18, 28, 33, 195, 220n36, 26n8; United States, 33-34, 35, 36, 87, 173, 180, 213-16, 233n75
Chase, Salmon P., 83, 84
Chesapeake, USS, 58
Chevers, Berry, 66
Chicago Conservator, 176
Christian Recorder, 96, 97
Christiana riot, 24-25
citizenship: in British North America, 11, 33, 240n9; in Canada, 184; in United States, 11, 26, 178, 218n2, 228n151
Civil War African American Sailors Project, 44, 60
Civil War Soldiers and Sailors System, 213, 215
Clayton, Charles L., 100, 244n82
Clunie, William, 252n1
Clymer, C., 160
Coleman, Jesse, 17
College of Physicians and Surgeons of Ontario (1869), 150
College of Physicians and Surgeons of Upper Canada (1839), 149, 163
Collison, Gary, 28
Colored Corps, 222n58. See also Runchey, Robert
Colored National Anti-Imperialist League, 174
commutation fee, 85, 127-28, 137
Congress, USS, 75
Connecticut: forms black regiments, 86, 96, 99, 101; 29th Connecticut Regiment, 3, 101-2, 151, 188; 30th Connecticut Regiment, 102
Constitutional Act of 1791, 13, 219n7
"contrabands," 62, 80, 235n33
contract surgeons, 158(i), 164-65, 258n121
Cooley, Chloe, 22
Coombs, Joseph, 75-76
Cornish, Dudley, 91
Cornish, Samuel, 226n128
crimping, 41, 67
crimps, 53, 68, 91, 242n37
Crosby, George, 136
Crosby, Margaret A., 204
Crowell, Daniel, 60, 234n24
Crowell, Joseph D., 187
Cuffee, Paul, 226n128

Cumberland, USS, 75

Da Costa, Mathieu, 218n1
Dawn settlement, 20, 21, 50
Day, William Howard, 31-32
Dean, George, 139(i)
Decoration Day, 184, 207
Dehart, William A., 234n22
Delany, Martin R., 158: and black emigration, 30, 31, 152-53, 226n131; as doctor, 147, 152-53; early life, 151-52; forced out of Harvard, 152; migrates to Chatham, 30-31, 152-53; pessimism of, 148, 153, 227n134; receives commission, 170; recruiting efforts, 88, 170; supports John Brown, 31
Dennis, Enoch, 47, 204
Dennis, James W., 266n121
desertion, 41, 131: Congress' reassessment of, 143; defined as, 122, 127, 140, 251n115; numbers of deserters, 109, 136; reasons for, 108-9, 110(i), 136, 140-43
Detroit, 50: offers bounties to black soldiers, 107-8; racism in, 109, 142
Detroit Advertiser and Tribune, 105-6, 107
Detroit Free Press, 108, 109
Detroit Liberty Guards, 106
Diggs, Seneca T.P., 23
Disability Pension Act (1890), 185-86
doctors (black), 9: ambition of, 146, 147, 152, 176; anger of, 208; numbers of, 147, 149; prejudice against, 147, 152, 153, 160-62, 168, 208; motivation of, 168; professional mobility, 153, 168, 176; and War Department's changing policy, 147, 159-63. See also Abbott, Anderson Ruffin; Augusta, Alexander Thomas; Delany, Martin; Purvis, Robert W.; Rapier, John H.; Riley, Jerome
Doleman, Israel N., 64
Donohoe, Denis, 102
Douglas, George, 76
Douglass, Frederick, 109, 115: effects of Fugitive Slave Act, 25; and recruiting efforts, 88, 89, 92, 241n26; sanctuary in New Brunswick, 32
Douglass' Monthly, 89, 241n26
draft districts: Fifth District (Mass.), 125; First District (Penn.), 125; Ninth

District (Penn.), 125, 126; Second District (Maine), 264n69; Seventeenth District (NY), 137; Sixteenth District (NY), 137; Sixth District (Mass.), 195; Tenth District (Mass.), 125; Thirtieth District (NY), 132; Thirty-first District (NY), 132; Twelfth District (NY), 126; Twenty-ninth District (NY), 126, 137, 204
draft lottery, 85, 121-22, 127
Duncan, Samuel, 190
Dunkerson, Nelson, 100-1

Easton, Hosea J., 72
Elgin settlement, 21-22, 223n77. *See also* Buxton settlement
Emancipation Proclamation, 4, 63, 147: final, 5, 85, 86, 96, 159, 210, 256n74; preliminary, 37, 240n13, 256n74; reaction for foreign black communities, 38-39; reaction of foreign press, 37-38 transnational dimensions, 37, 39, 209
Emilio, Luis, 87, 97-98
Enrollment Act (1863), 64, 198: and African Americans, 85-86, 121, 123, 242n32, 248n33; draft lottery, 85; immigrants and working class, 131; terms of, 85, 121, 127, 241n16, 242n32; and violence, 165-66
Eolus, USS, 69
European Squadron, 62-63, 78

families (of servicemen), 34: children, 193-94; lack of financial support, 89, 93, 135; parents, 47, 49, 135; problems in applying for pensions, 190-94; wives, 93, 101, 143, 193, 196-97, 201, 203-4
Farallones, USS, 68
Firman, James, 46
Fizer, Luke, 47
Florida, USS, 70, 75, 81
Foner, Eric, 5
Ford, Terry, 194
Foreign Enlistment Act (1819), 46, 49, 90, 165, 209: enforcement of, 50-53, 231n37
Forman, Henry, 79
Fort Fisher: attack on, 74, 76, 79
Fort Pillow: atrocities at, 119-20

Fort Wagner: attack on, 46, 112, 113, 135, 191, 201; reports of atrocities, 92
Foster, Charles W., 111, 163
Fourteenth Amendment, 5, 178
Freedmen's Bureau, 166-67, 171, 175
Freedmen's Hospital, 163, 166-67, 168, 169, 175
Freeman, George G., 107-8
Fry, James Barnet, 137, 249n59
Fugitive Slave Act (1850), 11, 21, 26, 223n72: factor in black emigration, 17, 26, 29-30, 221n44; numbers returned, 225n108; response of Northern states, 25, 33, 224n107; use of law to recapture fugitives, 22-23, 24, 25. *See also* fugitive slaves; slavery
fugitive slaves, 6, 19, 20, 29, 221n42, 226n127: attempted recapture of, 19, 22-23, 24-25, 26; gender balance, 16; escape rates, 25-26, 27, 225n110
Fuller, Samuel, 74

Galbraith, John Kenneth, 9
Gannon, Barbara, 183
GAR. *See* Grand Army of the Republic (GAR)
Gardner, William, 211
Garnet, Henry Highland, 88
Garrison, Albert R., 183, 187-88, 263n49
Garrison, Silas, 46, 250n94
Geary, James, 127
General Bragg, USS, 66
George, David, 14
Georgia, CSS, 78
Gibson, William, 185, 263n38
Gillmore, Quincy Adams, 112
Glatthaar, Joseph, 98
Going, Nettie, 192-93
Going, Samuel, H., 192
Goliah, Sampson, 115
Goosberry, John, 95(i)
Gorsuch, Edward, 24-25
Grand Army of the Republic (GAR), 182: black officers, 176, 183-84; Canadian posts, 176, 183-84, 260n165; eligibility for membership, 183; lobbies for greater pension benefits, 183, 185, 262n22; membership, 183, 263n56; as progressive institution, 183-84
Grant, Ulysses, 130, 131

Hackett, Nelson, 23
Haggerty, Annie, 93
Halifax British Colonist, 24
Halifax Morning Journal, 38
Hall, Earline, 35
Hall, John W., 35, 57
Hall, William, 57, 233n4
Hamilton Evening Times, 38, 52, 91-92
Hamilton Spectator, 184
Hammond, Edward W., 80-81,
Happy, Jesse, 23
Hardy, Isaac, 36, 203
Hardy, John, 34
Hardy, Pamela, 34
Hardy, William, 34
Hardy, William H., 187, 228n150
Harris, James, 211
Harris, Jennifer, 15
Harrison, James M., 36
Harrison, William, 142
Hart, John E., 47
Hartford, USS, 62, 64, 66, 235n32
Hartsill, Priscilla, 101
Harvard Medical School, 152, 253n24, 253n25
Hayden, Joseph, 235n25
Henderson, Joe, 265n115
Henderson, Sarah, 203, 265n115
Henry, Ralph, 15, 220n24
Henry (McHenry), William "Jerry," 24
Henson, Josiah, 21, 50-52, 126, 242n37
Henson, Tom, 235n25
Hepburn, Sharon A. Roger, 6,
Hodge (née Johnson), Lucinda, 196
Holly, James Theodore, 30
Holmes, Oliver Wendell, 152
Hope (steamer), 69
Hope, John, 138
Hornor, Caleb W., 169, 175
Howard, Franklin, 47. *See also* Hart, John E.
Howard, William E., 144
Howard University Medical Department, 171-72, 173
Howe, Samuel Gridley, 28, 241n24
Hughbanks, Robert, 204, 265n113
Hughes, Thomas, 52
Hunt, Harriot Kezia, 253n25

Illinois: 117th Illinois Volunteers, 105
Indiana: forms black regiment, 104
Iowa: black regiment, 115
Iowa College of Physicians and Surgeons, 158
Iverson, Gabriel P., 142

Jackson, Benjamin, 199(i): contested nature of disabilities, 199; discharged for disabilities, 198-99; early life, 197; enlists in navy, 60, 197-98, pension applications, 198-201; postwar life, 199, 205; prize money, 69, 200, 201
Jackson, John, 101
Jackson (née Martin), Mary Eliza, 201
Jackson, Moses, 135, 151
Jackson, Peter, 142-43
Jackson (née Carter), Rachael, 197, 201
Jackson, Thomas B., 74, 75
Jackson, Thomas H., 250n106
Jackson, William, 140
Jamaican maroons, 14
James, Mary, 34
James Adger, USS, 75
James S. Knowlton Post, No. 532 (Toronto), 176, 183-84
Jarvis, John A., 76
Java, USS, 58
Jerry Rescue, 24, 31
John M. Palmer Colored Democratic Club, 173-74
Johnson, Abraham, 25
Johnson, Andrew, 138
Johnson, Edward, 73, 238n81
Johnson, Elijah, 142
Johnson, Henry, 227n132
Johnson, James, 34
Johnson, James B., 262n19
Johnson, John (Sir), 18, 221n52
Johnson, John A., 66
Johnson, Leonard, 47
Johnson, Lucinda. *See* Hodge (née Johnson), Lucinda
Johnson, William, 77, 78(i)
Johnson, William B., 70
Joiner, Moses, 250n106
Jones, Amelia, 4
Jones, James, 143
Jones, John, 88
Jones, Thomas H., 33
Jones, William, 3, 4

Jordan, Aaron, 75
Juniata, USS, 76

Kearsarge, USS, 79
Keckley, Elizabeth, 175, 260n159
Keeler, William, 70, 75
Kennedy, George, 45, 138
Kennedy, Thomas, 105, 231n35
King, William, 21, 155-56
Kingston Chronicle and Gazette, 24
Kingston Daily News, 38

Lady Sterling (steamer), 69, 237n66
Laing, Daniel, 152, 253n24, 253n29
Landon, Fred, 26-27
Langston, John Mercer, 88
Layton, Isaac, 74
Le Jeaune, Olivier, 218n1
Leopard, HMS, 58
Lee, Robert E., 90, 130, 142, 188
Leslie, Thomas, 143
Levant, USS, 57
Lewis, George, 17
Lewis, John, 68, 140
Lewis, Lizzie, 17
Lincoln, Abraham, 5, 37, 61, 115, 121: articulates transnational dimensions of the war, 37; authorizes black enlistment, 5, 8, 85, 86, 93, 115, 159; calls for troops, 107, 116, 121, 123, 123-24, 127, 137; and Canadian press, 38, 86; death of, 174; defends substitutes and commutation fees, 127-28; greets Augusta and Abbott, 168-69; hires a substitute, 249n59; initially opposes use of black soldiers, 56, 84; threatens Confederates with retaliation, 92, 120, 210
Lincoln, Mary Todd, 168, 174, 175, 260n159
Lincoln, Robert, 168-69
Littlefield, John, 45
Lloyd, A.P., 189-90
London Spectator, 38
London Times, 37
Lower Canada: black population, 18; creation of, 13, 18, 219n7; early black immigration, 17; fugitive slaves, 24; slavery in, 13, 18
Lyons-Seward Treaty (1862), 79

Mackenzie, William Lyon, 19

Mackinaw, USS, 76
Mallory, George, 71
Marchand, John, 75
Marks, Jerry, 104
Marquis, Greg, 40, 57
Marston, Benjamin, 14
Martin, Mary Eliza. *See* Jackson (née Martin), Mary Eliza
Martin, William, 236n42, 238n85
Massachusetts: authorized to form black regiments, 86, 87; offers to pay difference in wages, 116; regiments keep state designation, 111; support for black soldiers and their families, 89, 93
- Fifth Massachusetts Cavalry, 46, 93, 96, 123, 142, 143: formed, 92, 98
- Twenty-fourth Massachusetts Infantry, 252n1
- Thirty-fifth Massachusetts Infantry, 142
- Fifty-fourth Massachusetts Infantry, 3, 40, 46, 122, 130, 135, 193: black officers, 169; excessive fatigue duty; 98; formed, 3, 87-89, 93-94; at Fort Wagner, 92, 112, 113, 191; at Honey Hill, 190; recruitment efforts, 93-95, 96, 99; threat of mutiny, 115
- Fifty-fifth Massachusetts Infantry, 93, 99, 115, 120, 142: anger in, 115, 117; black officers, 169; excessive fatigue duty, 98, 112; formed, 96; Reconstruction service, 195-96
Massasoit, USS, 77, 78(i)
Maxwell, William, 63
Maynard, Isaac, 136-37, 182
McCaul, John, 154, 155
McCoy, Elijah, 35
McCoy, George, 35
McCoy, Mildred, 35
McGill University, medical school, 150-51
McHenry, William "Jerry." *See* Henry, William "Jerry"
McIntosh, Alfred, 102
McKendrie, E. J., 108
Meade, George, 113
Medical and Surgical Reporter, 171
Medical Board of Upper Canada, 149, 155
Medical College of Queen's University, 150

medical education: by apprenticeship, 148, 152, 153, 157; "country doctor," 151, 153; doctors graduated, 149; in United Province of Canada, 149-51; in United States, 148-49
Medical Society of the District of Columbia, 171
Merrimack, USS, 75. *See* also *Virginia, CSS*
Miami, USS, 59(i),
Michigan: enlistment bounties in, 106-7; racial attitudes in, 106
— First Michigan Colored Infantry: in combat, 112; desertion in, 109, 110, 113; formed, 105-11, 123; opposition to, 106. *See also* United States Colored Troops (USCT), 102nd
— Eighth Michigan Colored Infantry, 106
— Tenth Michigan, 109
Michigan, USS, 67
Militia Act: (1792), 58; (1862), 85, 97, 240n11
Miller, Emily, 203
Miner (Minor), William H., 130-31, 138
Minkins, Shadrack, 24
Minnesota, USS, 62, 74
Mississippi Squadron, 75, 76
Mitchell, John W., 76
Mohican, USS, 78
Mohongo, USS, 64, 238n81
Monadnock, USS, 237n74
Monroe, James, 74
Monroe (Munroe), Joel, 3, 4, 188, 263n50
Monroe, Nelson, 188
Montreal: black population in 1861, 28
Montreal Gazette, 23, 24
Moore, John W., 93-94, 243n53
Moore's Rural New Yorker, 132
Morse, Joel, 161-62, 256n85, 257n89
Moseby (Molesby, Mosely), Solomon, 22-23
Moses, Daddy, 14
Mulder, Harriet A. *See* Nelson (née Mulder), Harriet A.
Mulder, John, 204
Murdock, Eugene, 131
Myers, James A., 102

Naden, William, 252n1
Nahant, USS, 80

Nancy (slave), 14
National Medical Society of the District of Columbia, 171
National Negro Anti-Expansion, Anti-Imperialist, Anti-Trust, Anti-Lynching League, 174
Nellis, Elijah, 70
Nelson (née Mulder), Harriet A.: marries Nelson, 203; receives widow's pension, 204; returns to Colchester with children during war, 204; as transmigrant, 205; and Ypsilanti, 203, 204
Nelson, John, 203-4, 266n121. *See also* Carter, Alexander
New Brunswick, 6: black population, 15; 17, 178, 221n38; black volunteers from, 48, 53; contested nature of slavery, 14-15; creation of, 13; discriminatory treatment of blacks, 15; early black immigration, 13, 14, 15, 16; emigration of blacks, 15; franchise, 15; fugitive slaves, 16-17; gender balance, 16, 221n40; nature of black population, 15-16; slaves in, 14, 15
New Brunswick Reporter, 38
Newby, Dalyce, 175
Newby, James, 40
New Hampshire, 130: and substitutes, 129; Third New Hampshire Regiment, 130
New York: 108th New York Infantry, 252n1; draft riots, 166; forms black regiments, 102; *New York Evening Post*, 37; *New York Herald*, 127; *New York Weekly African American*, 79, 97, 115, 119, 120, 163
Niagara, USS, 78-79, 239n107
Noble, William H., 143-44
non-commissioned officers (black), 44, 101, 130, 132, 138, 181, 192: anger at lack of commissions, 98, 113, 117, 141-42, 170; demotion of, 100-1, 104-5, 117, 132; offer of commissions by Andrew, 118, 142, 169; black commissions blocked by War Department, 118-19, 169. *See also* commissioned officers (black)
Northwest Ordinance (1787), 221n55
Nova Scotia, 6: black loyalists, 13; black population, 15, 16, 17, 178, 219n9; black volunteers from, 48, 53; complaints of neglect and discrimination, 13-14;

early black immigration, 11, 13, 15; early borders of, 219n6; fugitive slaves, 16-17; gender balance, 13, 16, 221n40; emigration of blacks, 14, 36; nature of black population, 15-16; postwar emigration, 178-79; postwar trends, 178; slaves in, 13; white treatment of blacks, 14, 16, 220n29
officers (black), 154(i): candidates appointed by Andrew but not released by War Department, 118-19, 142, 169; demands for, 117, 169-70; limited number commissioned, 159, 170, 230n27, 256n72; opposed by War Department, 159, 162-63, 255n71; purged from Louisiana Native Guard, 97, 255n71; white reaction to, 169, 170-71. *See also* Grand Army of the Republic (GAR). *See also* non-commissioned officers (black)
Olustee (Florida), 119
Onward, USS, 77-78
Oro Township settlement, 20

Pacific Squadron, 64, 68
Parker, William, 25
Patterson, Robert J., 17
Peak, James, 104-5
Pearson, Sarah Finer, 245n93
Pennsylvania: forms black regiments, 96, 102-3
Pension Examination Board of Surgeons, 189
pension system, veterans: concerns of fraud, 186, 263n43; difficulties facing female and minor dependents, 135, 190-94; difficulties facing veterans, 185, 187, 188-90, 200-1; eligibility, 143; examination by physicians, 189, 200-1; expansion of eligibility, 81-82, 185-86; formula for successful application, 186-87, 189, 190; lobbying of GAR, 183, 185; increased numbers, 186; payments, 187-88, 192, 193, 194, 199; prize money, 200; rating of disabilities, 190, 199; requirements for widows, 264n85
Pernell, Richard Bickerton (Lord Lyons), 49
Perry, Rufus Lewis, 178-79
Perth Courier, 119

Peters, Francis, 238n85
Peters, Thomas, 14, 15, 220n24
Philosophy of Negro Suffrage (Riley), 174
Plymouth (NC), 119-20
Pool, Alexander, 52, 126-27, 248n49
Pope, John H., 24
Poison Springs (Ark.), 119
Porter, Samuel, 250n106
Potomac, USS, 75
Powell, William, 159, 169
Powers, George, 74
Powhatan, USS, 79, 239n111
Preston, Richard, 178
Price, John, 47
Price, John W., 70, 184
Prince Edward Island: abolition of slavery, 16; black population, 16; black volunteers from, 48, 53; census, 16, 220n30; slavery in, 16
prize money, 45, 67, 68-71, 200, 264n76
Provincial Freedman, 32, 33, 152
Punch, 38
Purvis, Robert W., 171

Quaker City, USS, 76
Quebec Mercury, 127

Rachel Seaman, USS, 237n74
Ramold, Steven J., 64, 79
Randall, Reuben, 74
Rankin, Arthur, 50, 51(i)
Rankin's Lancers, 51(i)
Rann, Lorenzo, 111, 180
Rapier, Henry, 30
Rapier, James, 30, 156
Rapier, John H, (Jr.), 147, 155, 158(p): applies for commission, 158-59, 163, 167-68; at Buxton Mission School, 30, 156; calls for black officers, 170; and Central America, 156-57; changing attitudes of whites, 170-71; as contract surgeon, 168; death of, 170; early life, 156, 168; forced out of University of Michigan, 157-58; gets medical degree, 158-59; medical education plans, 157; moves to Jamaica, 157; prejudice faced, 158; pessimism of, 148, 156-57
Rapier, John H. (Sr.), 30, 156
Rapier, Richard, 30
Rapier, Susan, 156

Rattler, USS, 76
Ray, Stephen, 139
Refugee Home Society, 21
Reidy, Joseph P., 44
Release, USS, 74
regiments (black). *See also under* Connecticut; Illinois; Indiana; Iowa; Massachusetts; New Hampshire; New York; Pennsylvania; Rhode Island; South Carolina; United States Army, permanent black regiments; United States Colored Cavalry (USCC); United States Colored Heavy Artillery (USCHA); United States Colored Troops (USCT)
rendezvous, naval, 59, 60, 66-67
Rhode Island: forms black regiment, 86, 96, 99; Fourteenth Rhode Island Heavy Artillery, 99-101; offers large state bounties, 244n76. *See also* United States Colored Heavy Artillery, 11th
Richmond, USS, 60
Richmond Examiner, 91
Riggs, Thomas Peter, 250n94
Riley, Agnes, 173
Riley, Isaac, 155-56
Riley, Jerome R., 147, 148, 155, 167, 173(i): as author, 174; completes medical degree, 173; county coroner in Kansas, 172; as Democrat, 172-74, 208; denied commission, 163; early life, 155-56, 252n3; licensed to practise, 156, 168; moves to Washington, 168; opposes American imperialism, 174; postwar years, 172-73
Roberts, Charles L., 142
Robertson, John William, 17
Robinson, Amelia, 245n93
Robinson, James, 125
Robinson, John, 95, 243n56
Robinson, Joseph, 193-94
Robinson, Mary, 3,
Robinson, Matilda, 188
Robinson, Samuel J., 3, 4, 98, 113, 116, 117-18, 207
Rogers, R.V., 24
Rolph, John, 150
Rose, Major, 126
Rouse, Elias, 204

Royal College of Physicians and Surgeons, 149, 157
Runchey, Robert, 222n58
Ryde, John, 67

Sagamore, USS, 195
Sager, Eric W., 73
sailors (black): identifying, 44; image of, 73; monotony of naval life, 70, 75; motivation of, 39, 44-45, 66, 210; numbers of, 47-49, 59-60; pay, 65, 79; and pensions, 81-82, 189, 239n120; prejudice against, 79-81; previous occupations, 71-72; prize money, 45, 67; rating, 65-67, 71, 235n34; recruitment of, 54, 59, 62-65, 66-67; term of service, 64-66, 68. *See also names of individual sailors*
Saint John Morning Freeman, 38, 119
San Jacinto, USS, 70
Safford, Lyman, 35
Safford, Maloina, 35
Safford, Martha, 35
Safford, Mary Jane, 35
Safford, Richard, 35
Safford, William, 35
Sanborn, Franklin Benjamin, 241n24
Saunders, Lewis, 60, 197-98, 200. *See* Jackson, Benjamin
School of Medicine and Surgery of Montreal (l'École de médicine et de chirurgie de Montréal), 150-51
Scipio, Peter, 111
Scott, James, 157
Second Confiscation Act (1862), 84
Secord, Solomon, 252n1
"Secret Six," 32, 241n24
Seddon, James, 91
Shadd, Abraham D., 32, 118(i)
Shadd, Abraham W., 32(i), 118
Shadd, Emaline, 32
Shadd, I.D., 32
Shadd, Mary Ann, 32
Shaw, Robert Gould, 89, 93-94
Sherman, William T., 96
Sierra Leone, 14, 15
Silver Lake, USS, 236n47
Silverman, Jason H., 27
Simons, John, 144
Simpson, Levi, 203
Singer, Charles W., 39

Singleton, Holman, 145
slavery: abolished in British Empire, 18.
    See also Emancipation Proclamation;
    Fugitive Slave Act; fugitive slaves
Smith, James Y., 99, 244n76
Smith, Samuel, 236n47
Smith, Thomas, 181
Snowden, Isaac H., 152, 253n24, 253n29
soldiers (black): aid to families, 93, 107-8;
    authorization of, 5, 8; black agency,
    9, 89-90, 114, 119; dishonest recruiters,
    107, 126; excess fatigue duty, 96-97,
    112-13; frustration and anger of, 117,
    119; illness, 100, 102, 108, 110-11, 144,
    207, 244n82; motivation of, 39, 55,
    72-73, 83, 89, 113, 116, 123, 124, 133, 204,
    206-7, 210; numbers of, 47-49, 209,
    261n14; occupations of, 134-35; op-
    position to, 83-84; potential mutiny,
    98, 115; recruitment of, 54-55, 87-91,
    93-94, 99, 101, 266n7; terms of ser-
    vice, 135-36; timing of enlistment,
    122-24, 133, 209-10; unequal pay, 8,
    97, 98, 114-17, 133, 141; use of alias, 46-
    47, 204; white perception of, 85, 86,
    96, 99, 103, 106, 109, 146; white sup-
    port for, 99, 102, 146. See also name
    of individual soldiers; regiments;
    United States Colored Troops
    (USCT); substitutes
South Carolina: Third South Carolina
    Colored Infantry, 98. See also
    United States Colored Troops,
    Twenty-first
Spencer, William, 193
St. Catharines Constitutional, 128
St. Lawrence School of Medicine, 151
St. Mary, USS, 80
Staats (Stoats), Henry, 74
Stanton, Edwin M., 86, 97, 106, 116, 160,
    162, 163
Staples, John Summerfield, 249n59
Stearns, George L., 87-88, 90-91, 93-94,
    241n24
Stevens, Nelson, 184
Stoddard, Benjamin, 58
Stone, Thomas H., 17
Stonewall, CSS, 79
Stratton, William E., 125
Stump, Gideon H., 192. See also Bailey,
    Gideon

substitutes, 3, 34, 41, 46, 60, 85, 127: and
    African Americans, 47, 85-86, 129;
    allowed to select regiment, 130;
    allowing for black substitutes, 85-
    86, 129; British North Americans as,
    86, 128, 129, 130-31, 133, 138, 143, 145,
    197-98; Confederate substitution,
    249n61; perception of, 128, 131-32, 137;
    as non-commissioned officers, 130,
    138, 139, 144; number of black BNA,
    47, 136; oaths, 136; process of enrol-
    ling, 136-37
Sullivan, James, 71, 237n74
Sumner, Charles, 129, 161
Swails, Stephen A., 169
Sylvia, Samuel, 129-30

Talbot, Benjamin F., 43(i), 46-47
Talbot, John, 181
Thomas, Henry, 30, 156
Thomas, James, 178
Thomas, James P., 156
Thomas, William, 181
Thomas, William H., 77
Thompson, John H., 64, 73, 238n81
Thompson, Thomas, 211
Thurman (Therman), William, 43(i), 47.
    See also Talbot, Benjamin F.
Toombs, Robert, 84
Toronto General Hospital, 150, 154
Toronto Daily Globe: effect of Civil war
    bonuses, 132; and Emancipation
    Proclamation, 38, 86; Fort Pillow,
    119; rumours of enslavement or
    killing of black prisoners, 92; and
    Plymouth, 120
Toronto School of Medicine, 150
Toucey, Isaac, 58, 61, 235n27
transmigrants, 20, 35, 205, 222n65
transnationalism, 32, 39; and ties 4, 5, 6,
    209, 211
Travers, Amanda, 35
Travers, David, 35
Tremaine, William S., 252n1
Trinity Medical College, 153
Trust, Charles H., 64, 73, 238n81
Tucker, Jacob, 68, 78-79
Twenty-fifth Army Corps, 130, 143, 188,
    249n74

Underground Railroad, 19, 26, 222n64

United States Army
- discriminatory treatment of black soldiers, 114-17
- foreigners in, 7, 39-41, 125, 229n15
- more equitable treatment of black troops, 122, 124
- opposition to black officers, 118-19, 161-63, 169
- permanent black regiments, 182, 262n20; Ninth Cavalry, 182; Tenth Cavalry, 182, 196; Twenty-fourth Infantry, 182; Twenty-fifth Infantry, 182
- prewar prohibition of black soldiers, 57-58
- shortage of doctors, 146, 147, 159

United States Colored Cavalry (USCC): First, 126

United States Colored Heavy Artillery (USCHA): Eleventh, 120, 193, 243n58; Third, 45, 105

United States Colored Troops (USCT), 43-44; 102nd, 47, 105, 111, 139(i), 142, 181, 186, 192, 262n19; 104th, 170; 107th, 39; 117th, 257n89; atrocities against, 114, 119-20; deaths and illness, 100, 102, 130, 144-45, 244n82; Eighteenth, 34; Eighth, 130, 138; excessive fatigue duty, 96-97, 112-13; Fifth, 43(i), 47; First, 104, 144; Forty-third, 136-37; Forty-fifth, 143; harsh conditions in, 100, 105; hostility of West Pointers, 112; Nineteenth, 161; Ninth, 161; number of regiments, 230n34; re-designation of regiments, 43, 111, 230n28; Seventh, 161-62, 184; Sixth, 102-3, 126, 192, 204; Tenth, 252n1; Third, 4, 96, 102-3, 145, 181, 243n58; Thirty-first, 102, 252n1; Thirty-second, 252n1; Thirty-eighth, 143; threat of mutinies, 98, 115-16; Twelfth, 138; Twentieth, 96, 102, 112-13, 162, 181; Twenty-third, 46; Twenty-fourth, 125; Twenty-fifth, 102-3, 138, 139, 140, 184; Twenty-sixth, 102, 103(i), 32; Twenty-eighth, 104; Twenty-ninth, 36, 139, 144. *See also* soldiers (black)

United States Naval Academy, 61

United States Navy: "brown water" fleet, 62, 75; deskilling of, 62, 68; expansion of, 62; motivation of recruits entering, 44-45; modernization of, 61-62; numbers of vessels, 60-62; prewar navy, 60-61; prize money, 45, 66, 68-70; rating of sailors, 62, 65, 66-67, 235n34; reluctance to use foreign sailors, 58, 81; suppression of slave trade, 79; term of service, 64; tradition of black sailors, 44, 57-60; wages, 65, 79

University of Michigan: medical school, 157-58

Unpleasant, William, 140

Upper Canada: abolition of slavery, 18, 22, 221n55, 222n56; black population, 18; creation of, 13, 18, 219n7; fugitive slaves, 18-19, 22-23; slavery in, 13, 18; slaves fleeing to US, 18; white perception of black population, 19-20

Vail, Charles, 75
Valuska, David L., 60, 80
Vanderbilt, Cornelius, 66
Vanderbilt, USS, 66
veterans (black), 9: in Grand Army of the Republic, 183-85; linked across censuses, 180-81; occupations of, 181; pension applications, 187, 188-94; post-war lives, 177-78, 180-85, 194, 211
Virginia, CSS, 75-76, 238n94
Vogdes, Israel, 112
Voice of the Fugitive, 27, 32

Wafer, Francis W., 252n1
Walker, Barrington, 11
Walker, Hiram, 225n113
Walker, William, 98
Ward, Samuel R., 31, 32, 224n110
Ward, Thomas, 135
War of 1812, 11, 12, 14: black service in, 15, 19, 58; British encouragement of black emigrants, 15, 20
Warren, Francis, 126
Washington National Republican, 160
Watts, Spencer, 186
Wayne, Michael, 27-28, 29
Webber, Henry R., 80
Webber, Samuel Gilbert, 137
Weeks, Hannah, 135: difficulties applying for pension, 191-92, 264n62
Weeks, John, 135
Weeks, John, Jr., 135, 191-92

Welles, Gideon, 58, 61
Western, Paul, 125-26
Western Gunboat Flotilla, 77(i)
Wheeler, William, 52, 133
White, Garland H., 84, 103-4
White, Hattie, 193
White, John, 193
Whitfield, Harvey Amani, 6, 178
Whiting, William, 97
Whitman, W. H., 200
Widmer, Christopher, 149
Wilberforce settlement, 20, 223n69
Wilberforce Educational Institute, 175
William Badger, USS, 74
William Jennings Bryan Club, 174
William W. Cook Post No. 472 (Hamilton), 184
Williams, Henry, 132-33
Williams, James L., 144
Williams, Nathaniel, 99, 135, 244n75
Williams, Richard, 132-33
Williams, W. Henry, 181
Willis, Adam, 234n22, 237n60
Willis, Franklin, 250n94
Wilson, Henry, 161, 242n36
Wilson, Hiram, 21
Wilson, Isaiah F., 205: early life, 201; enlists in Fifty-fourth Massachusetts, 201; illnesses, 201-3; as sailor, 201, 203; returns to Brantford, 202; various treatments for illnesses, 202-3
Wilson, John T., 184
Winks, Robin, 27, 40, 41, 57, 131
Wright, Charles M., 252n1

Ypsilanti: Canadian-born residents in 1860, 34-35

Studies in Canadian Military History

CANADIAN WAR MUSEUM
MUSÉE CANADIEN DE LA GUERRE

John Griffith Armstrong, *The Halifax Explosion and the Royal Canadian Navy: Inquiry and Intrigue*

Andrew Richter, *Avoiding Armageddon: Canadian Military Strategy and Nuclear Weapons, 1950-63*

William Johnston, *A War of Patrols: Canadian Army Operations in Korea*

Julian Gwyn, *Frigates and Foremasts: The North American Squadron in Nova Scotia Waters, 1745-1815*

Jeffrey A. Keshen, *Saints, Sinners, and Soldiers: Canada's Second World War*

Desmond Morton, *Fight or Pay: Soldiers' Families in the Great War*

Douglas E. Delaney, *The Soldiers' General: Bert Hoffmeister at War*

Michael Whitby, ed., *Commanding Canadians: The Second World War Diaries of A.F.C. Layard*

Martin Auger, *Prisoners of the Home Front: German POWs and "Enemy Aliens" in Southern Quebec, 1940-46*

Tim Cook, *Clio's Warriors: Canadian Historians and the Writing of the World Wars*

Serge Marc Durflinger, *Fighting from Home: The Second World War in Verdun, Quebec*

Richard O. Mayne, *Betrayed: Scandal, Politics, and Canadian Naval Leadership*

P. Whitney Lackenbauer, *Battle Grounds: The Canadian Military and Aboriginal Lands*

Cynthia Toman, *An Officer and a Lady: Canadian Military Nursing and the Second World War*

Michael Petrou, *Renegades: Canadians in the Spanish Civil War*

Amy J. Shaw, *Crisis of Conscience: Conscientious Objection in Canada during the First World War*

Serge Marc Durflinger, *Veterans with a Vision: Canada's War Blinded in Peace and War*

James G. Fergusson, *Canada and Ballistic Missile Defence, 1954-2009: Déjà Vu All Over Again*

Benjamin Isitt, *From Victoria to Vladivostok: Canada's Siberian Expedition, 1917-19*

James Wood, *Militia Myths: Ideas of the Canadian Citizen Soldier, 1896-1921*

Timothy Balzer, *The Information Front: The Canadian Army and News Management during the Second World War*

Andrew Godefroy, *Defence and Discovery: Canada's Military Space Program, 1945-74*

Douglas E. Delaney, *Corps Commanders: Five British and Canadian Generals at War, 1939-45*

Timothy Wilford, *Canada's Road to the Pacific War: Intelligence, Strategy, and the Far East Crisis*

Randall Wakelam, *Cold War Fighters: Canadian Aircraft Procurement, 1945-54*

Andrew Burtch, *Give Me Shelter: The Failure of Canada's Cold War Civil Defence*

Wendy Cuthbertson, *Labour Goes to War: The CIO and the Construction of a New Social Order, 1939-45*

P. Whitney Lackenbauer, *The Canadian Rangers: A Living History*

Teresa Iacobelli, *Death or Deliverance: Canadian Courts Martial in the Great War*

Graham Broad, *A Small Price to Pay: Consumer Culture on the Canadian Home Front, 1939-45*

Peter Kasurak, *A National Force: The Evolution of Canada's Army, 1950-2000*

Isabel Campbell, *Unlikely Diplomats: The Canadian Brigade in Germany, 1951-64*